Laura Miller

Englische Übungsgrammatik

Grammatik, Übungen, Lösungen und Vokabelverzeichnis

Christian Asam Verlag

1. Auflage

Druck: Luthe Druck, Köln
ISBN 978-3-923954-19-3

Inhaltsverzeichnis

Vorwort

Nach meinem Englischstudium in Amerika bin ich nach Deutschland gekommen, um meine Muttersprache den Kindern eines Gymnasiums beizubringen.

Während meiner mehrjährigen Unterrichtserfahrung in der Unter- und Mittelstufe konnte ich feststellen, dass Kinder die englische Sprache nur dann richtig erlernen, wenn ihnen die Grammatik verständlich erklärt wird. Danach müsste eine gründliche Einübung der Grammatik erfolgen unter Zuhilfenahme vieler Übungssätze. Heute aber erklären viele Lehrer die Grammatik auf Englisch, und die Kinder verstehen oft nicht, worum es sich handelt. Viele englische Werke erklären die Grammatik entweder sehr knapp, sehr hochgestochen oder wiederum nur auf Englisch. Dann verstehen die Kinder wieder wenig. Die meisten Eltern haben entweder ihre englischen Sprachkenntnisse verlernt oder diese gar nie erworben, sodass sie ihren Kindern nicht weiterhelfen können. Hinzu kommt noch, dass der Stoff des englischen Lehrbuches innerhalb eines Jahres durchgenommen und dieses am Ende des Jahres abgegeben werden muss. Durch diesen Zeitdruck können die gewissenhaften Lehrer natürlich nicht die Grammatik so gründlich mit den Kindern einüben, wie sie gerne möchten; denn sonst kann das Unterrichtsbuch nicht rechtzeitig zum Ende des Schuljahres abgeschlossen werden.

Dieses Buch ist für Personen geschrieben, die Englisch durch richtiges Einüben erlernen oder lehren wollen. Die Grammatikregeln sind mit einem bewusst kleingehaltenen Wortschatz geschrieben. Die Sätze sind, so weit es geht, kurz.

Um Eltern zu helfen, die im Englischen nicht bewandert sind, werden die Lösungen zu sämtlichen Übungen im Beiheft angegeben.

Um Englisch zu lernen, muss man aber auch die Vokabeln beherrschen. Sonst kann man keine Sätze bilden und sich nicht verständlich machen. Ich habe meinen Kindern immer vorgeschlagen, kleine Zettel anzulegen. Auf der einen Seite soll das deutsche Wort stehen; auf der anderen Seite das englische. Dann sollen sie das deutsche Wort ansehen und das englische Wort aufschreiben. Nun können sie den Zettel umdrehen und vergleichen. Ist es falsch, soll der Zettel in einen Kasten kommen, den sie jeden Tag durcharbeiten. Ist das Wort ohne Zögern richtig, wird der Zettel in einen Kasten getan, den sie einmal im Monat wiederholen. Mussten sie überlegen, kommt der Zettel in einen dritten Kasten, den sie jede Woche durcharbeiten. Auf diese Weise sind die Kinder nicht auf ein Vokabelheft fixiert. Sie können nicht sagen, "Das ist das fünfte Wort von unten auf der linken Seite nach ... und vor ..., aber ich weiß die Bedeutung nicht." Auch überschlagen sie Seiten nicht, weil sie meinen, dass sie alle Wörter auf der Seite schon gelernt haben. Mit den Zetteln können sie die neuen Vokabeln erlernen und die alten wiederholen. Es ist jedes Mal neu. Nun auf zum Spaß des Lernens. Denn es macht wirklich Spaß, zu merken, dass man die Grammatik versteht und kann!

1 Personal Pronouns

1.1 Grammatik

Nominativ Subjekt Wer? Who?	Akkusativ Dativ Objekt Wen? Wem? Who(m)?	Genitiv Possessive Adjective Wessen? Whose?	Genitiv Possessive (without noun) Wessen? Whose?
I	me	my	mine
you	you	your	yours
he	him	his	his
she	her	her	hers
it	it	its	its
we	us	our	ours
you	you	your	yours
they	them	their	theirs

1. "Personal pronouns" ersetzen ein Wort.
   The doctor sees **Tom**. The doctor sees **him**.
2. "Personal pronouns" können in allen Fällen (Nominativ, Akkusativ, Genitiv, Dativ) gebraucht werden.
   a) Wenn man "**wer**" fragt, um die Antwort zu bekommen, ist es ein Wort aus der ersten Tabelle. Es ist ein Subjekt.

The doctor sees Tom.	**Who** sees Tom?	**The doctor**	Der Arzt sieht Tom.
He sees Tom.	Wer sieht Tom?	Der Arzt	Er sieht Tom.

   b) Wenn man "**wen**" oder "**wem**" fragt, ist es ein Wort aus der zweiten Tabelle. Es ist ein Objekt. Es ist egal, ob es Dativ oder Akkusativ ist.

The doctor sees **Tom**.	**Who(m)** does the doctor see?	**Tom**.	The doctor sees **him**.
Der Arzt sieht Tom.	Wen sieht der Arzt?	Tom.	Der Arzt sieht ihn.

The doctor gives **Tom** a book. **Who(m)** does the doctor give a book?
Der Arzt gibt Tom ein Buch. Wem gibt der Arzt ein Buch?

Tom. The doctor gives **him** a book.
Tom. Der Arzt gibt ihm ein Buch.

c) Wenn man "**wessen**" fragt, ist es ein Wort aus der dritten oder vierten Tabelle. Es zeigt Besitz an, ist also Genitiv. Wenn man die dritte Tabelle gebraucht, muss ein Substantiv (das, wovon geredet wird) nach dem Personalpronomen folgen (**my** book).

Wenn man die vierte Tabelle gebraucht, kommt kein Substantiv danach (**mine**).

The doctor sees **Sue's** hand. Der Arzt sieht die Hand von Sue.	**Whose** hand does the doctor see? Wessen Hand sieht der Arzt?
Linda's. Die Hand von Linda	The doctor sees **her** hand. Der Arzt sieht ihre Hand.
The doctor sees her **hands**. Der Arzt sieht ihre Hände.	The doctor sees **Linda's**. Der Arzt sieht Lindas.
Whose hand does the doctor see? Wessen Hand sieht der Arzt?	The doctor sees **hers**. Der Arzt sieht ihre.

1.2 Übungen

Setze die richtigen Fürwörter ein, bzw. ersetze die unterstrichenen Wörter durch die richtigen Fürwörter.

1. **Ben and Sarah** are here. ______ are here. ______ hats are here.
2. This is **Alan**. ______ is in the class. ______ is talking. I can see ______ . He has a pen in ______ hand.
3. **Father and mother** are leaving. ______ are walking. I shout to ______ .
4. Mother says, "**Jenny**, are ______ going home?"
5. **Ann**'s dress is here. ______ dress is here.
6. **Father** is here. ______ is here. I see ______ pullover.
7. **We** are going into ______ **classroom**. We are in ______ (the classroom).
8. Those are our **books**. ______ are on the table. I can see ______ .
9. Ann and Jane see **the cat**. ______ is here.
10. **Father** sees **Susan**. ______ sees ______ .
11. **Mother and I** see **the dog**. ______ see ______ .
12. **Jane**'s pen is here. ______ pen is here.
13. **Tom**'s pullover is here. ______ pullover is here.
14. **Father and I** are wearing shirts. ______ shirts are blue.
15. **The cats** are running. We see ______ . ______ are running.
16. **Andy**, ______ are nice.
17. **Pat and Pam**, can ______ come here?
18. Father sees **Tim and me**. He sees ______ .
19. **Pat's and my shoes** are here. ______ shoes are here. We see ______ .
20. **Ben** is here. ______ is here. I see ______ .

21. **Mary**'s sock is here. ______ sock is here.
22. **Jane's and Father's** jeans are here. ______ **jeans** are here. ______ are here. I see ______ .
23. **The girl** has **the book** in ______ hand. ______ is looking at ______ .
24. **The man** sees ______ **son**. ______ is buying **biscuits**. ______ are brown. He is eating ______ .
25. **Mother and I** are here. Father sees ______ . ______ dresses are blue. ______ are happy.
26. **Peter**, can ______ help **me**? ______ want ______ help. The table is too big for ______ to carry it alone; so please help ______ .
27. Look at **Father and Susan**. ______ are sitting at a table and reading. ______ books are interesting.
28. Do you see **Paul** and **Ann**? Yes, I see ______ . I see ______ and ______ . She has a pen in ______ hand. ______ has a pencil in his hand.

Ersetze die hervorgehobenen Wörter mit dem richtigen Pronomen.

29. **The man** sees me in the shop.
30. We are looking at **the girl's** dog.
31. We see **the girls** there.
32. **The women** go home.
33. She gives **the boy** a watch.
34. He sees **me**. ______ am here. It is ______ money.
35. **The dog** often barks .
36. **John**, ______ are very nice. Are ______ going home?
37. **Linda**, is this ______ book?
38. **Linda** is walking home.
39. Is this **Henry's** sock?
40. **Tom and I** are walking home.
41. This is **Dan's and my** book.
42. **Father and mother** wave to me.
43. They see **Linda and me**.
44. Peter is **my brother's** friend.
45. **Helen** is my friend.
46. **Helen and I** are in the same class.
47. **Helen and her sister** have a lot of books.
48. Do you know **Helen and her sister**?
49. This is **Helen's and her sister's** room.
50. **Helen**, take ______ toys and go home.
51. **Helen's mother** is not in the house.
52. **Peter** is at home.

53. There is **a letter**. Helen is reading ______ .
54. Helen gives **Peter** the letter.
55. **Peter and Helen**, ______ mother is in the garden.
56. **Father** is watching Bill.
57. **Susan**, ______ cat is sitting in a tree.
58. **Father**, are ______ still sleeping?
59. We are talking to **Dick and Debby**.
60. **Mother and Jane**, are ______ washing the car?
61. Jane is helping **Mary and me**.
62. **Sarah and Tom**, Linda can see ______ .
63. **The cat** is watching a mouse.
64. I am holding **Susan's and Tom's** books.
65. We go to **Mother** for help.
66. They can see **a table**.
67. Dick often goes home with ______ , **Betty**.
68. I see **Father**.
69. The boys are playing with **Jane's and my** toys.
70. Ann is looking at **Ben's** car.
71. **Betty's** book is on the table.
72. Mother and ______ are making a cake; she gives **me** a piece of cake.
73. **Peter and Ben** are in the bathroom.
74. **Mary** is riding a horse.
75. **The horse's** eyes are black.
76. **Linda and I** are eating apples.
77. **The girl** is throwing **a ball**.
78. **The boy** often laughs at **his brother**.
79. **The men** are writing **sentences**.
80. **Mother** says **a word**.
81. **Father** is reading **a book** now.
82. Is **mother** reading **two books** now?
83. Does **father** always read **books**?
84. **Father** sees **the girl**.
85. **Tom and Dick** are going to **school**.
86. I often drink **milk**.
87. **The children** are at **the windows**.
88. **The girls** sing **a song**.
89. **The girl** sings **songs**.
90. **The boy** is eating **an apple**.

91. **The parents** help **the boy**.
92. **Jane**, can ______ help me?
93. **Kitty and Sally**, I see ______ .
94. **Mother and I** are holding **the books**.
95. **The dogs** see **the cats**.
96. We are walking with **Tom**.
97. Let's help **Mother**.
98. **Betty** is talking to **Father**.
99. **Father and Mother**, we can help ______ .
100. **The dog's** mother is brown.
101. **Linda and Jane** are in the kitchen.
102. We can see ______ , **Paul**.
103. **Mary's** horse is brown and white.
104. Father and ______ go to the park; he holds **my** hand.
105. **Mary and I** are eating a cake.
106. **Mother** is looking at **Father and me**.
107. **Tom and Ben**, ______ hands are big.
108. **The dog** is looking at a cat.
109. I see **Dick and Betty**.
110. **Tom**, are ______ writing a letter?
111. Dick and Mary can write **a letter**.
112. **Linda** is playing with **Dick's** cat.
113. **Father and Mother**, are ______ buying **the picture**?
114. They are looking at **Mother's and my** dresses.
115. **Ben** is drawing **a picture**.
116. **Betty**, can ______ go to the window?
117. **The doctor** looks at **Tom and me**.
118. Do you see **that man**?
119. Can ______ come, **Mr. White**?
120. I am helping **my sister**.
121. Linda and ______ are here; **we** are here.
122. **Ben** is talking with **Tom and Jane**.
123. **Tom and Jane**, are ______ coming with me?
124. **The two men** are here.
125. Can you help **Betty**?
126. Tom is talking to ______ , **Christine**.
127. Here are ten pullovers. Is this **Linda's**?
128. **The two children** are swimming in the water.

129. **The little boy** is playing in the sand.
130. I see **my friends**.
131. There are 20 toy cars. There are **Linda's and Ben's**.
132. We can see **the apple**.
133. This is **the lady's** newspaper.
134. **Linda and Debbie**, are these ______ shoes?
135. Is this ______ book, **Mr. Brown**?
136. These are **Mark's and Ben's** books.
137. The doctors can see ______ now, **Dick and Linda**.
138. Can you see **the dog**?
139. **Ruth** is waiting for you.
140. These are Tom's and ______ cars; they are **ours**.
141. **The taxi** is coming.
142. Our friends see Tom and ______ ; they see **us**.
143. I am eating **cake**.
144. The cat is carrying **a mouse**.
145. We can help ______ , **Christian**.
146. **This tree** is big.
147. **My brother and sister** are reading **books**.
148. We are giving **Elizabeth** a pullover.
149. Tom and David can take ______ home, **Jenny**.
150. **Father** is carrying **the table**.
151. We are now washing **the dishes**.
152. Linda and ______ are here; **we** are here.
153. Tim's and ______ hats are here; **our** hats are here.
154. **Mother and Helen**, when are ______ going to get up?
155. Dan is talking to Linda and ______ ; he is talking to **us**.
156. **Jane's** dog is barking.
157. Can you count **Joan's and Rick's** arms?
158. **My sister and I** are sitting on **the sofa**.
159. **Father** is talking to **David**.
160. **The girl** can see **Robert's** car.
161. Tom sees **Linda and me**; he sees ______ .

2 Present Progressive

2.1 Grammatik

1. Die "progressive form" besteht aus 2 Teilen (eine Form von "to be" + die "-ing" Form des Verbes):

   am, are, is + -ing.

I am coming	I am beating
you are writing	you are telling
he/she/it is wiping	he/she/it is helping
we are taking	we are flying
you are swimming	you are doing
they are sitting	they are repairing

1. Die Bildung der "progressive form"

   - Wenn die Infinitivform mit einem stummen "e" endet, entfällt es und ein "-ing" wird angehängt.

     to com**e** ⇒ coming

   - Wenn die Infinitivform mit einem Konsonanten [1] und einem Vokal[2] endet, wird der letzte Buchstabe verdoppelt. Danach kommt ein "-ing".

     to **run** ⇒ running

   - Wenn die Infinitivform mit einem "y" endet, wird nur ein "-ing" an die Infinitivform angehängt.

     to fl**y** ⇒ flying
     to pla**y** ⇒ playing

   - Ansonsten wird nur ein "-ing" an die Infinitivform angehängt.

     to beat ⇒ beating
     to tell ⇒ telling
     to do ⇒ doing

2. Fragebildung

   - Wenn das Subjekt des Satzes "**he/she/it**" ist, kommt "**is + -ing**."

     Is he go**ing** home now?

     Where **is she** go**ing** now?

[1] Mitlaut
[2] Selbstlaut

- Wenn das Subjekt des Satzes "**I**" ist, kommt "**am + -ing**."
  Am I going home now?
  Where **am I going** now?

- Wenn das Subjekt des Satzes "**you/we/they**" ist, kommt "**are + -ing**."
  Are they going home now?
  Where **are you going** now?

3. Verneinung
   - Wenn das Subjekt des Satzes "**he/she/it**" ist, kommt "**is not + -ing**." (= isn't + -ing)
     He isn't going home now. (= **He is not going** home now.)

   - Wenn das Subjekt des Satzes "**I**" ist, kommt "**am not + -ing**." (= I'm not + -ing)
     I'm not going home now. (= **I am not going** home now.)

   - Wenn das Subjekt des Satzes "**you/we/they**" ist, kommt "**are not+ -ing**." (= aren't + -ing)
     They aren't going home now. (= **They are not going** home now.)

2.2 Übungen

1. Look, the dog ______ . (to bark)
2. Mother and father ______ posters for my room. (to get)
3. ______ a letter? (to write - you)
4. Tom and I ______ in the game. (to run)
5. You ______ a nice song. (to sing - not)
6. The tree ______ fast. (to grow)
7. We ______ the dog. (to keep - not)
8. I ______ the baby. (to feed)
9. You ______ in the sun. (to dance)
10. The man ______ the dishes. (to wash)
11. Sarah and Tom ______ loud words. (to shout)
12. I ______ my records. (to save - not)
13. ______ English now? (to speak - that boy)
14. The girl ______ to see you. (to hope)
15. Linda and I ______ our bikes. (to ride)
16. ______ the dog a biscuit? (to give - the girl)
17. The mother ______ the door. (to close)
18. Tom and Dick ______ the books. (to fetch)
19. We ______ your bikes. (to repair - not)
20. The children ______ the cake. (to eat)

21. Tom ______ the dog for a walk. (to take)
22. The man ______ to Berlin now. (to fly - not)
23. We ______ home late. (to come)
24. ______ a book? (to read - you)
25. The baby ______ to the table. (to walk)
26. The train ______ now. (to arrive)
27. Linda and I ______ the balls. (to throw)
28. My sisters ______ their room. (to tidy up)
29. The girls ______ fun. (to have)
30. The baby ______ the stairs. (to climb)
31. ______ at the cat? (to look - the dog)
32. You ______ ill. (to feel)
33. Father and I ______ the game. (to win)
34. The men ______ a chair. (to carry)
35. The dog ______ water. (to drink - not)
36. The children ______ on chairs. (to stand)
37. ______ nice things? (to say - I)
38. Linda and I ______ our clothes. (to change)
39. The girl ______ a cake. (to cut)
40. The boy ______ stamps now. (to collect - not)
41. The teachers ______ the doors. (to shut)
42. The dog ______ the cat. (to follow)
43. I ______ a new car. (to choose)
44. The girl ______ a film today. (to see)
45. ______ loudly? (to talk - I)
46. The boy ______ to the shop. (to run - not)
47. The shop ______ a rabbit. (to sell)
48. My sisters ______ to England. (to fly)
49. ______ with me? (to come - my sister)
50. My mother ______ my sister ice-cream. (to give - not)
51. The girl ______ her mother the new blouse. (to show)
52. ______ a bike for her birthday? (to get - the girl)
53. We ______ in Bonn. (to live)
54. ______ the dog home with you? (to take - you)
55. The boys ______ the girls letters. (to send - not)
56. You ______ your friends on the telephone. (to call)
57. The dogs ______ with the cats. (to play)
58. The telephone ______ . (to ring)

59. I _______ the letter on the desk. (to put - not)
60. _______ with his child? (to play - the man)
61. The two girls _______ to take a trip. (to plan)
62. Mother and I _______ father now. (to meet)
63. The boy _______ to dance. (to try)
64. It _______ now. (to rain - not)
65. The woman _______ her money. (to save)
66. _______ a joke? (to tell - the man)
67. I _______ the bed. (to move)
68. You _______ a new blouse. (to wear)
69. My brother _______ at your house. (to stay)
70. I _______ a new sofa. (to get - not)
71. _______ their blouses on the bed? (to put - the girls)
72. Linda _______ a knife. (to use)
73. You _______ your hands. (to clap - not)
74. The man _______ his car. (to push)
75. _______ in Berlin? (to live - he)
76. My friend _______ a birthday party. (to have - not)
77. The girl _______ the money. (to count)
78. When _______ to England? (to fly - we)
79. Sarah and I _______ many questions. (to ask)
80. I _______ the story. (to copy)
81. The girl _______ at the joke. (to laugh - not)
82. _______ home? (to run - they)
83. The children _______ very hard. (to work)
84. My friend and I _______ in the sea. (to swim)
85. The boy _______ bags into the car. (to put)
86. The women _______ the bird. (to watch)
87. The men _______ loudly. (to clap)
88. _______ the English words? (to learn - you)
89. That person _______ me. (to help)
90. I _______ the food. (to cook)
91. You _______ a present for her birthday. (to make)
92. _______? (to cry - the baby)
93. The people _______ to the radio. (to listen - not)
94. The child _______ on the chair. (to sit)
95. I _______ a bus to town. (to take - not)
96. You _______ in a new bed. (to sleep)

97. The girls ______ to the ball game. (to go - not)
98. ______ a lot of money? (to save - we)
99. Mother and father ______ food at the shop. (to buy)
100. The boy ______ his car door. (to shut)

3 Present Simple - Present Progressive

3.1 Grammatik

1. Simple:

   a) Wenn eines der folgenden Wörter im Satz vorhanden ist, kommt nur die "simple form":

always, every, often, sometimes, usually, in winter, in spring, in summer, in autumn, on Mondays, on Tuesdays, on Wednesdays, on Thursdays, on Fridays, on Saturdays, on Sundays.

   b) Wenn das Subjekt "**he, she, it**" ist oder ein Wort ist, das durch "he/she/it" ersetzt werden kann, dann kommt ein "s" oder "es" ans Verb. Nach -ss, -ch, -sh, -x, und -o wird ein "-es" angehängt.

   to make ⇒ he makes; to watch ⇒ he watches

   c) die Endung

   - Wenn das Subjekt des Satzes "**he, she, it**" ist und die Infinitivform mit einem Konsonanten[1] und "y" endet, wird der Konsonant in ein "ies" gewandelt.

     to **fly** ⇒ he flies

   - Wenn das Subjekt des Satzes "**he, she, it**" ist und die Infinitivform mit einem Vokal[2] und "y" endet, bleibt das "y" und ein "s" wird angehängt.

     to pl**ay** ⇒ he plays

   d) Nach Hilfsverben wie: "can, must" kommt "infinitive." Nach diesen Hilfsverben kommt nie ein "s". (**nie**: he musts)

   he **can come**; I **must run**

   e) Fragebildung

   - Wenn das Subjekt des Satzes "**he, she, it**" ist, kommt in der "present simple" "**does + infinitive**."

     Does he go home every day?

   - Wenn das Subjekt des Satzes "**I, you, we, they**" ist, kommt in der "present simple" "**do + infinitive**."

     Do they go home every day?

[1] Mitlaut
[2] Selbstlaut

f) Verneinung

- Wenn das Subjekt des Satzes "**he, she, it**" ist, kommt in der “present simple” “**does not + infinitive**.” (= doesn’t + infinitive)

  He doesn’t go home every day. (= **He does not go** home every day.)

- Wenn das Subjekt des Satzes "**I, you, we, they**" ist, kommt in der “present simple” “**do not+ infinitive**.” (= don’t + infinitive)

  They don’t go home every day. (= **They do not go** home every day.)

2. Progressive:

a) Wenn eines der folgenden Wörter im Satz vorhanden ist, kommt nur die "progressive form":

now, right now, at this moment, today, Look, Listen, in the picture

b) Die "progressive form" besteht aus 2 Teilen (eine Form von “to be” + die “-ing” Form des Verbes):

am, are, is + -ing.

I am coming	I am beating
you are writing	you are telling
he, she, it is wiping	he, she, it is helping
we are taking	we are flying
you are swimming	you are doing
they are sitting	they are repairing

c) Die Bildung der "progressive form"

- Wenn die Infinitivform mit einem stummen "e" endet, entfällt es und ein "-ing" wird angehängt.

  to com**e** ⇒ coming

- Wenn die Infinitivform mit einem Vokal (Selbstlaut) und einem Konsonanten (Mitlaut) endet, wird der letzte Buchstabe verdoppelt. Danach kommt ein "-ing".

  to sw**im** ⇒ swi**mm**ing

- Ansonsten wird nur ein "-ing" an die Infinitivform angehängt.

  to beat ⇒ beating;

  to tell ⇒ telling;

  to fly ⇒ flying

d) Fragebildung

- Wenn das Subjekt des Satzes "**he, she, it**" ist, kommt in “present progressive” “**is + -ing**.”

  Is he go**ing** home now?

- Wenn das Subjekt des Satzes "**I**" ist, kommt in "present progressive" "**am + -ing**."

  Am I go**ing** home now?

- Wenn das Subjekt des Satzes "**you, we, they**" ist, kommt in "present progressive" "**are + -ing**."

  Are they go**ing** home now?

e) Verneinung

- Wenn das Subjekt des Satzes "**he, she, it**" ist, kommt in "present progressive" "**is not + -ing**." (= isn't + -ing)

  He isn't go**ing** home now. (= **He is not** go**ing** home now.)

- Wenn das Subjekt des Satzes "**I**" ist, kommt in "present progressive" "**am not + -ing**." (= I'm not + -ing)

  I'm not go**ing** home now. (= **I am not** go**ing** home now.)

- Wenn das Subjekt des Satzes "**you, we, they**" ist, kommt in "present progressive" "**are not+ -ing**." (= aren't + -ing)

  They aren't go**ing** home now. (= **They are not** go**ing** home now.)

3.2 Übungen

Setze die richtige Form des Verbs ein. Manchmal ist das Verb hinten in Klammern angegeben; manchmal ist es in dem anderen Teil des Satzes vorhanden.

1. Look! Our dog ______ at the girls. He usually ______ only at animals. (to bark)
2. Grace and Barbara often ______ the same clothes on. (to have) But now Barbara ______ a blue dress and Grace ______ a skirt and a red blouse. (to wear)
3. We must ______ . We always ______ at half past nine. (to go)
4. The train always ______ at eleven. It ______ the station right now. (to leave)
5. My dog usually ______ on this chair. But right now I ______ on it. (to sit)
6. My parents sometimes ______ at six. They ______ now. (to get up)
7. The children often ______ the bus, but now they ______ a taxi. (to take)
8. English people always ______ English. We ______ English now. (to speak)
9. Every morning the clock ______ at six o'clock. It is six now: the clock ______ . (to ring)
10. Cars must ______ when the light is red. (to stop)
11. He ______ three cups of tea every day. He ______ his second cup now. (to drink)
12. What ______ Mike ______ right now? (to do) I think he ______ his bike. (to repair)
13. Uncle Henry and Aunt Jane always ______ the animals in the afternoon. They ______ them right now. (to feed)
14. Dick and his brother Tom ______ their faces every morning. They ______ them right now. (to wash)
15. Boys often ______ football. This boy never ______ football. (to play)
16. Tom ______ tennis every day. I ______ tennis right now. (to play)

17. We ______ home now. He usually ______ home at 2 o'clock. (to go)
18. They often ______ Mr. Clark. We ______ him today. (to see)
19. You ______ on Tuesdays. You ______ now. (to run)
20. I ______ up at 5 o'clock every day. My mother always ______ up at 4 o'clock. (to get)
21. He ______ near the door now. In winter they ______ near the window. (to sit)
22. We usually ______ upstairs. My father ______ in the bedroom now. (to sleep)
23. We ______ a party now because we ______ a party every Saturday night. (to have)
24. They usually ______ the bus, but today they ______ the taxi. (to take)
25. I ______ German now, but I often ______ English (to speak)
26. We often ______ tennis, but we ______ football now. (to play)
27. Tom ______ with Dolly now, but you usually ______ with her. (to dance)
28. I ______ my hands three times every day, but my sister always ______ her hands twice a day. (to wash)
29. Robert ______ his homework every evening; they ______ their homework every morning. (to do)
30. A bird ______ now; it ______ every day. (to fly)
31. I ______ TV now. Tom ______ TV every day. (to watch)
32. We ______ with Mr. Smith today. We often ______ with him. (to talk)
33. He always ______ well. He ______ well now. (to run)
34. My father ______ now. He always ______ at 6 o'clock. (to get up)
35. They usually ______ near the window. Now they ______ near the door. (to sit)
36. ______ (you) now? You always ______ until 7 o'clock. (to sleep)
37. I ______ Mrs. Jones on Thursdays. I ______ her today. (to see)
38. They ______ milk now. They ______ cornflakes every Wednesday. (to buy)
39. I ______ the bus today. I usually ______ the taxi. (to take)
40. You ______ your face every day. He often ______ his face. (to wash)
41. John ______ a trip every month. You ______ a trip at this moment. (to take)
42. The plane ______ to America now. The plane ______ to America every day. (to fly)
43. You always ______ German. My father and I ______ English right now. (to speak)
44. You ______ to school today. They only ______ to school in winter. But my sister ______ now. (to walk)
45. Look, there's Tom. He ______ at the bus stop. (to wait)
46. He always ______ the bus at 8 o'clock. (to get)
47. I ______ out in the park every afternoon. (to go)
48. In the picture the lady ______ a dog. (to push)
49. The taxi driver ______ the lady's bags at the moment. (to carry)
50. We ______ for a swim every week in summer. (to go)
51. The dog always ______ when people come to the house. (to bark)
52. Bill is always hungry. He ______ a lot of biscuits. (to eat)

53. The boys ______ in the garden now. (to play)
54. She ______ too much TV every evening. (to watch)
55. Look at the picture. Henry ______ to the house and the animals ______ . (to come; to run)
56. Some birds often ______ to warmer countries. (to fly)
57. This bird always ______ in our park. (to stay)
58. Mary ______ to school at 7 o'clock every day. (to go)
59. Susan ______ the apples in the basket right now. (to put)
60. They ______ with the girl right now. (to speak)
61. We ______ the apples on Wednesdays. (to eat)
62. My brother usually ______ TV. (to watch)
63. I ______ a letter now. (to write)
64. I always ______ on a chair. (to sit)
65. In summer they ______ in the river. (to swim)
66. Look, the boy ______ a bike. (to ride)
67. I ______ my father every day. (to see)
68. We always ______ tables. (to carry)
69. We ______ to America today. (to fly)
70. My brothers always ______ their faces after breakfast (to wash)
71. The man and the woman sometimes ______ the animals. (to feed)
72. In the picture the lady ______ in her bed. (to sleep)
73. The man ______ home at 2 o'clock every Wednesday. (to get)
74. You often ______ apples. (to buy)
75. The dog ______ away at this moment. (to run)
76. You ______ a picture of Father right now. (to take)
77. You ______ a letter now. (to write)
78. The dog always ______ into the garden. (to go)
79. Tom sometimes ______ my books. (to carry)
80. I often ______ home. (to run)
81. Mother and I ______ cornflakes in the picture. (to buy)
82. My sister and I ______ on a chair right now. (to sit)
83. You ______ late on Sundays. (to get up)
84. My brother and sister ______ the bus at this moment. (to take)
85. I ______ to our house right now. (to run)
86. My little sister always ______ TV on Sundays. (to watch)
87. In the picture the lady ______ apples into her car. (to put)
88. Look, the boy ______ a book. (to carry)
89. My sister and I ______ in the house in winter. (to play)
90. Today we ______ the new table. (to get)

91. My father ______ the animals today. (to feed)
92. The two girls usually ______ TV at home. (to watch)
93. My brothers ______ apples at this moment. (to eat)
94. In autumn the birds ______ south. (to fly)
95. The dog and cat often ______ away. (to run)
96. I ______ the door now. (to close)
97. The plane ______ to London on Mondays. (to fly)
98. We ______ for Berlin today. (to leave)
99. The lady ______ the shirts in the picture. (to hold)
100. My father and mother sometimes ______ in the sea. (to swim)
101. Jenny, you ______ on my pullover right now. (to sit)
102. Mac and Ben ______ their bikes now. (to ride)
103. My brothers always ______ their homework in the afternoon. (to do)
104. He must ______ his milk. (to drink)
105. Mike sometimes ______ his homework in the evening. (to do)
106. Linda and John, you ______ your faces every day. (to wash)
107. Susan and Jenny ______ on their heads in the picture. (to stand)
108. Dan, can you ______ your name? (to spell)
109. Tom and Mark ______ a car at this moment. (to drive)
110. My father usually ______ TV in the mornings. (to watch)
111. Look, the cat ______ to the house. (to run)
112. I ______ the cake for you now. (to get)
113. The two birds ______ at our window in winter. (to eat)
114. The old man often ______ milk. (to buy)
115. The boys ______ their sisters at this moment. (to help)
116. My sister and I usually ______ two books a week. (to read)
117. My sister must ______ her pullover. (to wash)
118. Alan and I ______ our children right now. (to feed)
119. He ______ to the seaside every year. (to go)
120. My brothers always ______ their shoes. (to carry)
121. They ______ tennis now. Usually they ______ golf. (to play)
122. Now the clock ______ . (to ring) Linda must ______ . (to get up)
123. Diane and Tom usually ______ to school. They ______ right now. (to walk)
124. Look, the cat ______ under the table. It sometimes ______ on the chair. (to sit)
125. We ______ an English lesson every Tuesday. We ______ one at the moment. (to have)
126. The pupils ______ for their teacher now. (to wait)
127. Robert always ______ paper in his pocket. (to have) He often ______ paper in the classroom. (to throw)
128. Look at Robert. He ______ a funny face. (to make)

129. Mr. Smith ______ the bus every morning. (to take)
130. My father can ______ all his friends. (to help)
131. You usually ______ tea, but you ______ milk now. (to drink)
132. Look, the plane ______ now. (to start)
133. My brother says, "You ______ your bike every week." (to repair)
134. Jenny says, "Look, I ______ home." (to run)
135. I ______ a cat now. I often ______ a cat. (to draw)
136. At this moment he ______ the animals. He always ______ them (to feed)
137. Tom ______ to the seaside every summer. Now Tom ______ to the seaside. (to go)
138. The buses always ______ from the bus stop. Right now the bus ______ . (to leave)
139. You usually ______ TV. At this moment you ______ TV. (to watch)

Übersetze!

140. Jetzt kommt er.
141. Die Jungen spielen oft Tennis.
142. Im Moment wäscht er sich das Gesicht.
143. Der Lehrer wartet jetzt in der Klasse.
144. Ich vergesse immer, mein Brot zu essen.

4 Question formation in the present (Fragebildung in der Gegenwart)

Um eine Frage zu stellen, muss man zwei Teile zum Verb haben. Das muss aber nicht zutreffen, wenn man nach dem Subjekt fragt oder wenn eine Form von “to be” das einzige Verb im Fragesatz ist.

Subjektfrage	Who comes every day?
	Who is coming now?
sonstige Fragen	Does he come every day?
	Is he coming now?
“to be”-Frage	Where is the water?

Fragewörter

Who	Wer?
When	Wann?
Where	Wo?
What	Was?
Why	Warum?
Whose?	Wessen?
How	Wie?
How many	Wieviele?
How much	Wieviel?

4.1 Grammatik

1. **present simple**

   a) Wenn man nach dem Subjekt fragt, braucht man kein weiteres Hilfsverb hinzuzufügen.

   Die Subjektfrage steht in der Einzahl und hat ein "-s"/"-es" am Verb, weil man bei der Fragestellung nicht weiß, ob die Antwort Einzahl oder Mehrzahl ist.

   Tom comes every day. **Who** comes every day?

   The girls come home. **Who** comes home?

   b) Bei allen anderen Fragen muss man zwei Teile zum Verb haben. Weil ein zweiter Verbteil fehlt, setzt man in der Gegenwart (present simple) "do" oder "does" als Hilfsverb dazu: bei "he, she, it" nimmt man "does" (+ Infinitiv), sonst "do".

   She comes home **every day**.
   When does she come home?

   They come home **every day**. **When do** they come home?

2. **present progressive** (=-ing)

a) Um Fragen in present progressive zu stellen, gebraucht man "am, are, is + -ing".

I am coming **today**. **When am** I coming?

They are coming **today**. **When are** they coming?

b) Wenn man nach dem Subjekt fragt, gebraucht man "is + ing", weil man bei der Fragestellung angeblich nicht weiß, ob die Antwort Einzahl oder Mehrzahl ist.

Tom is coming home. **Who is** coming home?

The girls are coming home. **Who is** coming home?

3. Die Wortstellung bei Fragen

Fragewort	*Hilfsverb*	*Subjekt*	*Hauptverb*	*Rest des Satzes*
When	are	you	coming	home?
When	do	they	come	home?
When	does	he	come	home?
Where	is	the water?		

bei Subjektfragen:

Fragewort	*Verb*	*Rest des Satzes*
Who	is coming	home?
Who	comes	home?
Who	is	that girl?

bei Ja/Nein-Fragen:

Hilfsverb	*Subjekt*	*Hauptverb*	*Rest des Satzes*
Do	they	come	home?
Is	she	coming	home?
Is	father		at home?

4.2 Übungen

Stelle je eine Frage zu den hervorgehobenen Wörtern.

1. **The boy** is running home now.
2. The boy is running **home** now.
3. The boy is running home **now**.
4. The boy is running **quickly**.
5. The boy is running quickly **because he is late**.
6. **Yes**, the boy is running home now.
7. The boy **is running home** now.
8. **The boy** can run home now.
9. The boy can run home **now**.
10. **Two girls** are running home now.

11. Two girls are running **home** now.
12. **Two** girls are running home now.
13. Two girls are running home **now**.
14. Two girls are running **quickly**.
15. Two girls are running quickly **because they are late**.
16. **Yes**, two girls are running quickly.
17. Two girls **are running home** now.
18. **Two girls** must run home now.
19. Two girls must run **home** now.
20. **I** am eating an apple now.
21. I am eating **an apple** now.
22. I am eating an apple **now**.
23. I am eating an apple **quickly**.
24. I am eating an apple quickly **because I am late**.
25. **Yes**, I am eating an apple.
26. I am eating an apple **in the kitchen**.
27. I **am eating an apple** now.
28. **I** can eat an apple now.
29. I can eat an apple **now**.
30. **The boy** runs home every day.
31. The boy runs **home** every day.
32. The boy runs home **every day**.
33. The boy runs **quickly**.
34. The boy runs quickly **because he is late**.
35. **Yes**, the boy runs quickly.
36. The boy **runs home** every day.
37. **The boy** can run home every day.
38. The boy must run home **every day.**
39. **Two girls** run home every day.
40. Two girls run **home** every day.
41. **Two** girls run home every day.
42. Two girls run home **every day.**
43. Two girls run **quickly**.
44. Two girls run quickly **because they are late.**
45. **Yes,** two girls run quickly.
46. Two girls **run home** every day.
47. **Two girls** can run quickly.
48. Two girls can run **quickly.**

49. **I** eat an apple every day.
50. I eat **an apple** every day.
51. I eat an apple **every day**.
52. I eat an apple **quickly.**
53. I eat an apple quickly **because I am late.**
54. **Yes,** I eat an apple quickly.
55. I **eat an apple** quickly.
56. **The man** is coming.
57. **Two** birds are flying.
58. Two birds **are flying**.
59. The father comes home **at night.**
60. The father **comes home** at night.
61. The boy is sitting **in the kitchen.**
62. **The boy** is sitting in the kitchen.
63. The boy **is sitting** in the kitchen.
64. The girl is drinking **milk.**
65. The girl **is drinking milk**.
66. I am writing **a letter.**
67. **I** am writing a letter.
68. I **am writing a letter.**
69. **The girl's** mother is here.
70. The boy is running **quickly.**
71. The birds are **in a tree.**
72. **The girls** are talking.
73. The girls **are talking**.
74. **Two** children are here.
75. The baby is crying **because it is afraid.**
76. **The girls** eat cake.
77. The girls eat **cake**.
78. The girls **eat cake**.
79. The men eat **in the kitchen.**
80. **The men** eat in the kitchen.
81. The men **eat** in the kitchen.
82. **Three** dogs bark every day.
83. Three dogs bark **every day**.
84. Three dogs **bark** every day.
85. **Yes**, we can drive the car.
86. **You** carry many chairs.

87. You carry **many chairs**.
88. You **carry many chairs.**
89. **I** see the tree in the morning.
90. I see **the tree** in the morning.
91. I **see the tree** in the morning.
92. I see the tree **in the morning.**
93. **The girls** are sleeping in their beds.
94. The girls **are sleeping in their beds**.
95. The girls are sleeping **in their beds.**
96. **The child** reads very slowly.
97. The child **reads very slowly**.
98. The child reads **very slowly**.
99. **The boys** are driving to school.
100. The boys **are driving to school**.
101. The boys are driving **to school.**
102. **I** sell books every day.
103. I sell **books** every day.
104. I **sell books** every day.
105. I sell books **every day.**
106. **You** are talking too loudly.
107. You are talking **too loudly.**
108. The tall man can carry **two** books.
109. **We** write five books.
110. We write **five** books.
111. We write **five books**.
112. We **write five books**.
113. **Yes**, the women are coming now.
114. **The little girl** writes letters.
115. The little girl **writes letters**.
116. The little girl writes **letters.**
117. You are sitting **because you are lazy.**
118. The dog must bark **ten** times.
119. **You** are standing on a chair.
120. You **are standing on a chair**.
121. You are standing **on a chair.**
122. **Yes**, he lives in a house.
123. **I** am wearing a pullover.
124. I **am wearing a pullover**.

125. I am wearing **a pullover.**
126. **The girls** often stand in the bus.
127. The girls often stand **in the bus**.
128. The girls often **stand in the bus**.
129. **I** fly a plane.
130. I fly **a plane**.
131. I **fly a plane**.
132. The cat is eating **its food.**
133. The cat **is eating its food.**
134. **Yes,** the little girl reads books.
135. **Yes,** she can read books.
136. **Yes,** the girl's reading books.
137. We are arriving **in London.**
138. **Yes,** the children talk.
139. **Yes**, the children can talk.
140. **Yes**, the children are talking.
141. **Yes,** I always walk.
142. **Yes**, I'm walking.
143. **Yes,** we're holding hands.

5 Some - any

5.1 Grammatik

1. **some, somebody, someone, something, somewhere**

   Diese Wörter werden in den folgenden Fällen gebraucht:

   - in Sätzen, wo kein "nein" vorhanden ist.
     I see **something**.

   - in Fragesätzen, wenn man erwartet, dass die Antwort "ja" sein wird.
     I heard the phone. Did **somebody** phone?

   - wenn man von einer unzählbaren Sache spricht.
     I would like **some** cheese.

2. **any, anybody, anyone, anything, anywhere**

   Diese Wörter werden in den folgenden Fällen gebraucht:

   - in Sätzen, in denen ein "nein" vorhanden ist.
     I do**n't** see **anything**.

   - in Fragesätzen, wenn man nicht weiß, was für eine Antwort kommt.
     Did she say **anything** about Tom when you asked her?

5.2 Übungen

Setze das richtige Wort (eine Form von "some" oder "any") in die Lücke ein.

1. Could we have ______ of the green apples, please?
2. (-thing). Haven't you heard ______ about the accident yet?
3. We will find ______ way of helping her.
4. Can't you see ______ way of helping her?
5. Would you like ______ pretty red apples?
6. (-thing). ______ must have happened to her!
7. The baby seems thirsty. Does he want ______ more milk?
8. (-where). We won't go ______ if you are so slow.
9. They don't have ______ TV any more.

10. You have so many stamps. Won't you give me ______ ?
11. (-thing). The child won't say ______ to me.
12. ______ of our pictures didn't turn out well.
13. We won't take ______ radio with us on holiday.
14. I would like ______ more cheese, please.
15. What's in the bag? ______ sweets?
16. We haven't seen ______ of them for a long time.
17. The girl's all wet! Have you got ______ other clothes for her?
18. (-where). You must be going ______ this summer!
19. The girl wanted ______ water.
20. You look hot. Would you like ______ water to drink?
21. (-thing). The baby hasn't eaten ______ yet.
22. (-body). ______ must be going!
23. I don't see the new balls. Have you got ______ more?
24. The clothes are dirty. Are you going to wash ______ today?
25. (-thing). No, I don't want ______ .
26. You could have ______ butter if you'd like.
27. Haven't you heard ______ good songs?
28. When Tom was quiet, he saw ______ rabbits.
29. (-body). It looks so empty. Isn't ______ home?
30. (-thing). You look funny. Do you have ______ to tell me?
31. (-where). I'm sure we'll meet ______ again.
32. (-where). They couldn't find the child ______ .
33. We still have ______ sandwiches if you want ______ .
34. It was so dark. Could you see ______ rabbits?
35. Where have you got ______ cornflakes?
36. Have you watched ______ of the football games?
37. (-where). His shoes must be ______ in the living-room.
38. Could we please have ______ biscuits, Mom?
39. (-thing). I read ______ about the accident yesterday.
40. (-where). We can't find her ______ .
41. Come, I've got ______ biscuits for you.
42. (-body). You mustn't tell ______ what I said.
43. (-body). ______ must have taken my chair.
44. We bought ourselves ______ new clothes yesterday.
45. You bought so many stamps yesterday. Have you still got ______ ?
46. He didn't want ______ money, did he?
47. (-thing). ______ woke her up.

48. (-body) The man hasn't helped ______ yet.
49. ______ hamsters were in the cage when we saw them.
50. You look hungry. Haven't you had ______ breakfast?
51. (-thing). We saw ______ nice over there.
52. Have you got ______ sugar?
53. (-where). Don't go ______ near that hole!
54. (-body). Can't ______ help me?
55. Did you take ______ pictures of us in the water?
56. They haven't met ______ interesting people.
57. (-where). We were ______ near that city.
58. That man doesn't like ______ dogs at all.
59. Tea's ready. Would you like ______ ?
60. Didn't you see ______ tigers at the zoo?
61. (-where). It was raining so hard. We couldn't go ______ .
62. Her mother likes only ______ of the music.
63. (-body). ______ has drunk my milk!
64. (-thing). Didn't you see ______ big?
65. That must have been ______ show last night!
66. (-body). Could you see ______ in the black night?
67. I'm sure she'll write to you ______ time soon.
68. (-thing). ______ loud woke me up.
69. I'd like ______ ice-cream, please.
70. This shop doesn't sell ______ milk.
71. (-body). The children are all dirty. ______ gave them cake.
72. You haven't seen ______ football for days.
73. We've got too much sand. Would you like ______ ?
74. The girls asked ______ interesting questions.
75. (-body). I surely hope ______ will be there when we arrive!
76. When she was 16, she hadn't driven ______ car yet.
77. (-thing). You'll get ______ nice when Grandma comes.
78. They have ______ children.
79. (-where). I'm sure they wouldn't have gone ______ near that house.
80. (-body). No, I don't think ______ saw me.
81. Dad, could I please have ______ money?
82. (-thing). Father won't buy ______ for you if you're bad.
83. Please give me ______ water.
84. (-thing). He's late but I don't think ______ has happened to him.
85. You're eating cake! Where did you find ______ ?

86. The children's mouths are dirty. Did you buy ______ ice-cream for them?
87. (-body). We didn't see ______ .
88. (-where). I've seen you ______ before.
89. (-where). She won't find you ______ .
90. Would you like to drink ______ tea, children?
91. She bought ______ shoes.
92. (-body). ______ is sleeping in my bed.
93. No, we don't want ______ apples.
94. ______ day my brother will come home.
95. (-where). The children are ______ in the house.
96. (-thing). No, she won't take ______ from you.
97. We didn't have ______ money yesterday.
98. (-where). The shoes must be lying ______ on the floor.
99. We met ______ very nice people at the party.
100. (-where). They wouldn't go ______ near the water.
101. (-thing). There was ______ I wanted to tell you.
102. (-body). I haven't seen ______ today.

6 They're - there - their

6.1 Grammatik

1. **They're** = they are = sie sind

   Dieses Wort besteht aus einem Subjekt (they) und einem Verb (are). Oft kommt ein "-ing" Form des Verbes danach.

   They're coming. = They are coming. = Sie kommen.

   Sonst ist das "'re" das einzige Verb im Satz.

   They're here. = They are here. = Sie sind hier.

2. **there** = dort, es gibt, es sind

   Es ist ein Adverb des Ortes und sagt, dass etwas "dort drüben" ist.

   I see them **there**.

   Oder es ist ein Füllwort (mit "There is/ There are"):

   There are two girls in the car. **There is** an apple on the table.

3. **their** = ihr

   Es ist ein Personalpronomen; die Mehrzahl von sein/ihr/sein. Ein Substantiv kommt danach.

   He is holding the children's dog. He is holding **their dog**.

6.2 Übungen

1. ______ bikes are old.
2. They are over ______ .
3. I see ______ cars.
4. ______ driving to Bonn.
5. When are they going ______ ?
6. Linda and Dan are helping ______ brother.
7. I am eating ______ cake.
8. ______ laughing at me.
9. They are sitting ______ .
10. ______ dogs are running after ______ cats.
11. ______ running fast.
12. ______ children are laughing.

13. ______ laughing.
14. ______ are two children.
15. We are sitting in ______ classroom.
16. ______ making costumes.
17. ______ costumes are funny.
18. They are making them over ______ .
19. ______ are many pupils in the classroom.
20. Are the pupils writing ______ words carefully?
21. They are dancing at ______ party.
22. ______ drinking water now.
23. Are they drinking water ______ ?
24. ______ climbing a tree.
25. The children are wearing ______ dirty clothes.
26. ______ playing with the dog.
27. Mother and father are eating with ______ neighbours.
28. The tourists are carrying ______ bags.
29. ______ going to the station now.
30. I see them ______ .
31. The men are working at ______ computers.
32. ______ reading ______ books.
33. ______ writing a story.
34. The boy and girls are eating from ______ dishes.
35. ______ feeding the baby.
36. We see it ______ .
37. The cats are closing ______ eyes.
38. ______ dreaming about birds.
39. ______ are three birds in the tree.
40. The men are holding ______ hats in the wind.
41. ______ is a big shop.
42. The men are putting ______ feet on the table.
43. ______ waiting for ______ children.
44. ______ at school.
45. The girls are seeing ______ friends.
46. ______ are many boys at the party.
47. ______ dancing with the girls.
48. The teachers are asking ______ pupils many things.
49. ______ books are new.
50. ______ on the desk over ______ .

51. The boys are doing ______ homework.
52. ______ helping the girls.
53. ______ are words we don’t know.
54. Are you helping them with ______ jobs?
55. ______ coming home today.
56. ______ jokes are funny.
57. ______ laughing at them.
58. ______ taking photos of the children.
59. The children are looking at ______ pictures.
60. ______ are many pictures.
61. Sarah and Robert are ______ .
62. ______ coming home.
63. ______ cars are red.
64. ______ getting ______ cars over ______ .
65. Look, ______ going to ______ car ______ .
66. ______ eating ______ apples.
67. Look, ______ are two people ______ .
68. ______ taking ______ hats.

7 to - two - too

7.1 Grammatik

1. **to** = zu

   Es ist ein Teil eines Ortsadverbs und beschreibt "wohin". Ein Substantiv folgt danach.

   She is going **to school**.

2. **two** = zwei

   Es ist eine Zahl und sagt "wie viele". Ein Substantiv folgt danach.

   Two children were walking.

3. **too** = auch, zu

   Mit der Bedeutung "zu" kommt ein Adjektiv oder Adverb danach.

   He is **too young** for the job.

   He is driving **too fast.**

   Wenn "too" mit der Bedeutung "auch" gebraucht wird, steht das Wort oft am Ende des Satzes.

   I am coming to the party, **too**.

7.2 Übungen

1. ______ girls are walking.
2. I am walking ______ .
3. We are writing ______ words.
4. There are ______ many words.
5. Are you writing ______ your sister?
6. Here are ______ animals, a dog and a cat.
7. They are running ______ the house.
8. We are running ______ .
9. ______ apples are on the table.
10. I am drawing ______ pictures.
11. My mother is giving presents ______ her brother.
12. He will give her a present ______ .
13. I have ______ aunts.
14. He has ______ aunts ______ .

15. The tourist is taking ______ bags.
16. She is taking them ______ the airport.
17. Our house has ______ bathrooms.
18. I am going ______ a bathroom.
19. We are cleaning them ______ .
20. The girl is reading ______ books.
21. I am taking ______ bottles ______ the supermarket.
22. ______ bottles are in the house ______ .
23. There are ______ candles on the cake.
24. We are bringing the cake ______ the party.
25. The girl is going ______ the window.
26. My parents have ______ cars.
27. They are driving the cars ______ Bonn.
28. We are driving ______ cars ______ .
29. ______ cats are following the birds.
30. The birds are flying ______ a tree.
31. Are the cats flying ______ ?
32. Have you got ______ children?
33. I have ______ children ______ .
34. ______ girls are going ______ the shop.
35. This school has ______ classrooms.
36. It has ______ teachers ______ .
37. We are going ______ the classroom.
38. My brother has ______ computers.
39. He is walking ______ his room ______ .
40. ______ days are nice: Saturday and Sunday.
41. The cats are closing ______ eyes.
42. ______ rabbits are looking at the cats ______ .
43. We are throwing the ball ______ our dog.
44. I can wash ______ dishes ______ .
45. He is putting ______ dishes on the table.
46. They are walking ______ the table with ______ dishes, ______ .
47. You are dancing on ______ feet.
48. We are singing ______ songs ______ .
49. ______ friends are coming, ______ .
50. Take the book ______ mother.
51. The girl is going ______ the house, ______ .
52. We are playing ______ games, ______ .

53. He is listening ______ the teacher.
54. Are you giving ______ blouses ______ your mother, ______ ?
55. I am learning ______ languages.
56. He is speaking ______ his father.
57. Are ______ languages ______ many for you, ______ ?
58. Can you see ______ men?
59. I see them ______ .
60. The pupil has ______ questions, ______ .
61. I have one ______ .
62. We are going on holiday ______ England for ______ weeks ______ .
63. Mother is reading ______ stories ______ you ______ .
64. ______ boys are going ______ school ______ .
65. Can you ______ boys walk ______ school ______ ?

8 Much - many

8.1 Grammatik

1. In positiven Sätzen werden "much" und "many" häufig durch "a lot of", "lots of", "plenty of" oder "a great deal of/ a large number of" ersetzt. Hier aber werden wir uns auf "much" und "many" festlegen und "a lot of" nicht gebrauchen.

   Bonn has **many** trees. - Bonn has a lot of trees.

   I drink **much** water. - I drink a lot of water.

   "Much" und "many" treten in bejahten Sätzen oft nach "**too**", "**so**", "**as**", "**very**", und "**how much**" / "**how many**" auf.

   The doctor says I am drinking **too much** tea.

   There are **so many** tourists in Bonn.

2. "**Much**" wird bei nicht zählbaren Substantiven gebraucht. Es zeichnet eine Menge aus, die nicht gezählt wird. Man zählt, z.B. "two pounds of cheese" aber nicht "two cheeses."

   Einige solche Wörter sind: air, bread, butter, cheese, chocolate, dirt, energy, food, fruit, fun, ice-cream, information, ketchup, milk, money, power, sand, sugar, tea, time, trouble, water,

   He has **much fun**.

3. "**Many**" wird bei Substantiven gebraucht, die gezählt werden können. Daher wird es bei der Mehrzahl gebraucht.

   He has **many friends**.

8.2 Übungen

1. I see ______ chairs.
2. I see ______ milk.
3. How ______ people are standing?
4. The girl has ______ teachers.
5. He eats ______ ice-cream.
6. How ______ sugar do you have in your tea?
7. The man is telling ______ jokes.
8. My mother eats ______ fruit.
9. ______ schools teach English.

10. We put ______ butter on our bread.
11. He hasn't got ______ time.
12. How ______ pieces of cake are you eating?
13. We are meeting ______ neighbours.
14. How ______ tea have you got?
15. The girls ask ______ questions.
16. How ______ sweets is he eating?
17. There are ______ weeks in a year.
18. How ______ sand is on the beach?
19. The book has ______ pages.
20. I know ______ names.
21. How ______ food was still there?
22. He sees ______ rabbits.
23. I see ______ bags.
24. How ______ water are you drinking?
25. I am not drinking very ______ water.
26. ______ windows in the house are open.
27. We have ______ fun on the beach.
28. The house has ______ rooms.
29. They are playing ______ games today.
30. How ______ money is on the table?
31. ______ sentences are easy.
32. There are ______ towns in Germany.
33. Put ______ cheese on your bread.
34. I eat ______ chocolate.
35. We are singing ______ songs.
36. The girl has ______ blouses.
37. How ______ cheese do you want?
38. I haven't got ______ money.
39. We see ______ cars every day.
40. How ______ milk is in the kitchen?
41. He has ______ sisters.
42. How ______ butter can I buy?
43. We eat ______ cheese every day.
44. How ______ doors are open?
45. There is ______ food on the table.
46. I have ______ sugar in my tea.
47. He is playing with ______ toys.

48. How ______ chocolate does he eat?
49. How ______ bedrooms are in your house?
50. I eat ______ fruit every day.
51. You have ______ friends.
52. We are eating ______ ice-cream now.
53. How ______ sandwiches does he eat?
54. In school we have ______ subjects.
55. We are drinking ______ tea now.
56. ______ tourists are shopping.
57. I have ______ time today.
58. We are helping ______ girls.
59. The children are playing with ______ sand.
60. You are writing ______ letters.

9 Little - few

9.1 Grammatik

1. "**Little**" und "**few**" werden oft nach Wörtern wie "**too**", "**so**", "**as**", "**very**", und "**how few**" / "**how little**" gebraucht.

   There are **very few cats** in our house.

   We have **very little time**.

2. "**Little**" / "**a little**" wird bei nicht zählbaren Substantiven gebraucht. Es zeichnet eine Menge aus, die nicht gezählt wird. Man zählt, z.B. "two pounds of cheese" aber nicht "two cheeses."

   little = wenig

   a little = ein wenig/ ein bisschen

   only a little = nur wenig

   Einige solche Wörter sind: air, bread, butter, cheese, chocolate, dirt, energy, food, fruit, fun, ice-cream, information, ketchup, milk, money, power, sand, sugar, tea, time, trouble, water,

   We have **little time**. (Wir haben wenig Zeit.)

   We have **very little time**. (Wir haben sehr wenig Zeit.)

   We have **a little time**. (Wir haben ein bisschen Zeit.)

   We have **only a little time**. (Wir haben nur wenig Zeit.)

3. "**Few**" / "**a few**" wird bei Substantiven gebraucht, die gezählt werden können. Daher wird es bei der Mehrzahl gebraucht.

   few = wenige

   a few = einige / ein paar

   only a few = nur wenige

   He has **few friends**. (Er hat wenige Freunde.)

   He has **a few friends**. (Er hat einige Freunde.)

   He has **only a few friends**. (Er hat nur wenige Freunde.)

9.2 Übungen

1. There are ______ animals in our house.
2. I have ______ money.
3. Here is a ______ cheese for your sandwich.
4. The woman is wearing ______ blouses this year.
5. Can I have a ______ sugar in my tea?
6. Sorry, I have very ______ time for you.
7. Have they got a ______ friends?
8. We see ______ good beaches at the seaside.
9. We have a ______ ice-cream for you.
10. There is too ______ tea for all of us.
11. The child is gettting a ______ balls for his birthday.
12. We are getting ______ information about the bad people.
13. ______ boys like washing dishes.
14. He is driving very ______ cars so fast.
15. There is ______ tea still in the cupboard.
16. He is eating a ______ fruit today.
17. Too ______ dogs like cats.
18. We often have a ______ trouble with the car.
19. There are ______ books in that box.
20. There is too ______ time for us to go to the shops.
21. There is very ______ food in our kitchen.
22. Put a ______ chairs in the living-room.
23. The baby is drinking very ______ milk now.
24. The cat is finding too ______ mice.
25. The child has ______ fun at school.
26. I want to eat a ______ chocolate.
27. We have got very ______ shopping bags.
28. Too ______ children eat fruit.
29. Can I have a ______ butter on my sandwich?
30. We have ______ bread at home.
31. The book has very ______ pages.
32. The men have very ______ money in their pockets.
33. I am looking at a ______ pictures of your trip.
34. He has a ______ time now.
35. The house has too ______ rooms for us.
36. I eat very ______ sugar.
37. We are listening to a ______ records.

38. Father is buying too ______ ice-cream.
39. The boy is telling very ______ jokes.
40. He has ______ friends.
41. ______ words are hard to understand.
42. I am bringing a ______ sand back from the seaside.
43. The girl has very ______ toys.
44. There is too ______ fruit on the plate.
45. Very ______ girls and boys don't like games.
46. I see ______ trees in the garden.
47. We have a ______ fun on the weekends.
48. Just drink a ______ water.
49. They are visiting a ______ cities on their trip.
50. You are giving me too ______ money for the present.
51. We have too ______ chairs to sit on.
52. I am writing a ______ sentences in my letter.
53. The child is drinking a ______ milk.
54. We have very ______ butter on our sandwiches.
55. The trees need a ______ rain.
56. She is buying a ______ tickets for the show.
57. We can see very ______ sand at the seaside.
58. He is eating a ______ food at the table.
59. Very ______ pupils are at school today.
60. The old women are drinking too ______ water in summer.

10 This - that - these - those

10.1 Grammatik

1. “**This** “ bezeichnet etwas, was in der Nähe ist und in der Einzahl ist.
   This cat is sitting **here** on my chair.

2. “**These**” bezeichnet etwas, was in der Nähe ist und in der Mehrzahl ist.
   These cats are sitting **here** on my chair.

3. “**That**” bezeichnet etwas, was weiter weg ist und in der Einzahl ist.
   That dog is standing over **there** near the door.

4. “**Those**” bezeichnet etwas, was weiter weg ist und in der Mehrzahl ist.
   Those dogs are standing over **there** near the door.

10.2 Übungen

Linda and Sarah are sitting on a sofa. They have 10 books, 1 blouse, 2 letters, 3 records and 1 apple on a bed near them.

Tom and Dick are standing at their desks. They have 11 pencils, 1 ruler, 5 pens, 1 tomato, 1 shirt and 4 balls on 2 chairs near them.

1. Sarah: “Linda, take ______ book to Tom.”
2. Linda: “______ is your book, Tom.”
3. Sarah: “______ records are new.”
4. Tom: “______ records are nice.”
5. Sarah: “______ balls are old.”
6. Dick: “Yes, ______ balls are old.”
7. Sarah: “______ ruler is long.”
8. Tom: “No, ______ ruler is not long.”
9. Sarah: “______ blouse is too big for me.”
10. Tom: “______ blouse isn’t pretty.”
11. Tom: “______ pencils are black.”
12. Sarah: “______ pencils look blue.”
13. Tom: “Are you reading ______ books, Sarah?”
14. Sarah: “Yes, I am reading ______ books.”
15. Tom: “Is ______ apple green?”

16. Sarah: "No, ______ apple is red."
17. Sarah: "But ______ tomato is also red."
18. Dick: "Yes, ______ tomato is red."
19. Dick: "______ pencil is old."
20. Linda: "Yes, ______ pencil is old."
21. Linda: "But ______ pencils aren't so old, are they?"
22. Dick: "No, ______ pencils aren't so old."
23. Dick: "Are ______ letters from your sisters?"
24. Linda: "Yes, ______ letters are from them."
25. Linda: " ______ letter is from Ann."
26. Dick: " ______ letter is long."
27. Linda: "______ shirt is dirty."
28. Dick: "Yes, ______ shirt is dirty."
29. Dick: "Can you see ______ pens?"
30. Dick: " ______ pen is green."
31. Dick: "And ______ four pens are blue."
32. Linda: "______ green pen is pretty."
33. Linda: "And ______ blue pens are nice, too."
34. Dick: "Is ______ sofa expensive?"
35. Linda: "Yes, ______ sofa is expensive."
36. Linda: " ______ desks are small."
37. Dick: "Yes, ______ desks are small."
38. Dick: "Can I have ______ apple, Sarah?"
39. Sarah: "Yes, you can have ______ apple."
40. Sarah: "Can I have ______ balls, Tom?"
41. Tom: "Yes, you can have ______ balls, Sarah."
42. Tom: Can I hear ______ record?"
43. Sarah: "Yes, you can hear ______ record."
44. Sarah: "Do you want to hear ______ records, too?"
45. Tom: "Yes, I want to hear ______ records, too."
46. Linda: "Can I have ______ green pen?"
47. Tom: "Yes, you can have ______ green pen."
48. Tom: "Do you want ______ blue pens, too?"
49. Linda: "No, I don't want ______ blue pens."
50. Linda: "But I like ______ ruler."
51. Tom: "You can have ______ ruler."
52. Tom: " ______ bed looks lovely."
53. Linda: "Come and sit on ______ bed here."

54. Linda: "______ chairs look hard."
55. Tom: "Yes, ______ chairs are hard."
56. Tom: "______ pencils on ______ chair are nice."
57. Linda: "Yes, ______ pencils on ______ chair are nice."

11 Past tense = Vergangenheit

11.1 Grammatik

1. Die Vergangenheit wird gebraucht, wenn wir etwas erzählen, was vorbei ist oder wenn wir eine Geschichte erzählen. Wörter wie "yesterday, last, when he was young" geben einen Hinweis auf die Vergangenheitsform.

2. **Simple form**

   a) Die meisten Verben bilden ihre Vergangenheit, indem ein "ed" zu der Grundform (infinitive) gesetzt wird.

      to walk ⇒ walked; to roar ⇒ roared

   b) Wenn ein stummes "e" am Ende der Grundform steht, wird nur ein "d" dazu gesetzt.

      to wip**e** ⇒ wiped

   c) Wenn die Grundform mit einem "vowel" (Selbstlaut) und einem "consonant" (Mitlaut) endet, wird der "consonant" verdoppelt. Dann kommt ein "ed" hinzu.

      to st**op** ⇒ stopped,

      to r**ob**, to r**ub**, to st**ep**

   d) Wenn ein Verb mit einem "y" endet und der vorletzte Buchstabe

      - ein "consonant" (Mitlaut) ist, wird das "y" in ein "ied" verwandelt.

        to car**ry** ⇒ carried; to reply ⇒ replied, to try ⇒ tried

      - ein "vowel" (Selbstlaut) ist, bleibt das "y" bestehen. Ein "ed" wird dazu gesetzt.

        to pl**ay** ⇒ played; to stay ⇒ stayed

   e) He/she/it haben kein "s" in der Vergangenheit

      he goes ⇒ he went; she wants ⇒ she wanted

   f) Die Vergangenheitsformen der unregelmäßigen Verben müssen auswendig gelernt werden.

   to see ⇒ saw; to go ⇒ went

3. **Progressive form**

   Die Vergangenheitsform wird mit "**was/were + ing**" gebildet.

I was walking	we were smiling
you were shaking	you were buying
he was feeding	they were crying

Das Verb "**to be**" wird wie folgt umgewandelt:

I	am	I	was
you	are	you	were
he,she,it	is	he,she,it	was
we	are	we	were
you	are	you	were
they	are	they	were

Vergleiche:

	Simple	**Progressive**
present	you hold	you are holding
past	you held	you were holding
present	it barks	it is barking
past	it barked	it was barking
present	he shakes	he is shaking
past	he shook	he was shaking
present	I take	I am taking
past	I took	I was taking

4. **Aussagesatz** in der Vergangenheit

   a) **Simple form**

   Die 2. Form des Verbes drückt die Vergangenheit aus.

present	I eat cake.	He writes books.	You play tennis.
past	I ate cake.	He wrote books.	You played tennis.

   b) **Progressive form**

   Die “progressive form” wird mit “was/were + -ing” gebildet.

present	I am going.	He is coming.	We are helping.
past	I was going.	He was coming.	We were helping.

5. **Fragestellung** in der Vergangenheit

   a) Die Wortstellung bei Fragen:

   bei ***Subjektfragen***:

Fragewort	**Verb**	**Rest des Satzes**
Who	went	home?
Who	was going	home?

   bei ***allen anderen Fragen***:

Fragewort	**Hilfsverb**	**Subjekt**	**Hauptverb**	**Satzrest**
Where	did	she	go	yesterday?
Why	were	they	roaring	loudly?

b) **Simple form**

Das "do/does + inf." in der Gegenwart wird in der Vergangenheit zu "**did + inf**". Bei "he/she/it" entfällt das "s”.

present	Do we see?	Does he go?
past	Did we see?	Did he go?

c) **Progressive form**

Das “am/are/is + -ing” in der Gegenwart wird in der Vergangenheit zu "**was/were + ing**".

present	Am I talking?	Are we shaking?
past	Was I talking?	Were we shaking?

6. **Verneinung** in der Vergangenheit

a) **Simple form**

Das "don’t/doesn’t + infinitive" von der Gegenwart wird in der Vergangenheit zu "**didn’t + inf.**" Bei he/she/it entfällt das "s".

present	I don’t go.	He doesn’t help.
past	I didn’t go.	He didn’t help.

b) **Progressive form**

Die verneinende Form in der Vergangenheit wird mit "**was/were + not + -ing**" gebildet.

present	I am not talking.	He isn’t going.
past	I was not talking.	He wasn’t going.

7. **Übersicht** / Beispiele

Aussagesatz:

present simple	**past simple**
1. Form des Verbes (bei he/she/it “s” am Ende des Verbes)	2. Form des Verbes (bei he/she/it kein "s" am Ende des Verbes)
I see, he sees, they see	I saw, he saw, they saw

Verneinender Satz:

present simple	**past simple**
don’t/doesn’t + inf.	didn’t + inf. kein “s” am Ende des Verbes bei he/she/it
I don’t see, he doesn’t see they don’t see	I didn’t see, he didn’t see they didn’t see

Fragesatz:

present simple	**past simple**
do/does + inf.	did + inf.
Do I see? Does he see? Do they see?	Did I see? Did he see? Did they see?

Aussagesatz:

present progressive	**past progressive**
am/are/is + -ing	was/were + -ing
I am seeing, he is seeing they are seeing	I was seeing, he was seeing they were seeing

Verneinender Satz:

present progressive	**past progressive**
am not/are not/ is not + -ing	was not/were not + -ing
I am not seeing he is not seeing they are not seeing	I was not seeing he was not seeing they were not seeing

Fragesatz:

present progressive	**past progressive**
am/are/is + -ing	was/were + -ing
Am I seeing? Is he seeing? Are they seeing?	Was I seeing? Was he seeing? Were they seeing?

11.2 Übungen

Ändere die Sätze in die Vergangenheit um.

1. My sister usually sees Mr. Smith.
2. The boys are swimming in the water at the moment.
3. You often leave your books on the floor.
4. We sometimes take her home in our car.
5. They always clean the board.
6. My brother holds his ear every day.
7. The boy is running into the water.
8. Do you often write letters?
9. The dogs always eat their food.
10. My brother always makes his bed.
11. We are driving home.
12. The teacher comes to school on Wednesdays.
13. I am drawing a picture.

14. My father has ten books.
15. He is writing a letter.
16. They always wash their faces in the morning.
17. The baby sleeps every night.
18. I usually feed the baby.
19. We always say what we do every day.
20. They often see the cat.
21. You always plan the games.
22. He is sitting in bed.
23. They usually have many friends in their room.
24. He dances every evening.
25. We always come to your party.
26. The boys are laughing at the girl.
27. The girl always shakes her head when she puts her hand on my arm.
28. That boy carries my books every day.
29. We buy bread at the shop.
30. The boys usually play football.
31. The father holds the baby every day.
32. She says, "You always stick your nose in the ice-cream."
33. Dogs always bark when they see the cats.
34. The child goes to the door when it sees that its mother is coming.
35. Does he leave the house when you tell him to go home?
36. The dogs bark because the men are running.
37. I make the cakes.
38. She gets up at 6:30.
39. You eat too much.
40. He drinks water when he is thirsty.
41. Who knows the answer?
42. He takes his dog out every day.
43. We eat the apples.
44. I know what he wants.
45. I see him every day.
46. When are you leaving the house?
47. The birds always fly.
48. You usually run to the bus.
49. My father leaves his car at home when he drinks.
50. She goes to Linda's house.
51. Ben is laughing at the clowns.

52. Mother and I count the money.
53. Mary is saying good-bye to her father.
54. Does she tell you everything?
55. Are we putting the plates on the table?
56. Do I always turn around?
57. Is father calling your sister?
58. What do you say to that?
59. Does Robert always watch the rabbits?
60. Does the girl shake her head?
61. Am I looking at Linda?
62. Are you reading that book?
63. Why do children always eat bananas?
64. Do we always shout at you?
65. Are the babies laughing?
66. It is a rainy day.
67. Tom sees his friend.
68. John comes to the bus stop every day.
69. A man and a girl are getting off the bus.
70. I do my homework.
71. Linda shows her friend her room.
72. We always leave the school at this time.
73. Peter has a lot of money.
74. We are looking for our books.
75. She takes the letter to her sister.
76. Mother goes shopping in the mornings.
77. I count the windows in my room.
78. Kate is cutting the cake.
79. We put our books here this morning.
80. Peter always waits for his friend.
81. The boys are sleeping on sofas.
82. They play tennis in winter.
83. She wants to tell me something.
84. We are singing songs.
85. Tom is riding a bike.
86. He cleans the windows.
87. Do they take their books home every day?
88. The men are repairing the bike.
89. The women help me.

90. Mary washes the socks.
91. She is eating the biscuits.
92. Mother and Linda are counting the shirts.
93. The children leave the school.
94. The women shake their heads.
95. John tells them a story.
96. The boy is feeding the animals.
97. They are eating sandwiches.
98. Do they always eat bread?
99. We listen to songs.
100. The child sometimes stands on the chair.
101. Why are you laughing?
102. Father says funny things.
103. Barbara knows how big the baby is.
104. You and I are leaving the house.
105. I always buy ice-cream.
106. The cat is washing its face.
107. They shake hands when they say good-bye.
108. We are taking you to school.
109. The girls come to school every morning.
110. I have a lot of work to do.
111. Are you happy when you go to school?
112. Do you like the dogs?
113. My brother often flies to London.
114. She sometimes finds money.
115. Do the people always buy apples?
116. Are they answering your question now?
117. He holds her hand when the dogs bark.
118. They clean the board when you tell them to do that.
119. Does he watch you when you are swimming?
120. Their father puts the newspaper on the table every morning.
121. We buy food for the cat.
122. The people see ten cars at the station.
123. Do you know my mother?
124. Why do the children eat in the morning?
125. Mother and I say, "You are shouting very loudly."
126. Where are you going in summer?
127. He tells them, "You eat very quickly."

128. The girl is wearing a pullover because it is cold.
129. When do you get up in the morning?
130. My mother throws the biscuit to the dog.
131. You are standing on my foot.
132. I go to school every day.
133. Linda and Mary say "hello".
134. Tina and I are watching TV.
135. My brother is holding a paper.
136. My father always buys the milk.
137. I sometimes write songs.
138. Helen and Jane are taking the test.
139. Does your father sing?
140. My sister and I carry our books.
141. You often throw the ball.
142. I'm playing with the ball.
143. Mother and I always feed the cat.
144. Do I talk too loudly?
145. Tom goes home.
146. We help our friends.
147. Do you collect stamps?
148. They are coming here.
149. I'm holding a pen.
150. Linda blows up a balloon.
151. Are you dreaming?
152. Does he eat apples?
153. Can you come?
154. Do the girls work hard?
155. That is a dog.
156. The lesson begins at 10 o'clock.
157. We catch balls.
158. Is he sleeping?
159. I'm making a castle.
160. Susan wants a cake.
161. Jane and Tim like dogs.
162. Does your dog bark?
163. Can I read the book?
164. We cut the cake.
165. Tom's swimming.

166. Am I pushing?
167. I hate cats.
168. You shout very loudly.
169. We stay in the house when it's hot.
170. Does your aunt ride a bike?
171. The men carry the table.
172. I work in the morning.
173. The monkey climbs a tree.
174. You talk too much.
175. Are the Millers flying to London?
176. My mother is washing the clothes.
177. We live in a house.
178. Is the plane arriving in Bonn?
179. The tree is growing.
180. Are we eating apples on Friday?
181. My brother calls his friend.
182. You are pulling my arm.
183. They can see the cat.
184. Is Diane drawing a picture?
185. You take a bike.
186. Do we know the Smiths?
187. Tom loves Jane.
188. The man cooks food.
189. You look funny.
190. The baby holds its finger.

Ändere die Sätze in die Gegenwart um.

191. My brother and I didn't break the plates.
192. Did the cat climb the tree?
193. We liked our sisters.
194. The dog hurt its eye.
195. I was eating cake.
196. Did they work hard?
197. The man fed the animals.
198. We met many people.
199. Was father learning English?
200. The men didn't cut their fingers.
201. Did I sometimes read your book?

202. Did your sister wash the clothes?
203. You were playing under the table.
204. The woman loved her child.
205. My father and mother sent many letters.
206. Was the dog living at your house?
207. We could talk with Tom.
208. I didn't help my brother.
209. Your brother often came to the door.
210. Was the lady drinking tea?
211. You ate the apples.
212. Did she sing that song?
213. My father was lighting the candle.
214. Were the girls shouting?
215. Our cat didn't forget the fish.
216. Did we sweep the kitchen every day?
217. My mother didn't hear the train.
218. The girl could feel the water.
219. You didn't carry the baby.
220. Was I wearing your dress?
221. Tom and Jean worked quickly.
222. My brother read a book.
223. Were we collecting stamps?
224. My sister was riding her bike.
225. Were you running to school?
226. I blew up a balloon.
227. The cat was shaking its head.
228. Did you fetch the chairs in the morning?
229. Did we want those books?
230. The man didn't start his car.
231. Did the girl swim every day?
232. The dog pulled my shoe off.
233. The girl didn't keep her books.
234. We were selling our house.
235. Did they stand at the table?
236. Did he often call you?
237. Was your brother buying a new car?
238. Her mother didn't cook the food.
239. The lady gave me an apple.

240. The women were speaking German.
241. The doctor arrived late.
242. Did you cry on Wednesday?
243. Was he holding your hand?
244. John and Barbara took us home.
245. We were shouting at the dog.
246. They bought their tickets.
247. Did he laugh at you?
248. Were you making a kite?
249. Yes, I made kites for my small brother.
250. The dog barked when it saw the cat.
251. We always ate the food.
252. You fed the cat.
253. Were you shouting at the animals?
254. Did your brother go to school?
255. Father was helping her.
256. They were laughing when I saw them.
257. He ran into the room when he saw me.
258. Did he drink his tea?
259. The cat shook its head when it stood.
260. We were dancing yesterday.
261. My mother put on her hat.
262. I was looking at the animals.
263. Did you laugh when Tom told you a funny story?
264. He was holding her hand while he said good-bye.
265. Did I see you in Berlin?
266. Did he sometimes carry the bags?
267. We held their hands.
268. They came home late.
269. The man left the school early.
270. Linda and I made very big pictures.
271. Did the lady run home?
272. Was the baby crying?
273. When did the cat eat the fish?
274. Did he leave the house?
275. My brother and sister were standing there.
276. I was shaking hands with her.
277. When did you tell your father?

278. That man was taking your chair.
279. Didn't I keep your book clean?
280. Were Linda and Sandy walking?
281. My mother and I didn't pay for our bread yesterday.
282. I was going home.
283. They fed their children some fish.
284. Weren't you coming to our house today?
285. The dog was running to the house.
286. I chose the red pullover on Monday.
287. Wasn't the boy doing his homework?
288. Were you helping mother yesterday?
289. Karen and I bought our food in the shop.
290. You didn't leave your shoes in the hall.
291. I wasn't shouting too loudly.
292. Didn't the girls stay in bed too long?
293. Was the woman speaking to your friend?
294. You drank your milk very quickly.
295. The girl didn't make her bed.
296. Tom and I were eating our breakfast.

12 Past simple - Past progressive

12.1 Grammatik

1. **Past simple** (=2. Form des Verbes) wird gebraucht

   a) bei Geschichten und Berichten. Mehrere Handlungen folgen nacheinander.

   I drove the car to the city yesterday, looked in the shops and bought many things.

   b) wenn man "when" fragt.

   When did you go to the city?

   c) Wenn eines der folgenden Wörter im Satz vorhanden ist, kommt nur die "simple form":

always, every, often, sometimes, usually, in winter, in spring, in summer, in autumn, on Mondays, on Tuesdays, on Wednesdays, on Thursdays, on Fridays, on Saturdays, on Sundays.

2. **Past progressive** (=was/were + -ing) wird gebraucht

   a) wenn eine Handlung zu einem bestimmten Zeitpunkt für einige Zeit in der Vergangenheit ablief.

   We were talking on the phone for two hours yesterday.

   b) wenn mehrere Handlungen zur gleichen Zeit abliefen.

   Linda was talking to her friends while her mother was washing the dishes.

   c) um Einzelheiten oder Personen in Erzählungen zu beschreiben.

   The man you saw was wearing a green hat, red pants and yellow shoes.

   d) wenn Wörter wie "at that moment", "at that time", "in the picture", "still" oder "right then" im Satz sind.

3. Wenn eine Handlung gerade ablief (progressive) und noch nicht zu Ende war, als eine neue Handlung (simple) anfing, wird die Handlung, die länger anhielt, in "progressive" gesetzt und die neue Handlung in "simple" gesetzt.

   Linda was eating her breakfast when the phone rang. (Linda war schon dabei, ihr Frühstück zu essen. Das Klingeln des Telefons unterbrach ihr Frühstück. Sie war länger am Frühstücken.

12.2 Übungen

Setze die richtige Zeitform in die Lücke!

1. She (to open) the window, (to look) out, and (to see) her mother.
2. The dog (to bark) when I (to come) home.
3. When (to see - I) you last?
4. You (to blow) your nose at that moment.
5. He (to fly) to London every week last year.
6. (to ride - they) a bike at that time yesterday?
7. I (to sweep - often) the kitchen.
8. While we (to sleep), the dogs (to bark).
9. (to meet - you) her on Mondays?
10. She (to sing) a song right then.
11. When I (to see - simple) mother, she (to buy) bread.
12. He (to leave) his house at 10 yesterday morning.
13. I (to bring - always) him his book in the morning.
14. We (to hold) hands when mother (to come) in.
15. (to feed - he) the cat at that moment?
16. We (to dig) a hole for two hours yesterday.
17. (to hide - she - always) her books?
18. You (to run) too quickly at this time yesterday.
19. Two people (to shake) hands when the third person (to shout).
20. The cat (to sleep - always) in winter.
21. My sister (to tell) me a story when you came.
22. My mother (to read) a book when I (to phone) yesterday.
23. You (to wake - always) me up at 7 o'clock.
24. The children (to take) the test for four hours yesterday.
25. (to learn - he) his vocabulary words yesterday?
26. We (to spread - usually) butter on our bread.
27. We (to wear) old clothes right then.
28. (to begin - she) to talk at that moment?
29. The children (to grow) so quickly last year.
30. The children (to run) around when the teacher (to call) them.
31. The dog (to break) its leg when it fell.
32. The children (to freeze) in the cold yesterday when I saw them.
33. (to get - the tree) enough water in summer?
34. (to come - mother and I) quickly enough yesterday?
35. The woman (to lie) in bed at that time yesterday.
36. While one girl (to read), the other girl (to write).

37. The woman (to pay) for the apples yesterday.
38. (to stand - you) in the cold while he (to drink) tea?
39. The boy (to win) the game when I came.
40. We (to sell - often) our own clothes.
41. (to show - the men - always) the women their books?
42. They (to sing) while mother (to wash) the dishes.
43. I (to ring - always) the bell at 5 o'clock.
44. The man and I (to speak) for two hours yesterday.
45. You (to bite - often) my finger when you were a baby.
46. (to cut - I) the cake when you (to come) in?
47. While the boy (to run), his sister (to sleep).
48. He (to eat - always) too much until he (to become) ill.
49. In the picture she (to fall) down the stairs.
50. (to choose - the men - often) the right toy?
51. Mother (to cut) the cake when father (to come) home.
52. Her nose (to bleed - often) in winter.
53. (to buy - we) shoes at that time?
54. The men (to sell) their cars in the picture.
55. You (to steal - often) my money!
56. They (to drive) to Bonn at that moment.
57. (to go - he - always) to the shop in the afternoon?
58. Father and I (to give - usually) the children a book.
59. Two days ago the dog (to bark), (to bite) the child and (to run) away. But then we (to find) it.
60. The dog and cat (to fight) when I saw them.
61. The girl (to catch) the ball every day.
62. While the man (to cook), the woman (to get) everything ready.
63. (to forget - the old man - always) his name?
64. I (to feel) sad when you phoned. Now I'm happy.
65. The balloon (to burst) when the child stuck a pencil in it.
66. My brother and I (to put) our pullovers on in winter.
67. The boy (to sleep - still) when we (to wake) up.
68. You (to write) letters when I (to see) you yesterday.
69. (to teach - the teachers) you to write when you were small?
70. My teacher (to let - always) me go home early on Mondays.
71. The child (to cry) and (to look) for its mother when she saw it.
72. She (to sell - always) apples in the supermarket.
73. I (to dig) a hole when you phoned me yesterday.
74. (to sit - the cat - sometimes) in the sun?

75. The man (to say) good-bye when you came.
76. We (to spend - always) our holiday in Spain.
77. (to lose - I) my hat yesterday?
78. You (to take) a test at that time yesterday.
79. The birds (to build) a nest every year.
80. (to do - she) her homework when you came?
81. You (to drink - sometimes) milk in the evenings.
82. I (to give) a party right then.
83. (to shake - they) their heads at that moment?
84. He (to spell - always) his name wrong.
85. Yesterday I (to phone) my sister, (to pack) my things and (to drive) to her house.
86. The cat (to catch - always) a mouse in summer.
87. The man (to draw) a picture when we saw him.
88. (to find - the girl - always) her books in her room?
89. You (to buy - sometimes) a blouse when you were in the city.
90. I (to fight) a cold for five days last week.
91. The bad boy (to steal - always) money from his mother.
92. (to hide - the children) when their mother looked for them?
93. You (to ride) a horse while your sister (to wash) the car.
94. (to sleep - the woman - usually) so late in the morning?
95. We (to stand) in the rain at that time.
96. I (to lie - sometimes) in bed until 10 in the morning last summer.
97. (to fly - the birds) to the south in the winter?
98. The teacher (to shut) her book when the pupils (to come) in.
99. The boy (to win - always) when he played cards.
100. (to begin - we) to talk at ten or nine?

13 Question formation in the past (Fragebildung in der Vergangenheit)

13.1 Grammatik

1. **past simple**

   a) Wenn man nach dem Subjekt fragt, braucht man kein weiteres Hilfsverb hinzuzufügen. Auch bei der Einzahl he/she/it kommt kein "-s" an das Verb.

   Tom came every day. **Who** came every day?

   The girls came home. **Who** came home?

   b) Bei allen anderen Fragen muss man zwei Teile zum Verb haben. Wenn ein zweites Verbteil fehlt, setzt man "did" als Hilfsverb dazu.

   She came home **every day**. **When did** she come home?

   They came home **every day**. **When did** they come home?

   Yes, they came home. **Did** they come home?

2. **past progressive** (= -ing)

   a) Bei "I/he/she/it" gebraucht man "was + -ing", um Fragen in "past progressive" zu stellen.

   She was running **home**. Where **was she** running?

   I was walking **yesterday**. When **was I** walking ?

   Yes, he was walking. **Was he** walking?

   b) Bei "you/we/they" gebraucht man "were + -ing", um Fragen in "past progressive" zu stellen.

   You were talking loudly. How **were you** talking?

   Yes, you were talking. **Were you** talking?

   c) Wenn man nach dem Subjekt fragt, gebraucht man "was + -ing", weil man bei der Fragestellung angeblich nicht weiß, ob die Antwort Einzahl oder Mehrzahl ist.

   Tom was coming home. **Who was** coming home?

   The girls were coming home. **Who was** coming home?

3. Wortstellung bei Fragen

Fragewort	**Hilfsverb**	**Subjekt**	**Hauptverb**	**Satzrest**
When	did	she	come	home?
Where	was	she	running	yesterday?

bei Subjektfragen dagegen:

Fragewort	**Verb**	**Rest des Satzes**
Who	came	home?
Who	was running	home?

bei Ja-/Nein-Fragen:

Hilfsverb	**Subjekt**	**Hauptverb**	**Rest des Satzes**
Did	they	come	home?
Were	you	talking	yesterday?

4. Fragewörter:

Who	Wer?
When	Wann?
Where	Wo?
What	Was?
Whose	Wessen
Why	Warum?
How	Wie?
How many	Wieviele?
How much	Wieviel?

13.2 Übungen

Stelle je eine Frage zu den hervorgehobenen Wörtern

1. He saw **two** houses.
2. **He** saw two houses.
3. He saw **two houses**.
4. He **saw two houses**.
5. **You** were eating pudding.
6. You **were eating pudding**.
7. You were eating **pudding**.
8. I sang a song **in the kitchen**.
9. **I** sang a song in the kitchen.
10. I sang **a song** in the kitchen.
11. I **sang a song** in the kitchen.
12. Mother and I were building **two** houses.
13. **Mother and I** were building two houses.

14. Mother and I **were building two houses.**
15. Mother and I were building **two houses.**
16. **Linda** was writing a letter.
17. Linda was writing **a letter**.
18. Linda **was writing a letter**.
19. I was biting **my** apple.
20. I was biting **my apple**.
21. I **was biting my apple**.
22. You wrote **ten** words.
23. **You** wrote ten words.
24. You wrote **ten words**.
25. You **wrote ten words**.
26. He gave you the present **because he loved you**.
27. He **gave you the present** because he loved you.
28. The three girls were singing **a song** this morning.
29. **The three** girls were singing a song this morning.
30. **The three girls** were singing a song this morning.
31. The three girls **were singing a song** this morning.
32. The three girls were singing a song **this morning**.
33. I read the book **loudly**.
34. **I** read the book loudly.
35. I read **the book** loudly.
36. I **read the book loudly**.
37. The little boy knew the answer **last week**.
38. **The little boy** knew the answer last week.
39. The little boy knew **the answer** last week.
40. You were sitting **on a chair**.
41. **You** were sitting on a chair.
42. You **were sitting on a chair**.
43. Tom and I ran **because we were late**.
44. **Tom and I** ran because we were late.
45. Tom and I **ran** because we were late.
46. Mother hung up **my dress**.
47. **Mother** hung up my dress.
48. Mother **hung up my dress.**
49. Linda and Gary rang us up **because they had not seen us**.
50. **Linda and Gary** rang us up because they had not seen us.
51. Linda and Gary **rang us up** because they had not seen us.

52. Mother bought a cat for **father**.
53. **Mother** bought a cat for father.
54. Mother bought **a cat** for father.
55. Mother **bought a cat** for father.
56. **I** began to read.
57. I began **to read**.
58. I **began to read**.
59. The cat was walking **very quietly**.
60. **The cat** was walking very quietly.
61. The cat **was walking** very quietly.
62. The cat **was walking very quietly**.
63. You were reading the book **when I phoned**.
64. **You** were reading the book when I phoned.
65. You were reading **the book** when I phoned.
66. You **were reading the book** when I phoned.
67. The woman was selling books **last night**.
68. **The woman** was selling the books last night.
69. The woman was selling **the books** last night.
70. The woman **was selling the books** last night.
71. The dogs and I were playing with **the children's** balls.
72. **The dogs and I** were playing with the children's balls.
73. The dogs and I **were playing** with the children's balls.
74. The dogs and I were playing with **the children's balls**.
75. You ate **too quickly**.
76. **You** ate too quickly.
77. You **ate** too quickly.
78. I was working **very slowly**.
79. **I** was working very slowly.
80. I **was working** very slowly.
81. My brother drove his car **to his sister**.
82. **My brother** drove his car to his sister.
83. My brother drove **his car** to his sister.
84. My brother **drove his car to his sister.**
85. We ate ice-cream **because it was a hot day.**
86. **We** ate ice-cream because it was a hot day.
87. We ate **ice-cream** because it was a hot day.
88. We **ate ice-cream** because it was a hot day.
89. **The girls** shook their heads.

90. The girls shook **their heads**.
91. The girls **shook their heads.**
92. You threw the ball **in the garden**.
93. **You** threw the ball in the garden.
94. You threw **the ball** in the garden.
95. You **threw the ball** in the garden.
96. I was walking **home**.
97. I **was walking home**.
98. The dogs were eating **two** dog biscuits.
99. **The dogs** were eating two dog biscuits.
100. The dogs were eating **two dog biscuits**.
101. The dogs **were eating two dog biscuits.**
102. The little dog caught **a ball**.
103. **The little dog** caught a ball.
104. The little dog **caught a ball.**
105. **The boys and I** were flying in a plane.
106. The boys and I were flying in **a plane**.
107. The boys and I **were flying** in a plane.
108. **Tom and Dick** went for a swim on Sunday.
109. Tom and Dick went for a swim **on Sunday**.
110. Tom and Dick **went for a swim** on Sunday.
111. The children took their toys **to their mothers**.
112. **The children** took their toys to their mothers.
113. The children took **their toys** to their mothers.
114. The children **took their toys to their mothers.**
115. The baby boy was wearing a pullover **because it was cold**.
116. **The baby boy** was wearing a pullover because it was cold.
117. The baby boy was wearing **a pullover** because it was cold.
118. The baby boy **was wearing a pullover** because it was cold.
119. I swam for **two** hours.
120. **I** swam for two hours.
121. I **swam** for two hours.
122. The books were lying **on a table**.
123. **The books** were lying on a table.
124. **You** broke the pencil.
125. You broke **the pencil**.
126. You **broke the pencil.**
127. Linda and Bob held hands **because they loved each other**.

128. **Linda and Bob** held hands because they loved each other.
129. Linda and Bob **held hands** because they loved each other.
130. Father and I held **mother's** hand.
131. **Father and I** held mother's hand.
132. Father and I held **mother's hand.**
133. Father and I **held mother's hand.**
134. The boy found the ball **under the tree**.
135. **The boy** found the ball under the tree.
136. The boy found **the ball** under the tree.
137. The boy **found the ball** under the tree.
138. Mother and I hung the picture up **in the living-room**.
139. **Mother and I** hung the picture up in the living-room.
140. Mother and I hung **the picture** up in the living-room.
141. Mother and I **hung the picture up** in the living-room.
142. I went **to school** every week.
143. **I** went to school every week.
144. I **went to school** every week.
145. I went to school **every week**.
146. The girl was buying **two** apples.
147. **The girl** was buying two apples.
148. The girl **was buying two apples.**
149. The girl was buying **two apples.**
150. Ben and I learnt the words **because the teacher told us to**.
151. **Ben and I** learnt the words because the teacher told us to.
152. Ben and I learnt **the words** because the teacher told us to.
153. Ben and I **learnt the words** because the teacher told us to.
154. You gave me a book **yesterday**.
155. **You** gave me a book yesterday.
156. You gave me **a book** yesterday.
157. You gave **me** a book yesterday.
158. You **gave me a book** yesterday.
159. Mother slept **poorly**.
160. **Mother** slept poorly.
161. The cat took a mouse **to its mother**.
162. **The cat** took a mouse to its mother.
163. The cat took **a mouse** to its mother.
164. The cat **took a mouse to its mother.**
165. His uncle carried **the chair**.

166. **His uncle** carried the chair.
167. His uncle **carried the chair.**
168. You went to Bonn **last year**.
169. **You** went to Bonn last year.
170. You went **to Bonn** last year.
171. You **went to Bonn** last year.
172. The children ran **quickly**.
173. The children **ran quickly.**
174. **The children** ran quickly.
175. My sisters and I met the man **two years ago**.
176. My sisters and I met **the man** two years ago.
177. My sisters and I **met the man** two years ago.
178. **My sisters and I** met the man two years ago.
179. You were laughing **because you were happy**.
180. You **were laughing** because you were happy.
181. **You** were laughing.
182. The men were selling **their** cars.
183. The men were selling **their cars.**
184. The men **were selling their cars.**
185. **The men** were selling their cars.
186. **My father** bought milk.
187. My father bought **milk**.
188. My father **bought milk**.
189. You saw **the house** yesterday.
190. **You** saw the house yesterday.
191. You saw the house **yesterday.**
192. You **saw the house** yesterday.
193. The monkeys ate **the child's** banana.
194. **The monkeys** ate the child's banana.
195. The monkeys ate **the child's banana.**
196. The monkeys **ate the child's banana.**
197. I fed the cat **every day**.
198. I fed **the cat** every day.
199. I **fed the cat** every day.
200. **I** fed the cat every day.
201. The women and I spoke **ten** words.
202. The women and I **spoke ten words.**
203. **The women and I** spoke ten words.

204. The women and I spoke **ten words.**
205. You were laughing **very loudly**.
206. **You** were laughing very loudly.
207. You **were laughing** very loudly.
208. **Susan** walked home yesterday.
209. Susan walked **home** yesterday.
210. Susan **walked home** yesterday.
211. Susan walked home **yesterday.**
212. The men were eating in the kitchen **last month**.
213. **The men** were eating in the kitchen last month.
214. The men were eating **in the kitchen** last month.
215. The men **were eating** in the kitchen.
216. The men **were eating in the kitchen** last month.
217. The old women were sitting down **because they were lazy**.
218. **The old women** were sitting down.
219. The old women **were sitting down** because they were lazy.
220. The children and I were riding horses **at the farm**.
221. The children and I were riding **horses** at the farm.
222. **The children and I** were riding horses at the farm.
223. The children and I **were riding horses** at the farm.
224. The boy held **a book**.
225. The boy **held a book.**
226. **The boy** held a book.
227. I was reading **twelve** books.
228. I **was reading twelve books.**
229. **I** was reading twelve books.
230. I was reading **twelve books.**
231. The children were quiet **in the supermarket**.
232. **The children** were quiet in the supermarket.
233. My father sometimes told **a story**.
234. **My father** sometimes told a story.
235. My father sometimes **told a story.**
236. Linda was throwing **a ball**.
237. Linda **was throwing a ball.**
238. **Linda** was throwing a ball.
239. The men were standing **at the door**.
240. **The men** were standing at the door.
241. The men **were standing** at the door.

242. The boys threw **four** balls.
243. **The boys** threw four balls.
244. The boys **threw four balls.**
245. The boys threw **four balls.**
246. **My sister and I** drew pictures.
247. My sister and I drew **pictures.**
248. My sister and I **drew pictures.**
249. **The boys** were selling cars.
250. The boys **were selling cars.**
251. The boys were selling **cars.**
252. You saw **Linda's** car.
253. **You** saw Linda's car.
254. You **saw Linda's car.**
255. You saw **Linda's car.**
256. We were reading a book to **the girl**.
257. **We** were reading a book to the girl.
258. We were reading **a book** to the girl.
259. We **were reading a book to the girl.**
260. I was reading the book **because it was interesting**.
261. I was reading **the book**.
262. They had lunch **at 1 o'clock**.
263. Tom was cooking for **his sister**.
264. Tom **was cooking** for his sister.
265. You were catching **Linda's** ball.
266. **You** were catching Linda's ball.
267. You were catching **Linda's ball.**
268. You **were catching Linda's ball.**
269. I was making a cake **yesterday afternoon**.
270. I was making **a cake** yesterday afternoon.
271. I **was making a cake** yesterday afternoon.
272. Father and I spoke **too quietly**.
273. **Father and I** spoke too quietly.
274. Father and I **spoke** too quietly.
275. The men were working **quickly**.
276. **The men** were working quickly.
277. The men **were working** quickly.
278. You were walking **at the park**.
279. **You** were walking at the park.

280. You **were walking** at the park.
281. We were driving **very fast**.
282. **We** were driving very fast.
283. The girl was holding **the ball**.
284. I took **Ken's** book.
285. I **took Ken's book.**
286. **I** took Ken's book.
287. Linda and Dick were buying toys for **their children**.
288. Linda and Dick **were buying toys** for their children.
289. **Linda and Dick** were buying toys for their children.
290. Linda and Dick were buying **toys** for their children.
291. **The man and his wife** were driving home.
292. The man and his wife were driving **home**.
293. The man and his wife **were driving home.**
294. The cat was hiding **under the tree**.
295. The cat **was hiding** under the tree.
296. **I** was driving the car.
297. I was driving **the car**.
298. I **was driving the car.**
299. The dogs barked **loudly**.
300. The dogs **barked** loudly.
301. I was washing the plates for **you**.
302. I was washing **the plates** for you.
303. I **was washing the plates** for you.
304. The man was feeding **the boy's** dog.
305. The man **was feeding the boy's dog.**
306. **The man** was feeding the boy's dog.
307. The man was feeding **the boy's dog.**
308. **The dogs and cats** were playing in the park.
309. The dogs and cats were playing **in the park.**
310. The dogs and cats **were playing** in the park.
311. You were hearing **ten** songs.
312. You **were hearing ten songs.**
313. **You** were hearing ten songs.
314. You were hearing **ten songs.**
315. **You** were talking on the phone.
316. You **were talking** on the phone.
317. You were talking **on the phone**.

318. My father and I drank milk **before school**.
319. My father and I drank **milk** before school.
320. My father and I **drank milk** before school.
321. **My father and I** drank milk before school.
322. I burnt my finger **on the hot plate**.
323. I burnt **my finger** on the hot plate.
324. I **burnt my finger on the hot plate.**
325. We gave the poor people **clothes**.
326. We gave **the poor people** clothes.
327. We **gave the poor people clothes.**
328. **We** gave the poor people clothes.
329. We were cleaning **the kitchen**.
330. **We** were cleaning the kitchen.
331. We **were cleaning the kitchen.**
332. **The girls** were writing many sentences.
333. The girls **were writing many sentences.**
334. The girls were writing **many sentences**.

14 Past - Present Perfect

14.1 Grammatik

1. **past**

   Wenn folgende Wörter im Satz vorhanden sind, kommt meist "past":

   ago, at ... o'clock, before (1980), in (1980), last (week), on (Tuesday), the other day, yesterday

   a) **simple**

   - Die Handlung ist abgeschlossen und hat keine Verbindung zu der Gegenwart. Man denkt an kein Ergebnis oder Folgen.

     I took the train yesterday.

   - Wenn mehrere Handlungen in der Vergangenheit aufeinander folgten und man berichtet über das vergangene Ereignis. Das wird besonders in Erzählungen, Geschichten und Romanen gebraucht.

     I drove the car to the city yesterday, looked in the shops and bought many new things.

   - Wenn man "when" fragt.

     When did you go to the city?

   b) **progressive**

   - Wenn eine Handlung in der Vergangenheit von einer anderen Handlung **unterbrochen** wurde. Die Handlung, die andauert, ist in "progressive". Die Handlung, die plötzlich eintritt, ist in "simple".

     Linda was telling a joke when the phone rang.

   - Bei Handlungen in der Vergangenheit, die **gleichzeitig** verlaufen sind.

     Linda was talking to friends **while** her mother was washing the dishes.

   - Wenn Handlungen oder Vorgänge **längere Zeit** verliefen.

     They were talking on the phone for two hours last night.

2. **present perfect**

Wenn folgende Wörter im Satz vorhanden sind, kommt meist "present perfect":

all day, already, ever, ever since, for, how long, just, lately, never, not yet, of late, recently, since ..., so far, the whole day, this (afternoon), today, up till now, up to now, yet

("Already" kann auch in den anderen Perfektformen gebraucht werden.)

- Die Handlung reicht von der Vergangenheit bis in die Gegenwart und ist **noch nicht beendet**. Diese Zeitform wird für aktuelle Berichte und Briefe gebraucht. Manchmal kommt "since + bis zum Zeitpunkt des Sprechens."

  I haven't heard from her since she left home.

- Die Handlung **wirkt** von der Vergangenheit bis in die Gegenwart, obwohl sie **vorher aufhörte**. Manchmal sieht man das Ergebnis noch. Aus dem Ergebnis der Handlung können Folgerungen oder weitere Handlungen entstehen.

  My dress is dirty. A car has splashed me.

- Als Einleitung für ein Gespräch über ein Ereignis, das in der Vergangenheit geschehen ist. Die weiteren Sätze über dieses Ereignis stehen in "past".

  There has been an accident at the corner. Two cars crashed and the police came.

a) **progressive**

In Kombination mit den Hinweiswörtern für "progressive" (z.B.: listen, look, now, right now, today) wird häufig "present perfect progressive" gebraucht.

Die Bildung davon: have/has + been + -ing

She has been talking ever since I entered the room.

He's been sitting there for ten hours now.

b) Vergleiche

I have never driven to London.

I have been driving **for** two hours **now**.

14.2 Übungen

Setze das Verb in Klammern in die richtige Zeitform!

1. Last week I (to visit) my uncle on Wednesday.
2. One day a boy (to meet) a girl in school. When (to meet - he) her?
3. When I was a child I (to play - not) with cars, but I (to play) with computers.
4. (to see - you - ever) the seaside?
5. I (to hear - never) a ghost.
6. One night Tom (to have) a terrible dream.
7. Mary (to give - just) the cat its milk.

8. The little girl (to take) my toys.
9. Yesterday a man (to come) into my house and (to break) all my chairs.
10. How often (to play - you) hockey since the holidays?
11. Tom (to feed) the animals three hours ago.
12. In 1968 Tom Jones (to write) his best book.
13. Bill (to repair) his bike yesterday.
14. During the holidays Linda (to go) for a swim every day.
15. I (to buy - just) a new blouse.
16. My mother (to write) three letters since seven o'clock.
17. When we were in London, we (to see - not) Big Ben, but we (to see) big buses.
18. How many times (to wear - you) your shoes since last weekend?
19. How many letters (to write - he) this month?
20. (to see - you) Mary last weekend? No, I (to see - not) her last weekend. But I (to see) her yesterday.
21. (you - to see - often) her this month? No, I (to see - not) her this month. But I (to see - often) her this year.
22. (I - to see - not) you the other day? Yes, I (to see) you yesterday.
23. (to eat - they - already) their breakfast?
24. The children (to sleep - not) yesterday.
25. (to see - we - not) you recently?
26. How long (he - to wait) for the bus up till now? He (to wait) for two hours now.
27. When (to buy - they) the fish yesterday? They (to buy) it at 4 p.m.
28. I (to speak - not) to her yet. But I (to speak) to her sister yesterday.
29. The girls (to do - not) their homework so far, but they (to play) for many hours.
30. I (to take) a taxi two days ago.
31. (to answer - we) all the letters up to now?
32. (you - to write) to her yesterday?
33. (to see - I - not) you already today?
34. The girls (to play) outside yesterday when I saw them.
35. We (to buy) a house before 1983.
36. (He - to visit - not) his mother last weekend?
37. You (to go - not) to the cinema with your friends lately.
38. (to eat - our friends) at nine o' clock? No. They (to eat) at ten o'clock.
39. (to be - I) good on Monday?
40. (to ride - he - not) his bike on Wednesday? No. He (to ride) on Thursday.
41. We (to fly) to America in 1980.
42. (I - not - to work) hard last month? Yes, you (to work) very hard.
43. (You - to drive - not) to Paris a month ago?
44. (to go - the lady) to Spain in 1970? No, she (to go) to France.

45. (to do - I) my homework correctly yesterday? Yes, you (to do) it correctly.
46. The men (to work) hard up till now.
47. (you - to see - not - ever) her before? No, I (to see - not) her before. But I (to see) you before.
48. (He - to see - not) Susan since the holidays? No, he (to see - not) Susan. But he (to see) Ann.
49. (to sit - they) there yesterday? No, they (to sit - not) there yesterday. But they (to sit) there on Saturday.
50. She (to wear) her blouse for two years now.
51. (to go - you) to the supermarket yesterday? No, I (to go) there on Monday.
52. (to eat - it) its food yet?
53. You (to watch - not) TV at 5 o'clock yesterday.
54. They (to see - not) my sister yet.
55. Where (to go - he) at 7 o'clock yesterday? He (to go) home.
56. (We - to see - not) the Smiths on Tuesday?
57. You (to go) to bed at 8 p.m. yesterday.
58. (They - to drink - not) their milk yet?
59. I (to feed - already) the cat.
60. (to go - my sister) shopping yet?
61. Mother and I (to go - not) to bed early last night.
62. (You - to see - not) Jane this week yet?
63. (to go - father and mother) dancing yesterday?
64. I (to see - never) the sea.
65. The boy (to eat - not) his breakfast yesterday.
66. (to hear - you - ever) a car?
67. The children (to see) their parents on Friday.
68. Where (to drive - you) the car last Tuesday? Well, we (to drive) it to Bonn.
69. She (to sleep) for five hours so far today.
70. (They - to phone - not) Linda before 6 p.m.? No, they (to phone) her at 7 p.m.
71. (They - to read - not) the newspaper so far?
72. I (to steal - never) a car, but I (to steal) a book yesterday.
73. The men (to go - just) to work.
74. The bad children (to steal) apples from the trees yesterday.
75. (to wash - you - already) your face?
76. Father (to buy - not) the milk the other day.
77. (to see - I - ever) you before?
78. We (to see) you yesterday.
79. No, she (to see - not) them two days ago.
80. You (to read - not) read a book recently. You (to read) a book two years ago.

81. Where (to live - they) before 1980? They (to live) in Spain.
82. (I - to speak - not) to you yet?
83. She (to go) home yesterday.
84. (to come - they - not - just) home from Japan?
85. We (to run - not) to the supermarket last week.
86. She (to talk - not) at that moment yesterday.
87. (to read - you) yesterday evening when I phoned?
88. The children (to play - not) cards when I came last evening.
89. (to find - you - not) your dog yet?
90. Why (the people - to eat - not) yet?
91. I (to sleep - not) well last night.
92. You (to watch) too much TV this week.
93. He (to be - never) to London.
94. They (to drive - not) a car before 1985.
95. We (to see - not) the film so far.
96. (to sleep - you) when your son arrived yesterday?
97. No, I (to be - not) home when he came.
98. He (to write - not) a book yet.
99. (They - to go - not) home yet?
100. My mother (to wash - not) the windows yesterday.

15 The Comparison of Adjectives = Die Steigerung der Adjektive

15.1 Grammatik

1. Ein Adjektiv mit nur **einer Silbe** wird mit "-er/-est" gesteigert.

   high - higher - highest

   Wenn die Adjektive mit **einem** Selbstlaut und **einem** Mitlaut enden, wird der Mitlaut verdoppelt, bevor man die Endung "-er/-est" anhängt.

   b**ig** - b**igg**er - biggest

   Ein stummes "e" am Ende des Adjektivs entfällt bei "-er/ -est".

   fin**e** - finer - finest

   Einige Adjektive:

   brave, bright, calm, cheap, clean, cold, cool, dark, deep, far, fast, fat, few, fine, flat, free, fresh, glad, great, high, hot, large, late, light, long, loud, low, mad, near, neat, nice, old, poor, proud, quick, sad, safe, short, shy, sick, slow, small, smart, soft, strong, sure, sweet, tall, thick, thin, tight, warm, weak, wet, wide, wrong, young

2. Adjektive mit **zwei Silben**.

   - Wenn sie mit "-er", "-le", "-ow" oder "y" enden, werden Adjektive mit zwei Silben mit "-er/-est" gesteigert. Wenn der letzte Buchstabe vor dem "y" ein Mitlaut ist, wird das "y" in ein "i" gewandelt. Dann wird "-er/-est" angehängt.

     hap**py** - hap**pi**er - happiest

     Einige Adjektive:

     angry, busy, cloudy, crazy, dirty, early, easy, funny, greedy, grumpy, handy, happy, hungry, juicy, lazy, little, lovely, lucky, narrow, naughty, noisy, pretty, rainy, shallow, silly, simple, steady, sunny, thirsty, tidy, ugly

   - Sonst werden Adjektive mit **zwei Silben** meist mit "more/ most" gesteigert. Auch Adjektive mit der Endung "-ful" oder "-re" werden so gesteigert. Sie haben die Betonung auf der ersten Silbe.

     famous - **more** famous - **most** famous

     Einige Adjektive:

     active, awful, basic, boring, careful, charming, childish, decent, dreadful, eager, famous, modern, nervous, perfect, special, splendid, thrilling, urgent, useful

- Manche zweisilbigen Adjektive können sowohl mit "-er/-est" als auch mit "more/most" gesteigert werden. Wenn sie vor einem Substantiv stehen, werden sie aber mit "-er/-est" gesteigert. In der Umgangssprache werden noch viele andere Adjektive auch mit "more/most" gesteigert, als hier unten angegeben.

  intense - intenser - intensest

  intense - more intense - most intense

  Einige Adjektive:

  able, bitter, clever, common, friendly, gentle, handsome, intense, pleasant, polite, precise, quiet, severe, sincere, stupid

3. Adjektive mit **drei oder mehr Silben** werden stets mit "more/most" gesteigert. Sonst ist das Wort für uns zu lang und kompliziert.

   interesting - more interesting - most interesting

   Einige Adjektive:

   ambitious, attentive, attractive, beautiful, colourful, comfortable, complicated, convenient, courageous, curious, delicious, difficult, efficient, exciting, expensive, fabulous, fantastic, fascinating, furious, generous, important, impressive, intelligent, interesting, musical, popular, possible, practical, radical, refreshing, reliable, terrible, unpleasant, wonderful

4. Einige Adjektive haben eine **unregelmäßige Steigerungsform**, die auswendig gelernt werden muss.

bad	worse	worst
far	farther	farthest
good	better	best
little	less	least
many	more	most
much	more	most
old	older	oldest
old	elder	eldest

5. Folgende Adjektive können theoretisch nicht gesteigert werden, da sie **einzigartig** sind; d.h. es gibt das nur einmal.

   almighty, certain, circular, complete, dead, empty, eternal, everlasting, heavenly, infinite, matchless, open, perfect, perpetual, round, single, square, supreme, triangular, unique, universal

   The box is empty. Wenn die Schachtel leer ist, kann eine zweite Schachtel nicht noch weniger drin haben.

6. **Die drei Formen der Adjektive**:

- Die **erste Form** (Grundform = positive) des Adjektivs wird gebraucht, um zu zeigen, wie etwas ist. Manchmal steht ein "very" vor dem Adjektiv.

  The man is **tall**.

  The girl is very **nice**.

  Oder ein Vergleich findet zwischen zwei Dingen, Sachen oder Personen wie in einer Waagschale statt. Der Vergleich kann

  - ausgeglichen sein und daher positiv ausfallen.

  as ... **as** (so ... wie)

  She is **as** tall **as** he. Sie ist so groß wie er.

  - nicht ausgeglichen sein und daher negativ ausfallen

  not as ... **as; not so**... **as** (nicht so ... wie)

  She is **not as** tall **as** he. She is **not so** tall **as** he. Sie ist nicht so groß wie er.

- Die **zweite Form** (Komparativ = comparative) wird gebraucht, wenn man zwei Sachen, Dinge oder Personen miteinander vergleicht. Der Vergleich fällt unterschiedlich aus. Meistens hat man ein "than" direkt nach der zweiten Form des Adjektivs.

  ...**er than** (...er als)

  more ... **than**

  That man is **taller than** his brother.

  A child is **more** active **than** an old person.

- Die **dritte Form** (Superlativ = superlative) wird gebraucht, wenn man drei oder mehr Sachen, Dinge oder Personen vergleicht. Die höchste Stufe (der Gewinner) ist die dritte Form. Vor der dritten Form des Adjektivs steht ein "the". Oft steht ein Vergleich mit "ever" danach.

  ... **est** (am ...sten)

  most ...

  That is the **most** interesting book of all.

  That is **the tallest** man I have ever seen. = Von allen Männern, die man je gesehen hat, ist er der Gewinner; d.h. der größte.

15.2 Übungen

Setze das Adjektiv, das hinten in Klammern angegeben ist, in der richtigen Form in den Satz ein.

1. Cologne is ______ than Berlin. (small)
2. Tokyo is ______ city in Japan. (big)
3. She is ______ than last year. (happy)
4. This is a ______ film than the other. (exciting)
5. This is ______ book in the world. (interesting)
6. Is your brother ______ my brother? (lazy; as ... as)
7. This is a ______ room. (cold)
8. He is ______ than I had hoped. (helpful)
9. Kindergarten classes are ______ than school classes. (noisy)
10. That is ______ of all my brothers. (old)
11. January has ______ days than February. (many)
12. The days in July are ______ the days in December. (dark; not... as)
13. Margarine is ______ than butter. (cheap)
14. Mt. Everest is ______ hill in the world. (high)
15. This a ______ man. (big)
16. Her father is ______ than her mother. (short)
17. That's ______ film on TV. (thrilling)
18. Are you ______ your father? (unhappy; as ... as)
19. Girls are ______ than boys. (careful)
20. She talked to ______ DJ in the city. (popular)
21. Tom is ______ than Jim. (loud)
22. A ______ woman is standing there. (wonderful)
23. That's ______ river of them all. (blue)
24. You are ______ your sister. (special; as ... as)
25. Stories are ______ than grammar. (interesting)
26. She rode to ______ corner of the world. (hot)
27. Today is ______ than yesterday. (cold)
28. How ______ of you to break the glass! (stupid)
29. This has been ______ English test this school year. (difficult)
30. I want to be ______ a bird. (free; as ... as)
31. A tortoise is ______ than a cat. (lazy)
32. This is ______ day of the month. (busy)
33. The orange is ______ . (sweet)
34. My car is ______ than your car. (dirty)
35. Is your sister ______ ? (old)

36. A cat is ______ a dog. (large; not ... as)
37. That's ______ car in Germany. (quick)
38. You stayed out ______ than we said you could. (late)
39. That man is very ______ . (special)
40. The man is ______ than the woman. (angry)
41. That was ______ song in the pop charts. (bad)
42. Are you ______ I am? (hungry; as ... as)
43. Your boy is ______ today than yesterday. (nice)
44. Betty is ______ of the children. (hungry)
45. June has ______ days than March. (few)
46. The film is ______ than the book. (thrilling)
47. Summer is ______ than winter. (good)
48. She was ______ I was. (surprised; not ... as)
49. That was ______ noise on December 31st. (loud)
50. Is the bike ______ than the book? (expensive)
51. I have a ______ sister. (good)
52. My brother is ______ than my sister. (popular)
53. That is ______ house in the town. (old)
54. Please come ______ possible. (early; as ... as)
55. Is a pencil ______ than a hammer? (useful)
56. She was ______ woman at the beach. (young)
57. That man was ______ than my husband. (exciting)
58. The sofa is ______ . (expensive)
59. This water is ______ than city water. (clean)
60. Tuesday was ______ Monday. (sunny; not ... as)
61. That is ______ light in the room. (bright)
62. The bike is ______ than the car. (dangerous)
63. We like ______ children. (clever)
64. Grandfather is ______ than a child. (careful)
65. She knows ______ of all the people I know. (much)
66. Are you ______ your sister? (tidy; as ... as)
67. Winter is ______ than summer. (bad)
68. The food was very ______ . (bad)
69. Is your husband ______ than that man? (clever)
70. I have eaten ______ apples. (many)
71. School is ______ than kindergarten. (interesting)
72. Is German ______ English? (difficult; as ... as)
73. That's ______ story in the book. (long)

74. Is school ______ than a party? (boring)
75. My brother is ______ . (bad)
76. German is ______ than English. (difficult)
77. That boy is ______ in his class. (clever)
78. Her story is ______ your story. (funny; not . . . as)
79. Is the film or the book ______ ? (exciting)
80. We know ______ people. (interesting)
81. Houses are ______ than cars. (expensive)
82. She has ______ money. (little)
83. The teacher is ______ woman in the room. (lovely)
84. That woman has ______ money than I. (little)
85. The story is very ______ . (terrible)
86. That is ______ song for me to sing. (easy)
87. My brother is ______ than his wife. (brilliant)
88. Is it ______ to London? (far)
89. Going to the doctor is ______ than going for a swim. (terrible)
90. Tom is ______ child in the class. (quiet)
91. That is a ______ story. (terrible)
92. A sofa is ______ than a chair. (expensive)
93. London is ______ from here than Bonn. (far)
94. Linda is ______ mother of all mothers. (wonderful)
95. Your mother is ______ than your grandmother. (young)
96. That man is very ______ . (silly)
97. Her husband has ______ books than mine. (many)
98. She was ______ of her class. (good)
99. The Mercedes was ______ than the VW. (fast)
100. His story was ______ of them all. (funny)
101. His sister is ______ than you. (old)
102. I want a ______ house. (modern)
103. This summer is ______ than last summer. (hot)
104. We are all ______ . (happy)
105. Is your mother ______ than your teacher? (pretty)
106. Your doctor was ______ than ours. (busy)
107. She has ______ money of all my sisters. (little)
108. Girls are ______ than boys. (quiet)
109. A teacher is often not ______ . (popular)
110. He's ______ man in the world. (strong)
111. I am ______ than you. (stupid)

112. Your child is ______ than our child. (big)
113. That is ______ person in the room. (surprised)
114. The boy is ______ than the girl. (thirsty)
115. Father is ______ person in the family. (brilliant)
116. Andrea was ______ child in the city. (dirty)
117. You are ______ person in the world. (lucky)
118. Have you got some ______ milk? (cool)
119. Bill was ______ than you today. (silly)
120. Is your room ______ enough? (tidy)
121. That day was ______ of them all. (warm)
122. That game was ______ of them all! (dangerous)
123. That is ______ book in the world. (useful)

16 Adverbs/Adverbials

16.1 Grammatik

1. Adverbials können aus einem Wort (**adverbs**) oder aus mehreren Wörtern (**adverbial phrases**) bestehen.
2. Adverbials geben Antwort auf die Fragen:

when, where, how, how often

a) **Adverbials of time** (Zeitadverbien)

Um ein "adverbial of time" festzustellen, fragen wir "**when**".

z.B.:

afterwards, already, before, early, for (3 weeks), ago, immediately, in 1980, in winter, just, last (night), late, lately, later, long ago, next (week), now, once, once upon a time, one day, recently, since (Easter), so far, soon, still, then, the other day, this (week), today, tomorrow, tonight, yesterday, yet

We went to the zoo **yesterday**. When did we go to the zoo?

We went to the zoo **in the morning**.

"Yesterday" ist das "adverb of time" in diesem Satz.

"In the morning" ist das "adverbial of time."

b) **Adverbials of place** (Ortsadverbien)

Die Frage dazu lautet: "**where**".

z.B.:

above, anywhere, below, everywhere, here, home, in, inside, near, nowhere, out, outside, somewhere, there, to the left, to the right

We went **home** yesterday. Where did we go?

We went **to the zoo** yesterday.

"Home" ist das "adverb of place."

"To the zoo" ist das "adverbial of place" in dem obenstehenden Satz.

c) **Adverbials of frequency** (Häufigkeitsadverbien) beantworten die Frage "**how often**".

z.B.:

always, continually, daily, each time, ever, ever so often, every (day), every now and then, for the most part, frequently, generally, hardly ever, hourly, monthly, never, occasionally, often, once, once a (month), periodically, rarely, repeatedly, seldom, several times, sometimes, three times, twice, usually, weekly

I **always** feed the cat. How often do I feed the cat? **always**

"Always" ist das "adverb of frequency" in diesem Satz.

“Adverbs of frequency”, insofern sie aus einem Wort bestehen, stehen in dem Satz vor dem Vollverb bzw. nach dem ersten Hilfsverb.

I have **never** been to Berlin.

He would **seldom** have taken a book.

d) **Adverbials of manner** (Adverbien der Art und Weise) Sie beantworten die Frage "**how**".

z.B.:

carefully, -fashion, fast, happily, hard, in a (funny) manner, in a (silly) way, long, -ly, -style, well, -wise

I always run **quickly**. How do you always run? **quickly**

"Quickly" ist das "adverb of manner" in diesem Satz.

- Meistens werden sie aus einem Adjektiv oder Partizip dadurch gebildet, dass wir die **Endung "ly"** hinzufügen.

  quick - quickly; slow - slowly

- Wenn das Adjektiv mit "y" endet, dann wird das **"y" durch "i" ersetzt** und danach die Endung "ly" hinzugefügt.

  happy - happ**ily**

- Ein "**le**", das nach einem Konsonanten kommt, wird **in "ly" umgewandelt**.

  z.B.:

  able, comfortable, gentle, idle, noticeable, possible, probable, reliable, sensible, simple, terrible

  gen**tle** - gen**tly**

- Adjektive, die mit "-ic" enden, werden zu "**ically**".

  z.B.:

  automatic, basic, dramatic, drastic, economic, fantastic, historic, realistic, scientific, specific, systematic

  realist**ic** - realist**ically**

  Ausnahme: public - publicly

- **Einige Ausnahmen**:

  Die folgenden Adjektive werden als Adverbien gleichlautend verwendet:

  hard - hard; fast - fast

  He takes hard tests. He works hard.

  Das Adjektiv "good" wird als Adverb zu "well".

  good - well

  That is a good car. Mother drives well.

3. **Position of adverbials**

	front	middle	end
Adverbial of time	x		x
Adverbial of place	x		x
Adverbial of manner		x	x
Adverbial of frequency		x	

Wenn in einem Satz sowohl ein **"adverbial of time"** als auch ein ***"adverbial of place"*** enthalten ist, dann lautet die Regel:

am Ende: ***Place*** before **time** (OZ = ***Orts***angabe vor **Zeit**angabe)

oder

time at the beginning (**Zeit**angabe am Anfang des Satzes)

place at the end (Ortsangabe am Ende des Satzes)

am Ende: We saw him ***at the zoo*** **yesterday**.

oder: **Yesterday** we saw him ***at the zoo***.

4. Beispiele:

Adverbial of time (Zeit = wann)

At 3 o'clock he went home. (front)

He went home **at 3 o'clock**. (end)

Adverbial of place (Ort = wo)

At school we sang happily. (front)

We sang happily ***at school***. (end)

Adverb of manner (Art und Weise = wie)

She **quickly** ran to her mother. (middle)

She ran to her mother **quickly**. (end)

Adverb of frequency (Häufigkeit = wie oft)

They **always** forget things. (middle)

Place/time:

We are going ***to church*** **at 7 o'clock**. (end/end)

Tomorrow morning we will go ***to our school***. (front/end)

5. **Unterscheidung zwischen Adjektiven und Adverbien in Sätzen**

a) Das Wort, das zwischen "the - noun" oder "a - noun" kommt, ist ein Adjektiv und hat kein "ly".

the loud **children**; **a** good **teacher**

b) Wenn das einzige Verb im Satz eine Form von "to be" ist (is/was/will be usw), kann kein Adverb folgen.

He is nice.

Das Verb "to be" kann man als Gleichheitszeichen (=) betrachten. Was danach kommt, sagt etwas über das aus, was vorher kam.

She is happy. She = happy.

Das "she" wird näher erklärt. Hier ist nur ein Adjektiv möglich.

Umgekehrt, wenn der Satz sonst nur aus einem Subjekt und einem Verb (außer dem Verb "to be") besteht, kann kein Adjektiv kommen. Nur ein "adverb of manner" kommt in Frage.

He talks quickly.

c) Um zu erkennen, ob ein Adjektiv oder Adverb im Satz vorkommt, muss man einiges bemerken oder fragen.

- Wie heißt das gesamte Verb? Wenn es nur eine Form von "to be" ist, kommt nur ein Adjektiv in Frage.

  The dog is loud.

  Wenn "to be" nur ein Hilfsverb ist, kann ohne weiteres ein Adverb kommen.

  The dog is barking loudly.

- Steht das Adjektiv/Adverb zwischen "the - noun" oder "a - noun", dann ist es ein Adjektiv.

  the nice man; a pretty girl

- Sonst muss man weiter fragen: Worauf gibt das gewünschte Wort eine Antwort?
  - Auf ein **Substantiv** (noun)? Dann ist es ein Adjektiv und hat kein "ly".

He has nice cars.	What sort of cars?	nice
	Was für Autos?	nette.

    Die Autos sind nett - nicht er.
  - Auf ein **Verb**? Dann ist es ein Adverb und hat meist ein "ly".

    He drives the car **quickly**. Wie ist sein Fahren?

    Das Auto ist nicht schnell. Er ist nicht schnell.

    Seine Fahrweise ist schnell.
  - Auf ein **Adjektiv**? Dann ist es wiederum ein Adverb.

    We saw the **extremely** beautiful girl.

    Beautiful sagt, was für ein Mädchen es ist.

    Extremely sagt, wie "beautiful" sie ist.
  - Auf ein **Adverb**? Dann ist es ebenfalls ein Adverb.

    The man drives the car **extremely** quickly.

    Quickly bezieht sich auf das "drives" und sagt, wie er fährt. Es ist ein Adverb. Extremely sagt, wie schnell er fährt.

16.2 Übungen

Adjektiv oder Adverb? Setze die richtige Form (Adjektiv oderAdverb) des Wortes, das in Klammern angegeben ist, in die Lücke ein.

1. They were very ______ and ran away ______ . (happy; fast)
2. They are very ______ boys. (nice)
3. We ______ threw the ball. (quick)
4. The ______ children listened ______ . (quiet; careful)
5. She shouted at Tom ______ . (angry)
6. I can't speak German very ______ . (good)
7. They asked the very ______ girl many things very ______ . (pretty; quick)
8. She was a very ______ girl. (noisy)
9. You walked to your desk ______ . (slow)
10. The little boy was very ______ to us. (nice)
11. He ______ showed us where to go. (quick)
12. The big man spoke ______ to the ______ woman. (loud; angry)
13. Our car is very ______ . We can drive it very ______ . (fast; fast)
14. The little girl worked ______ and ______ . (hard; careful)
15. The very ______ children asked questions very ______ . (sad; stupid)
16. The dancer is very ______ . She can dance very ______ . (good; good)
17. The man was talking ______ . (loud)
18. The ______ writer ______ read her ______ story. (young; happy; wonderful)
19. The ______ teacher asked the children to speak more ______ . (popular; slow)
20. He asked for food ______ . (hungry)
21. She was very ______ and ______ ran away. (stupid; quick)
22. He is a very ______ boy. (brilliant)
23. The boys drank the ______ water ______ . (dirty; thirsty)
24. Everything was very ______ . (dangerous)
25. He ______ followed the woman. (lazy)
26. She ______ opened the envelope. (quick)
27. The ______ child talked ______ . (happy; nice)
28. Dolly's teacher was ______ . (terrible)
29. He talked to her ______ . (boring)
30. She did her homework ______ . (easy)
31. Peter is so ______ . He walks ______ . (slow)
32. The teacher was ______ . He ______ sent Barbara to her seat. (angry)
33. You will never win if you play so ______ . You are always too ______ . (slow)
34. This story is very ______ . Betty has read it ______ . (interesting)
35. Your letter is ______ . You have written it ______ . (bad)

36. Mike is always ______ . Yesterday he wrote the letter ______ . (busy)
37. Dan is a ______ football player. He plays very ______ . (good)
38. Mr. Miller has a ______ car. It goes very ______ . (fast)
39. She is a ______ girl. She works ______ . (lazy)
40. He can run ______ . He ______ went round the corner. (quick)
41. Jane is a ______ worker. (good)
42. Clean the board ______ , please. (correct)
43. They are ______ children. (typical)
44. Are you ______ ? Is she a ______ girl? (polite)
45. She always cleans her room ______ . (tidy)
46. Your work is not ______ . (good)
47. Why are you so ______ ? (unhappy)
48. Did you watch an ______ film on TV? (exciting)
49. I am ______ because I have read an ______ book. (happy; exciting)
50. The children have been ______ this morning. They listened ______ . (quiet)
51. She left the room ______ . She was very ______ . (angry)
52. You are ______ girls. You welcomed your guests ______ . (funny)
53. That's a very ______ dress. She cleaned her room very ______ . (nice)
54. The cars drove ______ . They are ______ cars. (slow)
55. That boy is ______ . He reads ______ . (poor)
56. The birds sang very ______ . My girlfriends are very ______ . (happy)
57. He can work very ______ . (fast)
58. The ______ woman walked ______ . (angry; quick)
59. The ______ men worked ______ and ______ . (careful; hard; noisy)
60. The ______ teacher made us write the story ______ and ______ . (terrible; tidy; careful)
61. We talked ______ and ______ . (boring; poor)
62. I knew the lady very ______ . (good)
63. We took the ______ test very ______ . (hard; quick)
64. The ______ girls went into the water ______ . (pretty; happy)
65. My brother and I ran very ______ . (fast)
66. The ______ girl sang the song ______ . (sweet; sad)
67. A child sang the song ______ . (quiet)
68. The boy hit his sister very ______ . (hard)
69. The ______ dog walked very ______ . (fast; slow)

Position of Adverbials. Setze die angegebenen Wörter in die richtige Stelle des Satzes ein.

70. She has been here. (often)
71. We go for a walk. (never)
72. They take a walk. (before breakfast; never) 2x
73. We went. (to the shop; yesterday) 2x
74. My father works. (never; hard; at home) 2x
75. The young man swims. (often; in the morning) 2x
76. She will ride a bicycle to the shop. (careful) 2x
77. Ben has read a book. (seldom)
78. You have sung three songs. (today; in your room) 2x
79. We find our books. (never; on the table)
80. She comes. (to Cologne; always; at 12 o'clock) 2x
81. They went. (yesterday; quiet; to the zoo) 2x
82. I will open the door. (noisy; tomorrow) 3x
83. You helped us. (last year; seldom) 2x
84. We saw them. (this morning; in the kitchen) 2x
85. The old lady goes out. (seldom; in the evening) 2x
86. She goes for a swim. (after school; always)
87. I shall run to the doctor. (quick) 2x
88. She arrived. (yesterday; at the station) 2x
89. She has forgotten things. (often)
90. I have seen her. (this afternoon; at the circus) 2x
91. She works. (busy; at the office) 2x
92. I must go to bed. (at 8 o'clock) 2x
93. We shall visit you. (next week) 2x
94. Mike eats chocolate. (always; during the lessons) 2x
95. They go for a walk. (on Saturdays; always) 2x
96. They buy sweets. (at the supermarket; often)
97. Mr. Potter finished his meal. (quick) 2x
98. The old woman climbed the stairs. (slow) 2x
99. The boys went for a swim. (before lunch; in the sea) 2x
100. They have breakfast. (in the kitchen; at 8 o'clock) 2x
101. We spend our holidays. (in London; always)
102. We planned our holidays. (careful) 2x
103. She sunbathed. (on the beach; often)
104. Tim closed the window. (quick) 2x
105. I was at home. (yesterday) 2x
106. We saw her. (this morning; in the bus) 2x

107. She did her homework. (slow) 2x
108. We shall drive. (careful)
109. I ran to the bus stop. (quick) 2x
110. They went. (always; at 8 o'clock; to school) 2x
111. She talked to me. (never; angry; in the morning) 2x
112. We have sung a song. (often; noisily; in the bathroom) 2x
113. He got up. (at 5 o'clock; never)
114. The lady sat. (every day; in the sun) 2x
115. The men sang songs. (happily; always; at church) 2x
116. The children clapped their hands. (loudly; during the show) 2x
117. We wash our faces. (quick; in the bathroom; usually; in the morning) 2x
118. We will take the dog for a walk. (always; before school)
119. The children will have seen the cats. (by tomorrow; often)
120. The boys were eating apples. (happily; in their room; in the afternoon) 2x
121. I would have gone. (never; at night; to that house) 2x
122. My sister had cleaned her room. (sometimes; fast; on Saturday) 2x

17 Question Tags = Angehängte Fragen

17.1 Grammatik

1. Alle angehängten Fragen entsprechen den deutschen Wörtern "nicht wahr" oder "oder".

   He went home, didn't he? Er ging nach Hause, nicht wahr?

2. **Ein verneinendes Wort** muss vorhanden sein.

   a) Wenn im Hauptsatz ein verneinendes Wort vorhanden ist, kommt in der angehängten Frage keine Form von "not".

      He did**n't** go home, did he?

   b) Wenn im Hauptsatz keine Verneinung des Wortes vorhanden ist, wird in der angehängten Frage ein "not" gesetzt.

      He went home, did**n't** he?

3. **Bildung der angehängten Frage**

   a) Wenn im Hauptsatz eine Form von "to have" oder "to be" vorhanden ist, wird die entsprechende Form in der angehängten Frage verwendet.

      He **has** a car, **hasn't** he?

      She **is** here now, **isn't** she?

   b) Wenn im Hauptsatz ein Hilfsverb vorhanden ist, wird es in der angehängten Frage gebraucht. Wenn mehr als ein Hilfsverb vorhanden ist, ist nur das erste Hilfsverb maßgebend.

      They **will** go, **won't** they?

      They **won't** go, **will** they?

      You **can** help me, **can't** you?

      He **would** have taken it, **wouldn't** he?

4. Wenn im Hauptsatz ein anderes Verb (d.h. ein Vollverb) vorhanden ist, wird in der angehängten Frage ein "do/does" oder "did" verwendet.

   They took him home, **didn't** they?

   She drives to school, **doesn't** she?

   You don't cry, **do** you?

   We run quickly, **don't** we?

5. Das Subjekt des Hauptsatzes wird in der angehängten Frage wieder erwähnt.
   The girls often go there, don't **they**?
   Father and I went there, didn't **we**?
   My brother is going there, isn't **he**?

17.2 Übungen

Bilde die richtige angehängte Frage und setze sie am Ende des Satzes ein.

Nur present und past:

1. They are carrying books, ______ ?
2. He isn't going home now, ______ ?
3. My father and I sing many songs, ______ ?
4. I gave you the record, ______ ?
5. You have got many friends, ______ ?
6. The girl doesn't save money, ______ ?
7. There are many chairs in that room, ______ ?
8. The rabbit hasn't got its food, ______ ?
9. The baby throws its toys, ______ ?
10. The men didn't drive the car, ______ ?
11. The story has got many words, ______ ?
12. The children aren't playing, ______ ?
13. The car is here, ______ ?
14. Linda and I don't speak loudly, ______ ?
15. The plane is flying very high, ______ ?
16. The boys haven't got their tickets, ______ ?
17. You aren't reading a story, ______ ?
18. The woman repaired her bike, ______ ?
19. I have got much time, ______ ?
20. The girl does her homework, ______ ?
21. The dog is barking, ______ ?
22. The room hasn't got two windows, ______ ?
23. We are leaving soon, ______ ?
24. The men don't know the song, ______ ?
25. I took the train yesterday, ______ ?
26. The food is good, ______ ?
27. The girl doesn't eat salad, ______ ?
28. The woman has got a dog, ______ ?
29. The child isn't sleeping, ______ ?
30. They ride horses, ______ ?

31. The people didn't see you, ______ ?
32. Oranges are sweet, ______ ?
33. The women haven't got pencils, ______ ?
34. My father isn't here, ______ ?
35. Father and I left early, ______ ?

Bilde die richtige angehängte Frage und setze sie am Ende des Satzes ein.
alle Zeitformen:

36. Tim has big ears, ______ ?
37. They're wearing funny clothes, ______ ?
38. Tim doesn't look strong, ______ ?
39. The man isn't very strong, ______ ?
40. Tom hasn't got many friends, ______ ?
41. She can wait, ______ ?
42. He isn't coming, ______ ?
43. They look happy, ______ ?
44. She won't sing, ______ ?
45. They'd buy shoes, ______ ?
46. My sister and I often play, ______ ?
47. The dogs and I can run around the house, ______ ?
48. We hadn't ridden a bike before, ______ ?
49. I wasn't feeding the cat, ______ ?
50. You are going to school now, ______ ?
51. The woman took a picture, ______ ?
52. My father and I didn't hear you, ______ ?
53. The children aren't playing, ______ ?
54. He wouldn't have gone home, ______ ?
55. We understand you very well, ______ ?
56. I've come too early, ______ ?
57. You haven't been wearing that dress, ______ ?
58. We will go to the cinema, ______ ?
59. You won't give him the book, ______ ?
60. The dogs are running after the cats, ______ ?
61. She wouldn't be sleeping now, ______ ?
62. You will be writing soon, ______ ?
63. Father reads many books, ______ ?
64. We wouldn't hold your heads, ______ ?
65. You were eating that apple, ______ _?

66. The boys aren't driving too quickly, _______ ?
67. The teacher and I would carry the books, _______ ?
68. The driver didn't take the car, _______ ?
69. You're cutting the trees today, _______ ?
70. The boys can't be sleeping at this time, _______ ?
71. I've taught her well, _______ ?
72. You aren't driving away now, _______ ?
73. My sister will ride her bike, _______ ?
74. We can't go to your house, _______ ?
75. I grew quickly last year, _______ ?
76. Tom and Susan aren't collecting cassettes, _______ ?
77. I'd learn those words better, _______ ?
78. We don't work hard, _______ ?
79. You weren't feeding your sister, _______ ?
80. My brother has seen the sea, _______ ?
81. The cat didn't come home, _______ ?
82. The girls and I would've taken the bus, _______ ?
83. You won't be leaving early, _______ ?
84. I'd carry the table, _______ ?
85. Linda and Jean are cleaning the house, _______ ?
86. Father and I haven't seen the dog, _______ ?
87. You were feeding the animals, _______ ?
88. My sister had eaten her lunch, _______ ?
89. My brother and I wouldn't have taken your books, _______ ?
90. You didn't climb that tree, _______ ?
91. The dogs were dreaming, _______ ?
92. I don't call you often, _______ ?
93. He won't sing that song, _______ ?
94. We didn't thank the man, _______ ?
95. I'm not falling, _______ ?
96. The bird would fly to the tree, _______ ?
97. We haven't seen you before, _______ ?
98. You'd have been running if I hadn't stopped you, _______ ?
99. I'd found the box, _______ ?
100. My mother and sister couldn't be eating now, _______ ?
101. The boys and I had lost our money, _______ ?
102. You hadn't taken the dogs for a walk yet, _______ ?
103. My mother didn't wash the dishes, _______ ?

104. The man'd have written a letter, _______ ?
105. The children haven't eaten their food yet, _______ ?
106. Linda and I are carrying chairs, _______ ?
107. The cat hadn't caught the bird, _______ ?
108. You will be getting up at 8 o'clock, _______ ?
109. I couldn't build a house, _______ ?
110. Tom and Linda have been forgetting their homework a lot, _______ ?
111. You don't buy cheap cars, _______ ?
112. The boys and I won't talk loudly, _______ ?
113. Your dog can bark, _______ ?
114. You didn't help your sister, _______ ?
115. The girls would be hearing records now, _______ ?
116. I won't have to stay at your house, _______ ?
117. Their mother doesn't drink milk, _______ ?
118. You'd be sleeping when I came, _______ ?
119. Those people weren't thinking of us when they said that, _______ ?
120. I speak to everyone, _______ ?
121. The boy wouldn't forget you, _______ ?
122. You have been feeling better now, _______ ?
123. My mother and I have bought milk every day, _______ ?
124. I don't listen to records, _______ ?
125. The twins won't be coming early, _______ ?
126. My sister and I made the cake yesterday, _______ ?
127. The man hasn't cut his finger, _______ ?
128. You had been asking a question, _______ ?
129. My brother doesn't know you, _______ ?
130. The children'll be building sand castles, _______ ?
131. You didn't lose the book, _______ ?
132. The boy can't read, _______ ?
133. She could be sleeping now, _______ ?
134. The girls wouldn't fly to London, _______ ?
135. My father and I wash the car every day, _______ ?
136. We'll visit them, _______ ?
137. You hadn't eaten the apples yet, _______ ?
138. He's flying to Rome tomorrow, _______ ?
139. The radio's been broken for a long time, _______ ?
140. Tom goes to work early, _______ ?
141. Mother wouldn't sell the house, _______ ?

142. We'd left too late, ______ ?
143. You'd have given her that toy, ______ ?
144. They won't sleep at our house, ______ ?
145. I'd be welcome, ______ ?
146. I didn't eat your piece of cake, ______ ?
147. He's been reading for an hour, ______

18 If-clauses = Conditional clauses (Bedingungssätze)

18.1 Grammatik

If = falls, wenn (Möglichkeit)

I'll stay home if it rains.
nicht
when = als, wenn (zeitbedingt)
I went to a kindergarten when I was four.

1. Die drei Grundformeln:

If + present, future
If the weather is fine, I will go for a walk.
If + past, conditional 1
If you looked out of the window now, you would see the red car
If + past perfect, conditional 2
If I had learnt more, I wouldn't have had a "5".

a) **If + present, future** zeigt etwas an, das möglich ist. Es könnte durchaus passieren. Manchmal steht im Hauptsatz (main clause) " can / must + infinitive" statt "future" (Aber nur, wenn die Fähigkeit oder der Zwang betont werden soll).

If I am here today, I'll see you.

If he has enough money, he'll fly to Germany.

If he isn't coming now, he'll tell you.

If he goes home soon, he will see Sue.

If he doesn't go home soon, he won't see Sue.

b) **If + past, conditional 1** zeigt etwas an, das eventuell (halbwegs) möglich ist. Es könnte so werden, aber es könnte genauso auch nicht so werden. Manchmal steht im Hauptsatz ein "could", wenn die Möglichkeit ausgedrückt werden soll.

If I were (was) in Bonn today, I would see you.

If he had enough money, he would fly to Germany.

If he weren't (wasn't) coming now, he would tell you.

If he went home soon, he would see Sue.

If he didn't go home when his mother told him to, he wouldn't see Sue.

c) **If + past perfect, conditional 2** zeigt etwas an, das nicht mehr möglich ist. Die Gelegenheit wurde versäumt und das Geschehen ist abgelaufen. Es steht schon in der Vergangenheit und kann nicht mehr umgeändert werden.

If I had been at your house today, I would have seen you.

If he had had enough money, he would have flown to Germany.

If he hadn't been coming, he would have told you.

If he had gone home, he would have seen Sue.

If he hadn't gone home when his mother had told him to, he wouldn't have seen Sue.

2. **Die zwei Satzteile können umgetauscht werden**.

If + present, future	If she comes, I will be happy.

oder

future - if + present	I will be happy if she comes.

3. In dem Nebensatz (if-Teil) kann man folgendes sagen:

"if I were", "if he were" statt
"if I was", "if he was".

Das gilt natürlich nur für den "if + past, conditional 1" Satz, weil nur diese Form die Vergangenheit (past) hat.

4. Wörter wie "now" geben keinen Hinweis auf eine Zeit. Man kann ohne weiteres Sätze wie "if he saw her now" bilden, da die Vergangenheitsform in Bedingungssätzen nicht die Vergangenheit ausdrücken soll, sondern in welchem Maß etwas möglich ist.

18.2 Übungen

Ändere das Verb, das in Klammern angegeben ist, in die richtige Zeitform um.

1. If I (to be) you, I'd go to a doctor.
2. He (can help) you if he had wanted to.
3. He won't be late if he (to take) a taxi.
4. They (to give) you the book if they are at home.
5. She won't get the job is she (to speak - not) English.
6. He (to come) to see us if he had been able to.
7. If my brother were here, he (to know) what to do.
8. If you want us to, we (to repair) your radio tomorrow.
9. If he had done what I said, he (to win).
10. If he (to know - not) the answer, he would not speak.
11. I will come tomorrow if I (to have) time.
12. I (to help) you now if I could.
13. If they hadn't given him the money, the burglar (to shoot) them.
14. He (to invite) you to the party if you want to go.

15. What (you - to do) if the train is late?
16. What (he - to do) if he saw his sister?
17. I (to drink) water if I was thirsty.
18. What (we - to do) if the train had been late.
19. If he had broken his leg, he (can come - not) today.
20. What (you - to do) if you had no money?
21. I (to drink) my tea if it hadn't been so hot.
22. She'll have a problem if she (to learn English - not).
23. I (to buy) the shoes if I had had much money.
24. What (you - to do) if he doesn't come?
25. If he (to speak) five languages, he would be a very clever man.
26. If Karen (to speak - not) so quickly, we would understand her.
27. He (to speak) if he had known the answer.
28. We (to come) today if you had asked us.
29. When (they - can give) you the book if you asked?
30. If you (to eat - not) so much, you wouldn't be full.
31. We (to help) her if she were nice.
32. If father (to drive) fast, we'll be home soon.
33. If they (to see) John now, they would laugh at him.
34. If your uncle sees you, you (to run) away.
35. If we buy the car, we (must pay) much money.
36. If she (to have) the book, she would have known it.
37. Where (they - to go) if it had rained?
38. If Tom had seen the cat, he (can hold) it.
39. If I (to see) Jane, I'll say "hello."
40. If you (to give) Tom your book, he'll be very happy.
41. If you (to catch) the ball, you would have won the game.
42. If we (to find) the book, we would be able to read the story.
43. If Tom (to throw - not) the ball, he would have lost the game.
44. When (he - can come) if we invite him?
45. If I understood the sentences, I (to be) very happy.
46. If Bob had kept the car, he (can drive) it.
47. We (must go) home right away if mother tells us to.
48. Where (they - to hide) if they had run away?
49. If Linda (to feed - not) her dog, it would die.
50. If his brother (to teach) him English, he will be good.
51. I (to write) them a letter if I had had some paper.
52. What (you - to buy) if you had much money?

53. We (to fly) the new kite today if we had bought one yesterday.
54. If we (to see) the burglar, we would have fetched the police.
55. I would have helped you wash the car if you (to ask) me.
56. She will talk with him if she (to see) him.
57. I would not be hungry if I (to eat) a lot of food.
58. If we had a book, we (to read) it.
59. If she (to see) a mouse, she would shout.
60. Where (I - to find) the book if I had lost it?
61. We (to give) her the book if we had had it.
62. If Linda had seen the apple, she (can eat) it.
63. If we (to help) mother, she'll give us 10,- Euro.
64. Where (he - to go) if the shop closes?
65. If I (to eat - not), I would have been hungry.
66. What (you - can eat) if you had enough money?
67. If we (to live - not) there, she would come to visit us.
68. If father drove him home, he (to be) happy.
69. I (to see) the new teacher if I had gone to school early.
70. If you (to look) longer, you would have found the rabbit.
71. You (must wait) if I am late.
72. If your mother (to catch) you, you will cry.
73. If they (to talk - not) so much, they could listen better.
74. If I had known that you were ill, I (can visit) you.
75. If he (to help) her, she would have passed the test.
76. What (he - can win) if he tried?
77. If they run quickly, they (can catch) the girls.
78. If Karen (to take) the pencil, she would have cried.
79. You (to win) the prize if you had swum quickly.
80. If the dog (to run) away, you will cry.
81. If you (to run), you would catch the train.
82. She (to throw) the ball if she'd had one.
83. When (they - to come) if they don't come today?
84. We (to pay) much money if we bought the house.
85. If I (to catch) a mouse, you'll cry.
86. When (she - to drink) her tea if she had come late?
87. If they (to speak - not) German to her, she would have to learn English.
88. If he went home, he (to see) the new cat.
89. He (to get) a surprise if he goes home now.
90. If he had helped her yesterday, she (to buy) him a new toy.

91. If we drink our milk, we (can go) outside.
92. We won't break the girl's bike if she (to give) it to us.
93. If I had cleaned the board, the teacher (to be) happy.
94. They'd have spoken with her if they (to know) what to say.
95. If Bob (to read) the story, he could have answered the question.
96. If they came to the party, they (to eat) all the ice-cream.
97. If I (to fly) to America, I would see New York.
98. If you'd helped your mother, she (to give) you a present.
99. If they (to buy) a cat, the children could play with it.
100. If Linda sees a mouse, she (to shout).
101. If they took a picture, they (can show) their friends Big Ben.
102. If I (to go) to the zoo, I'd have seen the tiger.
103. If we see the film, we (to come) home late.
104. If you (to leave) the house now, you wouldn't be late.
105. If I had taken the book, I (can read) it tomorrow.
106. She'll hide behind a curtain if she (to hear) a burglar.
107. If I'd fallen down, I (can hurt) myself.
108. If she got up now, she (to be - not) too late.
109. If I (to eat - not) so much, I won't get too full.
110. If my sister (can drive) me home, I'll be there early.
111. You'd have gone to the cinema if you (to know) the film was good.
112. You'd catch the train if you (to run).
113. If John keeps the car, he (to drive) it.
114. They'd buy a dog if they (to have - not) one.
115. If I'd seen my brother, I (to say) "hello."
116. We (must eat) the pudding if she'd given it to us.
117. If the men came here, they (to see) my books.
118. If the girl comes, I (must talk) with her.
119. If you saw the film, you (to be) happy.
120. He won't be hungry if he (to eat) all the ice-cream.
121. The cat would have eaten the fish if it (to find) it.
122. Where (you - to go) if you had enough money?
123. If he'd known the girl, he (to bring) her sweets.
124. You'd catch the ball if he (to throw) it.
125. I'll wash her clothes if she (to bring) them.
126. You'll visit her if she (to ask) you to.
127. She won't run away if she (to like) you.
128. What (she - to buy) if she had no new clothes?

129. I'd have won the game if I (to play) hard.
130. We'd pass the test if we (to try).
131. If I'd eaten more, I (to be) ill.
132. Our dog would have barked if it (to see) the cat.
133. If Paul gives you the cake, you (to eat) it.
134. We'd drive home if we (to have) a car.
135. They (must drive) him home if he'd come.
136. If father (can catch) the ball, he'll give it to me.
137. If you see a burglar, you (must phone) the police.
138. I'd drive him home if he (to have - not) a car.
139. If she'd had a camera, she (to take) many pictures.
140. If they (to take - not) the train, they won't be able to visit Oma.
141. If he saw the girl, he (to know) where she is.
142. If Jim (can use) our pencil, he'll write a letter.
143. If I (to see - not) the girls soon, I won't be able to talk with them.
144. If they'd taken the book, the girl (to read) it.
145. I'd laugh if she (to come).
146. If you'd caught the ball, we (to play) with it.
147. I (must help) mother if she'd been ill.
148. If they saw the wolf, they (to run) away.
149. The baby'd have torn the book if it (to have) it.
150. If we find his bike, we (must give) it to him at once.
151. You'd have helped father if he (to come) and asked you.
152. When (she - to use) the ruler if she found it?
153. They'd buy a new car if the old car (to be) broken.
154. Father won't be angry if mother (to buy) a new blouse.
155. We'd ask who he is if we (to know - not) him.
156. They'll cry if he (to take) the dog away.
157. If you see the burglar, you (to call) the police.
158. If my mother'd seen the letter, she (to read) it.
159. They'd visit you if you (to talk - not) so much.
160. If you fetched some money, I (to buy) you a new bike.
161. If they hear the children, they (to laugh) at them.
162. If Tom'd seen Linda, he (to take) her home.
163. What (they - to sing) if they knew many songs.
164. You won't find the sweets if Sue (to hide) them.
165. He'd take the pencil if you (to hold) it out.
166. We'd have eaten the apples if we (to see) them.

167. If they see the teacher, they (must say) "hello."
168. If I (can help) you, you'll be finished sooner.
169. We (must pay) much money if we'd bought the house.
170. If you (to bring - not) the book, you won't be able to read it.
171. He'd eat all the food if he (to see) it.
172. We'll drink tea if he (to come) soon.
173. We'll see you come if Tom (to shut - not) the door.
174. If the babies cry, you (to hear) them soon.
175. If you wanted me to, I (to wear) that dress.
176. Linda wouldn't be thirsty if she (to drink) milk.
177. I would've kept the cat if father (to allow) it.
178. My sister'll clap if she (to see) the dog.
179. If you broke a glass, Mother (to shout) at you.
180. The salad wouldn't grow if it (to be) winter.
181. Father'll sleep long if the baby (to wake - not) him.
182. If they'd won, they (to be - not) so sad.
183. If I find your book, I (to phone) you right away.
184. If the boy sang a song, we (to run) away.
185. If mother'd burnt the toast, you (to have) nothing to eat.
186. It won't be dark at that time if the sun (to rise) early.
187. Don would've ridden the horse if he (to catch) it.
188. We'll find him soon if he (to hide - not) well.
189. If he hadn't made a big hole, the child (to fall - not) into it.
190. If he carries the glass quickly, you (to have) milk all over.
191. We wouldn't see her if she (to leave) the house early.
192. I'll choose the song if my brother (to want) me to.
193. We would've visited you if the car (to break - not) down.
194. If you bought the clock, it (to ring) tomorrow.

Übersetze die deutschen Sätze.

195. Er hätte dir helfen können, wenn er gewollt hätte.
196. Wenn du ihm das Buch jetzt gäbest, könnte er es übersetzen.
197. Wenn ich du wäre, würde ich meine Hände waschen.
198. Er hätte den Zug noch bekommen, wenn er seine Fahrkarte gefunden hätte.
199. Wenn er spät kommt, gehen wir nicht ins Kino.
200. Ich hätte Paul den Brief gegeben, wenn ich ihn gesehen hätte.
201. Wenn wir das täten, wäre er froh.
202. Ich würde Susan sehen, wenn ich in die Schule ginge.

203. Wenn wir den Brief gesehen hätten, hätten wir ihn gelesen.
204. Wenn er den Kuchen sieht, wird er ihn essen.
205. Wenn er Linda gesehen hätte, hätte er ihr Geld gegeben.
206. Wenn ich ihn sehe, gebe ich ihm den Brief.
207. Wir wären bald gegangen, wenn wir nicht so spät gekommen wären.
208. Ich hätte Vater geholfen, wenn ich ihn gesehen hätte.
209. Wenn die Frau käme, würden wir lachen.
210. Wenn wir sie besuchen, nehmen wir eine Blume (mit).
211. Wenn sie das Haus verkaufen, bekommen sie viel Geld.
212. Wenn ich die Kinder gesehen hätte, hätte ich gelacht.
213. Wenn der Mann hier wäre, würde er mir helfen.
214. Wenn er zu Hause gewesen wäre, hätte er den Einbrecher gefangen.
215. Falls ihr kommt, werdet ihr meine Pferde sehen.
216. Wenn ich jetzt aufhöre, kann ich ins Bett gehen.
217. Wenn ich du wäre, ginge ich ins Bett.
218. Wenn sie früher ins Bett gegangen wäre, wäre sie nicht so müde gewesen.
219. Wenn ihr zum Arzt geht, wird es euch nicht gefallen.
220. Wenn wir die Kamera gefunden hätten, hätten wir Bilder gemacht.
221. Ich hätte ihr helfen können, wenn sie gefragt hätte.
222. Er würde mit uns sprechen, wenn wir ihn anrufen würden.
223. Wenn sie kommen, trinken wir Kaffee.
224. Wir würden Briefe schreiben, wenn wir Bleistifte hätten.
225. Wenn ihr euch versteckt, finden wir euch.
226. Er hätte dir den Stuhl geben können, wenn er es gewusst hätte.
227. Wenn ich lange geschlafen hätte, wäre ich nicht so müde.
228. Wir hätten dorthin fahren können, wenn das Wetter besser gewesen wäre.
229. Wenn ich euch gesehen hätte, wäre ich froh gewesen.
230. Ihr würdet schlafen, wenn ihr Betten hättet.
231. Wenn er uns das Bild zeigt, zeigen wir ihm unsere Bilder auch.
232. Ich würde einen Kuchen backen, wenn ich Zucker hätte.
233. Wenn wir ihm helfen, geht es schneller.
234. Wenn er das gekauft hätte, wäre er unglücklich gewesen.
235. Sie hätten den König sehen können, wenn sie früher gekommen wären.

Verbinde die Sätze, indem die Bedeutung verknüpft und umgeändert wird.

We don't have enough money. We can't buy a car.
If we had enough money, we could buy a car.

236. He doesn't have a girl friend. He doesn't go dancing.

237. He didn't do his homework. He got a "5" in the test.
238. He wanted to go home. He said good-bye.
239. We don't like to walk. We take the bus.
240. We like to walk. We don't take the bus.
241. They wanted to walk. They didn't drive a car.
242. They didn't want to walk. They drove a car.
243. He is so quiet. I can't hear him.
244. I didn't do my homework yesterday. I went to the city.
245. I did my homework yesterday. I didn't go to the city.
246. He sits at home in the afternoon. He doesn't see his friends in the afternoon.
247. He didn't stay at home. He couldn't watch TV.
248. He stays at home. He can watch TV.
249. He doesn't stay at home. He can't watch TV.
250. He buys many things. He doesn't have much money.
251. He bought many things. He didn't have much money.
252. I don't run quickly. I don't get the bus.
253. I don't run quickly. I can't get the bus.
254. I didn't run quickly. I didn't get the bus.
255. I didn't run quickly. I couldn't get the bus.
256. I run quickly. I am very fast.
257. I didn't run quickly. I didn't win the game.
258. I ran quickly. I won the game.

19 Question formation = Fragestellung

19.1 Grammatik

1. Wenn man nach dem **Subjekt** des Satzes fragt, gebraucht man nur die Hilfsverben, die schon im Satz vorhanden sind. Keine zusätzlichen Hilfsverben dürfen dazukommen. (d.h. kein "do/does/did"). Wenn man mit "who" nach dem Subjekt fragt, weiß man (angeblich) nicht, ob das Subjekt Einzahl oder Mehrzahl ist. Deswegen steht eine Subjektfrage in der Einzahl. Das bedeutet, dass in der Gegenwart (present) ein "s" an die "simple form" des Verbes kommt oder ein "is + -ing" in der "progressive form" kommt.

   Two girls see a dog. **Who** sees a dog?

   Two girls are walking to school. **Who is** walking to school?

   Fragewörter:

who, how, what, whose

   The fathers come home. **Who** comes home?

   Two girls went to school. **How many** girls went to school?

   The dog barked. **What** barked?

   Ben's cat ran away. **Whose** cat ran away?

2. Bei **allen anderen Fragewörtern** muss das Verb im Fragesatz mindestens zwei Teile haben. Wenn das Verb im Aussagesatz nur ein Teil hat, muss ein Hilfsverb (do/does/did) dazugesetzt werden. Wenn aber ein Hilfsverb schon vorhanden ist, gebraucht man das vorhandene Hilfsverb und kein zusätzliches "do/does/did".

   Hilfsverben, die dazugesetzt werden, um Fragen zu stellen:

Present:	do	=	I, you, we, you, they
	does	=	he, she, it
Past:	did	=	I, you, he, she, it, we, you, they

   Fragewörter:

what, when, where, why, how (z.B. how many, how much, how long), who(m), whose

   Bill **made a kite**. **What** did Bill do?

   Julie went to school **yesterday**. **When** did Julie go to school?

   We see him **at church**. **Where** do we see him?

She is crying **because she has a "5"**. **Why** is she crying?

Linda bought **two** books. **How many** books did Linda buy?

They are helping **Jim** today. **Who(m)** are they helping today?

Tom took **Ben's** car. **Whose** car did Tom take?

Father can go home **now**. **When** can father go home?

3. Wenn das Verb "to be" das einzige Verb im Satz ist, braucht man kein zusätzliches Hilfsverb.

   Linda **is** 12 years old. How old **is** Linda?

4. Wortstellung im Fragesatz

   Bei "who" bzw. wenn man nach dem **Subjekt** des Satzes fragt:

Fragewort	**Verb**	**Rest des Satzes**
Who	went	home?
Who	is going	to the party?

Bei **allen anderen Fragen**:

Fragewort	**Hilfsverb**	**Subjekt**	**Hauptverb**	**Satzrest**
When	did	they	see	the cat?
Where	were	you	going	yesterday?

Wenn ein Hilfsverb mehr als einen Teil hat, wird nur der erste Teil vor das Subjekt gesetzt; alle anderen Teile kommen nach dem Subjekt.

Fragewort	**Hilfsverb**	**Subj.**	**Hauptverb**	**Satzrest**
	Is	he	going	home?
	Did	he	go	home yesterday?
	Will	he	go	home tomorrow?
Where	did	he	go	yesterday?
Why	is	he	walking	slowly?
How long	can	he	sing	that song?
What	would	he	have done	then?

5. **Verbindung: Hilfsverb/Hauptverb**

   a) Wenn das Hilfsverb eine Form von "to be" (am, are, is, was, were) ist, wird das Hauptverb mit "-ing" gebildet.

      Is he eat**ing** cake?

      When **were** they sitt**ing** under the tree?

      What **are** you talk**ing** about?

   b) **Wenn das Hilfsverb eines der folgenden Hilfsverben ist** (do, does, did, can, could, must, will, shall, would, had to, want to, may), **hat das Hauptverb die Infinitivform des Verbes** (to see, to go), nie die 2. Form des Verbes (saw, went). Auch kommt nie ein "s" an das Hauptverb.

      Does he always **eat** cake?

Do they **run** to school?

Did you **see** the bird?

Can I **help** you?

Could he **go** to school?

Will she **be** there tomorrow?

6. **Yes/No Questions**

Wenn man eine Frage stellt, die mit "ja" oder "nein" beantwortet wird, ist die Wortstellung

a) bei der **Frage**:

Hilfsverb	**Subjekt**	**Hauptverb**	**Satzrest**
Does	he	see	a book?

b) in der **Antwort**:

Yes/No,	**Subjekt**	**Hauptverb**	**Satzrest**
Yes,	he	sees	a book.

Ein Hilfsverb muss in der Frage vorhanden sein, außer wenn "to be" das Verb ist (z.B. Are you Jane?). Nur wenn sonst kein anderes Hilfsverb da ist, muss ein "do/does/did" dazugesetzt werden. Wenn in der Frage ein Hilfsverb (do/does/did) zusätzlich zum Verb gesetzt worden ist, entfällt es in der bejahenden Antwort.

Did he go home? (nicht: Went he home?)

Yes, he went home. (nicht: Yes, he did go home.)

present simple: do/does + infinitive

Does he play ball? (nicht: Plays he ball?)

Do you play ball? (nicht: Play you ball?)

past simple: did + infinitive

Did he play ball? (nicht: Played he ball?)

Did they play ball? (nicht: Played they ball?)

present progressive: am/are/is + -ing

Is he playing ball?

Are you playing ball?

Am I hurting you?

past progressive: was/were + -ing

Was he playing ball?

Were you playing ball?

7. In **verneinten Fragen oder verneinenden Antworten** muss ein Hilfsverb vorhanden sein. Wenn keins da ist, wird ein "do/does/did" dazugesetzt.

    Didn't he go home?

    No, he **did**n't go home. (nie: No, he went not home.)

8. **Beispiele**. Merke: Wenn ein Hilfsverb mehr als einen Teil hat, wird nur der erste Teil vor das Subjekt gesetzt; alle anderen Teile kommen nach dem Subjekt.

Fragewort	**Hilfsverb**	**Subj.**	**Hauptverb**	**Satzrest**
How	must	he	cut	the cake?
How long	can	he	sing	that song?
How many		girls	go	to the shop?
How many cats	did	he	see	yesterday?
To whom	will	he	have given	a book?
What	would	he	have done	then?
Where	are	you?		
Where	will	he	go	tomorrow?
Who	is		going	to the party?
Who			went	home?
Why	is	he	going	to school?
	Can	he	go	to my house?
	Did	he	go	there?
	Has	he	taken	my bike?
	Is	he	going	home?
	Will	he	have written	a letter?

present simple:

Father goes home **every day**.

When **does** father **go** home?

They go home **every day**.

When **do** they **go** home?

Father is at home **every day**.

When **is** father at home?

Father can go home **every day**.

When **can** father **go** home?

present progressive:

Father is going home **now**.

Father's going home now.

When **is** father **going** home?

past simple:

Father went home **yesterday**.

When **did** father **go** home?

past progressive:

Father was going home **when I saw him**.

When **was** father **going** home?

future simple:

Father will go home **tomorrow**.

Father'll go home tomorrow.

When **will** father **go** home?

future progressive:

Father will be going home **at this time tomorrow**.

Father'll be going home at this time tomorrow.

When **will** father **be going** home?

present perfect simple:

Father has gone home **every day so far**.

Father's gone home every day so far.

When **has** father **gone** home?

past perfect simple:

Father had gone home **every time he was able to**.

Father'd gone home every time he was able to.

When **had** father **gone** home?

future perfect:

Father will have gone home **by this time tomorrow**.

Father'll have gone home by this time tomorrow.

When **will** father **have gone** home?

conditional 1:

Father would go home **if you were there**.

Father'd go home if you were there.

When **would** father **go** home?

conditional 2:

Father would have gone home **if you had been there**.

Father'd have gone home if you had been there.

When **would** father **have gone** home?

19.2 Übungen

Entwirf eine Frage, so dass die hervorgehobenen Wörter die Antwort darauf bilden.

present tense:

1. This is **Mrs. Black**.
2. She is selling **newspapers**.
3. You can see her **every day**.
4. She sells **the newspaper**.
5. **In the evening** she sells the newspaper.
6. Mr. Jones is **a reporter**.
7. He is **driving to London**.
8. He often drives **to London**.
9. Peggy and Jill are walking **to work**.
10. They often **walk to work**.
11. **They** often walk to work.
12. **Yes**, they go to work by bus.
13. Mr. Summers is sitting **by the water**.
14. **Yes**, he sometimes watches the children.
15. He **reads a newspaper**.
16. He can sleep **by the water**.
17. **Miss Williams** is driving her car.
18. Mike and Joe live **in London**.
19. **Mike and Joe** live in London.
20. **Yes**, they are asking people about their jobs.
21. **Mr. Carter** lives in London.
22. Mike and Joe **are asking people about their jobs**.
23. **Mike and Joe** are asking people about their jobs.
24. Mrs. Pritchard is closing the supermarket **at half past five**.
25. Mr. Carter can catch **the bus**.
26. Mike and Joe get up **at seven o'clock**.
27. **Mike and Joe** get up at seven o'clock.
28. **Yes**, Mike is watching the people.
29. **Mr. Benson** can go to work by train.
30. Mr. Jackson drives to London **because he works there**.
31. Mr. Jackson **drives to London** because he works there.
32. Mr. Summer sees **two** children.
33. Mrs. Black sells **my father** a newspaper.
34. **Two** girls walk to work.

35. Two girls walk **to work**.
36. **Three children** watch Mr. Summers.
37. Three children watch **Mr. Summers**.

present und past tense:

38. **Yes**, he usually read to them.
39. **No**, he wasn't reading a book.
40. **You** are writing a letter.
41. **Yes**, I wrote one yesterday.
42. Mother and I always eat **cake** on Sunday.
43. My father and mother often **sing a song**.
44. Lois and Terry bought that **at the shop**.
45. The man can feed **the animal**.
46. They **drank their milk** yesterday.
47. **No**, he can't swim well.
48. I was wearing a pullover **yesterday**.
49. **No**, father and mother don't drive a car.
50. **The girls** are standing at the window.
51. My brother threw the books at **three** boys.
52. You were wearing a blouse **on Sunday**.
53. **Tom and Henry** ring them up every evening.
54. **The two** boys wrote a letter.
55. We **drink tea** every afternoon.
56. **Betty's** sister told me a story.
57. Tom and Carol always eat **apples** at school.
58. **No**, we can't give you that book.
59. They are running **to their mother**.
60. The animals **shook their heads**.
61. Mother and I went to the supermarket **yesterday**.
62. My brothers were singing **a song**.
63. My sister hears **that music** every morning.
64. **No**, my brother doesn't drink tea.
65. **The men** were helping the women.
66. The man drove me **to school**.
67. The man takes **Linda** along in his car.
68. I hate that music **because it is so loud**.
69. **The boys** always carry my books.
70. I help **my sister** with her homework.

71. The three birds flew **in the morning**.
72. The child was crying **because he broke his arm**.
73. The man is driving **his car**.
74. **I** am washing the dishes.
75. The girl works **in a supermarket**.
76. **In summer** the children go to the seaside.
77. We didn't want to sit there **because the chairs were dirty**.
78. The girls took **their pullovers**.
79. I ride a horse **at a farm**.
80. The woman gave **me** an apple.
81. His boy is helping him **because he is late**.
82. **The women** are cleaning the windows.
83. The cats always eat **their food**.
84. The boy is eating **bananas**.
85. **The man** brought his hat.
86. The baby walks to **his sister**.
87. Linda and Tom are picking **apples**.
88. The men were playing football **yesterday**.
89. I was eating a cake **at the restaurant**.
90. The baby cries **every day**.
91. **The cats** play on the floor.
92. You are telling **the child** a story.
93. Ted and I wanted to go to the beach **because it was so hot**.
94. The woman drank **a glass of milk**.
95. The three children were playing **in the sand**.
96. **The dogs** were barking at the cat.

alle Zeiten:

97. The child took **Ben's** toy.
98. **The child** took Ben's toy
99. The child **took Ben's toy**
100. The child took **Ben's toy**.
101. The man puts his hat **on a chair**.
102. The man puts **his hat** on a chair.
103. **The man** puts his hat on a chair.
104. The man **puts his hat on a chair.**
105. The people will come **because we asked them**.
106. **The people** will come because we asked them.

107. The people **will come** because we asked them.
108. **We** were running to the bus.
109. We were running **to the bus**.
110. We **were running to the bus.**
111. He is cutting your dress **because it is too long**.
112. You have often seen **my sister**.
113. **You** have often seen my sister.
114. You **have seen my sister** often.
115. You are blowing up **a balloon**.
116. **The dog** caught a ball.
117. The dog **caught a ball**.
118. The dog caught **a ball**.
119. The woman was holding **the baby** yesterday.
120. The woman **was holding the baby** yesterday.
121. The woman was holding the baby **yesterday**.
122. My brother **catches a ball** every day.
123. **My brother** catches a ball every day.
124. My brother catches **a ball** every day.
125. My brother catches a ball **every day**.
126. Their parents will hear **the cars**.
127. **Their parents** will hear the cars.
128. Their parents **will hear the cars.**
129. **My friends** go to school every day.
130. My friends **go to school** every day.
131. My friends go to school **every day**.
132. My friends go **to school** every day.
133. You take **Linda** to a show every week.
134. **You** take Linda to a show every week.
135. You take Linda **to a show** every week.
136. You take Linda to a show **every week**.
137. You **take Linda to a show** every week.
138. My brothers can run **home** after school.
139. **My brothers** can run home after school.
140. My brothers can run home **after school**.
141. My brothers **can run home** after school.
142. **Yes**, my sister is buying a new car.
143. We **threw the paper to them** yesterday.
144. **We** threw the paper to them yesterday.

145. We threw **the paper** to them yesterday.
146. We threw the paper to **them** yesterday.
147. We threw the paper to them **yesterday**.
148. **Tom's** sister has washed his shirts.
149. Tom's sister has washed **his shirts.**
150. Tom's sister **has washed his shirts.**
151. **Tom's sister** has washed his shirts.
152. We ring **Jean's** sister up every day.
153. **We** ring Jean's sister up every day.
154. We **ring Jean's sister up** every day.
155. We ring **Jean's sister** up every day.
156. We ring Jean's sister up **every day**.
157. The children must go to school **tomorrow**.
158. **The children** must go to school tomorrow.
159. The children **must go to school** tomorrow.
160. The children must go **to school** tomorrow.
161. My father must wake Mother up **every morning**.
162. **No**, I wasn't riding the pony when you saw me.
163. Linda will be holding **an apple** tomorrow.
164. **Linda** will be holding an apple tomorrow.
165. Linda **will be holding an apple** tomorrow.
166. Linda will be holding an apple **tomorrow**.
167. The men **had heard a car**.
168. **The men** had heard a car.
169. The men had heard **a car**.
170. **Yes**, the cat eats from his hand.
171. **The children** have seen many dogs.
172. The children **have seen many dogs**.
173. The children have seen **many dogs**.
174. Jim and I were taking **a test**.
175. **Jim and I** were taking a test.
176. Jim and I **were taking a test**.
177. They have taken a trip **today**.
178. **They** have taken a trip today.
179. They **have taken a trip** today.
180. They have taken **a trip** today.
181. They **have taken a trip today.**
182. Mr. Smith has held **the baby**.

183. **The cat** drinks milk.
184. The cat **drinks milk.**
185. The cat drinks **milk**.
186. Bob and Mary ran home **because they were late**.
187. **Nancy's** blouse was blue.
188. I'll walk home with **you** tomorrow.
189. **I**'ll walk home with you tomorrow.
190. **I'll walk home** with you tomorrow.
191. I'll walk **home** with you tomorrow.
192. I'll walk home with you **tomorrow**.
193. **Yes**, you are helping me now.
194. You are walking **to the supermarket**.
195. **You** are walking to the supermarket.
196. You **are walking to the supermarket**.
197. **Mary** was eating an apple.
198. Linda and I were taking **a bus**.
199. **Linda and I** were taking a bus.
200. Linda and I **could take a bus**.
201. Linda and I could take **a bus**.
202. **Linda and I** could take a bus.
203. **Yes**, he can help you today.
204. Mother and I were holding **an apple**.
205. Mother and I could have held **an apple**.
206. Mother and I **could have held an apple**.
207. I always see **three** girls.
208. **I** always see three girls.
209. I always **see three girls**.
210. I always see **three girls**.
211. I have always eaten **two** sandwiches.
212. I have always eaten **two sandwiches**.
213. **I** have always eaten two sandwiches.
214. I have always **eaten two sandwiches.**
215. **Yes**, Mary went to the supermarket.
216. The boy saw the dog **the day before yesterday**.
217. The boy saw **the dog** the day before yesterday.
218. The boy **saw the dog** the day before yesterday.
219. **Yes**, the dog often barks.
220. Mr. Smith is talking with **Mary**.

221. You will read **three** books tomorrow.
222. **You** will read three books tomorrow.
223. You will read **three books** tomorrow.
224. You will read three books **tomorrow.**
225. You **will read three books** tomorrow.
226. We are walking with **Tom**.
227. **We** are walking with Tom.
228. We should help **Mother**.
229. **We** should help Mother.
230. We **should help Mother.**
231. **Betty** is talking to her sister.
232. **Father and Mother** are here.
233. **Father and Mother** have been here.
234. **After breakfast** we will run to school.
235. After breakfast **we** will run to school.
236. After breakfast we will run **to school.**
237. After breakfast we **will run to school.**
238. After lunch he ran **to the station**.
239. After lunch **he** ran to the station.
240. **After lunch** he ran to the station.
241. After lunch he **ran to the station**.
242. **My brother** throws balls every day.
243. My brother throws balls **every day**.
244. My brother **throws balls** every day.
245. They have given her **a book**.
246. **They** have given her a book.
247. They **have given her a book.**
248. They have given **her** a book.
249. I am happy **because I have a "1"**.
250. They spoke to her **four times**.
251. They **spoke** to her four times.
252. **Ten** trees were growing near the river.
253. The dog **shook its head**.
254. The dog shook **its head**.
255. The dog **would have shaken its head.**
256. The dog would have shaken **its head.**
257. The dog **has shaken its head.**
258. The dog has shaken **its head.**

259. The dog **shakes its head.**
260. The dog shakes **its head.**
261. The dog **can shake its head.**
262. The dog can shake **its head.**
263. We are hiding **in the bedroom**.
264. **We** are hiding in the bedroom.
265. We **are hiding** in the bedroom.
266. We were hiding **in the bedroom.**
267. **We** were hiding in the bedroom.
268. We **were hiding** in the bedroom.
269. We will be hiding **in the bedroom.**
270. **We** will be hiding in the bedroom.
271. We **will be hiding** in the bedroom.
272. We drank milk **yesterday**.
273. **We** drank milk yesterday.
274. We **drank milk** yesterday.
275. We drink milk **every day**.
276. **We** drink milk every day.
277. We **drink milk** every day.
278. We have drunk milk **every day**.
279. **We** have drunk milk every day.
280. We **have drunk milk** every day.
281. We would drink milk **every day**.
282. **We** would drink milk every day.
283. We **would drink milk** every day.
284. We should drink milk **every day.**
285. **We** should drink milk every day.
286. We **should drink milk** every day.
287. We will drink milk **every day**.
288. **We** will drink milk every day.
289. We **will drink milk** every day.
290. We had drunk milk **every day**.
291. **We** had drunk milk every day.
292. We **had drunk milk** every day.
293. They took **an apple**.
294. **They** took an apple.
295. They **took an apple**.
296. She bought **five** books.

297. She bought **five books**.
298. I told you a story **because you wanted to hear one**.
299. **The two men** stood in the classroom.
300. The two men stood **in the classroom**.
301. **The two** men stood in the classroom.
302. The two men **stood** in the classroom.
303. He went **to the seaside**.
304. They eat **apples**.
305. **The little boy** ran home.
306. I went swimming **yesterday**.
307. You helped me **because you're my friend**.
308. **Two** girls bought books.
309. **Two girls** bought books.
310. Two girls **bought books**.
311. Two girls bought **books**.
312. We were flying a kite **at the beach**.
313. **We** were flying a kite at the beach.
314. **The old man** can help you.
315. The old man can help **you**.
316. The old man **can help you**.
317. We'll be visiting them **on Sunday**.
318. **We**'ll be visiting them on Sunday.
319. We**'ll be visiting them** on Sunday.
320. We'll be visiting **them** on Sunday.
321. **Yes**, I like him.
322. He eats **apples** every day.
323. She will call him **at 3 o'clock**.
324. **She** will call him at 3 o'clock.
325. She **will call him** at 3 o'clock.
326. She will call **him** at 3 o'clock.
327. Mother went to Bonn **yesterday**.
328. We'll talk with **him** tomorrow.
329. We**'ll talk with him** tomorrow.
330. **We**'ll talk with him tomorrow.
331. **Yes**, Don took his pullover with him.
332. You are running **to the bus stop**.
333. **You** are running to the bus stop.
334. I always eat **six** apples every week.

335. **I** always eat six apples every week.
336. I see **the red pencil**.
337. I'd seen **the red pencil**.
338. **I**'d seen the red pencil.
339. **I'd seen the red pencil.**
340. I'd see **the red pencil.**
341. **I**'d see the red pencil.
342. **I'd see the red pencil.**
343. **The little boys** have cars.
344. The supermarket opened **at 2 o'clock**.
345. The supermarket **opened** at 2 o'clock.
346. **Yes**, I can come to visit you.
347. They are walking **to the window**.
348. **They** are walking to the window.
349. He is looking at **Jane**.
350. I sang that song **twice**.
351. I **sang that song** twice.
352. I'd sing that song **twice.**
353. **I**'d sing that song twice.
354. **I'd sing that song** twice.
355. I'd sung that song **twice**.
356. **I**'d sung that song twice.
357. **I'd sung that song** twice.
358. She often **talks about her neighbours**.
359. **Yes**, they wore hats yesterday.
360. They bought **new clothes** last week.
361. She ran **quickly**.
362. She **ran quickly**.
363. The child hid behind the door **because he was bad**.
364. She will go **to school** tomorrow.
365. **She** will go to school tomorrow.
366. We listened to **the record**.
367. **Five** children are running down the street.
368. **Five children** are running down the street.
369. Five children are running **down the street**.
370. Five children **are running down the street.**
371. They always **fed the cats**.
372. They always fed **the cats**.

373. **I** forgot to take my pullover.
374. I forgot to take **my pullover**.
375. They had given her money **because she wanted to buy a record**.
376. **They**'d given her money.
377. They'd given her **money**.
378. They'd given **her** money.
379. They**'d given her money.**
380. **They**'d give her money.
381. They'd give her **money.**
382. They'd give **her** money.
383. They**'d give her money.**
384. **They**'d have given her money.
385. They'd have given her **money.**
386. They'd have given **her** money.
387. They**'d have given her money.**
388. You will be driving there **on Sunday**.
389. You **will be driving there** on Sunday.
390. She **has drawn a nice picture**.
391. She has drawn **a nice picture**.
392. He eats **six** pieces of cake every day.
393. He **eats six pieces of cake** every day.
394. We swam **in the dirty water**.
395. We **swam in the dirty water**.
396. You are buying a new blouse **tomorrow**.
397. **You** are buying a new blouse tomorrow.
398. **They** speak to me every day.

Entwirf Fragen, die du mit den unten angegebenen Fragewörtern einleitest. Du musst damit jeweils ein anderes Wort oder Wörter im Beispielsatz ersetzen.

399. The three boys saw the birds on the tree.
     a. Who? b. How many? c. What? d. Where?
400. Mother has driven two cars to Bonn.
     a. Who? b. What? c. How many? d. Where?
401. Father's sister is sitting on the chair.
     a. Who? b. Whose? c. Where?
402. The five boys would eat ten pieces of cake if you baked cake.
     a. How many? b. Who? c. How many? d. What? e. What?
403. We always give you books to read.
     a. Who? b. Whom?/Who? c. What?

404. I must go home now.

a. Who? b. Where? c. When? d. What?

405. The boys were eating apples in the garage.

a. Who? b. What? c. Where? d. What?

406. The children had thrown toys on the floor.

a. Who? b. What? c. Where? d. What?

407. Father will buy Susan five new books.

a. Who? b. Whom?/Who? c. How many? d. What?

408. My brother will be flying to London tomorrow.

a. Who? b. Where? c. When? d. What?

409. Pat's sister took Mike's car.

a. Whose? b. What? c. Whose? d. What?

410. The men would have given you many books if you had asked.

a. Who? b. Whom? / Who? c. What? d. What?

411. They go to Rome every summer.

a. Who? b. Where? c. When? d. What?

412. I have drunk a glass of milk.

a. Who? b. What? d. What?

413. Three boys were sitting on a chair in the kitchen.

a. Who? b. How many? c. On what? d. Where? e. What?

414. He sees four trees.

a. Who? b. What? c. How many?

415. I am going to Berlin tomorrow.

a. Who? b. Where? c. When? d. What?

416. Jane's sister wrote twenty letters yesterday.

a. Who? b. Whose? c. What? d. When? e. What?

417. They can talk for two hours today.

a. How long? b. When? c. What?

418. The class will go to the beach next week.

a. Who? b. Where? c. When? d. What?

419. John's brother helps me every day.

a. Who? b. Whose? c. Whom? /Who? d. When? e. What?

Stelle Fragen, um die angegebenen Wörter als Antworten zu bekommen:

420. Two boys are playing football.

a. Two boys b. two c. football

421. The girls have bought three pullovers.

a. The girls b. three c. three pullovers d. have bought three pullovers

422. The cat saw our dog yesterday.

a. The cat b. our c. our dog d. yesterday

423. The ten dogs would have barked loudly if they had seen the cats.

a. The ten b. The ten dogs c. loudly d. would have barked loudly

424. The three girls always eat six bars of chocolate.

a. The three girls b. The three c. six d. six bars of chocolate e. eat six bars of chocolate

425. We will be eating our food when you arrive tomorrow.

a. We b. our food c. will be eating our food

426. Mother and I can help you tomorrow.

a. Mother and I b. you c. tomorrow d. help you tomorrow

427. The man should drive the car into the garage.

a. The man b. the car c. into the garage d. should drive the car into the garage

428. My brother will go to school.

a. My b. My brother c. to school d. go to school

429. The men would work very hard every day if they had a job.

a. The men b. very hard c. every day d. would work very hard

430. The girl is throwing a ball into the air.

a. The girl b. a ball c. into the air d. is throwing a ball into the air

431. The boy often laughs at his two brothers.

a. The boy b. his two c. his two brothers d. laughs at his two brothers

432. The men were writing ten sentences.

a. The men b. ten c. ten sentences c. were writing ten sentences

433. The supermarket had sold ten apples.

a. The supermarket b. ten c. ten apples d. had sold ten apples

434. Mother said a word.

a. Mother b. a word c. said a word

435. Father'll read a book tomorrow.

a. Father b. a book c. tomorrow d. read a book

436. Tom would go to your party if Linda went there, too.

a. Tom b. your c. to your party d. would go to your party

437. Yes, father is reading.

a. Yes

438. Father always reads books.

a. Father b. books c. reads books

439. Father often read books when he was a boy.

a. Father b. books c. when he was a boy d. read books when he was a boy. e. read books

440. We often wash our cars.

a. We b. our c. our cars d. wash our cars.

Stelle die Frage nach dem/den hervorgehobenen Wort/Wörtern:

441. We're running **to school**.
442. **We**'re running to school.
443. We**'re running to school**.
444. **He**'s eaten his sandwich.
445. He**'s eaten his sandwich**.
446. **He**'s eating his sandwich.
447. He**'s eating his sandwich**.
448. **He**'d go to work if he had a job.
449. He**'d go to work** if he had a job.
450. **He**'d gone to work when he had a job.
451. He**'d gone to work** when he had a job.
452. Linda's sitting there **because she must see the doctor**.
453. **Yes**, we'll give you the paper.
454. They've taken **you** to school.
455. **They**'ve taken you to school.
456. They**'ve taken you to school**.
457. **They**'d taken you to school.
458. They**'d taken you to school.**
459. **They**'d take you to school.
460. They**'d take you to school**.
461. **We**'d helped you very often last year.
462. We**'d helped you** very often last year.
463. **We**'d help you if you asked us.
464. We**'d help you** if you asked us.
465. Mother's spoken with **Tom's** brother.
466. **Mother**'s spoken with Tom's brother.
467. Mother**'s spoken with Tom's brother**.
468. **Mother**'s speaking with Tom's brother.
469. Mother**'s speaking with Tom's brother**.
470. The girls'll feed **the cats**.
471. **Yes**, his sister'll swim next week.
472. **Tomorrow** mother's flying to Berlin.
473. Tomorrow **mother**'s flying to Berlin.
474. Tomorrow mother**'s flying to Berlin**.

475. **Mother**'s flown to Berlin very often.
476. Mother**'s flown to Berlin** very often.
477. Jerry's sleeping **on a sofa** now.
478. **Jerry**'s sleeping on a sofa now.
479. Jerry**'s sleeping on a sofa** now.
480. **Jerry**'s slept on a sofa very often.
481. Jerry**'s slept on a sofa** very often.

20 Verb tenses = Zeitformen

20.1 Grammatik

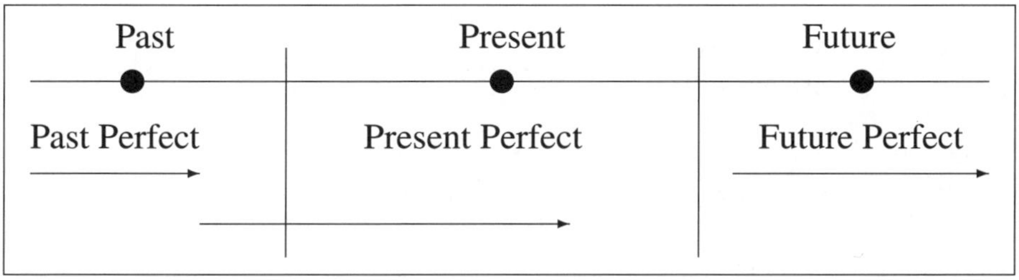

1. **Knappe Beschreibung**

   present: Ein Punkt in der Gegenwart

   past: Ein Punkt in der Vergangenheit

   future: Ein Punkt in der Zukunft

   present perfect: Eine Handlung fing in der Vergangenheit an und dauert bis in die Gegenwart an.

   past perfect: Eine Handlung fing in der Vergangenheit an und hörte in der Vergangenheit auf.

   future perfect: Eine Handlung fängt in der Zukunft an und

   a) dauert bis zu einem gewissen Punkt in der Zukunft oder

   b) man weiß nicht, wann die Handlung aufhören wird.

2. **Beispiele:**

present:	I go to school every day.
past:	I went to school yesterday.
future:	I will go to school tomorrow.
present perfect:	I have gone to school for six years now.
past perfect:	I had gone to school for six years when I was at the "Grundschule."
future perfect:	I will have gone to school for 13 years by the time I get my "Abitur."
conditional 1:	I would go to the university if I wanted to.
conditional 2:	I would have gone to school yesterday but I had a cold.

3. **Aussagesatz**

	simple:	
present:	1. Form (bei he/she/it: s/es)	
past:	2. Form	
future:	will	+ infinitive
pres.perf.:	have/has	+ 3. Form
past perf.:	had	+ 3. Form
fut.perf. :	will have	+ 3. Form
cond. 1:	would	+ infinitive
cond. 2:	would have	+ 3. Form
	progressive:	
present:	am/are/is	+ ing
past:	was/were	+ ing
future:	will be	+ ing
pres.perf.:	have/has been	+ ing
past perf.:	had been	+ ing
fut.perf. :	will have been	+ ing
cond. 1:	would be	+ ing
cond. 2:	would have been	+ ing

Beispiel: to eat, ate, eaten

	simple	
	englisch	**deutsch**
present	he eats	er ißt
past	he ate	er aß
future	he will eat	er wird essen
pres. perf.	he has eaten	er hat gegessen
past perf.	he had eaten	er hatte gegessen
fut.perf.	he will have eaten	er wird gegessen haben
cond. 1	he would eat	er würde essen
cond. 2	he would have eaten	er würde gegessen haben

	progressive	
	englisch	**deutsch**
present	he is eating	er ist dabei zu essen
past	he was eating	er war dabei zu essen
future	he will be eating	er wird dabei sein zu essen
pres. perf.	he has been eating	er ist dabei gewesen zu essen
past perf.	he had been eating	er war dabei gewesen zu essen
fut.perf.	he will have been eating	er wird dabei gewesen sein zu essen
cond. 1	he would be eating	er würde dabei sein zu essen
cond. 2	he would have been eating	er würde dabei gewesen sein zu essen

4. Merke die **Abweichungen in Fragen und Verneinungen**:

	Fragesatz		**Verneinung**	
present:	do/does	+ inf.?	don't/doesn't	+ inf.
past:	did	+ inf.?	didn't	+ inf.
future:	will	+ inf.?	won't	+ inf.

5. **Simple oder Progressive**:

   a) **simple**:

      - Wenn folgende Wörter im Satz sind: always, ever, every, never, often, sometimes, usually, in winter, in spring, in summer, in autumn, on Mondays, etc.

   b) **progressive**:

      - Wenn folgende Wörter im Satz sind: at this moment, at that moment, listen, look, now, right now, today
      - Handlungen, die gerade passieren
      - Wenn man Bilder ansieht und darüber spricht

6. **Ausführliche Erläuterungen zu den Zeiten**

   a) **present**

      - Handlungen, die jeden Tag in der Gegenwart geschehen

        I eat three times a day.

      - Handlungen in der Zukunft - gemäß einem Stunden- oder Fahrplan (timetable)

        My bus leaves in ten minutes.

      - Bei Bedingungssätzen (if-clauses), um etwas zu zeigen, was sehr möglich ist.

        If he **takes** his medicine, he will be well soon.

   b) **past =** Ein Zeitpunkt in der Vergangenheit.

      - Hinweiswörter: ago, before (1980), in (1980), last (week), yesterday

        We saw him yesterday.

      - Wenn man "when did" fragt.

        When did you go home? I **went** ...

      - Bei der indirekten Rede wird "present" in "past" umgewandelt.

        She said, "He is coming." She said that he **was** coming.

      - Bei Bedingungssätzen (if-clauses), um etwas zu zeigen, was eventuell möglich ist.

        If he **took** his medicine, he would be well soon.

      - In normalen Sätzen gebraucht man "was" bei "he/she/it.". In Bedingungssätzen gebraucht man "were" statt "was" bei "he/she/it".

        He was here yesterday. If he **were** here, I'd see him.

- **simple**
  - past simple (Die zweite Form des Verbes wird gebraucht.)

    to go - went - gone; he went home

  - Die Handlung ist abgeschlossen und hat keine Verbindung zu der Gegenwart. Man denkt an kein Ergebnis oder Folgen.

    I took the train yesterday.

  - Bei einer Geschichte und Berichten. Mehrere Handlungen folgen nacheinander gleichzeitig oder nacheinander. Das Verhältnis zueinander wird nicht betont.

    The man **went** into the room, **picked** up his hat, **left**...

- **progressive**
  - past progressive (= "was/were + -ing" wird gebraucht)
  - Bei Handlungen in der Vergangenheit, die **gleichzeitig** verlaufen sind.

    Linda was talking to friends **while** her mother was washing the dishes.

  - Wenn Handlungen oder Vorgänge zu einem bestimmten Zeitpunkt **längere Zeit** verliefen.

    They were talking on the phone for two hours last night.

  - um Einzelheiten oder Personen in Erzählungen zu beschreiben.

    The man you saw was wearing a green hat, red pants and yellow shoes.

  - Wenn eine Handlung in der Vergangenheit von einer anderen Handlung **unterbrochen** wurde. Die Handlung, die andauert, ist in "progressive". Die Handlung, die plötzlich eintritt, ist in "simple".

    Linda was telling a joke when the phone rang.

c) **future**

- Eine Handlung wird in der Zukunft stattfinden.

  Hinweiswörter: tomorrow, **next** week

  Father will go to work tomorrow morning.

- Bei Bedingungssätzen (if-clauses), um etwas zu zeigen, was sehr möglich ist.

  If he takes his medicine, he **will be** well soon.

- Eine Absicht/Entscheidung wird gefasst.

  I will visit you soon.

d) **present perfect**

- Wenn folgende Wörter im Satz vorhanden sind, kommt meist "present perfect":

  all day, already, ever, ever since, for, how long, just, lately, never, not yet, of late, recently, since ..., so far, the whole day, this (afternoon), today, up till now, up to now, yet ("Already" kann aber auch in den anderen "perfect" Zeitformen gebraucht werden. Es wird sogar auch manchmal in "past" gebraucht.)

  for = Zeitspanne angegeben. **for** five years

  since = Zeitpunkt angegeben. **since** 1985

- Wenn es in der Vergangenheit angefangen hat und noch anhält (Zeitspanne). Hinweise: **for ... now**, **since** the holidays, **this** week, **the past** two weeks.

  It has been raining for five hours now.

- Handlungen innerhalb einer Zeitspanne, die noch nicht abgeschlossen ist (since, for). Die Handlungen, die dabei abgelaufen sind, haben "past tense".

  Bob **hasn't heard** from Uncle Tom **for** two years now (Pres. Perf.), but last year he saw Aunt Jane. (Past)

- Wenn es in der Vergangenheit angefangen hat und gerade aufgehört hat, so dass man die Folgen noch sieht.

  Look at me. A lorry **has splashed** my dress!

  You look sick: Yes, I **have eaten** 20 apples.

- Wenn eine Inhaltsangabe in der Gegenwart erzählt wird. Dann werden alle Handlungen aus der Vergangenheit in "present perfect" erzählt.

e) **past perfect**

- Eine abgeschlossene Zeitspanne in der Vergangenheit

- Zwei Handlungen werden beschrieben. Ein Zeitpunkt ist vorbei, als der nächste anfängt. Der Zeitpunkt, der weiter zurückliegt, wird in "past perfect" ausgedrückt. Das Verhältnis zueinander wird oft durch Wörter wie "**when**, **after**" oder "**because**" betont.

  After mother **had eaten**, she left the house.

- Man denkt an die Resultate einer Handlung.

  You had no more money for you **had bought** a dress.

- Bei der indirekten Rede werden "past" und "present perfect" in "past perfect" umgewandelt.

  She said, "He has gone home."

  She said he **had gone** home.

  She said, "He went there yesterday."

  She said that he **had gone** there the day before.

- Bei Bedingungssätzen (if-clauses), um etwas zu zeigen, was nicht länger veränderbar ist.

  If he **had taken** his medicine, he would have been well, but now he is still very ill.

  "Already" kann auch in "past perfect" gebraucht werden.

f) **future perfect**

- Eine Zeitspanne in der Zukunft. Diese Zeitspanne fängt erst in der Zukunft an und wird bis zu einem gewissen zukünftigen Zeitpunkt beendet sein (I **shall have taken** my test **by this time tomorrow**), oder die Zeitspanne wird noch anfangen und auf ungewisse Zeit weiter anhalten.

  (She **will have been learning** English for half a year by December.)

- Eine Handlung in der Zukunft wird vollendet sein, bevor eine andere zukünftige Handlung stattfindet.

  (We **will have returned** from America before you get out of school in June.)

  "Already" kann auch in "future perfect" gebraucht werden.

g) **conditional 1**

- Bei Bedingungssätzen (if-clauses), um etwas zu zeigen, was eventuell möglich ist.

  If he took his medicine, he **would be** well soon.

- Bei der indirekten Rede wird "future" in "cond. 1" umgewandelt.

  She said, "I will come tomorrow." She said she **would come** the following day.

h) **conditional 2**

- Bei Bedingungssätzen (if-clauses), um etwas zu zeigen, was nicht mehr umänderbar ist.

  If he had taken his medicine, he **would have been** well soon, but now he is still very ill.

- Bei der indirekten Rede wird die "future perfect" in "cond. 2" umgewandelt.

  She said, "We will have taken the test by tomorrow."

  She said that they **would have taken** the test by the following day.

present simple:

Father flies a plane every day.

Does father fly a plane every day?

No, father does not (doesn't) fly a plane every day.

They fly a plane every day.

Do they fly a plane every day?

No, they do not (don't) fly a plane every day.

When do they fly a plane?

Father can fly a plane every day.

Can father fly a plane every day?

No, father cannot (can't) fly a plane every day.

When can father fly a plane?

Father is at home every day.
Is father at home?
No, father is not (isn't) at home.
When is father at home?

Father has a green plane.
Does father have a green plane? / Has father got a green plane?

present progressive:
Father is flying the plane now.
Is father flying the plane now?
No, father is not (isn't) flying the plane now.

past simple:
Father flew the plane yesterday.
Did father fly the plane yesterday?
No, father did not (didn't) fly the plane yesterday.

past progressive:
Father was flying the plane when I saw him.
Was father flying the plane when I saw him?
No, father was not (wasn't) flying the plane when I saw him.

future simple:
Father will fly the plane tomorrow.
Will father fly the plane tomorrow?
No, father won't (will not) fly the plane tomorrow.

future progressive:
Father will be flying the plane when I see him tomorrow.
Will father be flying the plane when I see him tomorrow?
No, father won't (will not) be flying the plane when I see him tomorrow.

present perfect simple:
Father has flown planes since 1980.
Has father flown planes since 1980?
No, father hasn't (has not) flown planes since 1980.

present perfect progressive:
Father has been flying the plane for two hours now.
Has father been flying the plane for two hours now?
No, father hasn't (has not) been flying the plane for two hours now.

past perfect simple:

Father had flown planes from 1980 until 1990.

Had father flown planes from 1980 until 1990?

No, father hadn't (had not) flown planes from 1980 until 1990.

past perfect progressive:

Father had been flying the plane when he heard a loud noise.

Had father been flying the plane when he heard a loud noise?

No, father hadn't (had not) been flying the plane when he heard a loud noise.

future perfect simple:

Father will have flown the plane by this time tomorrow.

Will father have flown the plane by this time tomorrow?

No, father won't (will not) have flown the plane by this time tomorrow.

future perfect progressive:

Father will have been flying the plane for ten hours by this time tomorrow.

Will father have been flying the plane for ten hours by this time tomorrow?

No, father won't (will not) have been flying the plane for ten hours by this time tomorrow.

conditional 1 simple:

Father would fly the plane if you wanted him to.

Would father fly the plane if you wanted him to?

No, father wouldn't (would not) fly the plane if you wanted him to.

conditional 1 progressive:

Father would be flying the plane now if he wasn't ill.

Would father be flying the plane now if he wasn't ill?

No, father wouldn't (would not) be flying the plane now if he wasn't ill.

conditional 2 simple:

Father would have flown the plane if you had wanted him to.

Would father have flown the plane if you had wanted him to?

No, father wouldn't (would not) have flown the plane if you had wanted him to.

conditional 2 progressive:

Father would have been flying the plane yesterday if he hadn't become ill.

Would father have been flying the plane yesterday if he hadn't become ill?

No, father wouldn't (would not) have been flying the plane yesterday if he hadn't become ill.

20.1.1 Unregelmäßige Verben:

Infinitiv	2. Form	3. Form	deutsch
arise	arose	arisen	entstehen, s. erheben
be	was/were	been	sein
bear	bore	borne/born	tragen, geboren
beat	beat	beaten	schlagen, übertreffen
become	became	become	werden
beget	begot	begotten	zeugen
begin	began	begun	anfangen, beginnen
bend	bent	bent	beugen, biegen
beseech	besought	besought	anflehen
bet	bet	bet	wetten
bid	bid/bade	bid/bidden	befehlen, bieten
bind	bound	bound	binden
bite	bit	bitten	beißen
bleed	bled	bled	bluten
blow	blew	blown	blasen
break	broke	broken	brechen, zerbrechen
breed	bred	bred	züchten
bring	brought	brought	bringen
broadcast	broadcast	broadcast	senden
build	built	built	bauen
burn	*burnt*	*burnt*	brennen
burst	burst	burst	explodieren, platzen
buy	bought	bought	kaufen
cast	cast	cast	werfen
catch	caught	caught	fangen
choose	chose	chosen	wählen
cling	clung	clung	festhalten, s. klammern
come	came	come	kommen
cost	cost	cost	kosten
creep	crept	crept	kriechen, schleichen
cut	cut	cut	schneiden
deal	dealt	dealt	austeilen, handeln
dig	dug	dug	graben
do	did	done	machen, tun
draw	drew	drawn	malen, ziehen
dream	*dreamt*	*dreamt*	träumen
drink	drank	drunk	trinken
drive	drove	driven	fahren
dwell	dwelt	dwelt	wohnen
eat	ate	eaten	essen, fressen
fall	fell	fallen	fallen
feed	fed	fed	ernähren, füttern
feel	felt	felt	fühlen, merken, wahrnehmen
fight	fought	fought	kämpfen
find	found	found	feststellen, finden
flee	fled	fled	fliehen
fling	flung	flung	schleudern
fly	flew	flown	fliegen

forbid	forbade/forbad	forbidden	verbieten
forecast	forecast	forecast	voraussagen
forget	forgot	forgotten	vergessen
forgive	forgave	forgiven	vergeben
forsake	forsook	forsaken	verlassen
freeze	froze	frozen	gefrieren
get	got	got	bekommen, kriegen, gewinnen
give	gave	given	geben,schenken
go	went	gone	fahren, gehen, reisen
grind	ground	ground	mahlen, schleifen
grow	grew	grown	wachsen
hang	hanged	hanged	sich aufhängen
hang	hung	hung	hängen
have	had	had	besitzen, haben
hear	heard	heard	hören
hide	hid	hidden/hid	verstecken
hit	hit	hit	schlagen
hold	held	held	halten
hurt	hurt	hurt	verletzen
keep	kept	kept	behalten
kneel	knelt	knelt	knien
know	knew	known	kennen, wissen
lay	laid	laid	legen, stellen
lead	led	led	führen
lean	*leant*	*leant*	lehnen, stützen
leap	*leapt*	*leapt*	springen
learn	*learnt*	*learnt*	erfahren, lernen
leave	left	left	abreisen, verlassen
lend	lent	lent	borgen, leihen
let	let	let	erlauben, vermieten, zulassen
lie	lay	lain	liegen
light	*lit*	*lit*	anzünden, leuchten
lose	lost	lost	verlieren
make	made	made	machen, verursachen
mean	meant	meant	meinen, vorhaben
meet	met	met	kennenlernen, treffen
mow	mowed	mown	mähen
overcome	overcame	overcome	besiegen, überwinden
overtake	overtook	overtaken	überholen
pay	paid	paid	zahlen
put	put	put	legen, stellen, tun
read	read	read	lesen
rebuild	rebuilt	rebuilt	wieder aufbauen
rend	rent	rent	zerreißen
rid	rid	rid	befreien
ride	rode	ridden	fahren, reiten
ring	rang	rung	klingeln, läuten
rise	rose	risen	aufstehen, s. erheben

run	ran	run	laufen, rennen
say	said	said	erzählen, sagen
see	saw	seen	erkennen, sehen, verstehen
seek	sought	sought	erbitten, suchen
sell	sold	sold	verkaufen
send	sent	sent	schicken, senden
set	set	set	legen, setzen
sew	sewed	sewn/sewed	nähen
shake	shook	shaken	schütteln
shed	shed	shed	vergießen,verlieren
shine	shone	shone	scheinen, strahlen
shoot	shot	shot	schießen
show	showed	shown	zeigen
shrink	shrank	shrunk	einlaufen, schrumpfen
shut	shut	shut	schließen, zumachen
sing	sang	sung	singen
sink	sank	sunk	sinken
sit	sat	sat	sitzen
slay	slew	slain	erschlagen, töten
sleep	slept	slept	schlafen
slide	slid	slid	gleiten, schlittern
sling	slung	slung	schleudern
slink	slunk	slunk	schleichen
slit	slit	slit	aufschneiden,schlitzen
smell	*smelt*	*smelt*	duften, riechen
sow	sowed	sown	säen
speak	spoke	spoken	reden, sprechen
speed	sped	sped	s. beeilen, beschleunigen, schnell fahren
spell	*spelt*	*spelt*	buchstabieren
spend	spent	spent	ausgeben, verbringen
spill	*spilt*	*spilt*	verschütten
spin	spun	spun	drehen, spinnen
spit	spat	spat	spucken
split	split	split	spalten, s. teilen
spoil	*spoilt*	*spoilt*	verderben, verwöhnen
spread	spread	spread	ausbreiten, streichen
spring	sprang	sprung	springen
stand	stood	stood	ausstehen, dulden, stehen
steal	stole	stolen	stehlen
stick	stuck	stuck	befestigen, heften, klebenbleiben
sting	stung	stung	stechen
stink	stank/stunk	stunk	stinken
stride	strode	stridden	schreiten
strike	struck	struck	schlagen
string	strung	strung	aufreihen, spannen
strive	strove	striven	s. bemühen, streben
swear	swore	sworn	fluchen, schwören

sweep	swept	swept	kehren
swell	swelled	swollen/swelled	schwellen, zunehmen
swim	swam	swum	schwimmen
swing	swung	swung	schaukeln, schwingen
take	took	taken	nehmen
teach	taught	taught	lehren, unterrichten
tear	tore	torn	reißen, zerreißen
tell	told	told	erklären, erzählen
think	thought	thought	denken, meinen
throw	threw	thrown	werfen
thrust	thrust	thrust	stoßen
tread	trod	trodden/trod	treten
understand	understood	understood	begreifen, einsehen, verstehen
upset	upset	upset	umwerfen, verwirren, aus der Fassung bringen
wake	*woke*	*woken/waked*	aufwecken,erwachen
wear	wore	worn	anhaben, tragen
weave	wove	woven	weben
weep	wept	wept	weinen
win	won	won	gewinnen
wind	wound	wound	(auf)drehen, wickeln, aufziehen
wring	wrung	wrung	wringen
write	wrote	written	schreiben

Anmerkung: Die mit *kursiv* gekennzeichneten Verben können ihre 2. und 3. Formen auch mit -ed bilden:

dream	dreamt	dreamt
dream	dreamed	dreamed

20.2 Übungen

Setze das Verb in die richtige Zeitform:

1. He (to sleep - past perf. prog.) for eight hours.
2. She (to write - past perf.) a letter before you came.
3. They (to break - fut. perf.) every record by the time they come tomorrow.
4. (to be - you - pres. perf. simple) to London this year?
5. Linda and Gary (to drink - past prog.) milk when I saw them.
6. She (to steal - always - not - cond. 1) things if she had enough money.
7. I (to drive - usually - pres.) to work on Mondays.
8. The dog (to bite - cond. 2) you if you had hurt it.
9. We (to catch - usually - past) the ball.
10. Father (to have - sometimes - past perf.) a bad day.
11. The little girl (to sleep - pres.) 10 hours every day.

12. You (to understand - always - past) what Tom said.
13. (to get - he - pres. perf. simple) everything?
14. (to blow - the wind - past prog.) very hard when you came home yesterday?
15. We (to speak - pres. perf.) to the teacher very often.
16. I (to leave - past perf. simple) Berlin when I was a child.
17. She (to meet - fut. simple) Ben at the party.
18. The girl (to blow - past prog.) a toy up.
19. He (to forget) to go home if you hadn't told him.
20. You (to keep) the horse if Father said "yes."
21. I (to begin - fut. perf.) to wash the dishes when you see me.
22. I (to buy - past simple) a hat.
23. They (to sleep - pres. prog.) at a hotel.
24. You (to fall - pres. simple) down the stairs.
25. You (to ride - past prog.) a bike yesterday.
26. (to speak - we - pres. perf.) to Linda?
27. They (to have - past perf.) to wait for two hours.
28. We (to ride - present) in a taxi now.
29. I (to get - sometimes - pres. perf.) homework.
30. We (to hold - past prog.) a cat.
31. The men (to begin - fut. perf.) to swim by next Monday.
32. Peggy (to eat - past simple) a banana.
33. We (to steal) apples if we were hungry.
34. They (to understand - often - past) their teacher.
35. I (to hear - past simple) a cat in the garden.
36. You (to be - pres. perf.) to school every day.
37. They (to take - present) the train to Rome every week.
38. Father (to drink - past prog.) milk.
39. Mac (to fly - pres.) to Paris once a month.
40. I (to read - pres. prog.) in the kitchen.
41. Father (to drive - past prog.) too slowly.
42. Peggy (to sell - past) books at that moment.
43. I (to leave - often - past perf.) school early.
44. Mother (to drive - pres.) a car now.
45. We (to eat - past prog.) cake.
46. They (to call - pres.) those people home every day.
47. My brother (to catch - past simple) a cold.
48. You (to get - past simple) some apples from the shop.
49. I (to have - always - past perf.) to buy bread on Saturday.

50. My brother (to go - pres.) to school every day.
51. They (to sing - fut. prog.) when we (to meet - pres.) them tomorrow.
52. If the man (to find) the money yesterday, he (to give - cond. 2) it to us.
53. The girls (to speak - pres. perf. prog.) on the phone for an hour now.
54. If father (to catch - past) some fish, we (can eat - cond. 1) fish tonight.
55. He (to see - not - pres. perf.) her yet.
56. You said that we (to ride - cond. 1 prog.) to Bonn tomorrow.
57. I (to run - past prog.) to the man because I (must talk - past) to him.
58. (to draw - you - pres.) a picture now?
59. They (to know - future) what I said when they (to hear - pres.) my father and mother.
60. When I saw them, the little children (to say - past prog.) that they (can build - past) a big sand castle.
61. When I (to sleep - pres. perf.) for two hours, I (to get up - fut.)
62. You (to swim - past perf. prog.) in the water for three hours.
63. She said that she (to buy - cond. 1) that house.
64. (to take - David - pres.) a test now?
65. I (to collect - pres. simple) records, but he (to collect- pres. simple) stamps.
66. He always (to go - pres.) to work at 8 a.m.
67. They (to see - just - pres.perf. simple) the picture.
68. He (to sit - past prog.) in the bedroom when I (to see - past simple) him.
69. We usually (to watch - pres.) TV, but now we (to listen - pres) to the radio.
70. If you (to help - past perf. simple) me, you (to get) some money.
71. If they (to come) here, they (to hear - fut. simple) a story.
72. If you (to know - past simple) the words, you (to understand) what I (to say - pres. perf. simple).
73. They (to talk - pres. perf.prog.) for an hour now.
74. I (to hope - past perf. simple) that you (to write - cond. 1 prog.) the letter when I (to come - past simple).
75. We (to drink - fut. prog.) tea when you (to find - pres. simple) us.
76. The house (to burn - cond. 2 prog.) at that time if the police (to catch - not - past perf. simple) that man.
77. She (to do - past prog.) her homework and (to say - past simple) that she (to play - cond. 1) tennis with me.
78. After we (to talk - past perf.) for an hour, she said that I (must go - past simple) so that she (can finish - past).
79. When I (to hear - past) that, I (to say - past), "I (to be - fut.) back at 3 o'clock."
80. (to see - you - pres. perf.) the newspaper today?
81. If he (to speak - past perf.) to me, I (to know) it.
82. If you (to take - pres.) me to the city, I (to make) a cake for you.
83. I (to leave - fut. prog.) home tomorrow.

84. If she (to buy) sweets, she (to eat - cond. 1) them right away.
85. She (to buy - not - past simple) any new clothes.
86. My teacher (to like - not - pres) bad pupils.
87. I (to clean - fut. perf.) the windows by the time you (to come - pres) back.
88. He (to think - past) that he (to see - past perf.) me yesterday.
89. He (to swim - pres. perf. prog.) for two hours now.
90. But we (to eat - not - past perf.) the cake yesterday.
91. They (to give - past perf.) Mary the book.
92. The clock (to strike - pres.) ten times a day.
93. She (to grow - pres. perf.) quickly this year.
94. I (to fly - pres. perf. prog.) the kite for only ten minutes now.
95. He (to put - past prog.) a fish in her clothes when I (to see - past) him.
96. I (to lie - pres.) in the chair now.
97. Who (to draw - past) this picture yesterday?
98. He (to open - past) the letter after they (to take - past perf.) it to him.
99. If she (to forget) to ring him up, he (to sleep - fut.) too long.
100. They (to repair - present) my car at the moment.
101. When I (to see - past) her, she (to learn - past perf. prog.) the words for three hours.
102. Mr. Smith (to have) a small car now, but next year he (to buy) a bigger one.
103. If she (to learn - past perf.) her vocabulary words, she (to have) a good test.
104. Betty (to do - pres. perf.) her homework. Now she (to play) with her dog.
105. She (to wash - past) her face when the telephone (to ring - past).
106. If she (to run - past) quickly, she (to catch) the bus.
107. When you (to come - pres.) to the beach, we (to build - fut.) a sand castle.
108. By the time you (to come - pres.) back, I (to draw - fut. perf.) a picture.
109. The teacher (to come - past) into the classroom.
110. The pupils (to do - past prog.) their homework.
111. After she (to help - past perf.) her mother in the kitchen, she (to go - past) out to play tennis.
112. If he (to read) the book, he (to know - cond. 2) the story.
113. When we (to arrive - past) at the birthday party, Barbara (to tell - past) a story.
114. We (to run - pres.) to school on Mondays.
115. (to run - your cat - pres.) away every night?
116. (to drink - he - past prog.) milk or tea?
117. He (to catch - not - past) the ball.
118. My father (to buy - pres.) a cake every day.
119. (to know - you - past) her mother?
120. Tom (to understand - not - pres.) that word.
121. My sister (to take - pres.) the train to Bonn every day.

122. We (to leave - fut. perf.) school by the time you come.
123. (to see - you - past) the newspaper yesterday?
124. Linda (to clean - not - pres. prog.) the board.
125. (to clean - he - past prog.) his bike?
126. Father and mother (to walk - pres.) to work on Mondays.
127. (to take - you - pres. prog.) the plane or train?
128. My brother (to teach - pres. perf.) us two songs.
129. (to bite - your dog - sometimes - pres.) children?
130. Father (to teach - not - pres. perf.) English.
131. (to be) it cold when you (to be - past) in Germany?
132. She always (to eat - pres.) quickly.
133. She said that she (to write - not - past perf.) the letter.
134. My father (to like - not - pres.) pudding.
135. (to make - your mother - pres.) dinner now?
136. He (to see - past) the car at once.
137. They (to ask - already - pres. perf.) many questions.
138. (to sing - the girls - past prog.) in the classroom?
139. His father (to give - pres. perf.) them many books.
140. (to drink - he - pres.) tea every morning?
141. I (to drink - sometimes - present) tea.
142. We (to eat - past) dinner at the moment.
143. We (to eat - cond. 2 simple) the cake if we (to find) it.
144. My mother (to carry - always - pres.) the milk home.
145. My father (to feed - often - pres.) the animals.
146. You (to cut - cond. 1 simple) your finger if you (to hold) the broken glass.
147. (to know - your sister) the burglar if she (to meet - past simple) him?
148. We (to hide - simple) the money tomorrow.
149. (can drive - he - present) the car?
150. If I (to catch) your shoe, I (to throw - cond. 2 simple) it into the water.
151. They (to think - usually - past) that we were coming soon.
152. We (to hold - progressive) hands in the future.
153. I (to eat) the apple if I (to keep - past perf. simple) it.
154. The man (to drive - not - usually - pres.) a VW.
155. (to eat - you) the apple if you (to buy - past simple) it?
156. The lady (to speak - not - often - pres.) German.
157. Tom (to bring - sometimes - past) his friends to breakfast.
158. My mother (to feed - pres.) the cat every day.
159. (to sell - he - cond. 1 simple) the picture if he (to draw) it?

160. You (to shut - past) your book at that moment.
161. (to wear - you - fut. prog.) your new blouse on Friday?
162. By when (to read - they - fut. perf. simple) the new book?
163. Last year we (to spend) our holidays in England, but next year we (to go) to France.
164. Father (to drive) a VW at this moment.
165. Father and Mother (to buy) a table yesterday.
166. Susan (to draw - often) pictures in the future.
167. My brother (to hear - simple) the song yesterday.
168. You (to sell) hats at the time I saw you yesterday.
169. (to speak - she) to them yet?
170. He (to go) to school every day at nine o'clock.
171. (You - to play) football when you were a little boy?
172. Which (to be) bigger: a dog or a tiger?
173. It (to start - already) to rain.
174. When I walked past the car, some men (to wash) it.
175. They (to catch) him last night.
176. She (to read) right now.
177. When (to arrive - you) home yesterday?
178. The baby (to cry) for an hour now.
179. We (to know) the Smiths for more than ten years now.
180. He (to leave) two hours ago.
181. They (must talk) to the teacher last week.
182. They (to talk - still - prog.) when I left.
183. She (to work - always) very hard up till now.
184. They (to go) home soon, won't they?
185. You (to want) to sing, do you?
186. He (to live) there, doesn't he?
187. She (to help) us often, hasn't she?
188. The food (to cook), isn't it?
189. He (to see) us last night, didn't he?
190. The police (to catch) the burglar last night.
191. It's still raining! It (to rain) for two days now.
192. (to work - your father) at this moment?
193. Please stop singing because I (to try) to work.
194. Listen! The teacher (to talk).
195. Her child ran away and she (to see - not) him for two years.
196. Last year she (to teach) all the children to read.
197. I saw that the man (to work - still - prog.) at seven o'clock last night.

198. Every day last week my aunt (to break) a plate.
199. Every day this week my aunt (to break) a plate.
200. When I saw you in the supermarket last week, you (to wear - not) your hat.
201. My mother told me not to come into the kitchen as she (to wash) the floor at the time.
202. He (to visit - not) the seaside once last year.
203. He (to play) golf for ten years now.
204. He (to phone) me last Monday.
205. They (to read) my book right now.
206. I (to meet) her when I was in New York last year.
207. Yesterday afternoon we (to go) to the supermarket and (to buy) a lot of things.
208. Betty can't play with you now. She (to help) her brother with his homework.
209. In September the Parkers always (to go) to the seaside.
210. Peter (to begin) his work at five o'clock. He (to work) for two hours now.
211. He always (to sing) a song when he is alone.
212. By the time you come back, we (to feed) the animals.
213. Last year we (to spend) our holidays in London.
214. He usually (to drink) milk. When he was at her birthday party yesterday, he (to drink) tea.
215. I (to write) letters since six o'clock and now I will stop.
216. The boys (to play) football for two hours now.
217. If they liked the book, they (to buy) it.
218. Tom (to eat - never) a tomato up till now.
219. You (to drive) to Bonn if you'd had a car.
220. I (to take) my dog for a walk now.
221. Mother (to fly) to London at this time tomorrow.
222. They (to shut) the shop by the time we come tomorrow.
223. (to write - you - not) the letter yet?
224. You (to read) the book if you had it.
225. The girls (to draw) pictures when we came in.
226. The girl (to find - already - past perf.) the lost book when I arrived.
227. Dan and I (to meet) Susan tomorrow.
228. The men (to steal) a TV when I saw them.
229. They (can sweep) the hall yesterday.
230. Linda and I (to swim) in the lake tomorrow.
231. I (to sweep) the floor for 20 minutes now.
232. If I saw a tiger, I (to hide).
233. He (to wash) his face now.
234. The girls (to read) books for five hours now.
235. I (to wear) the pullover if you had given it to me.

236. Linda (to tear - never) a book up to now.
237. (to find - you - not) the book yet?
238. I (to lose) my book. (to see - you) it?
239. I (to see - not) Tom for three months.
240. (to watch - you) TV last night?
241. I (to hear - not) from Linda since she (to have) a baby.
242. I always (to get) up early when I (to be) at school last year.
243. Linda (to move - just) to a new house.
244. Where (to be - you) until now?
245. (to see - he) you yesterday?
246. Yes, he (to see) me yesterday.
247. (to read - you) the book tomorrow?
248. No, I (to read - not) the book tomorrow.
249. I (to give) my child the book yesterday.
250. She (to come) home an hour ago.
251. He (to be - not) at school yesterday.
252. I (to know) her for the last ten years.
253. You (to tell) him the answer last night.
254. He (to forget - never) to bring her a present.
255. He (to swim) from England to France at this moment.
256. You (to drink) milk now if you had some.
257. I (to teach - simple) English since 1999.
258. My father (to buy) shoes when we saw him.
259. (to sell - they - ever) their bikes?
260. The girl (to learn - not - simple) her words yesterday.
261. I (to sit) here for two hours now.
262. The woman (to begin - simple) to write a letter by this time tomorrow.
263. We (to sing - simple) six songs this week.
264. The dogs (to bite) me now.
265. My sister (to fly - pres.) to Paris on Mondays.
266. (to leave - you) right now?
267. He (to write - never) a letter in his life.
268. The woman (to hear - not - simple) the music yesterday.
269. You (must drive) to Bonn last month.
270. They (to be) very happy when they heard that.
271. (to stick - you - ever) a picture on the wall?
272. (to play - she) the piano last night?
273. We (to do) our homework for two hours now.

274. The man (to pay - already) for the book when I saw him.
275. The man (to see - not - simple) his sister yesterday.
276. I (to hide - simple) the book tomorrow.
277. You (to hold) apples when we saw you.
278. How many hands (to shake - that man - simple) this week so far?
279. My sister (to teach - prog.) English for two years up to now.
280. You (to put) your clothes in a cupboard if you had one.
281. You (can feed) the cats yesterday.
282. They (to build - prog.) the castle in the future.
283. I (must catch) the ball last year.
284. He (to make - never) his mother angry.
285. I (to stand) here for ten minutes now.
286. We (to run) to school at this moment.
287. Father (can throw) the ball far yesterday.
288. I (to see - simple) my sister tomorrow.
289. He (to go - not - simple) home yesterday.
290. My sister (to hold - progressive) Tom's hand in the future.

Sieh die Tabelle genau an. Jede der folgenden Aufgaben hat nur eine richtige Antwort. Passe auf die Zeitformen in den Antworten auf!

1993	1994	1995	1996	1997	1998	1999	2000(now)
					married		
London		Brighton		York house			
VW	Opel		Ford				
bicycle							

291. a. Mr. Smith was in York for three years.
b. Mr. Smith had been in London for two years.
c. Mr. Smith had been in London since 1993.
d. Mr. Smith has been in Brighton for two years.

292. a. How long has Mr. Smith been in London?
b. How long is Mr. Smith in York?
c. How long had Mr. Smith been in Brighton?
d. Since when is Mr. Smith in England?

293. a. How long has Mr. Smith been in York?
b. How long has Mr. Smith been in London?
c. When has Mr. Smith been in York?
d. How long has Mr. Smith been in Brighton?

294. a. Mr. Smith hasn't lived in London for 1995.
    b. Has Mr. Smith been in York since three years?
    c. Has Mr. Smith been in Brighton for two years?
    d. Mr. Smith hasn't lived in Germany for seven years.
295. a. Mr. Smith has a bicycle since he is in England.
    b. Mr. Smith had a VW for one year.
    c. Mr. Smith has had an Opel from 1994 to 1996.
    d. Mr. Smith has had a VW for one year.
296. a. How long has Mr. Smith a VW?
    b. How long has Mr. Smith had a Ford?
    c. Since when has Mr. Smith a bicycle?
    d. How long has Mr. Smith had an Opel?
297. a. When has Mr. Smith a bicycle?
    b. When did Mr. Smith have a Ford?
    c. When has Mr. Smith had an Opel?
    d. When did Mr. Smith have a VW?
298. a. Mr. Smith has had a bicycle since six years.
    b. Has Mr. Smith had a Ford since four years?
    c. Mr. Smith had had an Opel for two years.
    d. Has Mr. Smith a Ford since 1996?
299. a. Mr. Smith has a house since 1997.
    b. Mr. Smith has had a house for three years.
    c. Mr. Smith has a house since three years.
    d. Mr. Smith has a house since he moved to York.
300. a. Mr. Smith has been married since 1998.
    b. Mr. Smith is married since 1998.
    c. Mr. Smith has married for two years.
    d. Mr. Smith has married since 1998.

Setze den folgenden Aussagesatz in die gewünschte Zeitform:
He eats many apples.

301. present progressive
302. past perfect simple
303. conditional 1 progressive
304. past simple
305. future perfect progressive
306. future simple
307. conditional 2 simple

308. present perfect progressive
309. present simple
310. past perfect progressive
311. conditional 1 simple
312. past progressive
313. present perfect simple
314. conditional 2 progressive
315. future progressive
316. future perfect simple

Setze den Satz als Fragesatz in die gewünschte Zeitform und frage nach "many apples":
He eats **many apples**.

317. future progressive
318. conditional 1 simple
319. past progressive
320. present perfect simple
321. present progressive
322. past perfect simple
323. conditional 2 progressive
324. future simple
325. future perfect progressive
326. present simple
327. conditional 1 progressive
328. past perfect progressive
329. conditional 2 simple
330. future perfect simple
331. present perfect progressive
332. past simple

Verneine den Satz in der gewünschten Zeitform:

He eats many apples.

333. present perfect simple
334. future progressive
335. conditional 1 simple
336. present simple
337. past perfect progressive
338. future perfect simple
339. conditional 2 progressive
340. past simple
341. present perfect progressive
342. future simple
343. conditional 1 progressive
344. past progressive
345. future perfect progressive
346. present progressive
347. past perfect simple
348. conditional 2 simple

Ändere den Aussagesatz in die gewünschte Zeitform um:

They drive quickly.

349. future simple
350. conditional 1 progressive
351. past simple
352. present perfect progressive
353. future perfect simple
354. conditional 2 progressive
355. present progressive
356. past perfect progressive
357. conditional 1 simple
358. present simple
359. future perfect progressive
360. present perfect simple
361. conditional 2 simple
362. past progressive
363. future progressive

364. past perfect simple

Ändere den Satz als Fragesatz in die gewünschte Zeitform um und frage nach “quickly”:
They drive **quickly**.

365. present perfect simple
366. future perfect progressive
367. past simple
368. conditional 1 progressive
369. past perfect simple
370. future progressive
371. conditional 2 simple
372. past perfect progressive
373. future simple
374. conditional 2 progressive
375. present simple
376. present perfect progressive
377. conditional 1 simple
378. past progressive
379. future perfect simple
380. present progressive

Verneine den Satz in der gewünschten Zeitform:
They drive quickly.

381. future perfect simple
382. present perfect progressive
383. conditional 1 simple
384. present progressive
385. past perfect simple
386. conditional 2 progressive
387. future simple
388. past progressive
389. future perfect progressive
390. present simple
391. conditional 1 progressive
392. present perfect simple
393. future progressive
394. conditional 2 simple

395. past perfect progressive
396. past simple

Ändere den Satz wie gewünscht um:

397. They drive **quickly**. (Frage - Verneinung - future perfect progressive - wie)
398. The man **shakes hands**. (Frage - Verneinung - present perfect progressive - was tun)
399. The girls would have gone **to school**. (Frage - Verneinung - conditional 2 simple - wo)
400. **The children** took a test. (Frage - Verneinung - present perfect simple - wer)

21 Relative Clauses = Relativsätze

21.1 Grammatik

1. **Es gibt fünf Relativpronomen** (relative pronouns)

who, whom, whose, which, that

   a) **who** (als Subjekt: der, die, das, welcher, welche) und **whom** (als Objekt: den, die, das, welchen, dem, der, welchen) werden bei Personen gebraucht.

   - The man **who** is here is my friend.

     Der Mann, der (welcher) hier ist, ist mein Freund.

   - The lady **whom (who)** I see is my sister.

     Die Dame, die (welche) ich sehe, ist meine Schwester.

   b) **whose** (Genitiv: dessen, deren) wird bei Personen, Tieren und Sachen gebraucht. Es geht um Besitz.

   - The child **whose** coat I have is my brother.

     Das Kind, dessen Mantel ich habe, ist mein Bruder.

   - The animal **whose** eye I see is a bird.

     Das Tier, dessen Auge ich sehe, ist ein Vogel.

   c) **which** (als Subjekt und Objekt: der, die, das, den, die das, dem, der, welche, etc.) wird nur bei Tieren und Sachen gebraucht.

   - The animal **which I** see is a bird.

     Das Tier, das ich sehe, ist ein Vogel.

   d) **that** kann für Personen, Sachen und Tiere gebraucht werden (als Subjekt und auch als Objekt). Aber bitte selten gebrauchen, weil es eher umgangssprachlich ist.

2. **Wie man Sätze kombiniert**:

   a) Suche das Wort oder die Wörter (Substantiv) heraus, die in beiden Sätzen gleich sind. Das Wort in dem zweiten Satz kann auch ein Personalpronomen sein.

   The man is talking to Linda. I gave a book to **him**.

   b) Schreibe den ersten Satz auf, wie er steht, bis direkt nach dem Wort, das gleich ist.

   The man

c) Lass den ersten Satz wegfallen und schreib den zweiten Satz, richtig umgewandelt hin. Das Wort, das gleich ist, muss durch "who/whom/whose/which" oder "that" ersetzt werden. Dann kommt diese Ersatzform (statt des eigentlichen Wortes) direkt **hinter** das Wort von dem ersten Satz, das schon auf dem Papier steht.

The man **whom (who)**

d) Schreib den 2. Satz zu Ende.

The man whom (who) **I gave the book to**

e) Jetzt schreib den 1. Satz zu Ende.

The man whom (who) I gave the book to **is talking to Linda**.

3. **Wie man zwei Sätze herstellt**:

The man whom (who) I gave the book to is talking to Linda.

a) Überprüfe, ob zwei Subjekte und zwei Verben vorhanden sind. Wenn ja, könnte es sich um einen Relativsatz handeln.

man is talking; I gave

b) Prüfe, ob ein Relativpronomen vorhanden ist. Manchmal ist es aber ausgelassen worden.

whom

c) Such den ersten Satz heraus, so dass er einen vollständigen Sinn hat.

The man is talking to Linda.

d) Was übrig bleibt, ist der zweite Satz.

whom (who) I gave the book to

e) Ersetze das "Relativpronomen" (oder das fehlende Relativpronomen) durch das Substantiv im ersten Satz, das direkt vor dem Relativsatz steht.

the man I gave the book to

f) Schreib die beiden getrennten Sätze richtig nieder.

The man is talking to Linda. I gave the book to the man.

21.2 Übungen

Setze das richtige Relativpronomen ein. (not "that")

1. The cat ______ eyes were green was called Tommy.
2. We can see the tree ______ is green.
3. We saw the man ______ was eating a piece of cake.
4. Do you know to ______ he wrote a letter?
5. That is the girl ______ book I read.
6. The woman ______ she had talked to ate an apple.
7. Those are the chairs ______ we carried.

8. The boy ______ he had given an apple to ran away.
9. There is the boy ______ car we drove.
10. The man ______ you had listened to took a pen.
11. This is the table ______ he ate at.
12. The girl ______ I had taken a photo of looked happy.
13. The dog ______ tail was black was lying on the chair.
14. Linda can hear the wind ______ is blowing.
15. You saw the girl ______ was drinking her milk.
16. Do you know ______ he gave a book to?
17. Bob has an uncle ______ lives near the sea.
18. I like to see my father ______ I love very much.
19. The girl ______ bike I have is my friend.
20. I read a book ______ was very interesting.
21. The house ______ I live in is large.
22. She doesn't want a dress ______ is worn by many women.
23. The car was bought by a man ______ has got much money.
24. People ______ can only talk about sports are not very interesting.
25. Did you see that Italian film ______ was on TV?
26. The men ______ the police caught are the burglars.
27. The pigs ate up the apples ______ fell down.
28. The man ______ our teacher told us about was my father.
29. The person ______ job it is to help us is my sister.
30. A thing ______ is hard to hear is quiet.
31. The woman ______ cut her finger was not nice.
32. The bag of apples ______ Dick was carrying fell.
33. The city ______ cathedral is large is Cologne.
34. The girl ______ is sitting next to me is very nice.
35. The dog ______ was barking was big.
36. The boy ______ took the money was 12 years old.
37. I saw the girl ______ bike was green.
38. The man ______ we talked to was very nice.
39. They watched the dog ______ food was hot.

Unterstreiche den Relativsatz.

40. The places we visited were full of tourists.
41. The milk we drank with our food was cold.
42. The hotel we stayed at was near a busy road.
43. The room we slept in was too quiet.
44. He gave the money to a man who has ten children.

45. Tim and Tom who filled a bag with their best apples drove a big car.
46. The table which Sam carried was too big for him.
47. The man they looked at sang a song.
48. They laughed at Tim who was walking by himself.
49. The bag the two brothers were taking to town was full of apples.
50. The town we live in is Cologne.
51. The animal we saw on the street was a dog.
52. The plates we ate from were dirty.
53. A man who was walking through a street in London stopped in front of a window which had dresses in it.
54. He went in and asked the man he saw how much the dresses cost.
55. The man whose shop it was answered his questions.
56. The man he had been talking to was very nice.
57. We walked to the shop mother worked in.
58. There we saw two women who wanted to buy the dress mother had put in the window.
59. The woman whose friend talked to her asked where she could pay for it.
60. My mother told them the name of the man whom they could give the money to and asked the woman whose blouse was on a chair to take the blouse with her.
61. The man they had heard of took the money they had given him.
62. The garden we worked in had twenty trees.
63. The doctor we had gone to went on holiday.
64. The boy whose bike was broken cried loudly.
65. The woman was talking about the radio programme we had heard.
66. The girl who was washing her face looked at us.

Verbinde die Sätze mit einem Relativpronomen. (not "that")

67. Peter said "thank you." He had helped Peter.
68. The pictures were interesting. We were looking at the pictures.
69. Mrs. Green asked Tom to lunch. We lived in her house.
70. The man is here. He ate a cake.
71. We took the apple. It was lying on the table.
72. Linda waved good-bye. They had taken Linda home.
73. You could see Mr. Twain. Ken has read his books.
74. We could talk to the woman. She was writing a letter.
75. The dog could not hear. Its ear was dirty.
76. We saw the boys. You had played with the boys.
77. Dick said "hello." We had brought Dick home.
78. You can speak to Linda. She is reading the newspaper.
79. They saw Mary Ann and me. Father played with us.

80. The songs were funny. We were listening to the songs.
81. The woman is there. She has eaten an apple.
82. Linda has stolen the money. It was lying under the chair.
83. We saw the Beatles. Tom has heard their records.
84. The cat cannot see. Its eye is bad.
85. Peter and Sue said "thank you." Jenny helped Peter and Sue.
86. Mr. Black will ask Laurie to lunch. We live in his house.
87. John is running to his brother. His brother gave him the bike.
88. Mr. Green sells many things. Mr. Green’s shop is in Cologne.
89. They drive along the street. The street is very busy.
90. Uncle John eats fish every day. Bob helps Uncle John with the work.
91. That is the man. The man took my car. My car is 5 years old.
92. The man is eating a sandwich. I see the man.
93. The girl always drinks water. The girl is my sister.
94. The dog is black. It is running down the street.
95. The chair is blue. I am sitting on the chair.
96. I am reading the letter. The letter is from my father.
97. The little boy is crying. My mother is holding the boy.
98. The man gave me a book. I drove the man’s car.
99. The woman was talking then. The woman’s husband stood up.
100. The child cried. The child’s arm was broken.
101. The child was young. The child’s shoe was open.
102. The man talked to me. His coat was black.
103. The girl was happy. It was her birthday.
104. The boy ran home. He had his own coat.
105. The man is my father. I gave the book to him.
106. His sister is 32. He bought a present for her.
107. The supermarket was open. The ice-cream was in it.
108. The shop was closed. He was walking to the shop.
109. The woman had a book. He was talking with her.
110. The tables were red. The chairs were between the tables.
111. The table was at the doctor’s. The man was lying on the table.
112. A man questioned her. He was a neighbour.
113. The woman rang him up. She was his mother.
114. The man drives a Mercedes. He is very good.
115. A house burnt down last night. It was very old.
116. The sock fell to the floor. It wasn’t clean.
117. The man stole money. They’ve caught him.

118. The man gave her a ring. She loved him.
119. The money was on the table. He took it.
120. The man did this. I know him.
121. I ate the food. It made me ill.
122. We had been waiting for the bus. The bus was full.
123. The knife is long. We cut our bread with the knife.
124. I was talking to the girl. The girl was my cousin.
125. The man is nice. The man is my father.
126. John is talking to his sister. His sister asked him to come home.

Mache zwei vollständige Sätze daraus.

127. The chair I sat on was expensive.
128. He likes the girl whose mother is now talking.
129. The man we took the books to is our uncle.
130. Can you see the man who is helping Jane?
131. We helped the woman whose car had stopped.
132. They talked to the child he had taken a banana from.
133. The girl who was looking at the dress when I saw her ran away.
134. Penny whose book I was reading walked to her mother.
135. The boy they had seen playing football threw the ball.
136. The animal which had eaten the cake was a cat.
137. The baby they heard crying had no mother.
138. The person I had seen was Tom.
139. The man I had helped was father.
140. The animal which had left its cage was a hamster.
141. Rosemary whose letter I have found ran to her father.
142. We spoke with the man you had taken a book from.
143. The shoes she had on were new.
144. Rita went to the man whose car was dirty.
145. The man who was looking at the car when we saw him walked away.
146. The girl you had watched gave me a ball.
147. The girl whose mother had left the house was sad.
148. If I had the camera which you gave me, I would take a photo.
149. The man to whom he gave the book was his father.
150. The woman I saw carried two books.
151. The bird whose tail was in the cat's mouth cried for help.
152. If they knew the man who had phoned, they would tell their mother.
153. The men with whom they were working ate their lunch.
154. The people you showed the picture to asked me questions.

155. If he had understood the woman who had called, he would have told his mother.
156. The shop I bought the chair from was closed yesterday.
157. The girl that was looking at you fell from her bike.
158. The man I saw walking down the street turned around.
159. The book she was reading when you came told about cats.
160. The radio we were listening to today is now broken.
161. If I wore the dress which she sold me, I would make her happy.
162. He likes the girl whose mother is now talking.
163. Is the man we took the books to our uncle?
164. Can you see the woman who is helping Jane?
165. The man we had spoken with wrote down our names.
166. Did the cat whose ball rolled away catch a mouse?
167. Were the babies who were crying hungry?
168. We heard the girls whose mothers had gone shopping.
169. The shop which we had bought cost much money.
170. The horses we rode walked slowly.
171. Why did the dog he was holding bark?
172. Didn't you see the man who gave me the camera?
173. Did the ball she was playing with roll away?
174. Have you seen the letters they've written?
175. When'll the cake they're making be cool?
176. Isn't that the biggest fish we've caught?
177. Did the cat he fed forget him?
178. Won't you be staying at the house they live in?
179. What was the day you dreamt about like?
180. Where's the book she's been reading?
181. The dogs they gave us grew quickly.
182. Didn't he hear the noise the dog made?
183. Will the picture they're drawing be pretty?

22 Passive

22.1 Grammatik

1. Das Passiv wird aus einer Form von "**to be**" und der **3. Form des Verbes** gebildet.
   The ball **is thrown**.

   Das Verb "to be":

present	am/are/is
past	was/were
future	will be
present perfect	have been/has been
past perfect	had been
future perfect	will have been
conditional 1	would be
conditional 2	would have been

2. **Tabelle der Zeitformen im Passiv**

	simple	
present	am/are/is	+ 3. Form
past	was/were	+ 3. Form
future	will be	+ 3. Form
present perfect	have been/has been	+ 3. Form
past perfect	had been	+ 3. Form
future perfect	will have been	+ 3. Form
conditional 1	would be	+ 3. Form
conditional 2	would have been	+ 3. Form
	progressive	
present	am/are/is + being	+ 3. Form
past	was/were + being	+ 3. Form

3. Ausführliches Beispiel in allen möglichen Zeitformen

Active		
simple		
	Deutsch	***Englisch***
present	Er sieht die Hunde.	He sees the dogs.
past	Er sah die Hunde.	He saw the dogs.
future	Er wird die Hunde sehen.	He will see the dogs.
present perfect	Er hat die Hunde gesehen.	He has seen the dogs.
past perfect	Er hatte die Hunde gesehen.	He had seen the dogs.
future perfect	Er wird die Hunde gesehen haben.	He will have seen the dogs.
conditional 1	Er würde die Hunde sehen.	He would see the dogs.
conditional 2	Er würde die Hunde gesehen haben.	He would have seen the dogs.
progressive		
present		He is seeing the dogs.
past		He was seeing the dogs.
alle anderen Zeiten		—

Passive		
simple		
	Deutsch	***Englisch***
present	Die Hunde werden von ihm gesehen.	The dogs are seen by him.
past	Die Hunde wurden von ihm gesehen.	The dogs were seen by him.
future	Die Hunde werden von ihm gesehen werden.	The dogs will be seen by him.
present perfect	Die Hunde sind von ihm gesehen worden.	The dogs have been seen by him.
past perfect	Die Hunde waren von ihm gesehen worden.	The dogs had been seen by him.
future perfect	Die Hunde werden von ihm gesehen worden sein.	The dogs will have been seen by him.
cond. 1	Die Hunde würden von ihm gesehen werden.	The dogs would be seen by him.
cond. 2	Die Hunde würden von ihm gesehen worden sein.	The dogs would have been seen by him.
progressive		
present		The dogs are being seen by him.
past		The dogs were being seen by him.
alle anderen Zeiten		———

4. **Die Bildung des Passivsatzes**:

   a) Das Subjekt des Aktivsatzes wird zum Objekt des Passivsatzes hinter einem "by".

   The man sees a table. A table is seen **by the man**.

   Manchmal wird das Subjekt des Aktivsatzes im Passivsatz ausgelassen.

   They offered a prize. A prize was offered.

   b) Das Objekt des Aktivsatzes wird zum Subjekt des Passivsatzes.

   The dog bit **the cat**. **The cat** was bitten by the dog.

   Wenn der Aktivsatz kein Objekt hat, kann kein Passivsatz gebildet werden.

   The man ran **around the corner**.

   Wenn zwei Objekte vorhanden sind, kann man auswählen, was als Subjekt gebraucht werden soll.

   The girl gave ***the boy*** **a ball**.

   The boy was given a ball by the girl.

   A ball was given to the boy by the girl.

c) Das Verb wird in derselben Zeitform gelassen, bloß umgewandelt.

Subjekt			Objekt
The girl	sees		**a cat**.
A cat	is seen	**by**	***the girl***.
The girl	gave		**me flowers**.
I	was given		**flowers** by ***the girl***.
Flowers	were given		**to me** by ***the girl***.

d) Die "progressive form" kommt nur in "present" und "past" vor. Im Passiv kann die "progressive form" in den anderen Zeiten nicht ausgedrückt werden.

He is reading a book. A book is being read by him.

He will be taking the train. —-

e) Wenn im Aktivsatz ein Hilfsverb wie "should, must, can, could" vorhanden ist, wird die Form im Passiv so gebildet:

I must throw the ball.

	Hilfsverb	+ be	+ 3. Form	
The ball	must	be	thrown	by me.

She could have thrown the ball.

	Hilfsverb	+ have been	+ 3. Form	
The ball	could	have been	thrown	by her.

22.2 Übungen

Setze den Satz von Aktiv in Passiv um. Vorsicht: einige Sätze können nicht umgestellt werden!

1. I write letters.
2. He wrote a book.
3. She will draw a picture.
4. He has found the light.
5. You will meet a friend.
6. She had sold her house.
7. He tore his letters up.
8. The man has stolen a radio.
9. The lady usually drives the car.
10. The cook beats Bob.
11. The policeman caught the thief.
12. The thief is running round the corner.
13. Professors visit the shop.
14. Linda has written a letter.
15. Some friends had met me at the station.
16. Jim always blows up the ball.
17. The man waited for the boys.
18. The girls had never heard of such a song.
19. The boys and girls have just eaten up all the cake.
20. The children laughed at the monkey.
21. An old man looked after the boy.
22. People talked about the project for a long time.
23. The keeper feeds the lions at noon.
24. Yesterday he fed them at noon.
25. Pumps carry the water to a higher place.
26. We expected him to come at three o'clock.
27. Jim cleans the house carefully.
28. Betty paints the walls beautifully.
29. Mac has cared for the baby every day.
30. John had washed the curtains well.
31. The doctor will give a lecture next week.
32. The doctor took the injured man to the hospital.
33. His friends call him Ted.
34. The mice have eaten all the bread.
35. The man will clean our windows tomorrow.
36. The secretary will type those letters.

37. They are now printing a new edition of the book.
38. Many people are visiting him in hospital.
39. Thieves were stealing fruit from the apple trees.
40. My father saw the lady at the counter.
41. The boy brings his books to school.
42. The girl has done her sums.
43. You will find the next book more interesting.
44. The clever man spoke seven languages.
45. Bob had thrown the ball quickly.
46. I shall now write eight words.
47. The old women point many fingers at Tom.
48. He helped the lady at the counter.
49. The boy hung the clothes up.
50. He gives much money to the church.
51. The old man has seen the setting sun.
52. He had spoken bad words.
53. Robbers stopped the train.
54. His wife is packing the suitcases.
55. They have often seen police officers.
56. A little girl had found the money.
57. Many people feed birds.
58. My boyfriend will hold my hand.
59. The little girl was watching the men.
60. Two friends wrote letters.
61. The teachers have read that book.
62. My sister eats apples every day.
63. The boys have often thrown the ball.
64. Will the men open the letter?
65. The little girl helps her father and mother.
66. The farmers would drive their children home.
67. The doctor had shut the doors.
68. You stole the cars.
69. You often wear a dress.
70. The artist is painting a picture.
71. They were repairing our radio.
72. She will have cleaned the windows by this afternoon.
73. They are selling his table.
74. You had often found the books.

75. I can read the book.
76. When did the boy drink the milk?
77. My brother is throwing new balls.
78. We had driven a car yesterday.
79. Did they buy a table?
80. You'll have eaten the cake by tomorrow.
81. How will they find the street?
82. My sister must blow a ball up.
83. You would have broken the dishes.
84. He has been catching balls.
85. Where do you hide your money?
86. My sisters were singing a song.
87. Why will they keep those books?
88. My brothers were hiding a book.
89. They have been drinking water.
90. We'll have put the forks away by tomorrow.
91. The dog would have bitten me.
92. Linda must bring a cake.
93. Where do you buy such clothes?
94. Did they break a chair?
95. My father would buy the ball.
96. They had found a pen yesterday.
97. When did the lion eat the man?
98. My mother is wearing a new dress.
99. Where do you see such pictures?
100. The man would hear a nice song.
101. You have been holding the baby.
102. Did they drive a car?
103. My father and mother were buying a new car.
104. We'll have found an answer by tomorrow.
105. My sister is eating a big cake.
106. Why will he bite the cat?
107. My sister had worn a dress yesterday.
108. We would have brought chairs.
109. When did the lady put the book on the shelf?
110. They must catch the ball.
111. I'll take the plates to mother.
112. Does the boy feed his cats?

113. The men were drinking coffee.
114. The babies would certainly catch my cold.
115. Has mother bought the presents?
116. Were the children carrying the tables?
117. The doctor can ring up the two patients.
118. Will the lady read those books?
119. Gangsters are following John everywhere.
120. I can't see the clock from here.
121. I have just bought a dress in London.
122. He is teaching me to swim.
123. He will have finished his homework at 9 o'clock.
124. I ate my dinner very quickly.
125. While I was feeding the dog in the kitchen, the cat caught a mouse in the garden.
126. The teacher had corrected the books very carefully.
127. Father took us to the zoo last week.
128. Many people watch television every evening.
129. They will tell us the reason soon.
130. She allowed him three minutes to get ready.
131. No one has ever taught me how to ride a bicycle.
132. You must pay the money by the end of the month.
133. You should fetch the cakes before the shops close.
134. He must paint the house in the summer.
135. You should have written the letter yesterday.
136. You must take the medicine every three hours.
137. You should buy tickets before you get on the tram.
138. You can no longer buy tickets from the driver.
139. If I had pulled the dog's tail, it would have bitten me.
140. They found a broken walking stick near his body.
141. That man took the policeman to Mr. Brown's house.
142. They had also found some burnt papers there.
143. They couldn't catch the man for a long time.

Wenn zwei Objekte in den folgenden Sätzen vorhanden sind, musst du zwei Sätze bilden.

144. The teacher gives Janet a pen.
145. Aunt Jane offered me a cup of tea.
146. The shops sold thousands of dolls to the visitors.
147. The teacher has just taught them a song.
148. Father told the girls a nice story.
149. The owner showed them the rooms.

150. The English girls wrote many letters to the German girls.
151. Father showed me a nice picture.
152. Mother has just given me a book.
153. He has just given me the book.
154. The little girl will show him pictures.
155. I told the children a nice story.
156. The woman showed me my room.
157. We always give them presents.
158. Linda and I have sold Mary new shoes.
159. Dick and Hank wrote their mothers a letter.
160. Father would bring you the books.
161. John and Tom sang their brothers a song.
162. Tina and I have given father many books.
163. Tom and I have thrown John three balls.
164. Ken and Dave fed their dogs a bone.
165. The boys have thrown Tom a ball.
166. Linda and I always show our mother the books.
167. The boys will have sold their sisters some books.
168. Dick is giving Jane new records.
169. Did the women tell the girls the story?
170. The little boy showed his father many pictures.
171. Tom threw the ball to Mary.
172. Mother was showing the house to the new guest.
173. Sally will give it to you later.
174. They gave her a prize.
175. Did they offer you a job?
176. They have given all the money to the workers.
177. Did they show you all the rooms?
178. They have offered him a cup of tea.
179. They promised John a new car for his birthday.
180. Did they give you enough money?
181. Someone lent me that book for the weekend.

Setze den Satz von Passiv in Aktiv um.Wenn nötig, musst du ein Subjekt erfinden.

182. That book has been read by many people.
183. What will the child be given?
184. The toy was blown up by father and mother.
185. Are the dogs always held by the man?
186. Was the car stolen by thieves?

187. No prizes will be won by bad students.
188. This meat is often eaten by lions.
189. Silly things have often been said by such men.
190. She said that a German song would be sung by a young lady.
191. All the people had been made happy by the good king.
192. Bad mistakes have never been made by those men.
193. The gifts for our friends will be brought by Tom.
194. The missing bag was found by the boys.
195. The meal is being prepared now.
196. The suitcases were being carried by two men.
197. You will be forgiven soon.
198. Such things are no longer sold.
199. We will be given a lesson tomorrow.
200. A prize was given to her.
201. Were you offered a job?
202. All the money was given to the workers.
203. Were you shown all the rooms?
204. Students have never been taught how to do that.
205. The house was sold for six thousand pounds.
206. He'll be arrested soon.
207. Where is the sugar kept?
208. The house was hidden by the trees.
209. Was the toy broken by the child?
210. Are those songs often sung by that class?
211. Where will the bad man be taken?
212. My sister has been sold books by those men.
213. Many songs were laughed at by the silly men.
214. The house was looked after by my father.
215. Are the balls often caught by my sister?
216. Was the letter written by my sister?
217. That car has been driven by many people.
218. When will the lions be fed?
219. Is that song sung every Sunday?
220. Those two dresses are often worn by that girl.
221. The ball would've been hit by the man.
222. The girl's song was heard by two men.
223. The pigs have often been seen by boys.
224. The apples are always eaten right away.

225. The dogs were beaten by the bad boy.
226. With what are the floors swept by the woman?
227. When were the dresses sewn by the girl?
228. How many hands are being held by me?
229. A big hole has been dug quickly.
230. The newspaper will be brought upstairs by father.
231. Old bombs are still found (by workmen) every year.
232. How is money stolen by thieves?
233. The candles were being lit (by the man) when I left.
234. The balls have been broken by the car.
235. Why were the rooms shown you (by him)?
236. How often are the children shaken by their father?
237. Skyscrapers are being built by that city every year.
238. How many slices of bread have been eaten (by him) tonight?
239. Is the horse being ridden by the owner at the moment?
240. The boy's words were being carefully chosen by him.
241. Yes, we will be met (by them) at the station.
242. The girls would have been bitten by the dogs if they had come near.
243. How long has the money been hidden by the thieves?
244. Your finger would soon be cut if you kept on.
245. When will the prizes be given to you?
246. Where were the deer shot by the hunter?
247. The leaves will have been blown by the wind tomorrow.
248. The birds were fed by the little girl.
249. Their voices could be heard by the teacher if they spoke louder.
250. Eight balls had been caught by that player.

23 Reported Speech = Indirekte Rede

23.1 Grammatik

Die Zeitformen der direkten Rede werden wie folgt umgewandelt, um die indirekte Rede zu bilden:

direkt		indirect
present	⇒	past
past	⇒	past perfect
present perfect	⇒	past perfect
past perfect	⇒	past perfect
future	⇒	conditional 1
future perfect	⇒	conditional 2

direkt		indirect
“I go”	⇒	she went
“I went”	⇒	she had gone
“I have gone”	⇒	she had gone
“I had gone”	⇒	she had gone
“I will go”	⇒	she would go
“I will have gone”	⇒	she would have gone

1. **Statements**.

   Aussagesätze werden, wie oben angegeben, umgewandelt. Man kann ein "**that**" (dass) einsetzen oder auch weglassen.

   - He said, "I go home."

     He said (that) he went home.
   - She stated. "We will go to London."

     She stated that they would go to London.

2. **Questions**.

   Statt "that" gebraucht man "**if**" oder "**whether**", wenn die Frage in der direkten Rede mit "yes" oder "no" beantwortet werden kann.

   - She asked, "Do you go home every day?"

     She asked if (whether) you went home every day.
   - She asked, "Will you be going home?"

     She asked whether (if) you would be going home.

   Wenn "interrogative words" (Fragewörter) (z.B. ***how, how many, what, when, where, why*** usw) vorhanden sind, gebraucht man diese auch in der indirekten Rede. In solchen Sätzen darf man weder "if" noch "whether" gebrauchen.

- She asked, "How old are you?"
  She asked how old you were.

3. **Commands**
   Wenn man "***said***" gebraucht, kommt "**that ... should**" danach.

   - She said, "Open your books."
     She ***said*** **that** we **should** open our books.

   Wenn man "***to ask, to order, to tell***" oder ein anderes Befehlswort gebraucht, kommt ein "**to + infinitive**".

   - She **told** them, "Open your books."
     She ***told*** them **to open** their books.

4. "Personal pronouns" müssen sinngemäß **umgewandelt** werden.

   - She said, "**I** like cake."
     She said that **she** liked cake.
   - Mary said, "**We**'ll go there."
     Mary said that **they** would go there.

5. **Wortumwandlungen**. Die Wörter in der linken Spalte sind Formen, die in der direkten Rede vorkommen. Sie werden in der indirekten Rede durch die entsprechenden Formen in der rechten Spalte ersetzt.

yet	⇒	up to that time
this/these	⇒	that/those
here	⇒	there
now	⇒	then; at that time
ago	⇒	before
last	⇒	the previous; the ... before
next	⇒	the next; the following; the ... after
today	⇒	that day
tonight	⇒	that night
yesterday	⇒	the previous day; the day before
tomorrow	⇒	the next day; the day after; the following day
the day before yesterday	⇒	two days before; two days earlier
the day after tomorrow	⇒	two days after; two days later; in two days time

6. Wenn das Verb in der Einführung nicht im "past" steht, bleibt die Zeitform im Hauptsatz bestehen: sie braucht nicht umgewandelt zu werden.

   - Mary ***asked***, "**Are** you going, John?"
     Mary ***asked*** John if he **was** going.

aber:

- Mary often ***asks***, "**Are** you going, John?"
  Mary often ***asks*** John if he **is** going.

23.2 Übungen

Ändere den Satz von der direkten Rede in die indirekte Rede um.

1. He said, "I went home at 2 o'clock yesterday."
2. He said, "I'll go home at 5 o'clock."
3. He said, "I always go home at 6 o'clock."
4. He said, "I've been going home at 8 o'clock."
5. He said, "I want to go home at 4 o'clock."
6. He said, "I wanted to go home at 4 o'clock."
7. He said, "I have to go home at 4 o'clock."
8. He said, "I had to go home at 4 o'clock."
9. He said, "I'll have to go home at 4 o'clock."
10. He said, "I must go home at 4 o'clock."
11. He said, "I'll be going home at 4 o'clock."
12. Peter asked Jim, "Will you send it back tomorrow?"
13. John said to Jane, "You forgot to send me a present."
14. John asked George, "Does your dog bite?"
15. Jim said to Dave, "Take the next street to the left."
16. John told Jim, "Don't tell Mary."
17. Tom said, "My brother's gone home."
18. Mary: "Are you laughing at me, Dick?"
19. Jim: "Please go with me, Linda."
20. Bill asked Harry, "How much did you pay for your coat?"
21. Mary told Bill, "Find me a nice book."
22. Ann told Jim, "This piece of cake is for you."
23. Fred told Helen, "You put your umbrella in my car yesterday."
24. Father told Mother, "Give Jim a bigger piece of cake."
25. Father told Mother, "I will see Jim tomorrow."
26. Mary asked Bill, "Have you heard the new song?"
27. Mary asked Bill, "Open the window."
28. Fred said, "I'm going to the city today and I'll fly to London the day after tomorrow."
29. Mary asked Jim, "Where have you hidden my shoe?"
30. Bill asked Ann, "How long have we known each other?"
31. The man told the girl, "If I catch you here again, I'll ring your father up."
32. Jim said to Tom, "I saw you here two years ago."

33. Mary asked Father, "Have you bought the books yet?"
34. Linda said, "I'll be going to school next year."
35. Jim: "Talk louder, Mary."
36. John said, "My sister flew to New York last week."
37. Mary asked, "Will they come at 3 o'clock?"
38. Mary: "Shall we be here at 3 o'clock to help her?"
39. Father: "You can't have a car, Bill."
40. Mother: "I'm sorry I can't help you with English, Linda."
41. The thief warned the boy, "If you shout, I'll kill you."
42. Your father promised us, "I'll go to the zoo with you."
43. Bill maintained, "I want to marry Betty."
44. Sue responded, "I knew them when they were young."
45. Tom and Lucy proudly said, "We have done everything ourselves."
46. The Taylors complained, "We had a terrible holiday."
47. Dotty asked us, "Were you at home on Wednesday?"
48. The men asked their wives, "Did we really go there last night?"
49. Peter: "I promise to be home at 10 o'clock."
50. The girl asked me, "Will you help me tomorrow?"
51. She asked him, "Did you read the newspaper yesterday?"
52. They said to us, "Walk slowly if you don't want to fall."
53. He told us, "Look at the shops and don't talk so loudly."
54. She said, "I bought this dress the day before yesterday."
55. He asked her, "Do you see that tree?"
56. She asked him, "Are you flying to Moscow tomorrow?"
57. He said, "I have read 20 books this year; last year I read only 15; next year I'll certainly read more."
58. The boy told the policeman, "I can't see them now."
59. She said to the boy, "I have cleaned the kitchen twice today. If you think I'm going to clean it again because you broke the dish, then you are wrong. I'll wait until tomorrow."
60. Mary said, "I'm going to the cinema tomorrow."
61. Mary told Jim, "You can have dinner with us this evening."
62. Mary said, "We'll go to the beach when we have had lunch."
63. Mary said, "I don't like cats, but I like dogs."
64. Mary told Jim, "Come quickly and see what I have done."
65. Mary asked Jim, "When will we arrive?"
66. Mary said, "I didn't finish my homework yesterday because I was so tired after the party the day before yesterday."
67. Mary said, "My aunt lives in this house over here."
68. Mary said to Jim, "Close the window before you leave."

69. Mary said, "Jim must hand in his book and then he can go home."
70. Mary asked her mother, "At what time will the party start?"
71. John said to Paul, "If we walk quietly, we can see the rabbits."
72. "Yesterday I was at the cinema and tomorrow I must visit my grandmother," said Mary.
73. "Susan will be in Bonn this afternoon, " she said.
74. "Are you going home at 4 o'clock?" my boss asked me.
75. "After we have had lunch, we'll be playing cards," they told us.
76. "Wipe your shoes before you come in," father told Mike.
77. "Why haven't you washed the cups?" the woman asked us.
78. Mary said, "I didn't see anyone here two hours ago."
79. "Mary and Peter are coming today and Bill's not leaving until next Wednesday," I said.
80. Aunt Jane said to Peter, "Switch the light off and close the door before you leave the house."
81. "When does the plane arrive in London?" we asked the stewardess.
82. The policeman asked the boy, "What's your name?"
83. You said to us, "Take your coats into the big room."
84. You said to us, "You have held it nicely."
85. He said, "I must go home at four o'clock."
86. "Does your toe hurt?" the doctor asked the man.
87. Father asked us, "How far are you walking today?"
88. The woman said, "I'll play tennis again soon."
89. The doctor asked Marie, "Why didn't you take your baby to the hospital last week?"
90. The teacher told us, "Leave the building."
91. Mother said to you, "You have done it very poorly."
92. The men asked the girls, "Did you go there yesterday?"
93. Martha said to me, "Don't work too hard."
94. "My sister lived here two years ago," the old woman said.
95. "If the weather doesn't change, we can't leave," the captain said to his men.
96. He said, "I'll come as soon as I've finished the book I'm reading."
97. Mrs. Jones said, "I'll help him if I can."
98. Their daughter said to them, "I'm not going to school today."
99. "Why didn't you try the other door?" her mother asked us.
100. He asked her, "Can you come?"
101. He said to us, "Get out of my house immediately."
102. She asked him, "Do you want anything else?"
103. My mother asked me, "Are you washing your face?"
104. John told us, "Someone broke into my house last night."
105. Jane said to us, "I'm glad to hear you're so happy."
106. She told her, "Have a good time."

107. Linda: "We haven't seen each other for a long time, Dave."
108. Dave: "What have you been doing, Linda?"
109. "I have something to show you," I said to her.
110. "Nothing ever grows in my garden," she said.
111. "I'm going away tomorrow, mother," he said.
112. "We have a lift, but very often it doesn't work," they said.
113. "I have an English lesson tomorrow and I haven't done my homework yet," said the small boy.
114. "I'm going fishing with my father this afternoon," said the boy.
115. "I'll wait until my boy comes in, but I hope he won't be too late," said Mrs. Small.
116. The policeman asked the man, "What's your name?"
117. The boys asked the girls, "Did you come here yesterday?"
118. Mother told him, "Look in the cupboard."
119. You said to us, "Take your dogs for a walk now."
120. They said to her, "You have written it neatly."
121. You asked me, "When will you come home tomorrow?"
122. "If you go there," she told us, "you will see two dogs."
123. He said to you, "If you had read that book, you'd have seen the word."
124. You said, "He didn't eat the apple after he'd stolen it."
125. He said to me, "If you are helping your mother now, you can go to the zoo with me the day after tomorrow."
126. He asked his wife, "Do you want me to come home at 4 o'clock?"
127. He said, "I promise I'll be home at 4 o'clock."
128. Judy told Bill, "I'll miss you very much."
129. Fred told Helen, "I've lost my key, but I've found yours."
130. George said, "I think I left it on my desk."
131. Peter was very late. He explained that... ("I missed the train.")
132. John asked Mary, "What are you doing?"
133. John asked Peter, "How did the film end?"
134. George asked Mary, "Why isn't my food ready?"
135. The waitress asked the lady, "Would you like tea?"
136. Tom asked Jane, "Can you catch the ball?"
137. We answered, "He's sitting over here."
138. Ruth: "Don't drink that water, Ken."
139. They asked us, "Haven't you bought a tree yet?"
140. They said, "He's sat here for two hours now."
141. Linda asked them, "Where will you sleep tomorrow?"
142. Tom said to Peggy, "If you taught me the words today, I would forget them again."
143. He said, "I spend all my money on horses."

144. Bob: "Hold my book, Dolly."
145. They said to us, "You threw the chair away three years ago."
146. She said to me, "I'd not say that if I were you."
147. She said, "I swim every day."
148. Linda said, "I must show you the book tomorrow, Bob."
149. They said to us, "You sat here two days ago."
150. Linda said, "The men've now shot five birds here this afternoon."
151. They told me, "You didn't sit here yesterday."
152. We said, "We won't bring you here again."
153. Tom said to Becky, "I'd not go with you if it weren't necessary."
154. Bill said, "He's learning the words."
155. Ben said to Linda, "If you flew to New York the day after tomorrow, you would see Carter."
156. She said, "I know all the people here."
157. Tom asked them, "When will you go next year?"
158. They said, "He was wearing a brown coat yesterday."
159. Ruth told Mac, "Sing the song."
160. Tom: "Don't drive too fast, Linda."
161. They said, "He was feeding the deer yesterday."
162. Ben asked, "When have you ridden on the bus, Peggy?"
163. Linda said, "I cut my finger the day before yesterday."
164. Mother told Father, "I'd not ask you to go if I could go."
165. Mom said, "They've now found ten toys under the chairs here."
166. She said, "I love my new book very much."
167. John said, "Take the dog out, Linda."
168. Linda said, "I must sell my books the day after tomorrow."
169. Linda told Tom, "Don't blow the candle out."
170. "I haven't kept your ring," Jenny told her boyfriend.
171. The man said to his sister, "I have bought two dresses for you this week."
172. Richard asked his mother, "What did you do two weeks ago?"
173. Bob said to Susan, "Don't begin to read."
174. My brother asked Linda, "Do you always throw your books in the corner?"
175. Tom reported, "I won't go there again."
176. Bob said to Linda, "I have known you for a long time."
177. Susan told Jenny, "Buy tomatoes today."
178. Linda said to me, "I'll hold your book here."
179. The boys asked us, "Did you sell your car?"
180. Cathy replied, "I'm drinking milk now."
181. Tom: "Please give me your pen, Peggy."

182. Carl told Susan, "You didn't think of that yesterday."
183. The woman told her husband, "I'll be singing that song the day after tomorrow."
184. Tom said to Peggy, "Catch this ball."
185. Daniel said, "I often take a bus."
186. The girls said to their mothers, "We were running to school when you saw us."
187. My sister asked me, "When will you wake up tomorrow?"
188. Cathy told Ben, "I don't understand what you said."
189. "At what time do you get up, Peter?" asked Mary.
190. The mother told her girl, "You can go to school when you are six years old."
191. "While I was on holiday this year, I visited the British Museum," said Tom.
192. "Hurry up or you'll be late for school," mother told us.
193. "If you have a dog, you'll have to take it out every day," the girl told me.
194. "Why didn't you stay at home last night?" the girl asked her boyfriend.
195. "I think I've seen you before, Miss Smith," said the doctor.
196. The teacher said to us, "Open your books and begin to read."
197. "I didn't see anyone here two hours ago," Jim told Linda.
198. "Did you see my pen?" the man asked his daughter.
199. "Do you like red dresses?" the lady asked me.
200. Bill told Mary, "You left your umbrella in my car yesterday."
201. "Have you been to the zoo this week?" the man asked the children.
202. Mary said that ... ("I saw the car accident"), but she denied that ... ("But I didn't cause it.")
203. "Can we take a piece of cake?" the children asked.
204. "Are you coming to my party tomorrow, Tom?" Peggy asked.
205. "Did you tell my sister to come, Linda?" Dan asked.
206. "Must we go to the doctor's tomorrow?" the boys asked their father.
207. Judy said to Tom, "I went there earlier than you."
208. Linda said, "I‘ll go there in March."
209. Dan said, "I‘ve heard that before."
210. Tom said, "We go there often, mother."
211. Andrea said, "They‘d seen the dog."
212. Ann said, "Linda and I threw her the ball two days ago."
213. Susan said, "You'll buy a car next week, father."
214. "I'm sure I left your book on my desk, Jane," Tom said.
215. "Don't stay too long or you'll have to go home in the dark," father warned the girls.
216. "If you don't work hard in class, you won't understand what I was saying," the teacher told us.
217. "Yesterday I was at home and tomorrow I'm going to the zoo," reported Mary.
218. "I visited my uncle three weeks ago," replied John.

219. "I'm leaving tomorrow, father," she said.
220. "I'll be with you as soon as I'm ready," Linda told Dick.
221. Dan explained, "We'll go on Friday."
222. "You've played very much today," the teacher told the children.
223. They shouted, "He's washing the car."
224. "Linda, you can't go out with Tom," said Father.
225. Tom's sister replied, "He always comes home at noon."
226. "We'll be taking the test tomorrow," said the boys.
227. "We went to church yesterday," their father said to the girls.
228. "I had seen you often," the neighbour said to Tom.
229. "The boy'll be going home soon," said the teacher.
230. "I have been here for three hours," she replied.
231. "We don't want to see you now, Tom," they said.
232. "I came home today," the daughter answered.
233. "Betty, I want to marry you," Tom said.
234. "You haven't played with any toys, Linda," mother said.

Wähle die richtige Antwort.

235. "I hope you are happy," she told him.
   a.) She told him she hopes you are happy.
   b.) She told him she hoped I am happy.
   c.) She told him that he hopes you are happy.
   d.) She told him she hoped he was happy.
236. "We'll take a test tomorrow," said the sad pupils.
   a.) The sad pupils said we'll take a test tomorrow.
   b.) The sad pupils said we would take a test tomorrow.
   c.) The sad pupils said they'll take a test the next day.
   d.) The sad pupils said they would take a test the next day.
237. "They went to church yesterday," the father said.
   a.) The father said they went to church yesterday.
   b.) The father said we went to church yesterday.
   c.) The father said that they have gone to church the previous day.
   d.) The father said that they had gone to church the previous day.
238. "We had seen them often," said the neighbour.
   a.) The neighbour said they had seen them often.
   b.) The neighbour said we had seen them often.
   c.) The neighbour said they saw them often.
   d.) The neighbour said they saw us often.

239. "He'll be going home soon," said the teacher.
    a.) The teacher said he was going home soon.
    b.) The teacher said he would be going home soon.
    c.) The teacher said that he will be going home soon.
    d.) The teacher said that he is going home soon.

240. "I have been here for two hours," she replied.
    a.) She replied that she had been there for two hours.
    b.) She replied that she has been there for two hours.
    c.) She replied that she has been here for two hours.
    d.) She replied that she had been here for two hours.

241. "They know our names," she stated.
    a.) She stated that they know your names.
    b.) She stated that we know our names.
    c.) She stated that they knew her names.
    d.) She stated that they knew their names.

242. "They'll run quickly next time," she remarked.
    a.) She remarked that we'll run quickly next time.
    b.) She remarked that we'd run quickly the next time.
    c.) She remarked that they'll run quickly the last time.
    d.) She remarked that they would run quickly the next time.

243. "I came home today," the daughter said.
    a.) The daughter said that she had come home today.
    b.) The daughter said that she had come home that day.
    c.) The daughter said that she came home today.
    d.) The daughter said that she came home that day.

244. "I want to marry Betty," he said.
    a.) He said he wanted to marry Betty.
    b.) He said he had wanted to marry Betty.
    c.) He said he wants to marry Betty.
    d.) He said he did want to marry Betty.

245. "He has stood for two hours," the man said.
    a.) The man said that he has stood for two hours.
    b.) The man said that he stood for two hours.
    c.) The man said that he had stood for two hours.
    d.) The man said that he stands for two hours.

246. "You paid high prices," he commented.
    a.) He commented that they have paid high prices.
    b.) He commented that they had paid high prices.
    c.) He commented that you paid high prices.
    d.) He commented that they paid high prices.

247. "He didn't play any tennis," his father said.
    a.) His father said that he doesn't play any tennis.
    b.) His father said that he hadn't played any tennis.
    c.) His father said that he didn't play any tennis.
    d.) His father said that he hasn't played any tennis.
248. "He has been working late," said his friends.
    a.) His friends said he had been working late.
    b.) His friends said he has been working late.
    c.) His friends said he was working late.
    d.) His friends said he had worked late.
249. "The wine tastes wonderful," the waiter said.
    a.) The waiter said the wine tasted wonderful.
    b.) The waiter said the wine tastes wonderful.
    c.) The waiter said the wine would taste wonderful.
    d.) The waiter said the wine had tasted wonderful.
250. "We found everything boring," they said.
    a.) They said they found everything boring.
    b.) They said they had found everything boring.
    c.) They said they would find everything boring.
    d.) They said they have found everything boring.
251. "I see her too often," he responded.
    a.) He responded that he has seen her too often.
    b.) He responded that he sees her too often.
    c.) He responded that he saw her too often.
    d.) He responded that he had seen her too often.
252. "I'll be here tonight," the boy promised.
    a.) The boy promised he'll be here that night.
    b.) The boy promised he'll be there tonight.
    c.) The boy promised he'd be there that night.
    d.) The boy promised he'd be here that night.
253. "We shall ring up the station now," he promised.
    a.) He promised we would ring up the station now.
    b.) He promised they should ring up the station now.
    c.) He promised they will ring up the station then.
    d.) He promised they would ring up the station then.
254. "Has he gone now?" she asked.
    a.) She asked that he had gone then.
    b.) She asked if he had gone then.
    c.) She asked if he had gone now.
    d.) She asked if he has gone now.

255. "Send an officer at once!" he commanded.
   a.) He commanded that an officer is sent at once.
   b.) He commanded them to send an officer at once.
   c.) He commanded them to sent an officer at once.
   d.) He commanded them that an officer should send at once.

256. "Hands up, Tom!" he yelled.
   a.) He ordered Tom to put his hands up.
   b.) He ordered that Tom should put his hands up.
   c.) He ordered if Tom had put his hands up.
   d.) He ordered Tom to have put his hands up.

257. "Did he go home?" he inquired.
   a.) He inquired whether he went home.
   b.) He inquired whether he did go home.
   c.) He inquired whether he had gone home.
   d.) He inquired that he had gone home.

258. "Do they often have tests?" the girls asked.
   a.) The girls asked if they often do have tests.
   b.) The girls asked that they often had tests.
   c.) The girls asked if they often have had tests.
   d.) The girls asked if they often had tests.

259. "Did he have much money?" asked the burglar.
   a.) The burglar asked if he had much money.
   b.) The burglar asked if he had had much money.
   c.) The burglar asked if he did have much money.
   d.) The burglar asked that he had had much money.

260. "I speak English and next year I'll learn French," she boasted.
   a.) She boasted that she would speak English and learned French the next year.
   b.) She boasted that she had spoken English and would learn French the next year.
   c.) She boasted that she spoke English and would learn French the next year.
   d.) She boasted that she spoke English and learned French the next year.

261. He said, "We will go next Tuesday."
   a.) He said we will go next Tuesday.
   b.) He said they will go the following Tuesday.
   c.) He said they would go the following Tuesday.
   d.) He said we would go the following Tuesday.

262. The reporters said, "They saw the last game."
   a.) The reporters said that they have seen the last game.
   b.) The reporters said that they saw the last game.
   c.) The reporters said that they had seen the previous game.
   d.) The reporters said that they were seen the last game.

263. The teacher said, "You have worked hard this week."
    a.) The teacher said that you had worked hard that week.
    b.) The teacher said that you have worked hard this week.
    c.) The teacher said that you worked hard this week.
    d.) The teacher said that you had worked hard this week.
264. They yelled, "He is washing the car now."
    a.) They yelled he is washing the car at that time.
    b.) They yelled that he was washing the car at that time.
    c.) They yelled that he is washing the car now.
    d.) They yelled that he was washing the car now.
265. Mother said, "I can't go out with George."
    a.) Mother said that she won't go out with George.
    b.) Mother said that she can't go out with George.
    c.) Mother said that she couldn't go out with George.
    d.) Mother said that she wouldn't go out with George.
266. His sister replied, "He comes home early."
    a.) His sister replied that he came home early.
    b.) His sister replied that he is coming home early.
    c.) His sister replied that he had come home early.
    d.) His sister replied that he would be coming home early.
267. The widow said, "My husband had always been kind."
    a.) The widow said her husband had always been kind.
    b.) The widow said her husband was always kind.
    c.) The widow said her husband has always been kind.
    d.) The widow said my husband had always been kind.

Ändere den Satz von der indirekten Rede in die direkte Rede um.

268. He said to Linda that she would be home soon.
269. He asked Don to help him.
270. He agreed with Nancy that her dress was nice.
271. He asked Peggy if she had been there the day before.
272. He said to the people that they should be quiet.
273. We asked Tom not to go with Dick the next day.
274. You said that we had been very quiet that day.
275. Linda asked us if we had been to London up to that time.
276. They said that Linda had helped them two days before.
277. You asked us if we would see Tom the following day.
278. They said to us that we should run to the bus that morning.
279. We agreed with Linda and said that she could write a letter.

280. She ordered Tom to write a book.
281. You asked us if we were going shopping the next day.
282. You said that Tom would be helping you in two days time.
283. I told the boy not to pick the apples there.
284. They told me that I had to take the bus the following day.
285. We asked them if they would have to drink alcohol at the party.
286. They agreed with Linda and said that it would have been better if she had gone to school earlier.
287. The man said he had driven the car the previous day.
288. The lady asked Tom to pick up his coat.
289. The boy asked whether Linda would be coming the following day.
290. The man told Dan to sit down.
291. The woman said the wind had been blowing very strongly there the previous day.
292. The teacher asked us if we would be flying to America two days after.
293. Peter asked us if we had gone by train the day before.
294. The doctor asked the child what she had done to the dog the previous day.
295. Dan told Jenny that it was her turn to feed the cat the following day.
296. They asked Don if he was building the garage then.
297. My girlfriend agreed to come to my house the following Friday.
298. The students asked the teacher if he would know the result of the test in two days time.
299. I asked my sister if she always bound those flowers.
300. Father asked Linda if she had drawn a picture the day before.
301. The boys asked the girls if they wanted to dig a hole that night.
302. The Smiths said that they had bought the table the previous week.
303. The girl told me that she cut her finger that day.
304. Our friends asked us when we would be meeting the people the next day.
305. The man asked me if I had begun to write the letter up to that time.
306. They told us that they would drive to the city the next day.
307. We asked the policemen if they had caught the thief the month before.
308. Tom's uncle asked him why he had fought with the other boy two days before.
309. Mother asked the boy if he had bitten that apple.
310. The stranger asked Carl what he had found two days before.
311. I told Mary that I was bringing her her milk at that time.

24 Reflexive Pronouns = das Reflexivpronomen

24.1 Grammatik

1. Die Reflexivpronomen heißen:

myself	ourselves
yourself	yourselves
himself	themselves
herself	
itself	

2. Sie werden wie folgt gebraucht:

   a) als **rückbezügliches Fürwort** (reflexive pronoun)

   Das Subjekt ist das gleiche wie das Objekt: dieselbe Person ist gemeint.

   He dressed **himself**.

   b) als **betonendes Fürwort** (intensive pronoun)

   Ein Substantiv (noun) oder Pronomen (pronoun) wird stark betont. Obwohl das Reflexivpronomen meistens am Ende des Satzes steht, kann es direkt hinter dem Wort stehen, das dadurch besonders betont wird.

   He showed me the house **himself**.

   He **himself** showed me the house.

   c) als **Redewendung** bei verschiedenen Präpositionen.

to see for ... self	I want to see the house for myself.
all by ... self	Are you going to travel there all by yourself?
beside ... self	She was beside herself with fear.

3. Bei den folgenden Verben wird das Reflexivpronomen gebraucht:

amuse, annoyed with, to be ashamed of, assert, behave, blame, control, convince ... of, cut, defend, devote, distinguish, enjoy, get .. a drink, help, hurt, injure, introduce, look after, look at, make ... understood, make ... useful, pay for, pull ... together, sit by, seat, see ... in a mirror, speak to, support, take care of, talk about, talk to, think of

4. Die folgenden Verben können mit oder ohne Reflexivpronomen gebildet werden. Wenn das Reflexivpronomen gebraucht wird, wird die bewusste Durchführung der Handlung betont.

   behave, dress, hide, prepare, prove, separate, settle, shave, submit, surrender, trouble, wash, yield

   Your children behaved very well.

   You must behave yourselves properly!

5. Die folgenden Verben, die im Deutschen Reflexivpronomen haben, haben im Englischen keine reflexive Form:

   approach, change, complain, imagine, lie down, move, recover, rely on, remember, sit down, turn to.

   Do you remember her? (Erinnerst du dich an sie?)

6. **Each other** ist ein reciprocal pronoun. Es zeigt eine wechselseitige Beziehung zwischen mindestens zwei Personen/Tieren/Sachen.

   The man and the woman liked **each other**. (Der Mann und die Frau mochten einander.)

7. Beispiel des Unterschiedes:

   The man and the woman can see **themselves**. (Der Mann und die Frau können sich selbst sehen.)

   The man and the woman can see **each other**. (Der Mann und die Frau können einander sehen.)

24.2 Übungen

Setze das richtige Fürwort (rückbezüglich = reflexive **oder** wechselseitig = reciprocal = each other) ein.

1. The woman devoted ______ to her children.
2. The water was so clear and still that we could see ______ in it.
3. We told her to amuse ______ .
4. Behave ______ , children.
5. The boy and girl liked talking to ______ .
6. We can spread the butter ______ .
7. They'll have to see for ______ .
8. Why don't you assert ______ more often?
9. I couldn't enjoy ______ at all.
10. The girl injured ______ .
11. The babies tried to see ______ in the mirror.
12. I always tried to make ______ useful.
13. The lady wants to see it for ______ .
14. May I help ______ to a cup of tea?
15. We have to think of ______ first.

16. The boy always kept to ______ .
17. We saw ______ in the mirror.
18. All she ever does is to think of ______ .
19. Linda and Tom, remember to behave ______ .
20. After we clapped, we all seated ______ .
21. Did you cut ______ ?
22. The woman introduced ______ .
23. That man is sick. He's talking to ______ .
24. As soon as we got there, we made ______ useful.
25. Let me do it ______ !
26. The people amused ______ at the party.
27. Did you shave ______ this morning?
28. The girls kept to ______ .
29. The lady told me to get ______ a drink.
30. You washed ______ very well, children.
31. Don't trouble ______ about that!
32. The man and woman who were in love looked at ______ .
33. That man will talk ______ out of a job.
34. The shy girl hid ______ quickly.
35. I tried to control ______ .
36. I hurt ______ yesterday.
37. Aren't you ashamed of ______ , children?
38. The men must defend ______ .
39. I have devoted ______ to writing.
40. The people seated ______ right away.
41. The girl cried because she had cut ______ .
42. I'll make ______ a new dress.
43. The boy wanted to see for ______ .
44. "Mommy, I'm really ashamed of ______ ."
45. The guests enjoyed ______ immensely.
46. I plan to travel all by ______ .
47. Linda got dressed all by ______ .
48. The man said, "Pull ______ together, man!"
49. I introduced the guests to ______ .
50. Can the boy dress ______ ?
51. The lady told me that I must assert ______ more often.
52. She talked ______ into self-pity.
53. Please help ______ to a piece of cake.

54. The woman had to support ______ .
55. The baby cried when it saw ______ in the mirror.
56. The boy wanted to travel all by ______ .
57. We all hid ______ during the game.
58. Did those two children wash ______ or ______ ?

Können die folgenden Sätze mit einem Reflexivpronomen gebildet werden? Wenn das möglich ist, ändere den Satz entsprechend um.

59. I didn't want to trouble the man.
60. Did you enjoy the picture, Sally?
61. I settled down for a long winter's nap.
62. The man supported his mother.
63. We prepared for the test.
64. Did you shave the boy's head?
65. The dog proved to be a good one.
66. We washed the girl's face.
67. The boy injured his head.
68. The girls dressed quickly.
69. The men defended their wives.
70. They settled into their new house.
71. You dressed your daughter quickly.
72. We amused the children.
73. Did you shave this morning?
74. I hurt my hand.
75. Should I introduce you?
76. Did the children behave?
77. I cut my finger.
78. The man controlled his temper.

Übersetze.

79. Die Mädchen zogen sich an.
80. Die kleinen Kinder freuten sich sehr.
81. Die Kinder schämten sich.
82. Wir mussten uns schnell waschen.
83. Die Kinder versteckten sich.
84. Das Mädchen führte Selbstgespräche.
85. Hast Du Dich verletzt?
86. Die mutigen Kinder behaupteten sich.
87. Der Junge hat sich geschnitten.

88. Benimm Dich!
89. Muss der Junge sich schon rasieren?
90. Hast Du es selber genäht?
91. Kann ich mich nützlich machen?
92. Wolltest Du es selbst machen?
93. Die Damen stellten sich vor.
94. Sie betrachteten ihr Spiegelbild.
95. Ich setzte mich.
96. Bediene Dich mit einem Stück Kuchen.
97. Der Junge und das Mädchen verliebten sich.
98. Wir sahen einander durch's Fenster.
99. Ich wollte die Stadt selbst ansehen.
100. Ich stellte die Damen vor.
101. Ihr sollt einander helfen.
102. Die weinenden Mütter mussten sich zusammennehmen.
103. Hat seine Frau sich selbst unterstützt oder ihren Mann?
104. Der Junge verletzte sich.
105. Das Mädchen ist alleine gefahren.
106. Wir dachten ständig aneinander.

25 Future = Zukunft

25.1 Grammatik

Die Zukunft kann durch verschiedene Zeitformen ausgedrückt werden.

1. **will + infinitive**

   Wenn man diese Form gebraucht, betont man keinerlei Absicht oder Plan. Das, was man sagt, wird geschehen, ob man es wünscht oder nicht. Es ist keine Zeitangabe notwendig. Es kann sich um die nahe oder entfernte Zukunft handeln.

   Father will certainly be happy when he sees you.

2. **present**

   Diese Form betont einen Plan. Die Form wird gebraucht bei Fahrplänen, festen Programmen, getroffenen Vereinbarungen und offiziellen Regelungen. Eine Zeitangabe der Zukunft ist fast immer vorhanden.

   When does the train to London leave?

   The train to London leaves at 7:10 p.m.

3. **present progressive**

   Diese Form wird gebraucht für eine schon beschlossene und vereinbarte Handlung. Eine Zeitangabe ist meistens vorhanden.

   in a few days, later this month, next week, next winter, soon, this morning, tomorrow, tonight

   Oft handelt es sich um ***Verben der Bewegung***:

   arrive, come, do, drive, fly, go, leave, play, remain, start, stay, travel

   I am flying to America this coming summer.

4. **be going to + infinitive**

   Diese Form drückt die nahe Zukunft aus. Der Sprecher ist wegen der jetzigen Situation sicher, was passieren wird. Die Form wird gebraucht bei einer

   - **Absicht**

     Die Handlung ist fest geplant, beabsichtigt oder sogar schon vereinbart. Die Vorbereitungen für die Handlung sind schon angelaufen.

     We are going to take the train to Munich next week.

     I'm going to be a doctor when I grow up.

     Are you going to buy new chairs for the living-room?

- **Voraussage** über die Wahrscheinlichkeit eines Geschehens. Man meint, etwas wird passieren. Es wird oft nach den folgenden Verben gebraucht:

  be afraid, be sure, believe, think

  I think it's going to rain today.

5. **will be + -ing** (future progressive)

   - Diese Form kann für die nahe oder weite Zukunft gebraucht werden. Es wird keine Absicht betont. Ein zukünftiges Ereignis wird bloß bekanntgegeben. Eine Zeitangabe ist nicht nötig, aber oft vorhanden. Gerade zu einem bestimmten Zeitpunkt in der Zukunft wird etwas passieren. Während einer Zeitspanne in der Zukunft wird etwas ablaufen.

     My sister will be coming to visit us in July.

     She will be working from 2 to 10 tomorrow.

   - Fragen wirken höflicher und nicht so direkt, wenn sie in dieser Form gestellt werden.

     When will you be coming to see us?

Form	Absicht betont	Absicht nicht b.	Zeitang. muß	Zeitang. muß nicht	nah	weit
present		x	x			
will + inf.		x		x	x	x
present prog.	x		x		x	
be going to + inf.	x			x	x	
will be + -ing		x		x	x	x

Diese Tabelle soll nur einen Anhaltspunkt geben. Abweichungen von der Tabelle sind möglich. Trotzdem trägt sie zum Verständnis der Zukunft bei.

25.2 Übungen

Setze die Verben in die angegebene Zeitform

present simple

1. When (to start - the show) tomorrow?
2. The plane from London (to arrive) at 9 p.m. this evening.
3. My boy (to start) school on Tuesday.
4. The Olympic games (to start) on June 1st.
5. The shops here (to close) at noon.
6. The shops (to open) at ten this Monday.
7. When (must read - you) a book today?
8. When (to leave - the train) this Wednesday?

present progressive

9. Do you know when (to go shopping - you) tomorrow?

10. My sister (to go) to school tomorrow.
11. (to go - you) to the cinema tonight?
12. Does he know what (to do - he) next June?
13. I (to take) my driving test next week.
14. Where (to take a walk - John) this afternoon?
15. When (to start - your child) school?
16. I'm so happy that I (to go) to school next year.
17. When (to work - father) next week?
18. What (to do - you) tomorrow?
19. When (to come - your friends) this afternoon?
20. Our friends (to drive) to Switzerland this summer.
21. I (to plan to wash) the clothes tomorrow.
22. When (to go - you) on holiday this year?

future simple (shall/will + inf.)

23. (to be - you) here tomorrow?
24. It (to snow - certainly) in winter.
25. They (to go) to sleep at 10 p.m.
26. (to see - we) your new house tomorrow?
27. The men (to drive) to Bonn this week.
28. When (to take - you) your holiday this year?
29. Mother (to make) a cake for her birthday.
30. What (to do - we) if you get ill?
31. Why (to be - father) angry?
32. The baby (to cry) when it is hungry.
33. What (to cook - you) when your friends come?
34. TV (to have) a new series which starts in September.
35. When (to wear - you) your new dress?
36. My sister (to have) a baby in June.
37. We (to eat) at 6 p.m.

future progressive

38. This time next week we (to land) in New York.
39. Christian (to start) school in August.
40. I (to sleep - probably) when you get home.
41. Don't ring the bell at 9 p.m. The baby (to sleep) then.
42. The doctor (to come) soon.
43. I'm sure your girl (to read) books by next summer!
44. You'll find him because he (to wear) a red hat.

45. My son (to work) at Ford as of October.
46. I'm to tell you that your sister (to arrive) at ten tonight.
47. In another week the patient (to go) home.
48. Can you tell me when you (to go) shopping next?
49. After we've gone to sleep, our parents (to go) to a party.
50. I'm sure we (to see) each other again soon.
51. It looks like it (to rain) soon.
52. When did you say you (to arrive)?

be going to + inf.

53. (to meet - he) you at the station?
54. What (to tell - you) her when she asks?
55. I've brought the cassettes. (to play - you) them now?
56. It looks like it (to rain) soon.
57. He (to get married) next year.
58. When (to visit - they) you?
59. Why (to feed - not - we) the hungry dog?
60. (to wash - your brother) the car today?
61. (to stop work - the men) soon?
62. I (to buy) my new car next Monday.
63. (to drive - your sister) or fly to Spain on holiday?
64. What (to be - you) when you grow up?
65. (to phone - not - your friend) this evening?
66. Where (to study - you) medicine?
67. We (to buy) that house soon.

Setze das Verb in die richtige Form.

68. And the children (all - to take) the test on the same day.
69. Even if he doesn't want to, he (must take) the test.
70. (to start - church) at 8 o'clock again this summer?
71. Don't worry. Your baby (to get) well soon.
72. I am sure you that you (to walk) normally in two weeks.
73. (to fly - he) to Spain on holiday this year again?
74. In 100 years people (to die - not) of cancer any more.
75. Look at your dog. It thinks you (to take) it for a walk.
76. Have you decided if you (to take) a pullover along on holiday?
77. Betsy (to grow up) to be a wonderful woman.
78. I'm sure we (to have) bad weather for our picnic today.
79. When (to arrive - Elvis) in Bonn on Wednesday?

80. My brother (to stay) with us when he comes to Europe this summer.

Übersetze die folgenden Sätze.

81. Ich werde dir heute abend helfen.
82. Die Hochzeit wird im Juni stattfinden.
83. Der Krieg wird kommen.
84. Ihr Zug fährt um 8 Uhr am folgenden Dienstag ab.
85. Wann geht ihr morgen in die Kirche?
86. Ich mache die Prüfung kommenden Mittwoch.
87. In 10 Jahren werden wir auf dem Mond landen.
88. Mein Bruder wird den Leuten zeigen, wie sie fahren müssen.
89. Das Baby meint, die Mutter wird es füttern.
90. Die Feier zum 4. Juli fängt in Amerika um 21 Uhr an.
91. Morgen werden wir länger schlafen.
92. Rufst du uns an, wenn du zu Hause angekommen bist?
93. Dan fährt am Freitag nach Bonn.
94. Die Katze hofft, dass die Maus aus dem Loch kommen wird.
95. Morgen werden wir heiraten.

Wähle die richtige Form.

96. a. Will you be taking the train on Friday?
    b. Do you take the train on Friday?
97. a. Are you coming to visit us in August?
    b. Are you going to come to visit us in August?
98. a. I'm sure it is raining this afternoon.
    b. I'm sure it's going to rain this afternoon.
99. a. We will be visiting Cologne on our trip to Germany this summer.
    b. We are visiting Cologne on our trip to Germany this summer.
100. a. Don't forget that the people are coming tomorrow.
    b. Don't forget that the people come tomorrow.
101. a. When are you planning to move?
    b. When are you going to move?
102. a. We buy fish this Friday.
    b. We will be buying fish this Friday.
103. a. My sister will be having a baby this year.
    b. My sister has a baby this year.
104. a. She doesn't wear a white dress.
    b. She isn't going to wear a white dress.

105. a. I think this man will feed the animals.
b. I think this man is going to feed the animals.

106. a. Are you going swimming tomorrow?
b. Will you be going swimming tomorrow?

107. a. Mother is cooking pancakes for lunch tomorrow.
b. Mother cooks pancakes for lunch tomorrow.

108. a. Tim is waiting for you at school tomorrow.
b. Tim is going to wait for you at school tomorrow.

109. a. When will you be going to bed tonight?
b. When do you go to bed tonight?

110. a. Will you feed our cat while we are gone?
b. Are you going to feed our cat while we are gone?

111. a. If I see you, I shout.
b. If I see you, I shall shout.

112. a. Many people will be coming in the future.
b. Many people are coming in the future.

113. a. What do you do then?
b. What will you do then?

114. a. The game begins at 8 p.m. this evening.
b. The game is going to begin at 8 p.m. this evening.

115. a. She is going to buy a new dress tomorrow.
b. She will buy a new dress tomorrow.

116. a. How will you leave if a fire starts?
b. How do you leave if a fire starts?

26 Auxiliaries = Modalverben

26.1 Grammatik

Ability (können) = Fähigkeit	
can/could	be able to
Possibility (es kann sein, dass/es könnte sein, dass) = Möglichkeit	
may/might	
Permission/Prohibition (dürfen) = Erlaubnis/Verbot	
may/might	be allowed to
can/could	be permitted to
may not	be not allowed to
cannot	be not permitted to
must not	be forbidden to
Compulsion (müssen) = Zwang	
must	be forced to
	be compelled to
	have to
	be obliged to
need not	
Duty, Obligation, Rules (sollen) = Pflicht, Regeln	
should	be expected to
ought to	be supposed to
	have to
	be to
	It is s.o. duty to
Necessity (notwendig sein) = Notwendigkeit	
must	have to
	It is necessary to
need not	There is no need to
	There isn't any need to

1. **Ability** = Fähigkeit (können)

present	can cannot	am/are/is (not) able to
past	could could not	was/were (not) able to
future	can can not	will (not) be able to
present perfect	—	have/has (not) been able to
past perfect	—	had (not) been able to
future perfect	—	will (not) have been able to
conditional 1	—	would (not) be able to
conditional 2	—	would (not) have been able to

2. **Possibility** = Möglichkeit

   present and future:

may (not)+ infinitive	(es kann sein,dass)
might (not) + infinitive	(es könnte sein,dass)

   past:

might (not) + infinitive	(bei indirekte Rede)

   past, present perfect, past perfect

may (not) have + 3. Form
might (not) have + 3. Form

   Dieses Modalverb ist ein ganz besonderes. Wie man sieht, werden nicht alle Zeitformen berücksichtigt. Stattdessen werden die Zeitmöglichkeiten in zwei Gruppen geformt: alles, was noch kommt und alles, was schon vorbei ist.

   In diesen zwei Gruppen wird weiter unterschieden. Wenn man sagen will, dass etwas ziemlich möglich ist, gebraucht man **may**. Wenn man sagen will, dass etwas eventuell möglich ist, aber doch nicht so sicher, gebraucht man **might**.

vorbei $\Leftarrow$	kommt noch $\Rightarrow$
may have + 3. Form = ziemlich möglich might have + 3. Form = eventuell möglich	may + inf. = ziemlich möglich might + inf. =eventuell möglich

3. **Permission - Prohibition**

Permission = Erlaubnis (dürfen)

present	can may	am/are/is allowed to am/are/is permitted to
past	could	was/were allowed to was/were permitted to
future	can may	will be allowed to will be permitted to
present perfect	—	have/has been allowed to have/has been permitted to
past perfect	—	had been allowed to had been permitted to
future perfect	—	will have been allowed to will have been permitted to
conditional 1	—	would be allowed to would be permitted to
conditional 2	—	would have been allowed to would have been permitted to

Prohibition = Verbot (darf nicht)

present	cannot may not must not	am not/aren't/isn't allowed to am not/aren't/isn't permitted to am/are/is forbidden to
past	couldn't	wasn't/weren't allowed to wasn't/weren't permitted to was/were forbidden to
future	cannot may not must not	will not be allowed to will not be permitted to will be forbidden to
present perfect	———	haven't/hasn't been allowed to haven't/hasn't been permitted to have/has been forbidden to
past perfect	———	hadn't been allowed to hadn't been permitted to had been forbidden to
future perfect	———	will not have been allowed to will not have been permitted to will have been forbidden to
conditional 1	———	wouldn't be allowed to wouldn't be permitted to would be forbidden to
conditional 2	———	would not have been allowed to would not have been permitted to would have been forbidden to

4. **Compulsion** = Zwang (müssen)

present	must	am/are/is forced to am/are/is compelled to have/has to
past	______	was/were forced to was/were compelled to had to
future	must	will be forced to will be compelled to will have to
present perfect	______	have/has been forced to have/has been compelled to have/has had to
past perfect	______	had been forced to had been compelled to had had to
future perfect	______	will have been forced to will have been compelled to will have had to
conditional 1	______	would be forced to would be compelled to would have to
conditional 2	______	would have been forced to would have been compelled to would have had to

(**Compulsion - 2**) = ***kein Zwang***, (brauchen nicht/ muss nicht)

present	need not	am/are/is not forced to am/are/is not compelled to do/does not have to
past	______	wasn't/weren't forced to wasn't/weren't compelled to didn't have to
future	need not	will not be forced to will not be compelled to will not have to
present perfect	______	have/has not been forced to have/has not been compelled to have/has not had to
past perfect	______	had not been forced to had not been compelled to had not had to
future perfect	______	will not have been forced to will not have been compelled to will not have had to
conditional 1	______	would not be forced to would not be compelled to would not have to
conditional 2	______	would not have been forced to would not have been compelled to would not have had to

5. **Duty, Obligation, Rules** = Pflicht (sollen)

present	should (not) ought (not) to	am/are/is (not) expected to am/are/is (not) supposed to have/has (not) to am/are/is (not) to It is (not) s.o. duty to
future	should (not) ought (not) to	will (not) be expected to will (not) be supposed to will (not) have to It will (not) be s.o. duty to
past		was/were (not) expected to was/were (not) supposed to had to/ didn't have to was/were (not) to It was (not) s.o. duty to
present perfect		have/has (not) been expected to have/has (not) been supposed to have/has (not) had to It has (not) been s.o. duty to
past perfect		had (not) been expected to It had (not) been s.o. duty to
past/perfect: (unerfüllt; in der Vergangenheit):		
	should (not) have + 3. Form ought (not) to have + 3. Form	
		was/were (not) expected to have + 3. Form was/were (not) supposed to have + 3. Form was/were (not) to have + 3. Form It was (not) s.o. duty to have + 3. Form

future perfect	will (not) have been expected to will (not) have been supposed to will (not) have had to It will (not) have been s.o. duty to
conditional 1	would (not) be expected to would (not) be supposed to would (not) have to It would (not) be s.o. duty to
conditional 2	would (not) have been expected to would (not) have been supposed to would (not) have had to It would (not) have been s.o. duty to

Diese Tabelle ist ungewöhnlich, weil sie eine zusätzliche Form hat:

Die "past/perfect".

Die Form ist immer schon abgelaufen. Man schaut zurück und gibt ein Urteil davon ab, wie es falsch gelaufen ist.

Durch diese zusätzliche Form wird etwas ausgedrückt, was hätte sein sollen, aber nicht geschehen ist.

He should have called by now.

Etwas wurde versäumt.

We were to have danced at the party.

Etwas hätte gemacht werden müssen, ist aber nicht gemacht worden.

I ought to have cleaned my room before you came.

Etwas hätte nicht sein sollen, ist aber jedoch passiert.

He shouldn't have hit her.

He wasn't supposed to have eaten the cake.

s.o. = someone's = my, your, his, her, its, our, your, their

6. **Necessity** = Notwendigkeit (müssen/brauchen/notwendig sein)

present	must	have/has to It is necessary to
past	______	had to It was necessary to
future	must	will have to It will be necessary to
present perfect	______	have/has had to It has been necessary to
past perfect	______	had had to It had been necessary to
future perfect	______	will have had to It will have been necessary to
conditional 1	______	would have to It would be necessary to
conditional 2	______	would have had to It would have been necessary to

Necessity - 2 = *keine Notwendigkeit* (brauchen nicht)

present	need not	don't/doesn't have to It isn't necessary to There is no need to There isn't any need to
past	______	didn't have to It was not necessary to There was no need to There wasn't any need to
future	need not	will not have to It won't be necessary to There will be no need to There won't be any need to
present perfect	______	have/has not had to It hasn't been necessary to There has been no need to There hasn't been any need to
past perfect	______	had not had to It hadn't been necessary to There had been no need to There hadn't been any need to
future perfect	______	will not have had to It won't have been necessary to There will have been no need to There won't have been any need to
conditional 1	______	would not have to It wouldn't be necessary to There would be no need to There wouldn't be any need to
conditional 2	______	would not have had to It wouldn't have been necessary to There would have been no need to There wouldn't have been any need to

26.2 Übungen

Setze die richtige Form des Verbes (entweder mit dem Modalverb oder seine Ersatzform als Hilfsverb!), das in den Klammern angegeben ist, in die Lücke ein!

Ability

1. A tiger ______ an elephant. (to kill)
2. The patient ______ now. (to walk)
3. Five years ago he ______ ten hours a day. (to work)
4. It will be dark and he ______ where he is going. (to see - not)
5. We ______ the lake from here. (to see)
6. He ______ for five years now. (to talk)
7. If they helped her wash the dishes, she ______ soon. (to play)
8. ______ English for three years now? (you - to talk)
9. ______ television tomorrow? (you - to watch)

Possibility

10. He ______ tomorrow, but I'm not sure. (to come)
11. They think that he ______ if we had asked him. (to come)
12. Do you think that they ______ home now? (to be)
13. We ______ her yesterday. (to see)
14. You are just afraid that the lions ______ you. (to eat)
15. Do you know what you ______ if you had been there? (to do)
16. Do you think he ______ the newspaper already? (to read)

Permission - Prohibition

17. You ______ now, children. (to go)
18. Father already said that you ______ to the cinema. (to go - not)
19. Do you think that I ______ tomorrow? (to go)
20. ______ to bed at midnight? (you - always - to go)
21. I? (to smoke)
22. ______ he really ______ that book yet? (to read - not)
23. You ______ alcohol. (to drink - not)
24. ______ a picture? (they - to paint - never)
25. No, they ______ that. (to do - never)
26. ______ her, if I spoke with his father? (he - to see)

Compulsion

27. You ______ your physics now! (to do)
28. No, you ______ it now. (to do)
29. He held a pistol and I ______ with him. (to go)
30. They ______ their homes next year. (to leave)
31. I ______ home up to now. (to run - often)
32. The burglars said, "If the police had come, we ______ " (to shoot)
33. We ______ hard for most of our lives. (to work)
34. He ______ there yesterday. (to go)
35. She says that you ______ your teeth the following day. (to brush)
36. He explained that they ______ liver the previous day. (to eat)
37. She says that you ______ at 7 a.m. the next Sunday. (to get up - not)
38. If he had gone there, you ______ with him. (to go)

Duty

39. He ______ yesterday, but he didn't. (to come)
40. They ______ us every day next week. (to help)
41. If I arrived tomorrow, I ______ to the show. (to go)
42. We ______ our homework every day. (to do - present)
43. He ______ at 5 o'clock today, and he did. (to arrive)
44. Since I turned ten, I ______ my own hair. (to comb - always)
45. If they had not seen the injured man, they ______ him. (to help - not)
46. She told me that I ______ there the previous day. (to go)
47. He told the woman that she ______ the dishes the following day. (to wash)
48. If we come tomorrow, we ______ father to the shop. (to take)

Necessity

49. We already have everything. You ______ anything. (to bring - not)
50. Yes, really, there ______ anything. (to bring - not)
51. Did you say that it ______ anything? (to bring - not)
52. Yes, and you ______ early tomorrow. (to come - not)
53. That's good! I thought it ______ two hours earlier. (to come)
54. Well, even if we hadn't already bought everything, there ______ early. (to come - not)

Setze das richtige Modalverb ein. ("present")

55. (ability) He is 80 and ______ still ride a bicycle.
56. (no necessity) You ______ write me a letter; you can phone me.
57. (compulsion) We ______ go to the hospital for the operation.

58. (necessity) You ______ water the flowers.
59. (duty) She ______ give her father a present for Christmas.
60. (prohibition) They ______ put shoes into the dishwasher.
61. (permission) You ______ call me Bill.
62. (compulsion) I ______ give the burglar our gold.
63. (duty) They ______ buy a ticket on a bus.
64. (necessity) You ______ hang the wash up.
65. (prohibition) He ______ break the window with a stone.
66. (no necessity) You ______ tell me their phone number; I know it.
67. (compulsion) They ______ take the English test now.
68. (prohibition) We ______ shoot the bird.
69. (no necessity) They ______ bring cola; we have enough.
70. (possibility) You ______ see Tom tomorrow, but I'm not sure.
71. (necessity) She ______ do the washing up.
72. (duty) I ______ wash my hands before I eat.
73. (prohibition) You ______ put the cat in the microwave.
74. (necessity) I ______ do my homework now.
75. (compulsion) He ______ do what the thief tells him to.
76. (duty) We ______ help our poor neighbours.
77. (possibility) They ______ phone us tomorrow, but I'm not sure.
78. (no necessity) I ______ water the plants for it's raining.
79. (permission) She ______ sing a song if she wants to.

Setze die richtige Ersatzform des Modalverbes ein. (alle Zeitformen)

80. (no necessity) It ______ to water the flowers tomorrow.
81. (prohibition) I ______ talk during the test yesterday.
82. (duty) ______ say "thank you" for a present? (you - never)
83. (ability) ______ fly to America if they were invited? (they)
84. (compulsion) He ______ work hard next year.
85. (no necessity) There ______ write a letter if you had known your grandmother was coming.
86. (permission) ______ read that book up to now? (you)
87. (their duty) It ______ to cut the grass every week.
88. (no necessity) They ______ wash their car yesterday.
89. (compulsion) I ______ take a test next week.
90. (ability) ______ visit mother if we invited them? (they)
91. (necessity) I ______ sleep enough every night so that I'm not tired.
92. (duty) We ______ do our homework alone up to now.
93. (his duty) It ______ to go shopping every day.

94. (no necessity) We ______ go to the dentist's two weeks ago.
95. (ability) ______ pass the test if you worked hard? (you)
96. (compulsion) They ______ have a shot the day after tomorrow.
97. (duty) ______ wash their own hair? (they - ever)
98. (your duty) It ______ clean up your room every day.
99. (duty) I ______ iron my own clothes. (never)
100. (compulsion) You ______ go to the dentist's tomorrow.
101. (no necessity) There ______ have a "6" if you had worked hard.
102. (necessity) She ______ eat daily in order to live.
103. (prohibition) We ______ steal the apples yesterday.
104. (ability) ______ talk in German if we asked him? (he)

Welcher der Sätze zeigt folgendes an:

105. ability:
   a) He won't be able to go to school next week.
   b) She was allowed to read the newspaper.
   c) They could do their homework.
106. permission:
   a) He is forced to go shopping.
   b) The doctor said he would have to stay in bed.
   c) She may go to the park on Sunday.
107. compulsion:
   a) He had to leave school at 14.
   b) They were compelled to visit the headmaster.
   c) You ought to eat something.
108. possibility:
   a) You may arrive at 3 o'clock if the train isn't late.
   b) I can't ring you up if I haven't got your number.
   c) You might be able to speak to him tomorrow.
109. necessity:
   a) You don't have to run; the bus doesn't leave for half an hour.
   b) I'm not forcing you to come with me.
   c) You should tidy your room; it looks terrible.
110. obligation:
   a) I will be allowed to go swimming tomorrow.
   b) I am supposed to play with my little brother.
   c) I was expected to have written three sides.

111. prohibition:
   a) You can't go to the zoo.
   b) You aren't obliged to go swimming.
   c) He was not permitted to drink alcohol.

In welche Tabelle gehören die folgenden Sätze?

112. If I had seen the car, I might have written down the number.
113. It has always been my duty to clean the bathroom.
114. I often need to ask my father for money.
115. No one can force me to wear a skirt.
116. If it doesn't rain, my mother will allow me to go.
117. My little brother asked when he would be able to go to school.
118. Will I be expected to finish before 5 o'clock?
119. I must go home now because I have to cook the dinner.
120. Smoking is forbidden in German cinemas.
121. You might see the queen in London.
122. She must leave now because she has to be home soon.
123. If we had seen you, we might have spoken with you.
124. Will we be expected to write the letter before Wednesday?
125. I can't force them to go home.
126. Your mother will permit you to go if it doesn't rain.
127. We have to go to bed now because we have to get up early tomorrow.
128. She need not make the dinner.
129. If I had read the book, I could have told you the story.

Ändere die folgenden Sätze in die angegebene Zeitform um.

130. future: I can help you.
131. present perfect: We need not wash the curtains every week.
132. future: The baby must really go to bed.
133. future: Father said I may not go swimming tomorrow.
134. past: We shouldn't drink so much water.
135. future: We must be going now.
136. past: You ought to wash the dishes.
137. future: The children needn't be so quiet.
138. present perfect: Could he walk without help?
139. future: The plane must land soon.
140. past: You mustn't touch the pictures!
141. future: We can't see the sun at night.

142. present perfect: I must do my homework every day.
143. future: Couldn't you write your name?
144. past: You should go to bed.
145. Conditional 1: May Tom go with us?

Setze die richtige Form des Modalverbes bzw. seine Ersatzform in die Lücke ein.

146. My brother can walk now, but last year he still ______ (to walk).
147. We still aren't sure, but maybe we will go to France this summer; yes, we ______ . (to go - possibility)
148. Although he thinks that nobody can force him to do his homework, he ______ it. (to do - future)
149. We have enough sugar here; you ______ any more. (to buy - not)
150. We ______ speak perfect French when we were eight.
151. You ______ drive so fast. It's dangerous.
152. It ______ to be hard to find the dog; it barks continually.
153. The waitress said, "You can pay now if you want to, but you ______ ."
154. Usually they are forbidden to, but yesterday the boys ______ swim to the island.
155. Tomorrow there will be very many people at your house, so you probably ______ help your mother.
156. As there was no other room free, we ______ to sleep in the small room.
157. I don't know where Jane is; she ______ home already. (to go - possibility)
158. If Tom had come, I ______ there alone, but he didn't come; so I had to go there alone. (to go - not)
159. You really ______ do your homework, you know that is your duty.
160. He held a gun in my back and so I ______ do what he said.
161. You've already asked your father ten times if you may go; you know that you ______ tomorrow. (to go - not)
162. We have guests coming. If there isn't enough coffee there, we ______ buy some more.
163. If he doesn't want to do that, he ______ . (not)
164. We were afraid that there ______ wolves in the forest, but there weren't any. (to be)
165. You must go to school now; ______ to school when you are 35? (to go - you)
166. When Ursula arrived in England, she ______ a word. (to understand - hardly); now she can understand everything.
167. As it is very cold outside, I ______ a coat. (to wear)
168. Now I may go dancing, but when I was younger, I ______ dancing. (to go - not)
169. You're lucky. If you moved in, you ______ (to paint - not = brauchen); your brother already painted it for you.
170. If they had phoned me, I ______ them (to help = können); I had enough money to lend them; but they didn't phone; so I ______ them. (to help = können).

Ability, permission, prohibition or compulsion?

171. The children ask their parents if they ______ go swimming.
172. In a museum you ______ touch the pictures with your fingers.
173. The girl ______ (not) tell me the way to the shop when I asked her.
174. ______ you tell me what the thief looked like? No, I ______ but I hope you ______ catch him soon.
175. In England most pupils have no school on Saturdays, but when Mary was in Germany last year, she ______ go to school every Saturday.
176. The patient ______ take the medicine twice a day, but he ______ (not) stay in bed.
177. Peter ______ (not) run fast, but he is practising hard so that he ______ run faster next year.
178. In our last holidays I ______ go for a swim whenever I wanted to.
179. ______ I go to England? No, you ______ because you are too young. But next summer you ______ go there.
180. Must I run to get the train? No, you ______ ; you have much time.
181. You ______ steal the pictures from a museum.
182. I don't want to, but tomorrow I ______ take an English test.
183. The students ask their teacher if they ______ talk in class.
184. The doctor is telling the patient he ______ rest a lot.
185. You ______ (not) tell me where the dog was yesterday. ______ you tell me now?

Possibility or duty?

186. We ______ help blind people to cross the street.
187. I don't know where Tim is. He ______ be at Bill's house.
188. A pen-friend ______ write all the letters with care.
189. We aren't sure, but the baby ______ all the time we were gone. (to cry)

Übersetze!

Ability

190. Ich kann nicht schwimmen.
191. Als ich zwei Jahre alt war, konnte ich nicht schwimmen.
192. Mit 80 Jahren werde ich nicht schwimmen können.
193. Bis meine Oma starb, konnte ich jeden Sonntag zu ihr gehen.
194. Kannst du Klavier spielen?
195. Er kann seit 5 Jahren sprechen.
196. Sie konnte mit einem Jahr schon laufen.
197. Sie werden in 2 Stunden nach Hause fahren können.

Possibility

198. Es kann sein, dass ich um 17 Uhr nicht hier bin.
199. Es könnte sein, dass ich das Flugzeug nicht nehme.
200. Es kann sein, dass sie früher gegangen ist.
201. Sie hatten Angst, dass Wölfe im Wald sein könnten.
202. Es könnte sein, dass das nicht geschehen wäre, wenn sie hier gewesen wäre.
203. Es kann sein, dass du in der Küche warst.
204. Sie fürchteten, er ginge nicht.
205. Sie meinte, er könnte tot sein.
206. Es könnte regnen.

Permisssion - Prohibition

207. Darf ich gehen?
208. Du darfst in der Straßenbahn nicht rauchen.
209. Mit 10 Jahren durfte ich allein in eine andere Stadt gehen.
210. Du wirst heiraten dürfen, wenn du 18 bist.
211. Seit 1 Jahr habe ich um 22 Uhr ins Bett gehen dürfen.
212. Wenn er 18 wäre, dürfte er wählen.
213. Wir durften nicht zu laut sprechen.
214. Du hast mir nicht geholfen; deshalb darfst du kein Eis haben.
215. Kinder dürfen die Baustelle nicht betreten.
216. Die Passagiere durften das Flugzeug nicht verlassen.
217. Das Kleid darf nicht zu oft gewaschen werden.
218. Ihr dürft noch nicht nach Hause gehen.

Compulsion

219. Ich muss Einkäufe machen.
220. Du musst zum Arzt gehen.
221. Er musste zu Hause bleiben.
222. Er muss morgen nach München fliegen.
223. Hast du je Rasen essen müssen?
224. Du brauchst noch nicht zu gehen.
225. Doch, ich muss jetzt gehen.

Duty

226. Du sollst um 20 Uhr zu Hause sein.
227. Er soll nicht so laut sprechen.
228. Wenn sie 18 wird, muss sie ihren Geburtstag feiern.
229. Ich hätte das nicht tun sollen.
230. Ihr hättet uns helfen sollen.
231. Sie hätten gestern kommen sollen.
232. Ich soll eigentlich nicht hingehen.

Necessity

233. Er muss essen, um zu leben.
234. Du musst das nicht tun, wenn du nicht willst.
235. Ich brauchte gestern nicht mitzugehen.
236. Wir werden mit dem Bus nicht zu fahren brauchen, wenn wir ein Auto haben.
237. Sie muss zweimal im Jahr zum Zahnarzt.

Alle Tabellen

238. Es könnte sein, dass er morgen kommt.
239. Du darfst das Zimmer nicht verlassen.
240. Er sagte, er könne morgen kommen.
241. Wir brauchen nicht früh da zu sein.
242. Ihr sollt nicht so viel essen.
243. Durfte er gestern schwimmen gehen?
244. Du musst morgen früh aufstehen.
245. Wenn er jetzt käme, dürftest du dann mit mir gehen?
246. Wenn er hier gewesen wäre, hätte es sein können, dass er mit uns gegangen wäre.
247. Ich hätte dir helfen können, wenn du mir Bescheid gesagt hättest.
248. Wann hast du gestern ins Bett gehen müssen?
249. Ich hätte ihr helfen sollen.

250. Was kann ich schreiben?
251. Es wurde von ihr erwartet, dass sie hilft.
252. Wirst du das Buch lesen müssen?
253. Es ist uns verboten worden, hier zu rauchen.
254. Es wird nicht notwendig sein, das Auto zu verkaufen.
255. Es kann sein, dass wir morgen fahren.
256. Wir werden morgen kommen können.
257. Es könnte sein, dass er geschrieben hätte.
258. Würden sie uns morgen besuchen dürfen?
259. Es könnte sein, dass wir geholfen hätten.
260. Er wird nächstes Jahr lesen können.
261. Ihr hättet früher ins Bett gehen sollen.
262. Es kann sein, dass ich morgen krank bin.
263. Es könnte sein, dass ich gekommen wäre, wenn du mich gefragt hättest.
264. Als ich krank war, musste ich im Bett bleiben.
265. Der Arzt sagte, ich dürfe nach drei Tagen aufstehen, dann würde ich wieder normal essen können.
266. Kinder unter 18 Jahren dürfen keinen Alkohol trinken.
267. Ich kann dir im Moment nicht helfen, weil ich mein Zimmer aufräumen soll.
268. Er sagte, dass er nicht kommen konnte, weil er die Fenster putzen musste.
269. Er hätte die Fenster putzen müssen, aber stattdessen ging er schwimmen.
270. Müssen wir das machen, ist es wirklich notwendig?
271. Warum kannst du nächste Woche nicht kommen?
272. Ich darf nicht, weil ich dazu verpflichtet bin, mit meinem kleinen Bruder zu spielen.
273. Dürftest du kommen, wenn meine Schwester mit deinem Bruder spielte?
274. Hoffentlich wird sie bald nach Hause gehen können.
275. Letztes Jahr konnte sie noch nicht sprechen.
276. Es kann sein, dass wir morgen gehen können.
277. Es könnte sein, dass er hätte gehen dürfen.
278. Wir dürfen nicht dorthin gehen.
279. Er durfte gestern nach Hause gehen.
280. Dürfen wir das Kind sehen?
281. Er wird nächstes Jahr nach London reisen dürfen.
282. Weil keine Bahn kam, musste ich zu Fuß gehen.
283. Ihr werdet morgen früh zu Hause bleiben müssen, weil eure Mutter krank ist.
284. Sie hätten eigentlich gestern zu Hause sein sollen.
285. Er soll morgen eigentlich um 17 Uhr hier sein.
286. Da es regnet, muss ich einen Regenschirm tragen.

287. Der Mann mit dem gebrochenen Arm fragte: "Wann werde ich wieder schreiben können?"

288. Du solltest am Montag zum Zahnarzt gehen. Warum warst du nicht da?

289. In der Schule durften wir nicht auf dem Tisch sitzen.

290. Sie soll ihr Bett machen, aber sie braucht ihr Zimmer nicht aufzuräumen.

291. Wenn ich das Buch verloren hätte, wäre ich gezwungen gewesen, ein Neues zu kaufen.

292. Zu Hause darf ich nicht auf dem Bett herumspringen.

Suche die richtige Form des Modalverbes aus!

293. They ______ sing a song tomorrow.

a) will be supposed
b) ought
c) should be to
d) will be expected to

294. You ______ a letter, but you didn't.

a) should write
b) should have written
c) should be written
d) should have write

295. They ______ drive a car for 5 years now.

a) have permitted to
b) will be permit to
c) will have been permitted
d) have been permitted to

296. He isn't sure, but he thinks they ______ here yesterday.

a) may be
b) were
c) might have been

297. I ______ take this test for ten minutes up to now.

a) was forced to
b) have been forced to
c) am forced to
d) have forced to

298. If you turned the TV off, you ______ write a letter tonight.

a) will be able to
b) would have been able to
c) would be able to
d) would

299. You ______ work hard next year.

   a) will have to
   b) will
   c) would be
   d) had to

300. You ______ ten bars of chocolate, but you did.

   a) should eat
   b) should have eaten
   c) should not have eaten
   d) should not eat

301. I ______ swimming tomorrow.

   a) may go
   b) may be gone
   c) might have gone
   d) may will go

302. They ______ drive a car for two months by this time next year.

   a) will be allowed to
   b) have been allowed to
   c) can
   d) will have been allowed to

303. We ______ go to bed early tomorrow.

   a) will have to
   b) will
   c) would be
   d) had to

304. Du wirst morgen deine Hausaufgaben machen müssen.

   a) You will do your homework tomorrow.
   b) You are forced to do your homework tomorrow.
   c) You will have to do your homework tomorrow.
   d) You were compelled to do your homework tomorrow.

305. Werdet ihr morgen den Brief lesen dürfen?

   a) Would you be allowed to read the letter tomorrow?
   b) Were you been allowed to read the letter tomorrow?
   c) Will you been allowed to read the letter tomorrow?
   d) Will you be allowed to read the letter tomorrow?

306. Wir brauchen nicht laufen. - Das Auto ist da.

   a) We need not to walk. - The car is there.
   b) We aren't necessary to walk. - The car is there.
   c) We need not walk. - The car is there.
   d) There is any need to walk. - The car is there.

307. Wir müssen vier Klassenarbeiten schreiben.

   a) We have taken four tests.
   b) We must took four tests.
   c) We must take four tests.
   d) We must compelled to take four tests.

308. Nein, du musst jetzt nicht ins Bett; du kannst aufbleiben.

   a) No, you don't have to go to bed now; you can stay up.
   b) No, you need not to go to bed now; you can stay up.
   c) No, you must not go to bed now; you can stay up.
   d) No, you mustn't to go to bed now; you can stay up.

309. Werden wir morgen auf der Fahrt essen können?

   a) Should we eat on the trip tomorrow?
   b) Could we eat on the trip tomorrow?
   c) Will we eat on the trip tomorrow?
   d) Will we be able to eat on the trip tomorrow?

310. Es kann sein, dass sie gestern da waren.

   a) It may be, that they have been there yesterday.
   b) They may be there yesterday.
   c) They may have been there yesterday.
   d) They could have been there yesterday.

311. Darf ich morgen spät ins Bett gehen?

   a) Would I be allowed to go to bed late tomorrow?
   b) Was I supposed to go to bed late tomorrow?
   c) Will I be supposed to go to bed late tomorrow?
   d) Will I be allowed to go to bed late tomorrow?

312. Ihr werdet morgen gezwungen sein, das Auto zu Hause zu lassen.

   a) You will leave the car at home tomorrow.
   b) You are forced to leave the car at home tomorrow.
   c) You will have to leave the car at home tomorrow.
   d) You were compelled to leave the car at home tomorrow.

313. Haben die Leute gestern genug essen können?

   a) Have the people enough to eat yesterday?
   b) Have the people been able to eat enough yesterday?
   c) Did the people have enough to eat yesterday?
   d) Were the people able to eat enough yesterday?

314. Sie soll ihre Hausaufgaben machen.

   a) She would be expected to do her homework.
   b) She has to do her homework.
   c) She should be expected do her homework.
   d) She ought do her homework.

315. Ich hätte mit ihm sprechen sollen.

   a) I would have spoken with him.
   b) I should have spoken with him.
   c) I should speak with him.
   d) I should had speak with him.

316. Ihr werdet die Milch für uns kaufen müssen.

   a) You should be supposed to buy the milk for us.
   b) You have been expected to buy the milk for us.
   c) You'll have to buy the milk for us.
   d) You would be expected to buy the milk for us.

317. Wir müssen die Schweine jetzt füttern.

   a) We should feed the pigs now.
   b) We must compelled to feed the pigs now.
   c) We must feed the pigs now.
   d) We have feed the pigs now.

27 Gerund = das Gerundium

27.1 Grammatik

1. Ein "gerund" (verbal noun = -ing form of a verb used as a noun = substantiviertes Verb) kann wie folgt gebraucht werden:

   a) als **Subjekt** (subject)

   Hockey is fun. ***Swimming*** is fun.

   b) als **prädikative Ergänzung** zum Subjekt nach dem Verb "to be". Andere Bezeichnungen hierfür sind: Subjektergänzung, subject complement, predicate nominative, predicate complement.

   The woman was my mother. Her job was ***washing up***.

   c) als **Objekt** (object)

   She likes the Beatles. She likes ***swimming***.

   d) als **Substantiv nach Präpositionen** (noun after prepositions): without, by, etc.

   I always see him without a car.

   She always takes my dresses without ***asking***.

   Instead of **helping** he went out to play.

2. Nach dem "gerund" kann

   - ein **Objekt** folgen.

     Watching **birds** is fun.

   - ein **Adverb** folgen.

     She likes ***swimming*** **quickly**.

3. Ein "gerund" kann einen bestimmten Artikel (the) oder ein Adjektiv vor sich haben.

   She did most of **the *talking***.

   He received a warning for **bad *driving***.

4. Ein "gerund" wird oft nach den folgenden Verben gebraucht:

admit, adore, anticipate, appreciate, avoid, be busy, catch, cease, consider, cut out, defer, delay, deny, detest, discontinue, dislike, dread, enjoy, escape, excuse, fancy, favour, finish, forgive, how about, imagine, include, involve, justify, keep, loathe, mention, mind, miss, no good (It is no good), no use (It is no use), not much use, oppose, pardon, postpone, practise, prevent, propose, recall, recollect, recommend, regret, reject, remember, resent, resist, resume, risk, save, can't stand, stop, suggest, understand, value, what about, It is worth

5. Ein "gerund" wird gebraucht nach den folgenden Kombinationen:

accuse of, be accustomed to, adjust to, admit to, advantage of, be afraid of, agree on/to/with, alternative of,be amazed at, amount to, angry about/at, apologize for, approve of, be ashamed of, ask about, assist in, be astonished at, be bad at, begin by, believe in, benefit from, blame for, boast about, be busy, bother about, be capable of, care about/for, be certain of, chance of, choice between, be clever at, complain about/of, concentrate on, congratulate on, be conscious of, consist of, convince of, cope with, count on, be crazy about, be in danger of, a great deal of, decide against/on, delight in, be delighted about/at, depend on, devote to, die of, difference between, difficulty in, be disappointed about/at, disapprove of, dislike for/of, doubt about, dream about/of, be enthusiastic about, escape from, be excited about, excuse for, experience in, fail in, be famous for, for fear of, be fed up with, feel like, be fond of, forgive for, be frightened of, get around to, get sick of, get tired of, give up, be glad about, go on, be good at, be grateful for, grumble at, be guilty of, habit of, be happy about, hear about/of, hope of, impressed with, indulge in, insist on, intention of, take an interest in, be interested in, be keen on, keep from/on, know about, be late for/in, leave off, listen to, look forward to, means of, method of, necessary for, necessity for, need for, be nervous about, object to, objection to, occasion for, opportunity of, pay for, persist in, place for, be pleased about/at/with, have the pleasure of, take pleasure in, be on the point of, There's no point in, possibility of, prevent s.o. from, privilege of, problem about/in/of, profit by/from, be proud about/of, punish for, put off, quarrel about, reason for, refrain from, rely on, be right in, There's no risk of, be sad at, be satisfied with, see about, be serious about, be shocked at, be sick of, sorry for, speak of, specialize in, spend on, succeed in, be sure of, be surprised at, suspect of, take part in, talent for, talk about/of, taste for, tell about, thank for, think about/of, be tired of, trouble in, be used to, useful for, warn against, way of, be weary of, worry about

6. **perfect gerund**

Hier bezieht sich ein "gerund" auf eine vergangene Handlung.

It's no good, It's worth(while), It's no use, It's useless, What's the use of?

What's the use of ***saying*** you're sorry? The coffee is spilt and my dress is wet and dirty.

7. Ein "gerund" ersetzt ein "**adverbial clause**" nach den folgenden Präpositionen:

after, at, apart from, be against, be for, before, besides, by, for, from, in, in spite of, instead of, on, since, with, without

Before he did his homework, he went outside to play.

Before ***doing*** his homework, he went outside to play.

After he had done his homework, he went outside to play.
After ***having done*** his homework, he went outside to play.

8. **Entweder ein "gerund" oder ein "infinitive"** darf nach den folgenden Wörtern gebraucht werden:

advise, allow, attempt, begin, can't help, cease, continue, dislike, encourage, forbid, forget, go on, hate, intend, like, love, mean, neglect, opportunity, permit, prefer, propose, recommend, regret, require, remember, start, stop, try, used to

a) **like, dislike, hate, love, prefer**

- like + gerund = Etwas, das immer wahr ist.

  I like ***going*** dancing.

- would like + infinitive = Man denkt an einen bestimmten Zeitpunkt, einen Einzelfall.

  I would like **to go** dancing tonight.

b) **forget, remember**

- remember + gerund = Man denkt an etwas in der Vergangenheit

  Do you remember ***having*** ... as a teacher?

- remember + infinitive = Etwas in der Gegenwart oder Zukunft; oft ein Befehl oder Hinweis. Es kann aber auch eine Frage bezüglich der sehr nahen Vergangenheit sein.

  Please remember **to go** to the post office today.
  Did you remember **to go** to the post office this afternoon?

c) **stop**

- stop + gerund = Bloß eine Tätigkeit aufhören, ohne etwas anderes unbedingt anzufangen.

  He stopped ***reading*** when I came in.

- stop + infinitive = Etwas aufhören, um etwas anderes anzufangen.

  The driver stopped the car **to ask** for the way.

d) **regret**

- regretted + gerund = (active present) Es tat jemand leid, etwas getan zu haben.

  She regretted ***telling*** me her secret.

- regret(s) + gerund (active perfect) = Es tut jemand leid, etwas getan zu haben.

  She now regrets ***having told*** me her secret.

- regret(s) + infinitive = Es tut jemand leid, etwas sagen zu müssen.

  She regrets **to inform** you that she can't come.

e) **advise, allow, encourage, forbid, permit, recommend, require**

- Wenn kein Objekt vorhanden ist, kommt das "gerund".

  We allow ***smoking***.

- Wenn im Satz ein Objekt vorhanden ist (wem etwas erlaubt/geraten/verboten ist), kommt "to + infinitive".

  We allow him **to smoke**.

f) **attempt, intend** = Beide Formen dürfen gebraucht werden; der "infinitive" ist aber gebräuchlicher.

g) **begin, cease, continue, start** = Es ist egal, welche Form gebraucht wird.

h) **can't help**

- Wenn "can't help" die Bedeutung von "nicht umhin können" (ich kann nicht verhindern) hat, kommt das "gerund".

  It was so funny. I couldn't help ***laughing***.

- Wenn es die Bedeutung "nicht helfen" und dann auch ein Objekt hat, kommt "to + infinitive".

  I can't help him **to do** his homework.

i) **go on**

- gerund = Dieselbe Tätigkeit weiterhin tun; weiter machen.

  You can go on ***playing*** until I call you.

- infinitive = Eine andere Tätigkeit als nächstes tun.

  After the children had cleaned up their rooms, they went on **to help** their mother wash the dishes.

j) **means**

- gerund = Etwas muss getan werden.

  It's pouring outside. That means ***wearing*** raincoats again.

- infinitive = Beabsichtigen, etwas zu tun.

  We meant **to walk**, but as it was pouring, we couldn't.

k) **need**

- gerund = passive Form = benötigt

  My car needs ***washing***.

- infinitive = active Form = muss

  I need **to wash** my car.

l) **opportunity**

- to have the (an) opportunity of + gerund

  You will have the opportunity of ***seeing*** her alone.

- There will be (It will be) an opportunity to + inf.

  There will be an opportunity for you **to see** her alone.

m) **try**

- gerund = Ein Experiment machen; etwas ausprobieren.

  Try ***adding*** water to your drink.

- infinitive = Ein Versuch machen; sich bemühen (sich anstrengen), etwas zu tun.

  Try **to understand** what I am saying.

n) **used to**

- to be used to = Wenn eine Form von "to be" vor dem "used to" erscheint, hat es die Bedeutung "gewohnt" und wird nur als "gerund" ausgedrückt.

  I am used to ***taking*** the bus.

  Ich bin es gewohnt, mit dem Bus zu fahren.

  Don't worry; soon you will be used to ***working***.

  Mach dir keine Sorgen. Bald wirst du daran gewöhnt sein zu arbeiten.

- used to. Wenn das Verb ohne "to be" erscheint, bedeutet es "pflegte zu tun", "hat früher getan" und wird mit dem Infinitiv gebildet. Diese Form erscheint nur in der Vergangenheit.

  I used **to take** the bus; then I bought a car.

9. Wenn ein "**personal pronoun**" vor dem "gerund" steht, hat es die Besitzform (3. Tabelle):

my, your, his, her, its, our, your, their

He closed the door. I didn't mind **his *closing*** the door.

Father closed the door. I didn't mind **father's *closing*** the door.

Can't the children stop **their *fighting***?

10. **Übersicht**

	active	*passive*
present	taking driving	being taken being driven
perfect	having taken having driven	having been taken having been driven

active

present	Driving a car is fun.
perfect	Please forgive me for having driven so quickly.

passive

present	I like being driven to my school.
perfect	The old man mentioned his having been driven everywhere all of his life.

27.2 Übungen

Kommt das Gerundium oder der Infinitiv? Setze die richtige Form in den Satz.

1. I am looking forward to (to see) you.
2. I wish (to see) the manager.
3. It's no use (to wait).
4. He warned her (to touch - not) the wire.
5. Don't forget (to lock) the door before (to go) to bed.
6. My mother told me (to speak - not) to strange men.
7. At dinner she annoyed me by (to smoke).
8. Would you mind (to show) me how (to work) the lift?
9. After (to walk) for three hours, we stopped (to let) the others catch up.
10. The boys like (to play) games but hate (to do) lessons.
11. I couldn't help (to overhear) what you said.
12. She doesn't allow (to smoke) in her house.
13. He doesn't allow his family (to smoke) at all.
14. He surprised us all by (to go) away without (to say) "good-bye."

a) Kombiniere die Sätze mit der richtigen Form;

b) Ändere den Satz um, indem die richtige Gerundium-Form gebraucht wird.

15. He has improved his French; he learns a few hours every day. (by)
16. Alfred succeeded; he defeated the Danes. (in)
17. Father laughed heartily; he could not help it.
18. You must come at once; I insist on it.
19. He opened the window; I did not mind it.
20. Do not talk, Tommy, stop!
21. Father reads the newspaper after dinner; he is fond of doing so.
22. After he had returned from school, Tom did his homework.
23. The girl got an expensive stamp; she paid a great sum for it. (by)
24. Before we go to school, we say good-bye to Mother.
25. Nobody can be put into jail before he has been tried.
26. He left the room; he did not say a word. (without)
27. Charles got a prize; he had written the best exercise. (for)
28. After he had arrived in London, Tom at once visited the Tower.
29. To swim is healthy.
30. The Normans continued to speak French.
31. He finished (to speak) and sat down.
32. We are looking forward to (to read) your new book.
33. They don't allow (to smoke) in this theatre.

34. He is thinking of (to leave) his job and (to go) to America.
35. He was accused of (to steal) cars.
36. Do stop (to talk); I am trying (to finish) a letter.
37. The police accused him of (to set) fire to the house, but he denied (to have been) there.
38. I could not but laugh.
39. To travel by ship is more pleasant than to travel by train.
40. I have always liked (to learn) poems.
41. I prefer to walk.
42. Billy had won a prize; he was very proud of it.
43. I have written a letter; I have finished it.
44. You may go alone; I don't mind it.
45. You can do that; nobody will prevent you. (from)
46. He is not lazy; you can't accuse him of it.
47. After he had finished his work, he went home.
48. Tom frightened me; he banged the door behind him.
49. I shall come in time; you may depend on it.
50. I am in a great hurry; please excuse me.
51. To see is to believe.
52. I hate to listen to such talk.
53. Monika is a German; she is proud of it.
54. What is the (to mean) of this word?
55. To write books is hard work.
56. She remembers (to go) to school for the first time.
57. Did you remember (to lock) the car?
58. After (to spend) two days (to argue) about where to go for their holidays, they decided (to go - not) anywhere.
59. He said, "I'm terribly sorry for (to keep) you (to wait)."
60. The teacher began by (to tell) us where the island is.
61. Would you like (to come) to a lecture?
62. What about (to buy) two dresses?
63. When would you like (to start)?
64. Let's wait until it stops (to rain).
65. He succeeded in (to climb) out of the window.
66. Remember (to bring) your balls.
67. What about (to have) a picnic?
68. After (to spend) a week in the cottage, he decided that he didn't really enjoy (to live) in the country.
69. The town was captured without a shot (to be) fired.
70. You still have a lot (to learn) if you'll forgive my (to say) so.

71. Why do you keep on (to look) back?
72. Is he afraid of (to walk) home alone?
73. He had given an impolite answer. We regret it.
74. Do you remember (to hear) that story last year?
75. What about (to come) with us, Ann?
76. The story was so interesting that the girls stopped (to talk) (to listen) to it.
77. We go to the cinema often. We are interested in it.
78. They don't allow girls (to wear) trousers at school.
79. They don't allow girls (to wear) trousers to enter the church.
80. Did she remember (to phone) you yesterday?
81. We had phoned them yesterday. Do you understand it?
82. She watched TV before (to do) her homework.
83. You were on television. Could they imagine it?
84. They hurt you. Please forgive them. (for)
85. Linda, don't eat; stop!
86. Mr. Smith didn't permit (to talk) in his class.
87. I sewed my dress. I didn't use a machine. (without)
88. I went to school for one year. I could write my name. (after)
89. You'll get up at 5 a.m. Do you think you'll succeed in it?
90. They'll always prefer (to drink) milk to (to drink) rum.
91. I read his book. He didn't mind it.
92. Would they mind (to help) him to wash the car?
93. Does he want to clean his room? Does he feel like it?
94. To help you wash dishes is fun.
95. Would you mind (to tell) me what time it is?
96. They didn't allow their children (to watch) television.
97. Sally, don't run; stop!
98. She had taken English for four years. She could speak it well. (after)
99. To ride a boat on a sunny day is fun.
100. He was suspected of (to shoot) the man.
101. I'll always dislike (to write) letters.
102. They smoked cigarettes. I didn't mind it.
103. I read her letter before (to write) an answer.
104. Did you remember (to buy) shoes yesterday?
105. During their walk they stopped (to have) a cup of coffee.
106. They don't permit (to run) in the halls.
107. She went home. He regrets it.
108. I collect stamps. I am interested in it.

109. Do you remember (to climb) trees when you were a boy?
110. He had helped her. I understand it.
111. They will get a good mark. They will, of course, succeed in it.
112. Do you want to go to bed? Do you feel like it?
113. I drank oil. Can you imagine it?
114. He did his homework. He didn't ask his mother for help. (without)
115. They had left us so soon. I regret it.
116. Do you remember (to read) that book three years ago?
117. We slept for two hours. We woke up. (after)
118. He reads many books. He is interested in it.
119. Do they want to go for a picnic? Do they feel like it?
120. They washed their hands. They didn't use soap. (without)
121. Are you proud of (to be) a German?
122. We don't allow (to cheat) on our tests.
123. She ran away from home. We understand it.
124. Would he mind (to show) her where the cathedral is?
125. The TV programme was so exciting that the children stopped (to play) in the snow (to see) it.
126. I'll write a book. I'll succeed in it.
127. You sat on a camel. Could he imagine it?
128. I love to ride a pony.
129. She had seen him often before (to talk) to him.
130. I was late. Please forgive me. (for)
131. He always liked (to help) his mother and father.
132. We won't permit our boy (to smoke) at home.
133. Do they always remember (to go) to the dentist?
134. We talked loudly. They didn't mind it.
135. I watch birds. It is an interesting hobby.
136. He talks a lot. He does most of it.
137. She works in the office. She likes it.
138. Father was angry because we had stopped (to help) him.
139. Although he was busy, the man stopped (to help) us.
140. Because he thought he was too big for such work, the boy stopped (to help) his mother with her work.
141. I always like (to see) a good film.
142. Right now I'd prefer (to be) alone.
143. I dislike (to take) such tests.
144. He avoided (to meet) her as long as he could.
145. Although nobody was listening, he kept on (to talk).

146. Would you like (to go) for a walk?
147. I want you (to read) that book.
148. I remember (to see) the film in 1980.
149. My mother always expects me (to make) my bed.
150. If you don't stop (to make) that sound, I'll hit you.
151. I couldn't help (to feel) sorry for the injured boy.
152. I like (to play) records.
153. Will you please remember (to bring) me my book tomorrow?
154. You're not asleep now. Why can't you help me (to make) the coffee?
155. My brother's trying (to draw) a picture, but he's only two years old now.
156. If we stop (to buy) a book on the way, we won't get to school on time.
157. Don't try (to move) your arm. It might be broken.
158. When I asked her, she said she hadn't remembered (to phone) him in time.
159. I can't help (to sing) that tune. I like it so much.
160. He said he was too young to remember (to go) to America when he was a child.
161. I'm fond of (to draw) pictures and I'd like you (to draw) one, too.
162. I hope you enjoyed (to watch) the film.
163. Did you forget (to write) the letter?
164. After an hour the baby finally stopped (to cry).
165. When we saw a lady in distress, we stopped (to help) her.
166. She wants (to go) for a walk this afternoon.
167. He prefers (to eat) chocolate to liver.
168. Although they heard her, they kept on (to walk).
169. He avoided (to see) me this afternoon.
170. She would hate (to hurt) her brother.
171. We did not mind (to go) to the store.
172. After ten minutes he finished (to write) the letter.
173. Tom encouraged Susan (to read) the difficult book.
174. Please try (to tell) me why I can't go.
175. I'd like (to hear) that woman sing!
176. Don't forget (to write) your name on that page.
177. Stop (to talk) when your mouth is full.
178. Father hates (to be) late.
179. I couldn't help (to cry) when I saw the sad film.
180. Try (to talk) without yelling.
181. Child, do you now regret (to take) Susan's money?
182. Father used (to take) the bus before he had a car.
183. We advised him (to go) to a doctor.

184. I'm sure we'll forget (to leave) on time.
185. We were used (to go) to bed early when we were children.
186. We used (to go) to bed early when we were children.
187. The police required us (to tell) them where we live.
188. If you're so tired, try (to go) to bed earlier. Maybe then you won't be so tired.
189. We stopped (to help) the injured man.
190. I was used (to work) late when I was a teacher.
191. I advised (to write) a letter.
192. My sister likes (to take) pictures every day.
193. Father couldn't help me (to learn) the new English words.

28 Participles

28.1 Grammatik

1. **present participle** = -ing Form des Verbes (Präsenspartizip)

   Die Form kann sowohl in der aktiven als auch in der passiven Form gebraucht werden.

   Als **aktive Form** führen die Personen selbst eine Handlung aus. Die Form wird gebraucht:

   a) als "**object complement**" (Ergänzung zum direkten Objekt)
   - nach Verben der Sinneswahrnehmung (verbs of perception)
   feel (fühlen, spüren), find (feststellen), hear, notice, see, smell, watch

   Vergleiche:

   - Der Verlauf des Geschehens wird festgestellt und beobachtet.
     The teacher heard us ***talking*** in class.
   - Ein kurzer Punkt wird beschrieben. Eine bloße Tatsache wird festgestellt.
     The teacher heard Jane ***say*** something.

   - in Verbindung mit den Verben "catch", "find"

   catch/find + D.O. + participle
   If I catch ***him smoking***, he'll get a spanking.

   - nach den Verben "to have", "to get"

   He had ***me diving*** in no time.

   - nach Verben wie: to keep, leave (lassen), find

   Don't keep Tom ***waiting***.
   Did your father leave you ***sitting*** there?
   I found my baby ***crying*** when I came home.

   - nach Verben der Ruhe und Bewegung:

   to come, go, lie, remain, sit, stand, stay
   I stood ***waiting*** for his girlfriend to get ready.

b) Wenn das "present participle" ein **eigenes Subjekt** hat, wird es

- häufig durch die Präposition "**with**" eingeleitet.

  It was very loud with the baby ***crying***.

- von dem Hauptsatz mit einem ***Komma*** abgetrennt.

  The children left the house, each ***going*** in a different direction.

c) als **Adjektiv**

I like ***running*** water.

We'll see you in the ***coming*** days (in the days which are coming).

d) als **Verkürzung für einen Relativsatz**

- Das Verb ist eine -ing-Form.

  We saw the men who were carrying the chairs.

  We saw the men ***carrying*** the chairs.

- Das Verb bezeichnet eine Handlung, die gewohnheitsmäßig oder durchgehend ist. Das Verb zeigt etwas, das ständig der Fall ist.

  The road which leads along the field is narrow.

  The road ***leading*** along the field is narrow.

  People who drive cars should not drink.

  People ***driving*** cars should not drink.

- Das Verb äußert einen Wunsch.

  desire, hope, want, wish

  Linda, who hoped to get a good grade, studied hard.

  Linda, ***hoping*** to get a good grade, studied hard.

- Das Verb drückt Erwarten oder Denken aus:

  believe, expect, know, think

  Tom, who expected it to be a sunny day, suggested a picnic.

  Tom, ***expecting*** it to be a sunny day, suggested a picnic.

e) als **Verkürzung für adverbial clauses**.

Das Subjekt des Haupt- und des Nebensatzes muss gleich sein.

time before, when, after, until, till, while

Der "participle"-Teil des Satzes steht meist vor dem Hauptsatz. Wenn ein Objekt im Hauptsatz vorhanden ist, muss oft "when, while" vor dem "participle" stehen, um Missverständnisse zu vermeiden.

When we arrived at the seaside, we went to the water right away.

Arriving at the seaside, we went to the water right away.

The thief shot the policeman while he was trying to escape.

The thief shot the policeman trying to escape.

Wer wollte entkommen?

The thief shot the policeman while ***trying*** to escape.

reason Keine Konjunktion wird gebraucht.

Ebenfalls steht der "participle"-Teil des Satzes meist vor dem Hauptsatz.

Since the woman was tired, the woman went to bed.

Being tired, the woman went to bed.

concession though, although

Although he thought she was gone, he phoned.

Though thinking her to be gone, he phoned.

manner (Art und Weise). ohne Konjunktion

Im Deutschen werden die zwei Satzteile oft durch "und" verbunden. Der "participle"-Teil steht gewöhnlich hinter dem Hauptsatz.

Hans ran away and left his mother alone.

Hans ran away, ***leaving*** his mother alone.

f) um **einen Satz oder Hauptsatz zu ersetzen**.

- Zwei Handlungen werden gleichzeitig von demselben Subjekt ausgeführt.

  The girl drove away. The girl sang as she went.

  The girl drove away, ***singing*** as she went.

- Einer Handlung folgt sofort eine zweite Handlung. Das Subjekt der beiden Sätze bleibt gleich. Im Deutschen werden die zwei Sätze mit "und" verbunden. Die erste Handlung wird als "participle" ausgedrückt.

  The burglar broke the window. The burglar climbed into the house.

  Breaking the window, the burglar climbed into the house.

- Die zweite Handlung ist ein Teil oder ein Resultat der ersten Handlung. Die zweite Handlung wird als "participle" ausgedrückt.

  The girl stumbled. The girl hit her head on the table.

  The girl stumbled, ***hitting*** her head on the table.

Als **passive Form** wird das **“present participle passive”** gebildet durch die Verbindung von “to be” in Kombination mit dem Past Participle.

being + 3. Form

z.B. being taken

The exams now being taken will continue until Friday.
The question now being asked is whether ....

2. **past participle** = 3. Form des Verbes = Perfektpartizip = Partizip Perfekt

Die Form ist eine **passive Form**. Eine Handlung wird ausgeführt. Die Form wird gebraucht

a) als “**object complement**” (Objektergänzung)

Hier haben die Sätze eine passive Bedeutung.

- nach den Verben "to have, to get" (lassen, veranlassen)

I	***had***	**my house**	***repaired***.	
Subj.	Verb	Objekt	Perfektpartizip	**passiv**
Ich	ließ	mein Haus	reparieren.	

(Vergleich den Satz mit:)

I	***had repaired***	**my house**.		
Subj.	Verb	Objekt		**aktiv**
Ich	hatte	mein Haus	repariert.	

Der zweite Satz ist aktiv. Wenn man "to have, to get" + Objekt + 3. Form gebraucht, ist der Satz passiv. Jemand anders - nicht die Person, die als Subjekt genannt wird, - macht die Sache. Wenn man die Sätze genau vergleicht, sieht man, dass die Wörter identisch sind, bloß in einer anderen Wortstellung. Bei der aktiven Form tritt das Verb als Einheit (had repaired) auf. Das Objekt (my house) kommt nach dem Verb. Bei der passiven Form ist das Verb auseinandergerissen (had ... repaired). Das Objekt ist dazwischen (my house). An dieser Wortstellung erkennt man, dass die Bedeutung von "tun lassen" angebracht ist. (Ich ließ es machen.)

- nach Verben, die "wünschen" und "wollen" ausdrücken:

to want, to wish

He ***wants*** the letter ***written*** by tomorrow.

- nach Verben der Sinneswahrnehmung:

feel (fühlen, spüren), find (feststellen), hear, notice, observe, see, smell, watch

Linda ***heard*** her name ***called***.

- nach "to keep, to leave, to make"

Can father ***make*** himself ***understood*** with all the noise?

- nach "to catch, to find" + D.O.

I ***found*** her dress all ***torn*** into pieces.

b) Wenn das "past participle" ein **eigenes Subjekt** hat, wird es:

- häufig durch die Präposition "**with**" eingeleitet.
  Father and I sat **with** our hands ***folded***.

- von dem Hauptsatz mit einem **Komma** abgetrennt.
  We all sat there, our faces ***covered*** by our hands.

c) als **Adjectiv**

Das Verb eines Satzes wird zum Adjektiv.

I saw the car. It was stolen.

I saw the ***stolen*** car.

He has broken his leg. He has a ***broken*** leg.

d) als **Verkürzung für einen Relativesatz**

Hierbei stehen die eingeschobenen Wörter direkt hinter dem Substantiv, zu dem sie gehören.

The boy was taken to the doctor. The boy was injured on his head.

The boy ***injured*** on his head was taken to the doctor.

e) als **adverbiale Bestimmung**

- Bei **aktiver** Bedeutung wird der Satz mit "having + 3. Form" gebildet.
  I saw the film. I went home.
  Having ***seen*** the film, I went home.

- Bei **passiver** Bedeutung wird der Satz meistens ohne "being" bzw. "having been" gebildet.
  Having been given a choice, I'd prefer steak, please.
  Given a choice, I'd prefer steak, please.

  Seen from a distance, the dress doesn't look bad.
  I heard a song. It was sung by a man.
  I heard a song ***being sung*** by a man.
  I heard a song ***sung*** by a man.

time

While I was being driven in a car, I read a book.

While ***driven*** in a car, I read a book.

reason

As Tom had been driven to the city, he was home sooner than we expected.

Driven to the city, Tom was home sooner than we expected.

concession though, although

Although the fire was discovered immediately, it spread quickly.

Although ***discovered*** immediately, the fire spread quickly.

manner

Opened slowly and carefully, the door didn't hurt anyone.

condition if. Die Konjunktion ist erforderlich.

If I were asked, I would go along.

If ***asked***, I would go along.

3. **perfect participle**

   a) **perfect participle active** = having + 3. Form

   Diese aktive Form zeigt, dass eine Handlung vorbei war, bevor die nächste Handlung anfing.

   The men had done the work. The men went home.

   Having done the work, the men went home.

   - Diese Form ist nötig, wenn eine Unklarheit entstehen könnte, falls man bloß die "-ing"-Form (present participle = z.B. cleaning) gebrauchen würde.

     Cleaning the windows, I went shopping.

     (Ging man einkaufen, während man die Fenster putzte?)

     Having cleaned the windows, I went shopping.

     (Es ist eindeutig, dass man zuerst die Fenster fertig geputzt hatte. Dann ging man einkaufen.)

- Die Form ist notwendig, wenn eine Zeitspanne zwischen den zwei Handlungen existiert.

  Not ***having visited*** my niece for five years, I was surprised to see how tall she had grown.

- Die Form wird gebraucht, wenn die erste Handlung sich über eine lange Zeitspanne erstreckt.

  Having gone to school for 13 years, I was glad to be finished.

b) **perfect participle passive** = having been + 3. Form

Diese passive Form betont, dass eine Handlung vor einer anderen Handlung geschehen ist.

The children were warned not to go to bed too late.

The children went upstairs right after supper.

Having been warned not to go to bed too late, the children went upstairs right after supper.

The work had been done. The men went home.

The work ***having been done***, the men went home.

The work ***done***, the men went home.

4. Ein **Objekt** kann nach "participles" folgen.

Hearing the teacher's **voice**, we hurried to our seats.

After ***having eaten*** so many **chickens**, Max and Moritz were very full.

5. Ein **Adverb** kann nach "participles" folgen.

Riding the horse **quickly**, I arrived home before my sister.

Having learnt the words **poorly**, I forgot them rapidly.

Being thrown in the air **unexpectedly**, I screamed loudly.

6. **Übersicht**

	active	passive
present participle	taking eating	being taken being eaten
past participle	—	taken eaten
perfect participle	having taken having eaten	having been taken having been eaten

present participle

active **Taking** a bath, the child was happy.
I caught the child **eating** the cake.

passive I heard a bath **being taken** by the child.
He saw the cake **being eaten** by the child.

past participle

I want the bath **taken** by 8 p.m.
We didn't want the cake **eaten** before the party.

perfect participle

active **Having taken** a bath, the child went to bed.
Having eaten the cake, the child wasn't hungry.

passive The bath **having been taken** early,
we had a lot of time in the evening.
The cake **having been eaten**, we had no more food.

28.2 Übungen

Ändere die Sätze in Partizipkonstruktionen um.

1. The girls looked at the pictures which had been taken long ago.
2. The girl who was waiting for the bus was reading a book.
3. Since I knew that we had no school today, I stayed in bed.
4. He sat at his desk while he was writing a letter.
5. The boy snatched his coat and ran out the door.
6. We went through the door and found that we were surrounded by our friends.
7. The woman who was waiting at the bus stop was very nervous.
8. They found us outside where we were lying in the sunshine.
9. We bought pictures that were drawn by a famous artist.
10. I found that the girls acted very grown-up.
11. After Linda had finished her homework, Linda went to bed.
12. That's my brother who is riding a bicycle.
13. When my mother saw the spider, mother ran away.
14. As I knew that the children were cold, I gave them their coats.
15. If the little girl was asked her name and address, she couldn't tell it.

16. That's the cake that was baked by my mother.
17. They'll visit us in the year which is coming.
18. We like children who are swimming.
19. Because I didn't see the baby, I called everywhere.
20. The woman couldn't hear her husband because of her child which was screaming.
21. Though we paid for the lesson, we didn't go there.
22. We found the car which was stolen.
23. Since the girl saw that she wouldn't catch the bus, the girl stopped running.
24. The teenager yelled that she was late and ran to the bus.
25. The boy who was writing a letter didn't hear his mother.
26. We counted the toy cars that were given to us by our friends.
27. Because I felt lonely, I went to my friend's house.
28. The children did their homework while they listened to the radio.
29. The girl woke up and found that her mother was sleeping.
30. As they hoped to get more money from us, the children behaved very nicely.
31. The mother said good-night to the children and left their room.
32. After we had eaten our meal, we took a walk.
33. When I looked through the window, I saw the sad girl.
34. While the man took a shower, the man sang.
35. Though we wanted to go to bed early, we went to bed late.
36. When the cat saw the mouse, the cat chased it.
37. We searched and saw the cat where it was sitting in a tree.
38. If the medicine is taken at once, it will help you in minutes.
39. Because I wasn't told exactly how to get there, I got lost.
40. The woman saw the man who was riding on a horse.
41. The injured man found that the doctor was helping him.
42. We looked at the horse which was ridden by the blind child.
43. After our friends said good-bye, they drove away.
44. The man took his money and went to the shop.
45. When the man had closed the door, he locked it.
46. The children hunted and found the boy where he was hiding from them.
47. We tickled the baby who was held by its mother.
48. The taxi drove away and left the strange people at our house.
49. Since the child didn't feel good, the child stayed in bed.
50. After the work had been completed, the people drove home.
51. As we had gone to bed very late, we didn't want to get up early.
52. After the mother had bathed the baby, she put it to bed.
53. The player caught the ball and ran to the goal.

54. The people saw the tiny bird which was caught by the cat.
55. When it had rained, the air was cooler.
56. The men in the crashed airplane found that they were surrounded by friendly natives.
57. Though the mother expected her child to phone in the evening, she waited all day near the telephone.
58. The child took a pencil and drew a picture.
59. Because we thought it would rain, we didn't go swimming.
60. When the woman had taken her shower, she went to bed.
61. After the men had finished their job, they ate their lunch.
62. Since the man didn't want to be late, the man drove quickly.
63. If the cold milk is drunk too quickly, it will give you a stomach ache.
64. Until I came here, I didn't know how bad the situation was.
65. The baby climbed on a chair and started to play the organ.
66. The mother saw the dirt which was swept under the rug by her daughter.
67. After the girl had drunk her milk, she was happy.
68. As I thought the baby would be sleeping, I entered the room quietly.
69. The woman opened the door and looked outside.
70. The milk will turn sour unless it is drunk at once.
71. When the house had been painted, it looked pretty.
72. Though the girl started her homework early, she wasn't done until late at night.
73. After the cake had been baked, it was eaten quickly.
74. The children looked at the pictures which were taken long ago.
75. Since he didn't know where to turn, the driver asked the policeman for help.
76. Because the children had not worked hard for the test, they were afraid to take it.
77. The trees didn't move in the wind, as if they had been held back by a hand.
78. As the sky was so dark, we expected it to rain soon.
79. After the cat had caught the bird, the cat carried it home.
80. The man will die unless he is given the medicine right away.
81. When the rain was finished, we took a walk.
82. They were ungrateful till they had heard that others had lost everything.
83. Though the girl ate twice as much as anyone else, she didn't gain weight.
84. If the exercises are faithfully performed every day, they will help you to lose weight.
85. Since they didn't wish to be alone, the man and his wife went to visit friends.
86. The teacher corrected the homework which was written the previous night.
87. After the book had been read, it was returned to the library.
88. Because we couldn't see where we were going, we drove very slowly.
89. When they had thrown the ball, they ran to get it again.
90. We left the concert last night and each went his own way home.
91. Since I hoped to be invited to his home, I phoned my friend.

92. As the music was so loud, the people left the room.
93. The father held his child by its leg and swung it around.
94. If the baby is forced to eat, it will vomit.
95. The lady wore the dress which was sewn especially for her.
96. After the tree had been cut down, it was made into a table.
97. Because the woman couldn't buy anything cheap, she went home empty-handed.
98. Since we expected you to be home, we drove over without phoning first.
99. Though the garden was watered every day, it dried up very quickly.
100. I cried and hid my face in my hands.
101. When the children had understood the sentences, they were happy.
102. As I couldn't go to sleep, I went outside and took a walk.
103. Since he expected to be hit, the naughty boy ran away.
104. After the woman had slept for a long time, she felt better.
105. If the English words are practised every day, they will soon be learnt.
106. Because the visitors didn't want to impose, they didn't even ask for a glass of water.
107. Though the pupil had studied very hard, he failed the exam.

Verbinde die Sätze mit einem Partizip.

108. We heard her. She was talking to her husband.
109. I spent my time. I took care of the children.
110. The woman listened to the piano. It was being played by a famous man.
111. The people found the baby. It was sleeping quietly.
112. A dog came. It ran up to its master.
113. The man left me. I was standing at the door.
114. Tina ate her food. Then she left for school.
115. We cleaned up. We sang as we worked.
116. The father opened the door. He saw the mess.
117. The tourists had seen so many churches. They no longer wanted to enter another one.

Übersetze.

118. Meine Mutter hörte, wie ich mit dem Mann sprach.
119. Ich werde meine Haare nächste Woche schneiden lassen.
120. Der Mann ließ sein Auto laufen.
121. Kann der Junge sich verständlich machen?
122. Ich hörte, wie mein Name gerufen wurde.
123. Sie möchte, dass das Zimmer bis heute Abend aufgeräumt ist.
124. Ich fühle, wie die Ameisen meine Beine hochkrabbeln.
125. Der Mann ließ seine Schuhe reparieren.

126. Ich will, dass es sofort weggebracht wird.
127. Ich ließ meinen Zahn letzte Woche ziehen.
128. Wir werden unser Auto nächste Woche waschen lassen.
129. Da die Katze mit dem besten Fleisch gefüttert wurde, wollte sie die Reste vom Tisch nicht fressen.
130. Der Junge kam nach Hause, gefolgt von seinen Freunden.

Verbinde die Sätze mit Partizipkonstruktionen.

131. I eat breakfast. I go to school. (after)
132. I ate breakfast. I went to school. (after)
133. Father reads the newspaper. He eats his food. (while)
134. My brother brushes his teeth. He goes to bed. (before)
135. The people were looking out of the window. They saw a police car. (when)
136. I turned the radio on. I couldn't hear the music. (until)
137. The man thought his friends were gone. He phoned them anyway. (though)
138. We heard the music in the morning. We sang the song all day. (after)
139. The man sang in the bathroom. He washed his face. (while)
140. You leave the room. You say good-bye. (before)
141. The man drove away. He gave his children a present. (before)
142. The famous man was driven in a car. He looked out the window. (while)
143. You take the medicine every day. The medicine will help you. (if)
144. They had been given tickets. They didn't go to the show. (though)
145. The girls bought a CD. They listened to it.
146. She took her jeans off. She washed them.
147. The jeans had been taken off. The jeans were washed.
148. I felt sad. I cried.
149. I didn't know his telephone number. I couldn't phone him.
150. The woman was tired. She went to bed.
151. The car hit the man. The car was going too fast.
152. The car was driven too fast. It couldn't stop.
153. I saw the road. The road leads to Bonn.
154. I talked to a man. The man was wearing a coat.
155. The girl was driven home. She was home early.
156. The books are gone. They were stolen from the shops.
157. They saw the child. The child was eating cake.
158. We saw the dog. The dog was being fed.
159. The girl had done her homework. She watched TV.
160. The homework had been done quickly. The girl still had much time left.

29 The infinitive with and without "to"

29.1 Grammatik

1. Der Infinitiv mit "to" steht

   a) als **Subjekt**

   To go horse-back riding is exciting.

   Wenn ein besonderes Ereignis dadurch ausgedrückt werden soll, wird diese Form benutzt. Wenn aber etwas Allgemeines, sich immer Wiederholendes gemeint ist, kommt das "gerund".

   Going horse-back riding is exciting.

   b) als **direktes Objekt**.

   - **Nach den folgenden Verben** kommt nur der Infinitiv, ohne dass ein Substantiv oder Personalpronomen davorgesetzt wird. Manchmal kommt ein Substantiv nach dem Infinitiv.

     afford, agree, aim, appear, arrange, attempt, be bound, begin, care, chance, claim, come, consent, continue, dare, decide, demand, determine, endeavour, fail, forget, guarantee, happen, hesitate, hope, hurry, learn, manage, neglect, offer, plan, pretend, proceed, promise, propose, prove, refuse, remember, resolve, seem, swear, tend, threaten, trouble, try, undertake, volunteer, vow.

     She agreed ***to come***.

     I hope ***to see*** him.

     She dared ***to ride*** his horse.

   - **Nach den folgenden Verben** kann auch ein "gerund" folgen:

     begin, continue, forget, hate, intend, like, love, mean, prefer, propose, remember, try

     Would you please begin reading.

     Would you please begin ***to read***?

- **Nach den folgenden Verben** folgt manchmal nur der Infinitiv (gelegentlich mit einem Substantiv danach). In dem Fall will das Subjekt die Handlung selbst ausführen. Manchmal aber kommt zuerst das Objekt und dann der Infinitiv (gelegentlich mit einem Sustantiv danach). In dem Fall will das Subjekt die Handlung nicht selbst ausführen; das genannte Objekt führt die Handlung aus.

ask, beg, choose, desire, expect, hate, would hate, help, intend, would like (= enjoy), would love, long for, mean, prefer, prepare, promise, want, wish

I want ***to read*** a book.
I want ***to read*** **them** a book. — Ich lese vor.

I want **my children *to read*** a book.
I want **them *to read*** a book. — Sie lesen selbst.

c) als **Ergänzung zum direkten Objekt** (object complement)

- **Nach den folgenden Verben** des Befehlens, Bittens, Erwartens, Veranlassens, Wünschens und Zulassens. Das Subjekt des Satzes möchte oder erwartet etwas von dem Objekt. Was er will, möchte oder befiehlt wird hinter dem Objekt mit "to + infinitive" ausgedrückt.

advise, allow, bribe, cause, command, compel, enable, encourage, entitle, forbid, force, get, hire, implore, induce, instruct, invite, lead, let, oblige, order, permit, persuade, press, remind, request, require, send, shout at, show how, teach, teach how, tell (befehlen), tell how, tempt, trust, urge (zwingen), warn

The teacher reminded **the children *to do*** their homework.

Im Deutschen drückt man diesen Gedanken oft durch ein "dass" aus.

Ich möchte, dass du dein Zimmer aufräumst.

I would like **you *to clean*** up your room.

- **Nach den folgenden Verben** folgt ein Objekt. Dann kommt entweder das Verb "to be" oder "to have" als Infinitiv. Die Sätze können manchmal anders - ohne Infinitiv - ausgedrückt werden.

acknowledge, assume, believe, calculate, consider, declare, estimate, find, guess, know, maintain, reckon, see, suppose, take (= presume), think, understand

We consider **him *to be*** a good person.

He is considered to be a good person.

She found **him *to be sleeping***.

She found that he was sleeping.

d) **statt einer indirekten Frage**. Nach den Fragewörtern:

how, what, when, whether, where, which, who, whom, why

Der Infinitiv kommt in diesem Fall nach den folgenden Verben vor:

ask, decide, discover, find out, forget, know, learn, remember, see (= understand, perceive), show (+ object), teach, tell, think, understand, want to know, wonder.

The girl wondered **where *to go***.

e) **statt Relativsätzen**

Der Infinitiv wird häufig gebraucht nach

- **Zahlwörtern**

  the first, the second, the third, ... the last, the only

  He was the last person who finished the race.
  He was **the last *to finish*** the race.

- **der dritten Steigerungsform der Adjektiv**
  (superlative)

  the best, the slowest, the fastest, etc.

  We were the slowest of all the people who came home.
  We were **the slowest *to come*** home.

f) als **Teil einer Adjektivgruppe**

- **Adjektive, die Freude, Unmut oder Überraschung** zeigen. Adjektive, die nach dem Verb "to be" oder eines Verbes wie "appear, become, seem" kommen, können durch einen Infinitiv erweitert werden. Einige solche Adjektive sind:

  amazed, angry, anxious, ashamed, astonished, delighted, disappointed, disgusted, glad, great, happy, horrified, interesting, lucky, overjoyed, pleased, proud, relieved to, sad, shocked, sorry, surprised, upset

  I would be **happy *to take*** your car.

- **Nach "It is/was + adjective"**
  z.B. bei den Adjektiven:

  awkward, dangerous, difficult, dreadful, easy, hard, impossible, lovely, nice, possible, stupid

  It is lovely *to see* you again.

  It is lovely for me ***to see*** you again.

- **Nach noun/pronoun + to be + adjective + infinitive**

  Adjektive: siehe die gerade erwähnten Adjektive und noch weitere Adjektive:

  able, anxious, apt, bound, due, inclined, liable, prepared, ready, reluctant, unwilling, willing

  The **dog is impossible** ***to teach*** anything.

  Are you ready ***to go***? **I am ready** ***to go***.

- **Nach "too; enough"**

  - **too + adjective + infinitive**

    We were **too sad** ***to talk***.
  - **too + adjective + a + noun + infinitive**

    That was **too heavy a tree** ***to move***.
  - **too + adverb +infinitive**

    You walk **too quickly** ***to follow***.
  - **adjective/adverb + enough + infinitive**

    The boy was **big enough** ***to write*** his name.

    The dog barked **loudly enough** ***to be heard*** for miles.

- **Nach "It + to be + adjective + of + noun/pronoun + infinitive**
  "It/that + to be + a/an + adjective + noun + infinitive"
  "What + a/an + adjective + noun + infinitive"

  Die folgenden Adjektive werden oft so gebraucht:

  amazing, astonishing, bad, brave, careless, clever, cowardly, crazy, funny (= odd), generous, good, honest, kind, mad, nice, odd, pointless, queer, ridiculous, rude, selfish, silly, strange, stupid, wicked, wise

  It was wise of him ***to go*** home that early.

  That was a funny way ***to talk***.

  What an odd man ***to talk*** to!

g) in **speziellen Fällen mit "for"**

- **Nach "for + noun/pronoun + infinitive"**

  The best way **for me *to learn*** this is to do the sentences.

- **Nach folgenden Redewendungen am Anfang des Satzes**:

  It's better for s.o. to

  It's best for s.o. to

  It's more difficult for s.o. to

  It's most important for s.o. to

  It's more difficult for him *to learn* the words than for her.

- **Nach Verben, die mit "for" verbunden werden**.

  verb + for + object + infinitive

  Im Deutschen werden diese Sätze entweder mit einem Substantiv statt Verb oder mit "dass" ausgedrückt.

  ask for, look for, wait for

  We are **waiting for** my sister ***to arrive***.

  Wir warten auf die Ankunft meiner Schwester.

  Wir warten darauf, dass meine Schwester kommt.

- **Nach Adjektiven oder Adverbien, die mit "enough" oder "too" verbunden sind**.

  enough + for + noun/pronoun + infinitive

  too + adjective + for + noun/pronoun + infinitive

  Did she have **enough** food **for** you ***to eat***?

  The sun is so bright that I can't look at it.

  The sun is **too bright for** me ***to look*** at.

- **Nach Substantiven am Anfang des Satzes, die mit "for" verbunden sind**:

  Here is/are, It is, There is/are, This is

  There are some biscuits **for** you ***to eat***.

  It is not necessary **for** him ***to phone*** us.

h) **Nach Substantiven oder Pronomen**

- um zu **zeigen, wie sie gebraucht** werden können.

  We have many **books *to read***.

  Oft sind die Verben mit einer Präposition verbunden.

  drink out of, keep in, open with, talk about/to, write on/with

  Here is **the man *to talk*** to.

- nach einer Reihe von Substantiven oder Verben + Substantiven, um **Ursache, Folge oder Möglichkeit auszudrücken**, wie z.B.:

  Will we **have** enough **time *to see*** our friends?
  It is my **responsibility *to teach*** you English.
  You **have no right *to punish*** your sister.

to have the ability to
    You have the ability to learn a great deal.
to take action to
    You should take immediate action to catch the thieves.
to follow/take s.o. advice to
    I took his advice to write a letter.
of age to/to have the right age to
    She is of age to vote.
It is/was s.o. aim to
    It was my aim to become a doctor.
to have an/no/the ambition to
    He has no ambition to better himself.
to make an/no attempt to
    The doctors made an attempt to save his life.
to have the/to give s.o. the/It is in my authority to
    The police have the authority to put you in prison.
    The man gave me the authority to sign for him.
    It is in my authority to punish you.
to have the brains to
    You have the brains to learn this quickly.
to have a burden to
    Everyone has a burden to carry.
capacity to
    The hall had the capacity to seat 200 people.

cause to

You have no cause to worry.

to have/want/ a/no/the chance to

I had the chance to learn Russian.

to have the charm to

She has the charm to make everyone do what she wants.

to give s.o. the/to have the choice to

We gave them the choice to fight or to run away.

to have no/the courage to

Does he have the courage to fight like a man?

to have a craving to

I have a craving to eat chocolate.

day to

This is the day to take the test.

(a great) deal to

We have a great deal to talk about.

to have the decency to

Would you have the decency to close the door while I am dressing?

to make the decision to

Father made the decision to take a new job.

to have a/no/the desire to

I have no desire to meet her again.

to have the determination to

She had the determination to help the poor people.

distance to

It's a long distance to travel with children.

It is/was s.o. dream to

It was her dream to see India.

It is/was s.o. duty to

It's my duty to teach you this.

to make an/no effort to

He made no effort to do his homework nicely.

to give s.o. the encouragement to

We must give her the encouragement to pass her test.

experience to

She had no experience to fall back on.

experiment to

The pupil made an experiment to see if he could solve the problem.

freedom to

Do you have the freedom to do what you want?

It is/was fun to

It was fun to play with the children.

to have the heart to

Did you have the heart to tell him?

It is/was the hour to

It was the hour for the thieves to steal the people's money.

to feel the/to have the inclination to

I have the inclination to lose my temper.

to have/be the/no inducement to

His helping her was still no inducement to work for the test.

instinct to

A cat has the instinct to catch mice.

to have/to give s.o. the instructions to

I was given the instructions to start cooking at 12.

to have the intelligence to

You have the intelligence to go to the university.

It is/was s.o. intention to

It was my intention to phone you.

It is/was in s.o. interest to

It was in his best interest to get a new job.

invitation to

She extended an invitation to visit them.

to have the kindness to

Would you have the kindness to help me?

to beg/get/have/take leave to

May I have leave to go home now?

He got leave to visit his wife in hospital.

She begged leave to visit her sick mother.

to be at/ have/take the liberty to

I hope you don't mind my taking the liberty to phone you.

just a few lines to

Here are just a few lines to thank you.

to find/have the/ It is within s.o. means to

I don't have the means to buy each child a present.

She found the means to get there then.

It is within our means to buy this house.

to have a mind to/to make up one's mind to

I have a mind to tell him what I think.

I made up my mind to go soon.

There is no need to/There isn't any need to

There is no need to get up so early.

to have an/the obligation to

We have the obligation to inform her.

occasion to

This is not the right occasion to talk about that.

to have the/no opportunity to

I had no opportunity to see her.

to give/have permission to

We gave her permission to stay up late.

perseverance to

She had the perseverance to learn the difficult language.

to form the plan/to make plans to

We made plans to visit her.

to be in a/no position to

I am in no position to scold her.

to have no possibility to

I had no possibility to visit her.

privacy to

Do you have the privacy to meditate?

It is/was s.o. privilege to

It's father's privilege to get up late.

question to

Do you have a question to ask him?

to have a race to

The children had a race to see who was the fastest.

to have a/no/ to see a/no/

There is a/no reason to

I have no reason to feel sad.

She can see no good reason to call him.

There is no reason to get up early tomorrow.

It is/was s.o. responsibility to

It was father's responsibility to earn money.

to have no/the right to

We have the right to say what we want to.

There is/was/will be a scramble to

There will be a scramble to get the best seats.

This is the season to

This is the season to buy strawberries.

It is/was a shock to

It was a shock to hear that your child is in hospital.

a sight to

That was a sight to soothe my eyes.

to have the/no strength to

We in ourselves have no strength to handle such hard problems.

to need s.o.'s support to

We need God's support to have such strength.

to make/take a survey to

The city officials are making a survey to find out what we think.

to have the technology to

The Western countries have the technology to overcome disease.

to make a test to

We made a test to see if your idea was correct.

It is/was a thrill to

It was a thrill to hear her play the piano so well.

to have/make/take/ It is/was time to

We have time to visit you on Monday.

I'll make the time to come and see you.

It is time to go home now.

to know/play a trick to

She knew a trick to make the people laugh.

to take the trouble to

Would you take the trouble to listen to us?

to take it in s.o. turn to/ It is/was s.o. turn to

He took it in his turn to wash the dishes.

It was my turn to clean up.

to have an/the urge to

I have the urge to phone my mother.

to make a wager to

They made a wager to see who could run the fastest.

That is the/no way to/ It’s a long way to/s.o. has a long way to

That is no way to to treat your mother.

It’s a long way to walk.

Tom has a long way to go before he gets home.

to have the willpower to

She had the willpower to study hard.

to have no/the wish to

I had no wish to fight with him.

years

He has enough to do for years to come.

i) **bei der Passivform**

Die Passivform wird immer mit "to" gebildet.

We saw the man cross the street. (Aktiv - ohne to)

The man was seen ***to cross*** the street. (Passiv - mit to)

j) Nach den folgenden Verben oft in der -ing-Form:

appear, happen, hope, manage, plan, pretend, seem

The girl **pretended *to be sleeping*** when we entered her room.

2. **Die Zeiten in dem Infinitiv**

a) **Present Infinitive**

Die Handlung geschieht zur gleichen Zeit wie die Handlung im Hauptverb.

I **planned *to write*** the letter **while** we **were** on vacation.

b) **Perfect Infinitive**

Die Handlung geschah vor der Handlung, die mit dem Hauptverb ausgedrückt wird.

I **planned *to have written*** the letter **before** we **left** home.

3. **Übersicht**

	active	passive
present	to take	to be taken
perfect	to have taken	to have been taken

active	
present	I want to write the letter while you are here.
perfect	I wanted to have written the letter before you came.
passive	
present	The letter is to be written today.
perfect	The letter was to have been written yesterday.

4. Beide Formen (mit und ohne "to") sind geläufig bei dem Verb "help".

   She **helped** me ***to carry*** the table.

   She **helped** me ***carry*** the table.

5. **Der Infinitiv ohne "to"** als

   Ergänzung zum direkten Objekt.

   Ein Infinitiv ohne "to" steht

   a) **Nach Verben der Sinneswahrnehmung**.

   Der Infinitiv nach den "direct object" hat kein "to".

   feel, hear, listen to, look at, notice, observe, overhear, see, watch

   - **Verb + object + infinitive**

     We saw her ***go*** into the water.

     Wenn man den Infinitiv (ohne "to") gebraucht, zeigt es, dass man den ganzen Vorgang gemerkt und verfolgt hat. Das gesamte Ergebnis steht fest. Ein Ergebnis ist oft dabei. Der Ablauf ist oft kurz.

   - **Verb + object + present participle**

     We saw her ***going*** into the water.

     Wenn man das Präsenspartizip gebraucht, zeigt es, dass man einen Teil der Handlung gesehen oder wahrgenommen hat. Man bemerkte die Handlung, die gerade geschah. Ob die Handlung beendet ist, wird nicht gesagt. Die Handlung kann ein längerer Vorgang sein, ohne Ergebnis bleiben oder zur gleichen Zeit mit anderen Vorgängen geschehen.

b) **Nach den folgenden Verben**.

Der Infinitiv nach dem "direct object" hat kein "to".

bid, have, let (zulassen), make (veranlassen)

When we saw how tired she was, we **made** her ***go*** to bed at once.
We **let** her ***use*** our car.
She was **let** ***go***.

c) **Nach den folgenden Ausdrücken**:

cannot but, had better, rather than, sooner than, would rather, would sooner

You **had better** ***wash*** your hands before you eat.
Rather than ***see*** you waste your money, I'll spend it for you.

d) **Nach den folgenden Hilfsverben**:

can, could, dare, do, does, may, might, must, need, shall, should, will, would

I **dared** not ***talk*** too loudly.

29.2 Übungen

Setze die richtige Form (mit oder ohne "to") in den Satz ein.

1. We saw her (to go) into the shop.
2. I asked him (to help) me.
3. Did you remember (to tell) her the story?
4. We will expect you (to be) home on time.
5. He plans (to leave) on vacation soon.
6. She listened to them (to tell) us how to drive.
7. The captain commanded the beggar (to get) off his boat.
8. He invited us (to go) home with him.
9. How did you manage (to get) the children ready so soon?
10. I don't like (to wear) that dress.
11. You dare not (to go) near the water.
12. She agreed (to let) me go.
13. We happened (to be) passing through.
14. I ordered them (to return) at four.
15. He made me (to jump) over the chair.
16. I hope (to see) them soon.
17. The baby appears (to want) you near him.
18. Has he ever offered (to help) you?

19. We could not (to come) yesterday.
20. Did he hesitate (to open) the door?
21. I aim (to leave) soon.
22. We urged them (to walk) quickly.
23. I let her (to wear) my coat.
24. She showed me how (to bake) that cake.
25. I failed (to pass) the test.
26. You need not (to go) so early.
27. We helped them (to load) the car.
28. He swore (to stop) smoking.
29. They forbad him (to tell) me the answer.
30. I'd advise you (to go) to bed.
31. He continued (to read) his book.
32. They bid me (to leave) the shop.
33. Do you promise not (to tell) anybody?
34. He neglected (to do) his homework.
35. I can't afford (to take) you along.
36. We heard the clock (to strike) noon.
37. This will entitle you (to enter) without paying.
38. The dog caused me (to be) late.
39. Who permitted them (to come) in?
40. She'll let you (to use) her books.
41. It threatened (to rain) at any moment.
42. Children only learned (to read) and (to write) earlier.
43. The teacher encouraged the boy (to go on) reading.
44. We noticed the thief (to take) a watch.
45. He really tried (to remind) me.
46. I've begun (to understand) English now.
47. He'll tell me how (to open) the camera.
48. They made me (to work) until dark.
49. Did you persuade the old man (to go) to the doctor?
50. I'd love (to go) along!
51. We implored him (to stop) smoking.
52. It proved (to be) too much for us.
53. I reminded him (to go) to the post office.
54. He need not (to write) his name in his books.
55. Would you care (to see) Bonn today?
56. We want (to help) you.

57. I refuse (to do) the washing up.
58. He demanded (to know) what was happening.
59. Did the man wish (to come) today?
60. We'll make her (to go) to the doctor this afternoon.
61. He made her (to eat) that food.
62. They hurried (to catch) the bus.
63. I have resolved (to write) my mother once a week.
64. We felt the wind (to blow) our hair.
65. The boy proceeded (to do) what he wanted.
66. The plan will seem (to be) absurd to you.
67. I dare not (to tell) my father.
68. Did Dick forget (to come) yesterday?
69. Did you see Tom (to put) on his coat?
70. When did you decide (to go) on vacation?
71. She had better (to come) home quickly.
72. He'd tempt them (to swim) far out.
73. We'll have to force them (to open) the door.
74. I intend (to marry) Betty.
75. We have tended (to be) rather easy on you.
76. Rather than (to drink) beer, we drank nothing.
77. Has she volunteered (to work) in the hospital?
78. Did your father teach you how (to write) your name?
79. He shouted at me (to hurry) up.
80. I was always warned (to wear) my boots when it rained.
81. Have they always trusted you (to be) on time?
82. The teacher shouted at the children (to be) quiet.
83. I would rather (to eat) outside, if you please.
84. The money will enable you (to get) home.
85. My cold compelled me (to stay) in bed.
86. I don't think you'll get her (to come).
87. You had better (to pay) attention.
88. The little girl's parents instructed her not (to drink) any alcohol.
89. The little boy endeavoured (to swim) across the lake.
90. Did the woman consent (to marry) you?
91. She would sooner (to do) it herself than let me (to do) it.
92. I was determined (to pass) the difficult test.

Ändere die Sätze in "infinitive with to" Sätze um.

93. I showed him how he should write his name.
94. The teachers decided where they could have their picnic.
95. We were pleased when we heard that you were coming.
96. I bet she'd be surprised if she got a letter!
97. How often have we told you that you shouldn't say that word?
98. Did he understand how he could get to Bonn?
99. Did they tell you when you should come?
100. We didn't remember whether we should come today or tomorrow.
101. We had hoped that we could have left early.
102. Did the children know where they could buy pancakes?
103. Has he remembered what he should ask them?
104. We forgot which road we had to take.
105. Has the new mother found out when she has to bathe the baby?
106. Did the boy forget how he had to unlock the door?
107. Has the girl understood why it is important that she should brush her teeth?
108. Did you decide whom you should tell the story?
109. We were sorry when we heard that you had been ill.
110. I'd be glad if I could shake his hand.
111. Has the man discovered what he should take home?
112. Did they ask where they should meet us?
113. Do the children know which man they could ask for help if they are lost?
114. I would be delighted if I could go with you!
115. He was surprised when he saw his son driving a car.
116. They must have decided whether they should eat now or later.
117. I found out whom I could ask for money.
118. Did you ask if you could take John with you?
119. How did you know whether you could speak or should stay silent?
120. We would be delighted if we might visit them.
121. Did your teacher tell you which words you had to learn?
122. I wonder when I could phone her.
123. They showed us whom we should help.
124. She didn't know where she could turn for help.
125. Has the man thought of what he could give his wife for her birthday?
126. The last person who is outside is a donkey.
127. She supposed that he was sleeping.
128. We found that it was very difficult to do.
129. The only person who finished the race was a big boy.

130. Did you estimate that it would cost too much?
131. We considered that matter was finished.

Übersetze.

132. Es war schwierig für mich, einen Brief auf deutsch zu schreiben.
133. Bist du vorbereitet, die Prüfung zu machen?
134. Ich erwarte, dass er lieb ist.
135. Die Leute würden es hassen, wenn du spät wärst.
136. Versprichst du mir, dass du mir morgen hilfst?
137. Er wäre froh, dein Bild zu haben.
138. Wir möchten, dass du bald wieder kommst.
139. Du brauchst morgen nicht dorthin zu gehen.
140. Ich möchte, dass mein Sohn Arzt wird.
141. Der Mann bat mich darum, ihm zu helfen.
142. Ich würde gern mit dir gehen.
143. Würdest du es vorziehen, Wein zu trinken?
144. Die Frau fragte, ob sie mit dir sprechen könnte.
145. Er sucht nach einer Möglichkeit, dorthin zu kommen.
146. Es scheint, als ob du so schnell erwachsen wirst!
147. Ich flehe dich an, mir zu helfen.
148. Wärest du überrascht, wenn du sie hier treffen würdest?
149. Wir warten, bis der Regen aufhört.
150. Er hat es vorgezogen mitzugehen.

30 Adverbial clauses

30.1 Grammatik

Hiermit werden zwei Sätze miteinander verbunden. Der Nebensatz (subclause), der mit einer Konjunktion anfängt, liefert dem Hauptsatz (main clause) zusätzliche Information. Diese Informationen können folgender Art sein:

1. **Folge** (result)

   Der Nebensatz erzählt das Resultat des Hauptsatzes.

so ... that

   Nach "so" kommt ein Adjektiv oder Adverb. Kein Substantiv darf auftreten. Manchmal erscheint "much", "many" oder "few".

   I was **so** good at spelling **that** I won a prize.

   The children had **so many** toys **that** they didn't know what to play with.

   The girl always talked **so** quietly **that** nobody could hear her.

such (a) ... that

   Nach "such (a)" kommt ein Adjektiv + Substantiv.

   She had **such a** bad cold **that** she had to stay in bed.

   It was **such** cold weather **that** we had to wear coats.

2. **Zweck** (purpose)

   Der Nebensatz erklärt den Zweck oder Absicht der Handlung, die im Hauptsatz beschrieben wird.

so that + will/can/should + inf.	(present, future, present perfect)
so that + would/could + inf.	(past)

   You have to take an umbrella **so that** you won't get wet.

   The boy got up early **so that** he could get to school on time.

3. **Zugeständnis, Einräumung** (concession)

Ein Gegensatz wird zwischen dem Haupt- und dem Nebensatz ausgedrückt. Der Hauptgedanke ist im Hauptsatz.

although though

Although I was ill, I went to work.

4. **Ursache** (reason)

Der Grund der Handlung, die im Hauptsatz beschrieben wird, wird bekanntgegeben.

as because since

The boy went to bed **because** he was tired.

5. **Zeit** (time)

Das zeitliche Verhältnis zwischen dem Hauptsatz (= HS) und dem Nebensatz (= NS) wird beschrieben. Mehr Information über den Hauptsatz wird gegeben. Die folgenden Zeitkombinationen sind häufig:

after	past perf.(NS)-past (HS)
as soon as	past-past; pres-pres.; pres.(NS)-fut.(HS)
before	past(NS)-past perf(HS)
since	past(NS)-pres. perf.(ing)(HS) past(NS)-pres.perf.(HS)
until/till	past-past; past(NS)-past perf(HS) fut.(HS)-pres.(NS)
when	pres.-pres; past-past; past perf (NS)- past(HS
whenever	pres.-pres.; past-past
while	past (HS)-past(ing)(NS); pres(HS)- pres(ing)(NS) past(ing)-past(ing); pres(ing)-pres(ing) past-past

After the burglar had taken many things, he left the house.

6. **Bedingung** (conditional clauses = if-clauses)

Siehe Kapital über Bedingungssätze.

if

If I go to bed now, I won't be tired tomorrow.

7. **Ort** (place)

where wherever

I'll go **wherever** you go.

30.2 Übungen

Kombiniere die Sätze, indem du das richtige Verbindungswort aussuchst und gebrauchst. Die Zeit in den Satzteilen darf nicht umgeändert werden. Die Satzteile dürfen nicht umgetauscht werden.

purpose, time, concession, condition

1. Carl turned the radio off. We couldn't hear music.
2. Carl had turned the radio off. We couldn't hear music.
3. Tom had eaten ten pieces of cake. His stomach hurt.
4. Father was very busy. He helped us anyway.
5. We'll save our money. We can buy new records.
6. I had gone to school earlier. I would have seen Jim.
7. They were going to help mother. She would be finished more quickly.
8. Dan was not nice. He was bad.
9. We'll wait at the corner. You come.
10. The baby climbed onto a chair. It could get the chocolate.
11. The baby had climbed onto the chair. It could get the chocolate.
12. The tree died. We had watered the tree.
13. We should go to bed now. We can get up early tomorrow.
14. She had 20 Euro. She would buy a new blouse.
15. You bought paper. You can write letters.

reason, time, concession, condition

16. Mother bought a dishwasher. We needn't wash the dishes.
17. Daniel moved to Bonn. He has met many boys.
18. The food smelled bad. The women ate the food.
19. It was raining. We stayed home.
20. We were very tired. We went to bed.
21. He went to school. He would get a good job.
22. Susan ran to the bus stop. She couldn't see the bus.
23. Susan got a "2". She received 2 Euro.
24. Mother was cooking. Father was reading the newspaper.
25. Harry wanted to write letters. He bought paper.

26. Linda liked the colour red. She bought two red dresses.

result, time, condition, concession

27. Jim was so good at sports. He won a medal.
28. We come to town. We visit our friends.
29. Linda was so pretty. She became "Miss World."
30. We helped him. He got a "6."
31. Tom made so few mistakes in his tests. He always got a "1."
32. Linda has seen us twice. Linda moved to Bonn.
33. I have learnt English for such a long time. I must speak it well.
34. Dick was such a nice person. Everyone liked him.
35. There were so many people at the cinema. We had to stand.

Die Satzteile dürfen nicht vertauscht werden. Jedes Wort wird einmal gebraucht. Die Zeitformen des Verbes dürfen auch bei"after" nicht umgewandelt werden.

Verbinde mit "although, because, since, until, while"

36. Dan liked cars. He bought a new Ford.
37. We were talking on the phone. The door bell rang.
38. Tom wanted a new car. He didn't buy one.
39. White knocked the bar down. Lee was left.
40. Dick bought a Ford. He had driven a VW.

Verbinde mit "after, if, so ... that, such a ... that, whenever"

41. Don was a stupid person. He didn't know his own name.
42. Ben helped his mother. She would be happy.
43. We see our friends. We shake hands.
44. Linda had got the bad test back. She cried.
45. Tom is tall. He can touch the sky.

Verbinde mit "before, since (seitdem), so that, so ... that,when"

46. He talked very loudly. We should hear him.
47. Tom talked to me yesterday. I have been very happy.
48. You could take the bus. You had to get out of bed.
49. Father had a cold. He stayed home.
50. Bess has written many letters. Her hand hurts.

Verbinde mit "after, if, since (seitdem), so that, though"

51. I wonder how much time has passed. We started to take this test.
52. I read the book. I should be allowed to go swimming.
53. They had finished reading the book. They would have gone swimming.
54. She hadn't started to read the book. She went swimming.
55. We had read the book. We went swimming.

Verbinde mit "because, when"

56. It gets dark. We go home.
57. He ate too much. He is sick.
58. We closed the book. It was open.
59. The desks are dirty. We clean them.
60. Helen left the room. The door banged.
61. He was happy. He got a "1."
62. It was dark. It was raining.
63. The music started to play. Robert turned the radio on.
64. He cried. He had lost his car.
65. He reached home. He was hungry.

Verbinde mit "if, though."

66. He failed. He tried hard.
67. You are good. You will get a new pair of shoes.
68. You walk quickly. You will not be late.
69. You walk quickly. You will be late.
70. You want to grow tall. You must eat your food.
71. You want to go home. You must stay here.
72. My room is dirty. It was cleaned yesterday.
73. He wants to go to the university. He must study hard.
74. I would ask a policeman. I got lost in London.
75. He got lost. He had a map of the city.
76. Mother went to the grocer's. She would buy peas.

Verbinde mit "because, if, though, when"

77. She was happy. She got a "6."
78. We go home now. We can eat.
79. It strikes 8. We can leave.
80. You are ill. You were in the cold rain too long.
81. He is a teacher. He acts like a child.

82. The girl cried. She had lost her doll.
83. You are good. You will get an ice-cream cone.
84. The film was over. We went home.
85. They all go. We will also go.
86. The car stopped suddenly. A person stepped in front of it.
87. I met the film star. I would ask for an autograph.
88. You did your lessons. You would know more words.
89. She tried very hard. She failed.
90. She has tried very hard this time. She failed last time.
91. He works hard. He can get a "1."
92. They had worked hard. They got a "1."
93. Some people had got in. The doors closed.

Kombiniere mit passenden Verbindungswörtern.

94. The girls didn't study. They failed the test yesterday.
95. I was three years old. I couldn't talk.
96. He ran quickly. He should catch the tram.
97. The lady was standing. I stood up.
98. She looked like 16. She was only 13.
99. The boy saw the mouse. He began to scream.
100. The student was very (so) tired. She fell asleep while standing up.
101. It was dark. We lit candles.
102. It was dark. We still didn't get lost.
103. It was dark. We lit candles. The children should not be afraid.
104. I turned off the radio. I could hear what Father was saying.
105. They were very tired. They went to bed.
106. It was raining. The children went out to play.
107. We went swimming. It was so hot.
108. He bought records. He had little money.
109. I heard the phone ring. I was reading a book.
110. I went to the phone. I had heard it ring.
111. He got a bad grade. He had worked very hard.
112. I have no dress to wear. I can't go dancing.
113. We bought a dishwasher. We don't have to wash the dishes.
114. Mother was preparing the food. The children were playing outside.
115. It was cold. The children couldn't go outside. (so)
116. It was rainy. We had a lot of fun.
117. All the girls worked hard. They should be the best.

118. She is smiling all over. It is her birthday today.
119. The girl spoke in such a low voice. She had to repeat the questions.
120. They installed a new traffic light. A lot of accidents would be avoided.

Setze das richtige Verbindungswort ein.

121. ______ I came to school this morning, I got up.
122. He kept on walking ______ he reached home and could go to bed.
123. She cooked dinner ______ we did our homework so that we could eat as soon as we were finished.
124. ______ he had drunk ten glasses of water, he was no longer thirsty.
125. I wonder how much time has passed ______ we started school this morning.

31 Adverbials

31.1 Grammatik

1. Adverbs/Adverbials sind Wörter (Umstandswörter) oder Wortgruppen (Umstandsbestimmung, adverbiale Bestimmung), die ein Verb, Adjektiv, ein anderes Adverb oder einen Satz näher beschreiben, indem sie zusätzliche Information über Zeit, Ort, Art und Weise, Häufigkeit, Ursache, usw. liefern.

2. Adverbials können folgender Natur sein:

   a) Umstandswörter
   aus einem Wort bestehen (adverbs)

   quickly, here, tomorrow, etc.

   b) Umstandsbestimmung = adverbiale Bestimmung
   aus mehreren Wörtern bestehen

   - nominals groups
     mit einem Substantiv verbunden

     last year

   - prepositional phrases = adverbial phrases
     eine Präposition-Substantiv-Verbindung

     at night, in the house, at the moment

   - adverbial clauses = subclauses. Nebensätze
     Zwei Sätze werden miteinander verbunden, um mehr Information zu liefern.

     although he ran quickly
     because they helped her
     whenever he came home

     Es gibt adverbial clauses of concession (though, although), of purpose (so that), of reason (because, as, since. Sie beantworten die Frage "why"), of result (so - that, such a - that), of place, of time, conditional clauses (if).

     Diese Sorte Adverbien werden in Kapitel 30 behandelt.

3. Zusätzlich zu den Adverbien in Kapitel 16 gibt es folgende Sorten:

   a) **Adverbs of degree** (Gradadverbien = Grad/Ausmaß)

   Sie beantworten die Frage "how much".

   a bit, absolutely, a good deal, a great deal, a little, all but, a lot, almost, apparently, as good as, at all, badly, barely, by far, certainly, clearly, completely, considerably, deeply, definitely, enough, entirely, especially, even, evidently, extremely, fairly, for certain, for sure, greatly, hardly, indeed, in part, in the least, just, kind of, little, much, nearly, obviously, only, particularly, partly, perfectly, perhaps, possibly, presumably, pretty, quite, rather, really, scarcely, simply, so, sort of, such a, surely, terribly, thoroughly, too, totally, undoubtedly, utterly, very, very much, well, wholly

   - Wenn sie ein **Adjektiv oder ein anderes Adverb beschreiben**, werden sie davorgesetzt.

     She is ***extremely*** **beautiful**.

     He ***almost*** **never** comes.

   - **enough** wird nach dem Adjektiv oder Adverb, das es beschreibt, gesetzt.

     Did we come **quickly** ***enough***?

   - Adverbien, die sich **auf Verben beziehen**, werden vor das Hauptverb bzw. hinter das erste Hilfsverb gesetzt.

     I ***almost*** **won** that game.

     He **had** ***scarcely*** **spoken** a word before she came.

   - **"just"** soll am besten vor das Wort gesetzt werden, das es beschreibt.

     I have seen ***just*** **one** monkey so far.

   - **"only"** kann sich auch auf Verben beziehen.

     The child ***only*** **wants** to be near you.

     Dieses Adverb soll vor/neben das Wort gesetzt werden, worauf es sich bezieht. Sonst kann leicht eine andere Bedeutung entstehen.

     Only our child played with the ball.

     (sonst kein Kind)

     Our ***only*** child played with the ball.

     (Wir haben sonst kein Kind.)

Our child ***only*** played with the ball.
(Es hat nichts Falsches getan - bloß gespielt.)

Our child played ***only*** with the ball.
(mit keinem anderen Gegenstand.)

b) **Focusing adverbs** (hervorhebende Adverbien)
Sie heben ein Wort oder Wortgruppe hervor.

alone, also, as well, at least, chiefly, either, especially, even, exactly, exclusively, mainly, merely, mostly, neither, nor, only, particularly, too

c) **Adverb of viewpoint and comment**
(Adverbien des Standpunktes und Kommentars)

Sie beziehen sich auf einen ganzen Satz und geben eine Beurteilung über eine Aussage ab. Der Standpunkt des Sprechers (ob etwas richtig oder falsch, etc ist) wird bekanntgegeben.

apparently, as a matter of fact, bluntly, briefly, certainly, correctly, evidently, fortunately, frankly, honestly, hopefully, in brief, in general terms, in short, justly, morally, naturally, obviously, of course, perhaps, personally, politically, possibly, presumably, probably, psychologically, reportedly, rightly, strangely, surely, technically, typically, understandably, undoubtedly, unluckily, -wise, wrongly

d) **Linking adverbs**
(Verknüpfende Adverbien = conjunctive adverbs)

Sie verbinden zwei Sätze mit einer logischen Beziehung.

above all, accordingly, additionally, after all, again, all in all, all the same, also, altogether, anyhow, anyway, at any rate, besides, consequently, equally, finally, first of all, first(ly), for example, furthermore, hence, however, in addition, in comparison, in conclusion, in contrast, indeed, in fact, in other words, in short, in sum, in that case, in the same way, last, likewise, moreover, namely, nevertheless, next, otherwise, on the contrary, on the one hand, on the other hand, or rather, second(ly), similarly, so, still, that is, then, therefore, though, thus, yet

4. Einige Adverbien haben die gleiche Form (keine Endung) wie die Adjektive, aus denen sie gebildet werden. Andere haben die "-ly"-Endung.

a) Die folgenden **Adverbien** werden genau **wie deren Adjektive geschrieben**. Die **Bedeutung** ist ebenfalls **gleich**.

daily, deep, early, easy, extra, fair, far, fast, fine, free, fresh, hard, high, hourly, last, late, little, long, low, monthly, near, pretty, right, short, straight, tight, weekly, wide, yearly adj.: We were the ***last*** people to come.

adv.: We came ***last***.

adj.: The ***little*** water we'd had was gone. = wenig

adv.: The boy worked very ***little***. = wenig

b) Die folgenden **Adverbien** haben **die gleiche Form wie die Adjektive**, aus denen sie gebildet werden. Aber die **Bedeutung** ist **verschieden**.

clean

adj. rein	That's a ***clean*** room.
adv. gänzlich	He's ***clean*** forgotten it.

even

adj. glatt, flach, gerade	The ground was ***even***.
adv. noch	She's ***even*** nicer than we'd heard.

ill

adj. krank	Linda was ***ill***.
adv. schlecht	I can ***ill*** afford to get another "6".

just

adj. gerecht	That's her ***just*** punishment.
adv. gerade	Father's ***just*** come home.

only

adj. einzig	He's our ***only*** child.
adv. nur, erst	We'll ***only*** go if you go.
	We'll go ***only*** if you go.

pretty

adj. hübsch	The girl is ***pretty***.
adv. ziemlich	We were in a ***pretty*** bad situation.

right

adj. recht haben	Linda was ***right*** yesterday.
adv. gerade,sofort	I'll come ***right*** away.

sharp

adj. scharf	The knife was ***sharp***.
adv. punkt	Be here at four ***sharp***.

still

adj. ruhig, still	The girl was ***still***.
adv. immer noch	Are you ***still*** doing your homework?

very

adj. rein, richtig, wirklich	You must tell the ***very*** truth.
adv. sehr	You have a ***very*** good idea.

well

adj. gesund, wohl	She was ***well*** again.
adv. gut	You did that very ***well***.

c) Die folgenden Adverbien können **mit oder ohne "-ly"** geschrieben werden.

- **Beide Formen haben die gleiche oder eine ähnliche Bedeutung wie das Adjektiv**:

  cheap, dead, dear, deep, direct, easy, full, high, loud, new, quick, right, safe, slow, sound, thick, tight, wrong

  adj. There was a ***loud*** noise.

  adv. That woman talked so ***loud***.

  adv. The children shouted ***loudly***.

  - **Das Adjektiv und die "-ly" Form des Adverbs haben die gleiche Bedeutung. Das Adverb ohne Endung hat die gleiche Form, wie das Adjektiv aber eine andere Bedeutung.**

adj./adv. mit "-ly"	**Adv. ohne Endung**
just/justly = gerecht	just = gerade
pretty/prettily = hübsch	pretty =recht/ ziemlich

just

adj. gerecht	She came to get her ***just*** reward.
adv. gerecht, mit Recht	The boy was ***justly*** spanked.
adv. gerade	It has ***just*** turned nine.

pretty

adj. hübsch	That's a ***pretty*** dress.
adv. hübsch	The girl was dressed up ***prettily***.
adv. ziemlich	You did that ***pretty*** well.

- **Das Adjektiv und das Adverb ohne Endung haben die gleiche Bedeutung. Das Adverb mit der "-ly" Endung hat eine andere Bedeutung.**

adj./adv. ohne Endung	**Adv. mit -ly**
close = eng, nah	closely = genau, scharf
deep = tief	deeply = sehr (emotionell)
fair = anständig, ehrlich, schön	fairly = recht, ziemlich
hard = schwer	hardly = kaum
high = hoch, laut	highly = sehr empfehlend, höchst lobend
late = spät	lately = kürzlich, neulich
low = niedrig	lowly (humble) = bescheiden
near = nah	nearly (almost)= beinahe, fast

close

adj. eng, nah	That woman is a ***close*** friend.
adv. eng, nah	We wanted to be ***close*** to him.
adv. genau, scharf	The thief was ***closely*** followed.

deep

adj. tief	We saw a ***deep*** hole.
adv. tief	You'll have to dig very ***deep***.
adv. sehr	They are ***deeply*** in love.

fair

adj. anständig	That was a ***fair*** game.
adv. anständig	You'd better play ***fair***.
adv. ziemlich	Father is ***fairly*** certain that he saw Mother.

hard

adj. schwer	Father has a ***hard*** job.
adv. schwer	We had to work very ***hard***.
adv. kaum	We were ***hardly*** able to see him.

high

adj. hoch	I stood on a ***high*** ladder.
adv. hoch	The bird was flying quickly and ***high***.
adv. sehr lobend	They spoke very ***highly*** of her.

late

adj. spät	He gave us a ***late*** date.
adv. spät	We got home very ***late***.
adv. neulich	***Lately*** I've had a funny feeling.

low

adj. niedrig	The baby sat on a ***low*** chair.
adv. niedrig	The bird flew slowly and ***low*** near the earth.
adv. bescheiden	Jesus was born in a ***lowly*** stable.

near

adj. nahe	Linda is a ***near*** relative.
adv. nahe	The man was standing very ***near*** to us.
adv. fast beinahe	It's ***nearly*** time to go home now.

5. Die folgenden Adverbien weisen **Unregelmäßigkeiten in der Bildung** auf:

   due-duly, dull-dully, full-fully, true-truly, whole-wholly

6. **Steigerung der Adverbien**

   a) **Germanisch** gesteigert werden einsilbigen Adverbien + early.

   –, -er, -est

   early, fast, hard, late, often, soon

   soon - sooner - soonest
   early - earlier - earliest

   b) **Romanisch** gesteigert werden

   —, more –, most –

   - Adverbien, die mit "-ly" enden. Sie haben alle zwei oder mehr Silben.

     carefully - more carefully - most carefully

   - alle Partizipien

     interesting - more interesting - most interesting
     delighted - more delighted - most delighted

   c) Die Adjektive, die **unregelmäßig gesteigert** werden, bleiben auch als Adverbien unregelmäßig.

far	-	farther	-	farthest
far	-	further	-	furthest
ill/badly	-	worse	-	worst
little	-	less	-	least
much	-	more	-	most
well	-	better	-	best

32 Verzeichnis der grammatikalischen Begriffe

Absichtssatz siehe purpose, clauses of

A.c.I. = Akkusativ mit Infinitiv

Nach dem Verb kommt ein Objekt und danach eine Infinitivkonstruktion.

She has the desire to go with you.

accusative case = Wenfall = Akkusativ

Die Antwort auf die Frage "wen" oder "was" steht im Akkusativ.

I saw the man. Ich sah den Mann. Wen sah ich? den Mann

Akkusativobjekt siehe direct object

active voice = Tätigkeitsformen = Aktiv = Tatform

Aktionform des Verbes

Ein Subjekt führt eine Handlung aus = macht etwas.

The man writes two words.

adjective = Adjektiv = Eigenschaftswort

Ein Wort beschreibt oder begrenzt ein Substantiv oder Pronomen näher.

We see a big table.

adverb = Adverb = Umstandswort

Ein Wort beschreibt ein Verb, Adjektiv oder ein anderes Adverb näher.

The child shouts loudly.

The extremely beautiful girl was sleeping.

The man ran extremely quickly.

adverbial = Adverbien = adverbiale Bestimmung = Umstandsbestimmung

Ein Wort (adverb) oder mehrere Wörter (adverbial phrases) beantworten die Fragen: when (wann, Zeit, time), where (wo, Ort, place), how (wie, Art und Weise, manner), how often, (wie oft, Häufigkeit, frequency).

I wrote two letters yesterday.

We drove him to school.

Adverbial clauses = adverbialer Nebensatz = Adverbialsatz = Umstandssatz

Ein Nebensatz gibt dem Hauptsatz umfangreiche Informationen über Folge (result), Zweck (purpose), Einräumung (concession), Grund und Ursache (reason), Zeit (time), Bedingung (condition), oder Ort (place - Lokalsätze) einer Handlung.

Although I was tired, I studied for the test.

While I was doing my homework, my brother was playing.

adverbial phrase = Adverbialbestimmung = Umstandsbestimmung

Eine Gruppe von zwei oder mehreren Wörtern (nicht aber eine Subjekt-Verb-Verbindung), die einem Satz mehr Information über wann (when), wo (where), wie (how), wie oft (how often) gibt.

adverbial of time adverbiale Bestimmung der Zeit

We will see you in September.

adverbial of place adverbiale Bestimmung des Ortes

My boy is at school.

Adverbialsatz des Ortes siehe place, adverbial clauses of

Akkusativ siehe accusative case

aktiv siehe active voice

angehängte Fragen siehe question tags

article = Artikel = Geschlechtswort

bestimmt definite : the

Bestimmte Artikel weisen auf bekannte Substantive hin. Sie heben einzelne Personen/Sachen aus einer Gruppe heraus.

the dog

unbestimmt indefinite : a/an

Unbestimmte Artikel bezeichnen noch nicht bekannte Wörter.

an apple, a book

Art und Weise adverbiale Bestimmung der siehe adverbial

attribute = Attribut = Beifügung

Ein Adjektiv steht vor einem Substantiv, um es näher zu beschreiben.

She is a good girl.

auxiliary = Hilfsverb = Modalverben = unvollständige Hilfsverben

Ein Verb, das nicht alleine stehen kann, sondern nur mit einem Hauptverb vollständig ist. Es hilft die Zeiten zu bestimmen.

The man can go home.

Bedingungssätze siehe conditional clause

Begründungssatz siehe reason, adverbial clauses of

Beifügung siehe attribute

besitzanzeigendes Fürwort siehe possessive pronoun

betonendes Fürwort siehe intensive pronoun

bezügliches Fürwort siehe relative pronoun

causal siehe reason, adverbial clauses of

concession = concessive clauses = Konzessivsatz = Einräumungssatz = Zugeständnis = Adverbialsatz der Einräumung = Konzessivbestimmung

Ein Gegensatz wird zwischen den Aussagen in dem Hauptsatz und dem Nebensatz ausgedrückt.

Although she loved the man, she didn't marry him.

conditional = Bedingungsform = Konditional

Das "conditional" sagt, was passieren würde/könnte, wenn eine Bedingung oder Voraussetzung erfüllt oder nicht erfüllt wäre.

he would have come; he would phone; he couldn't have heard you

conditional clause = Bedingungssatz = adverbiale Bestimmung der Bedingung = Konditionalbestimmung = Konditionalsatz = Zugeständnis

Der Nebensatz enthält eine Bedingung

If I come to Germany, I'll visit you.

continuous form siehe progressive form

dative case = Wemfall = Dativ

Die Antwort auf die Frage "wem" steht im Dativ

The man gave me his hat. Der Mann gab mir seinen Hut. Wem gab der Mann seinen Hut? mir

Dingwort siehe noun

direct object = direktes Objekt = Akkusativobjekt

Die Antwort auf die Frage "wen" oder "was" ist ein "direct object" und steht in dem Akkusativ. Das ist das Ziel einer Handlung.

The man hit the ball.

direkte Rede siehe direct speech

direct speech = direkte Rede = wörtliche Rede

Dieselben Worte, die gesprochen wurden, werden exakt wiedergegeben.

He said, "I love you."

Eigenschaftswort siehe adjective

Einräumungssätze siehe concession

Finalbestimmung siehe purpose, clauses of

Finalsatz siehe purpose, clauses of

Folge siehe result, clauses of

frequency, adverb of = Häufigkeitsadverb

Ein Adverb besagt wie oft etwas passiert.

We have seldom been there.

Fürwort siehe pronoun

future (tense) = Futur = Zukunft

Eine Handlung, die in der Zukunft noch stattfindet, wird beschrieben.

The man will come tomorrow.

A letter will be written.

The man will be writing a letter when you come.

future perfect = vollendete Zukunft

Bis zu einem Punkt in der Zukunft wird etwas vollbracht sein.

Next year I will have been married for 5 years.

Gegenwart siehe present (tense)

genitive case = Wesfall = Genitiv

Dieser Fall zeigt Besitz an und beantwortet die Frage "wessen"

This is his book. This is Tom's book.

gerund = Gerundium = hauptwortliches Zeitwort

Die "-ing"-Form des Verbs wird als Substantiv gebraucht, und um Nebensätze zu ersetzen.

He likes books. He likes reading.

When the people saw the ships, the people shouted.

On seeing the ships, the people shouted.

Geschlechtswort siehe article

Grund siehe reason, adverbial clauses of

Grundform siehe infinitive

Hauptwort siehe noun

Häufigkeitsadverb siehe frequency, adverb of

Hilfsverben siehe auxiliary

Imperfekt siehe past (tense)

indirect object = indirektes Objekt = Dativobjekt = dative = Wemfall

Wenn ein Satz zwei Objekte hat, ist das Dativobjekt die Person oder Sache, der etwas gegeben/getan wird. Es beantwortet die Frage "wem".

The man gave me his hat.

indirect speech siehe reported speech

indirekte Rede siehe reported speech

infinitive = Infinitiv = Nennform = Grundform = to-infinitive

Das ist die Grundform des Verbes

to see

Sie wird auch gebraucht als Substantiv oder um Nebensätze zu ersetzen.

I wanted to see her.

We came because we wanted to see you.

We came to see you.

ing-Form

Die "-ing"-Form des Verbes wird gebraucht als:

Gerundium = Substantiv

I like reading.

Präsenspartizip = Adjektiv

A barking dog won't bite.

Verlaufsform in den verschiedenen Zeiten des Verbes, um zu zeigen, dass etwas gerade abläuft/ablief/ablaufen wird.

I am writing a letter.

intensive pronoun = betonendes Fürwort

Ein Substantiv oder Pronomen wird durch ein "-self"- pronoun stark betont.

She herself wrote that book.

irregular verbs = unregelmäßige Verben = strong form of verbs = starke Verben

Ein Verb dessen 2. und 3. Form nicht mit "-ed" gebildet wird.

to see, saw, seen

Kausalsätze siehe reason, adverbial clauses of

Konditionalsatz siehe conditional clause

Konsekutivsätze siehe result, clauses of

Konzessivsätze siehe concession

Kurzfragen siehe question tags

Leideform siehe passive voice

local clauses siehe place, adverbial clauses of

Lokalsätze siehe place, adverbial clauses of

manner, adverb of siehe adverbial

Mittelwort siehe participle

Modalverben siehe auxiliary

Nennform siehe infinitive

Nennwort siehe noun

nominal group = Nominal-/Substantivgruppe

hat ein Substantiv als Bezugswort

the heavy table; many working people

nominative case = Werfall = Nominativ

Der Fall zeigt/bezeichnet ein Subjekt und beantwortet die Frage "wer" oder "was".

The man saw me.

noun = Substantiv = Hauptwort = Nennwort = Dingwort

Ein Wort, das eine Person, Tier, Gegenstand oder abstrakten Begriff bezeichnet.

table, man, friendship

object = Objekt = Satzergänzung

Ein Satzteil, der die Handlung, die im Verb ausgedrückt ist, ergänzt. Ein Substantiv, das die Handlung des Verbes empfängt.

He kissed the girl. He kissed her.

Hinter einer Präposition steht ebenfalls ein Objekt.

She stood behind the man. She stood behind him.

Ortsadverb siehe place, adverbial clauses of

participle = Partizip = Mittelwort

Die "-ing"-Form und 3. Form des Verbes werden als Adjektiv gebraucht und um Nebensätze zu ersetzen bzw. zu kürzen.

The crying girl couldn't talk.

He found his lost letter.

As she had no car, she couldn't drive to town.

Having no car, she couldn't drive to town.

Partizip siehe participle

Partizip Perfekt siehe past participle

Partizip Präsens siehe present participle

Passiv siehe passive voice

passive voice = Leideform = Passiv

Eine Handlung wird am Subjekt des Satzes ausgeübt. Es wird auf das Subjekt eingewirkt. Das Subjekt ist der Empfänger der Handlung des Verbes. Etwas passiert mit/oder an dem Subjekt.

The letter was written by the little girl.

past (tense) = Präteritum = Vergangenheit = Imperfekt

Eine Handlung ist in der Vergangenheit geschehen. Es ist vorbei und hat keine wesentliche Auswirkungen in der Gegenwart.

I wrote a letter.

I was writing a letter.

A letter was written.

A letter was being written.

past participle = Partizip Perfekt = Mittelwort der Vergangenheit = Die 3. Form des Verbes = Perfektpartizip

Diese Form kann wie ein Adjektiv gebraucht werden. Sie wird gebraucht, um die 3. Form des Verbes zu bilden. Sie steht nach to have, to get, nach Verben des Wünschen und Wollens, nach Verben der Sinneswahrnehmung; anstelle von Adverbialsätzen.

stolen He has stolen. the stolen car

I have to get my picture taken.

past perfect = vollendete Vergangenheit = Plusquamperfekt = Vorvergangenheit

Eine Handlung lief vor einer anderen Handlung ab. Von zwei Handlungen in der Vergangenheit liegt diese weiter zurück.

She had already written a letter before you came.

I had been writing a letter.

A letter had been written.

past progressive = past continuous = Verlaufsform der Vergangenheit

Eine Handlung in der Vergangenheit war gerade im Gange, meistens als etwas anderes passierte.

She was washing the dishes when the children came home.

The babies were being fed when the phone rang.

perfect participle active: having + 3. Form des Verbes: having eaten

passive: having been + 3. Form des Verbes: having been told

Diese Form eines Partizips zeigt, dass eine Handlung vorbei war, bevor die nächste Handlung anfing.

Having eaten, we decided to take a walk.

Having been told not to go too close to the water, the children stayed away from the river.

Perfekt siehe present perfect

Perfektpartizip siehe past participle

persönliches Fürwort siehe personal pronoun

personal pronoun = Personalpronomen = persönliches Fürwort

Eine Gruppe Fürwörter, die eine Person, einen Namen oder Sache ersetzt.

We saw the man. We saw him. He was there.

place, adverbial clauses of = Lokalsatz = Ortssatz = Adverbialsatz des Ortes = local clauses = Ortsadverb

Diese Nebensätze liefern dem Hauptsatz mehr Information über einen Ort, als eine adverbiale Gruppe es tun könnte. Er beantwortet die Fragen: wo, wohin, woher, wie weit.

The man knew how far I was walking.

She was standing where I had left her.

Plusquamperfekt siehe past perfect

possessive adjective = Possessivpronomen = adjektivisches Possessivpronomen = besitzanzeigendes Fürwort

Dieses Wort bezeichnet Körperteile und Gegenstände, die einer Person gehören. Das Substantiv, was einer Person gehört, steht immer nach dem Possessivadjektiv.

That is my book.

possessive form = Genitiv

Die Besitzform eines Substantivs. Sie beantwortet die Frage "wessen".

The boy has Linda's book. He has her book.

possessive pronoun besitzanzeigendes Fürwort substantivisch gebrauchtes Possessivpronomen substantivisches Possessivpronomen

Dieses Wort bezeichnet Körperteile oder Gegenstände, die einer Person gehören. Das Substantiv, das einer Person gehört, wird nicht nach dem Possessivpronomen ausgedrückt. Es fehlt.

That book is mine.

Präsens siehe present (tense)

Präsenspartizip siehe present participle

Präteritum siehe past (tense)

preposition = Präposition = Verhältniswort

Diese Wörter drücken eine räumliche, zeitliche, logische oder übertragende Beziehung zwischen Personen, Sachen oder Vorgängen aus. Sie verbinden ein Substantiv oder Pronomen mit einem anderen Teil des Satzes.

The man is on the chair.

Here is a chair for you.

present (tense) = Präsens = Gegenwart

Eine Handlung geschieht in der Gegenwart; sie ist aktuell.

She writes books. She is writing a book.

Books are written. Books are being written.

present participle = Partizip Präsens = Mittelwort der Gegenwart = Präsenspartizip

Diese Form wird gebraucht, um eine Verlaufsform zu bilden; sie wird auch als Adjektiv gebraucht und kommt nach "Here is/ There is"; nach Verben der Sinneswahrnehmung hinter einem Objekt; anstelle von Relativsätzen; anstelle adverbialer Nebensätze; usw.

running. The boy is running. The running car

I saw her running.

present perfect = Vorgegenwart = Perfekt = vollendete Gegenwart

Eine Handlung fing in der Vergangenheit an und reicht bis in die Gegenwart oder die Folgen sind noch sichtbar.

We have been talking for two hours now.

That car has made my dress dirty.

present progressive = present continuous = Verlaufsform des Präsens

Eine Handlung ist gerade im Gange.

She is helping her mother.

The pigs are being fed now.

progressive form = Verlaufsform = continuous form

Diese Form zeigt, dass eine Handlung zur Zeit des Erzählens gerade abläuft/ablief/ablaufen wird.

I am reading a book now.

I will/shall be reading a book tomorrow.

I have been reading books for 10 years now.

Pronomen siehe pronoun

pronoun = Fürwort = Pronomen

Ein Substantiv wird durch ein solches Wort ersetzt.

We saw the man yesterday. We saw him yesterday.

purpose, clauses of = (Final-/Zwecksätze) = Adverbialsatz des Zweckes = Absichtssatz = Finalbestimmung

Der Zweck oder die Absicht der Handlung des Hauptsatzes wird in dem Nebensatz erklärt oder angegeben. Der Nebensatz beantwortet die Fragen "wozu", "zu welchem Zweck"

You must get up early so that you won't be late for school.

question tags = Kurzfragen = angehängte Fragen

Eine "ja-nein"-Frage wird an einem Aussagesatz angehängt. Sie entspricht das Deutsche "nicht wahr", "oder?"

She went home, didn't she?

reason, adverbial clauses of = Kausalsatz = Begründungssatz = causal = Kausalbestimmung = adverbiale Bestimmung des Grundes = Grund = Adverbialsätze der Ursache

Der Grund/Die Ursache/Die Begründung der Handlung vom Hauptsatz wird angegeben. Er antwortet auf die Fragen "warum", "weshalb"

The girl fell asleep because she was very tired.

reciprocal pronoun = gegenseitiges/ wechselseitiges/ reziprokes Pronomen

one another, each other

Zwei Personen/Sachen/Substantive tun dasselbe einander gegenüber; es ist eine gegenseitige Handlung. Sie geschieht also wechselseitig.

The boy and girl looked at each other.

reflexive = (zu)rückbezüglich

Das Subjekt und das direkte Objekt sind gleich.

I myself

he himself

reflexive pronoun = Reflexivpronomen = rückbezügliches Fürwort

Sie enden auf -self/-selves.

Das Subjekt und das direkte Objekt bezeichnen dieselbe Person. Personen oder Dinge werden dadurch betont. Die Handlung des Satzes bezieht sich auf das Subjekt.

She dressed herself.

reflexive verbs = rückbezügliche Verben

Das Reflexivpronomen hinter dem Verb bezieht sich auf das Subjekt.

He shaved himself.

regelmäßige Verben siehe regular verbs

regular verbs = regelmäßige Verben

Ein Verb, dessen 2. und 3. Form mit "-ed" gebildet wird.

to walk - walked - walked

relative clause = Relativsatz = bezüglicher Satz = Bezugssatz = Beifügungssatz

Zwei Sätze, die ein gemeinsames Substantiv oder Pronomen besitzen, werden verbunden, indem ein Satz als Nebensatz untergeordnet wird. Das gemeinsame Wort wird durch ein Relativpronomen ersetzt.

The man, whom I saw, was my father.

relative pronoun = Relativpronomen = bezügliches Fürwort

Das Wort, das einen Relativsatz einführt. Das Verbindungswort zwischen den zwei Satzteilen eines Relativsatzes.

who, whom, whose, which, that

reported speech = indirekte Rede = indirect speech

Die Mitteilungen anderer Personen werden wiedergegeben oder etwas wird weitererzählt.

My friend said, "I love you."

My friend said that he loved me.

result, clauses of = Adverbialsatz der Folge = consecutive = Konsekutivsatz = Konsekutivbestimmung = Folge

Der Nebensatz erzählt das Resultat/die Folge der Handlung des Hauptsatzes. Er beantwortet die Frage "mit welcher Folge”

He was so friendly that the children went with him.

He was such a friendly man that the children went with him.

reziprokes Pronomen siehe reciprocal pronoun

rückbezügliche Verben siehe reflexive verbs

rückbezügliches Fürwort siehe reflexive pronoun

Satzgegenstand siehe subject

simple form (of the tenses) = einfache Form (der Zeiten)

Diese Form des Verbes zeigt, dass eine Handlung immer/oft/manchmal/im Frühling/gewöhnlich/usw. passiert/passierte/ passieren wird. Diese ist oft eine wiederholte Handlung.

Tom always does his homework nicely.

Tom has sometimes done his homework nicely.

simple past = einfaches Präteritum

Diese Form des Verbs zeigt, dass in der Vergangenheit etwas immer/oft/manchmal, usw. passierte.

We sometimes played tennis.

simple present = einfaches Präsens = einfache Zeitform der Gegenwart

Diese Form des Verbs zeigt, dass in der Gegenwart etwas immer/oft/manchmal/usw. passiert.

We often play tennis.

strong form of verbs siehe irregular verbs

subject = Subjekt = Satzgegenstand

Der Substantiv oder Pronomen des Satzes, worüber etwas gesagt wird. Im Aktivsatz geht die Handlung von diesem Wort aus. Er beantwortet die Frage "wer" oder "was".

The man drove the car.

subject complement = Prädikativum

Nach einer Form von "be" oder einem anderen Gleichsetzungsverb stehendes Substantiv, Adjektiv oder dergleichen.

That man is my father.

That man is nice.

Substantiv siehe noun

Tatform siehe active voice

Tatwort siehe verb

Tätigkeitsformen siehe active voice

Tätigkeitswort siehe verb

Temporalsätze siehe time, adverbial clauses of

tenses = Zeitformen = Tempus = Zeiten

Die Form des Verbes, die die Zeit der Handlung zeigt. Sie zeigt, ob die Handlung sich in der Gegenwart, Vergangenheit oder Zukunft abspielt.

He is coming. He came. He will be driven.

time, adverbial clauses of = temporal clauses = Temporalsätze = adverbiale Bestimmung der Zeit = Temporalbestimmung = Temporalsätze = Umstandssatz der Zeit = Zeitadverb = Zeitsatz

Diese Nebensätze geben dem Hauptsatz mehr und neue Informationen über eine Zeitangabe, als eine Adverbialgruppe es tun könnte. Das zeitliche Verhältnis zwischen dem Haupt- und dem Nebensatz wird beschrieben. Er beantwortet die Fragen "wann", "wie lange", "wie oft", "seit wann".

The boy did his homework while his mother was cooking.

to-infinitive siehe infinitive

Tuwort siehe verb

Umstandsbestimmung siehe adverbial/adverbial phrase

Umstandssatz siehe adverbial clauses

Umstandswort siehe adverb

unregelmäßige Verben siehe irregular verbs

unvollständige Hilfsverben siehe auxiliary

Ursache, Adverbialsätze der siehe reason, adverbial clauses of

verb = Verb = Zeitwort = Tatwort = Tätigkeitswort = Tuwort

Ein Wort, das eine Handlung/ein Geschehnis oder bloß Existenz (Da-Sein) ausdrückt.

He is working. Is he here? The dog barked.

Vergangenheit siehe past (tense)

Verhältniswort siehe preposition

Verlaufsform siehe progressive form

vollendete Gegenwart siehe present perfect

vollendete Vergangenheit siehe past perfect

vollendete Zukunft siehe future perfect

Vorgegenwart siehe present perfect

Vorvergangenheit siehe past perfect

Wemfall siehe dative case

Wenfall siehe accusative case

Werfall siehe nominative case

Wesfall siehe genitive case

wörtliche Rede siehe direct speech

Zeiten siehe tenses

Zeitadverb siehe time, adverbial clauses of

33 Vokabelverzeichnis Englisch-Deutsch

a	ein
a bit	ein bisschen, etwas, ein wenig
a cup of	eine Tasse
a few	einige, ein paar
a good deal	viel
a great deal of	viel
a large number of	viel, viele
a little	ein wenig, ein bisschen
a lot of	viele, viel
a piece of	ein Stück
ability	Fähigkeit
able	fähig
about	über, von, ungefähr, etwa
above	über
absolutely	absolut, vollkommen, vollständig
absurd	absurd, albern, lächerlich
accident	Unfall
accordingly	entsprechend, folglich, gemäß
to accuse of	anklagen, beschuldigen
to be accustomed to	an etw gewöhnt, gewohnt zu tun
ache	Schmerz
to acknowledge	anerkennen, eingestehen
across	über
to act	sich benehmen, spielen, darstellen, schauspielern
action	Aktion, Handlung
to take action	in die Tat setzen, in Bewegung setze
active	aktiv, belebt, rege
to add	hinzutun
additionally	außerdem, ergänzend, zusätzlich
address	Adresse, Anschrift
to adjust to	anpassen an
to admit	zugeben, gestehen
to adore	anbeten, lieben, verehren
advantage of	im Vorteil sein
adverbial	Adverbien
advice	Rat
to take advice	einen Rat befolgen, auf Rat hören
to advise	raten, beraten
to afford	sich leisten
afraid	ängstlich, besorgt, fürchten
after	nach, nachdem
after all	nach allem, schließlich
afternoon	Nachmittag
afterwards	nachher
again	wieder, noch einmal

against	gegen
age	Alter
of age	mündig sein, volljährig
ago	vor
to agree	vereinbaren, zustimmen, sich einigen, übereinstimmen
aim	Ziel, Absicht
to aim	zielen auf, beabsichtigen, vorhaben, Absicht erstreben
air	Luft
airplane	Flugzeug
airport	Flughafen
alarm clock	Wecker
alcohol	Alkohol
all	alle, ganz
all day	den ganzen Tag
to allow	erlauben
almighty	allmächtig
almost	fast, beinahe
alone	alleine
along	entlang, mit
already	schon, bereits
also	auch
alternative	Alternative, Wahl
although	obwohl
altogether	insgesamt, durchaus, ganz und gar
always	immer
am	bin
amazed	erstaunt, überrascht
amazing	erstaunlich, verblüffend
ambition	Ziel, Bestreben, Ambition, Ehrgeiz
ambitious	ehrgeizig
America	Amerika
to amount to	sich belaufen auf, hinauslaufen
to amuse oneself	sich amüsieren, sich gut unterhalten, vergnügen
and	und
angry	zornig, wütend, verärgert, böse, sauer
animal	Tier
to annoy	ärgern, belästigen, irritieren, stören
another	noch eine, ein anderer
to answer	antworten, beantworten
answer	Antwort
ant	Ameise
to anticipate	erwarten, erhoffen
anxious	besorgt, bedacht
any	keine, welche, irgendwelche
anybody	irgend jemand
anyhow	jedenfalls, immerhin
any more	(nicht) länger
anyone	irgend jemand, irgend etwas
anything	irgend etwas
anyway	trotzdem, jedenfalls, auf irgendeine Weise, wie dem auch sei
anywhere	irgendwo
apart from	abseits, ausserdem, abgesehen von
to apologize	sich entschuldigen, Vergebung bitten
apparently	offenbar, anscheinend
to appear	erscheinen, auftauchen

apple	Apfel
to appreciate	zu schätzen wissen, würdigen
to approach	sich nähern
to approve	billigen, gutheißen, zustimmen
apt	dazu neigen, geneigt
are	sind
to argue	streiten, diskutieren
to arise	entstehen, sich erheben
around	herum, rund um, rum, rund ums, umher
to arrange	ordnen, arrangieren, anordnen
to arrest	verhaften
to arrive	ankommen, eintreffen
artist	Künstler
as	da, weil, als, so ... wie
as if	als ob
as of	ab
as... as	so ... wie
ashamed	beschämt, schämen
to ask	stellen, fragen, bitten
to ask for	bitten um, fragen nach
asleep	schlafend, schlafen
to assert	behaupten, bestehen auf, geltend machen
to assist	helfen, unterstützen
to assume	annehmen
assure	versichern
astonished	erstaunt
astonishing	erstaunlich
at	an, am
at least	wenigstens
at once	sofort
attempt	Versuch
to attempt	versuchen
attention	Aufmerksamkeit
attentive	aufmerksam
attractive	reizend
aunt	Tante
authority	Autorität, Vollmacht
autograph	Autogramm, Unterschrift
automatic	automatisch
autumn	Herbst
to avoid	vermeiden, meiden. ausweichen
to awake	aufwecken, wecken, wach
away	weg, fort
awful	schrecklich
awkward	peinlich, ungeschickt, schwierig, verlegen
back	zurück, hinten, Rückseite, Rücken
bad	böse, schlecht, unartig, schlimm
bag	Tasche, Tüte, Sack, Beutel
to bake	backen
balloon	Ballon
to bang	knallen, schlagen
bar	Tafel, Riegel
barely	kaum
to bark	bellen
basic	wesentlich

basket	Korb
bath	Bad
to bathe	baden
bathroom	Bad, Badezimmer
to be	sein
beach	Strand
to bear	tragen, geboren
bear	Bär
to beat	schlagen, übertreffen
beautiful	schön
because	weil, da
to become	werden
bed	Bett
bedroom	Schlafzimmer
beer	Bier
before	vorher, vor, schon einmal, bevor, ehe
to beg	betteln, bitten um
to beget	zeugen
beggar	Bettler
to begin	beginnen, anfangen
beginning	Anfang
to behave	sich benehmen, sich verhalten
behind	hinter
to believe	glauben, meinen
bell	Glocke, Klingel
below	unter
to bend	beugen, biegen
benefit	Vorteil, Nutzen
to beseech	anflehen
beside oneself	außer sich
besides	außerdem
best	beste, am besten
to bet	wetten
better	besser, verbessern
between	zwischen
bicycle	Fahrrad
to bid	befehlen, bieten
big	groß, groß und breit
bike	Fahrrad, Rad
to bind	binden
bird	Vogel
birthday	Geburtstag
biscuit	Plätzchen, Keks
to bite	beißen
bitter	bitter, schmerzhaft
black	schwarz
to blame	Schuld geben, tadeln
to bleed	bluten
blouse	Bluse
to blow	blasen, putzen
to blow up	aufblasen
blue	blau
bluntly	freiheraus, barsch, grob, stumpf
board	Tafel, Brett, Spielbrett, Wandtafel
to boast	prahlen, sich rühmen

boat	Boot, Schiff
body	Körper
bomb	Bombe
bone	Knochen
book	Buch
boots	Stiefel
boring	langweilig
born	geboren
boss	Chef, Boss, Vorgesetzter
to bother about	sich kümmern um, sich aufregen über, sich bemühen
bottle	Flasche
to be bound	bestimmt, muss so
box	Schachtel, Kiste, Dose, Kasten, Karton, Kästchen
boy	Junge
boyfriend	Freund
brains	Gehirn, Verstand, Intelligenz
brave	mutig
bread	Brot
to break	brechen, zerbrechen, kaputtgehen
break	Pause
breakfast	Frühstück
to breed	züchten
to bribe	bestechen
briefly	kurz, kürzlich, kurz zusammengefasst
bright	schlau, leuchtend, glänzend, hell
brilliant	großartig, brillant
to bring	bringen, mitbringen
to broadcast	senden
broken	zerbrochen, kaputt
brother	Bruder
brown	braun
to brush	putzen, bürsten
to build	bauen
building	Gebäude
burden	Last
burglar	Einbrecher
to burn	brennen, verbrennen
to burst	bersten, zerplatzen, platzen, explodieren
bus stop	Bushaltestelle
busy	beschäftigt, belebt, verkehrsreich, hektisch
but	aber
to buy	kaufen
by	bei, bis, indem, von, mit, mit dem
cage	Käfig
cake	Kuchen, Torte
to calculate	berechnen, kalkulieren
to call	rufen, nennen, heißen, anrufen
calm	ruhig
camel	Kamel
camera	Kamera
can	können, dürfen
cancer	Krebs
candle	Kerze
cannot but	kann nicht anders als; kann nicht umhin zu
can't help	kann nicht anders als

capable of	fähig sein, imstande sein
capacity	Kapazität, Aufnahmefähigkeit, Umfang
captain	Kapitän, Mannschaftsführer
to capture	erobern, gefangennehmen, fangen
car	Auto
card	Karte
care	Sorge, Sorgfalt
to care about	Wert auf etwas legen, besorgt sein, sich etwas daraus machen
to care for	sich kümmern um, pflegen, sorgen für
careful	vorsichtig, sorgfältig, achtsam
careless	unvorsichtig
to care to	Wert darauf legen
to carry	tragen
cassette	Kassette
to cast	werfen
castle	Schloss, Burg
cat	Katze
to catch	fangen, kriegen, bekommen
to catch up	aufholen
cathedral	Dom, Kathedrale
cause	Ursache, Grund, Anlass, Zweck
to cause	verursachen
to cease	aufhören
certain	bestimmt, sicher
chair	Stuhl
chance of	Chance, Aussicht, Gelegenheit
to change	wechseln, ändern, umsteigen
charming	reizend, entzückend
to chase	verfolgen, jagen
cheap	billig, preiswert
to cheat	betrügen, mogeln, pfuschen
cheese	Käse
chicken	Huhn, Hähnchen
chiefly	hauptsächlich
child	Kind
childish	kindisch
children	Kinder
chocolate	Schokolade
choice	Wahl, Auswahl
to choose	wählen, aussuchen
Christmas	Weihnachten
church	Kirche
cigarette	Zigarette
cinema	Kino
circular	rund
circus	Zirkus
city	Großstadt, Stadt
to claim	behaupten, beanspruchen
to clap	klatschen
class	Klasse, Schulklasse, Kurs
classroom	Klassenzimmer, Klassenraum
to clean	säubern, saubermachen, reinigen, putzen, sauber machen
to clean up	aufräumen
clean	sauber, rein, gänzlich
clear	klar, deutlich

clever	gescheit, klug, schlau, intelligent
to climb	klettern, steigen
to cling	festhalten, sich klammern
clock	Standuhr
close	eng, nah, genau, scharf
to close	schließen, zumachen
closed	geschlossen
clothes	Kleidung, Bekleidung, Klamotten
cloudy	bewölkt
coat	Mantel
coffee	Kaffee
cold	kalt, die Kälte, Erkältung
to collect	sammeln, abholen, einsammeln
Cologne	Köln
colour	Farbe
colourful	farbenfroh, bunt
to comb	kämmen
to come	kommen
comfortable	bequem, behaglich
to command	befehlen
to comment	sich äußern, bemerken
common	alltäglich, gewöhnlich
to compel	zwingen
compelled	gezwungen
to complain	sich beklagen
complete	ganz, vollständig
completed	fertig, abgeschlossen
complicated	kompliziert
compulsion	Zwang
to concentrate	konzentrieren
concert	Konzert
concession	Zugeständnis, Einräumung, Ermässigung
condition	Bedingung, Zustand
cone	Kegel, Eistüte, Speiseeis
to congratulate	gratulieren, beglückwünschen
conscious of	bewusst
to consent	zustimmen
consequently	folglich, folgerichtig
to consider	überlegen, erwägen, der Meinung sein
considerably	beträchtlich, bedeutend
to consist of	bestehen aus
continually	ununterbrochen
to continue	weitermachen, fortsetzen
to control	kontrollieren
convenient	günstig, passend
to convince of	überzeugen
to cook	kochen, zubereiten
cook	Koch
cool	kühl, scharf, stark
to cope with	zurechtkommen mit, mit etwas fertig werden, bewältigen
to copy	kopieren
corner	Ecke
to correct	berichtigen, verbessern, korrigieren
correct	korrekt, richtig
to cost	kosten

costume	Kostüme
cottage	Häuschen, Hütte, Landhaus
could	könnte, konnte
to count	zählen
counter	Ladentisch, Theke, Spielstein, Spielmarke
country	Land
courage	Mut
courageous	mutig
cousin	Kusine
to cover	zudecken, bedecken
cowardly	feige, ängstlich
to crash	zusammen krachen, einstürzen, zerbrechen
craving	Verlangen
crazy	verrückt
to creep	kriechen, schleichen
to cross	überqueren
to cry	weinen, rufen, schreien
cup	Tasse
cupboard	Schrank
curious	neugierig
curtain	Vorhang, Gardine
to cut	schneiden
Dad	Vati, Papa
daily	täglich
to dance	tanzen
dancer	Tänzer
dancing	Tanzen
Danes	Dänen
danger	Gefahr
dangerous	gefährlich
to dare	wagen
dark	dunkel, Dunkelheit
date	Datum, Verabredung, Termin
daughter	Tochter
day	Tag
dead	tot
to deal	austeilen, handeln
dear	lieb, teuer, Schatz
December	Dezember
decency	Anstand, Anständigkeit
decent	anständig
to decide	entscheiden
decision	Entschluss, Entscheidung, Beschluss
to declare	erklären
deep	tief, sehr (emotionell)
deer	Reh
to defeat	schlagen, besiegen
to defend	verteidigen
to defer	verschieben, verlegen, nachgeben, sich beugen
definitely	bestimmt, endgültig, deutlich
to delay	verschieben, aufschieben, verzögern
delicious	lecker
to delight in	Freude bereiten, Freude haben, Spaß haben
delighted	erfreut, entzückt
to demand	verlangen

dentist	Zahnarzt
to deny	bestreiten, ableugnen, verneinen, dementieren
to depend on	abhängen von, sich verlassen auf
desire	Wunsch, Verlangen
to desire	wünschen, begehren, verlangen
desk	Schreibtisch, Pult, Schülertisch
determination	Entschlossenheit
to determine	bestimmen, entscheiden
determined	entschlossen, unbedingt tun wollen
to detest	hassen, verabscheuen
to devote	widmen, aufopfern, hingeben
to die	sterben
difference	Unterschied
different	anders, verschieden, unterschiedlich
difficult	schwierig
difficulty	Schwierigkeit
to dig	graben
dinner	Hauptmahlzeit, Abendessen
direct	direkt, gerade
direction	Richtung
dirt	Dreck, Schmutz
dirty	dreckig, schmutzig
disappointed	enttäuscht
to disapprove	missbilligen
to discontinue	aufgeben, abbrechen, aufhören, unterbrechen
to discover	entdecken
disease	Krankheit
disgusted	angeekelt, sich über einen ärgern
dish	Schale, Schüssel
dishes	Geschirr
dishwasher	Geschirrspülmaschine
to dislike	nicht mögen
distance	Entfernung, Strecke
to distinguish	unterscheiden, sich auszeichnen
distress	Not, Elend, Leiden, Verzweiflung
to dive	springen, tauchen
to do	machen, tun
doctor	Doktor, Arzt
dog	Hund
doll	Puppe
donkey	Esel
door	Tür
doubt	Zweifel
down	herunter, hinunter, runter
dramatic	dramatisch
drastic	drastisch
to draw	malen, zeichnen, ziehen
to dread	sich fürchten vor
dreadful	schrecklich
to dream	träumen
dream	Traum
dress	Kleid
to dress	sich anziehen
to drink	trinken
to drive	fahren

driver	Fahrer
to dry up	austrocknen
due	fällig, gebührend, angemessen, geziemend
dull	trüb, träge, stumpf, dumm, geistlos, langweilig
during	während
duty	Pflicht
to dwell	wohnen
each	jede(r), jede einzelne
each other	einander
each time	jedes Mal
eager	begierig
ear	Ohr
early	früh, zu früh
to earn	verdienen
earth	Erde
Easter	Ostern
easy	leicht, einfach
to eat	essen, fressen
economic	wirtschaftlich
edition	Ausgabe
efficient	leistungsfähig, wirksam
effort	Versuch, Anstrengung
eight	acht
either	auch nicht, entweder
elephant	Elefant
eleven	elf
else	sonst, noch
empty	leer
empty-handed	mit leeren Händen
to enable	ermöglichen, befähigen
to encourage	ermutigen
encouragement	Ermutigung, Ansporn
to end	beenden, aufhören
end	Ende
to endeavour	sich bemühen
energy	Energie
English	englisch
to enjoy	genießen
enough	genug
to enter	eintreten, betreten
enthusiastic	begeistert
entirely	ganz, ausschließlich, durchaus, völlig
to entitle	berechtigen, Anspruch haben auf
envelope	Briefumschlag
equally	ebenso, genauso, gleich
to escape	flüchten, entfliehen, entkommen
especially	besonders
to estimate	einschätzen, schätzen, veranschlagen
eternal	ewig
Europe	Europa
even	sogar, noch, flatt, flach, gerade, glatt, selbst
evening	Abend
ever	je, jemals, schon mal
ever since	seitdem
everlasting	ewig

every	jeder, alle
everybody	jedermann, jeder, alle
everyone	alle, jedermann, alle
everything	alles
everywhere	überall (hin)
evidently	offensichtlich, einleuchtend, klar, offenbar
exact	genau
exam	Prüfung, Examen
excited	aufgeregt
exciting	aufregend, spannend
exclusively	exklusiv, ausschließlich
to excuse	entschuldigen
exercise	Übung
to expect	erwarten, annehmen
expected to	sollen
expensive	teuer
experience	Erfahrung
experiment	Versuch, Experiment
to explain	erklären, erläutern
to extend	aussprechen
extremely	extrem, äußerst
eye	Auge
fabulous	toll
face	Gesicht
to fail	versagen, durchfallen, misslingen, scheitern
fair	anständig, ehrlich, schön, gerecht, fair
fairly	recht, ziemlich
faithful	treu, genau
to fall	fallen, stürzen. hinfallen
to fall asleep	einschlafen
to fall back on	zurückgreifen auf
family	Familie
famous	berühmt
to fancy	einbilden, glauben, vorstellen, gern haben
fantastic	fantastisch, toll
far	weit
farm	Bauernhof, Farm
farmer	Bauer
fascinating	bezaubernd
fashion	Mode, Art
fast	schnell
fat	dick, fett
father	Vater
to favour	bevorzugen, vorziehen, begünstigen
fear	Furcht, Angst
February	Februar
to be fed up with	etw satt haben, die Nase voll haben
to feed	füttern, ernähren
to feel	sich fühlen, fühlen, merken, wahrnehmen, spüren, empfinden
feeling	Gefühl
to feel like	Lust haben auf
to feel sorry for	Leid tun
to fetch	holen, abholen
few	wenige
field	Wiese

to fight	kämpfen, bekämpfen
finally	schließlich, endlich, zum Schluss
to find	finden, feststellen, suchen
fine	fein, gut, schön, prima
to finish	beenden, fertig machen, aufhören, zu Ende machen
to fire	abfeuern, abgeben
fire	Feuer
first	erste, als Erstes, zunächst, erst, zuerst
fish	Fisch
five	fünf
flat	flach, platt
to flee	fliehen
to fling	schleudern
floor	Fußboden
flower	Blume
to fly	fliegen
to fold	falten
to follow	folgen
following	folgend
fond of	gern haben, gerne mögen
food	Essen, Lebensmittel, Futter, Nahrung
foot, feet	Fuß, Füße
football	Fußball
for	für, seit, lang
for certain	ganz sicher, sicherlich
for example	zum Beispiel
for sure	ganz sicher, ganz bestimmt, gewiss, sicherlich
to forbid	verbieten
to force	zwingen
to forecast	voraussagen
forest	Wald
to forget	vergessen
to forgive	vergeben
fork	Gabel
to forsake	verlassen
fortunately	glücklicherweise
four	vier
France	Frankreich
frankly	offen, ehrlich, offen gesagt
free	frei
freedom	Freiheit
to freeze	frieren, gefrieren
French	französisch
frequency	Häufigkeit
frequently	häufig
fresh	frisch
Friday	Freitag
friend	Freund
friendly	freundlich, nett
frightened	verängstigt
from	aus, von, woher
fruit	Obst, Früchte, Frucht
full	satt, voll
fun	Spaß, Freude, es macht Spaß
funny	komisch, lustig, witzig

furious	wütend
furthermore	außerdem
future	Zukunft
to gain	gewinnen, erlangen, zunehmen
game	Spiel
gangster	Gangster, bewaffneter Verbrecher
garden	Garten
generally	normalerweise
generous	großzügig
gentle	sanft
German	deutsch
Germany	Deutschland
to get	bekommen, gewinnen, kriegen, holen, veranlassen, gelangen, besorgen, abholen, nehmen
to get around to	zu etw kommen, dazukommen etw zu tun
to get lost	sich verlaufen
to get married	heiraten
to get off	aussteigen
to get ready	fertig machen
to get up	aufstehen
ghost	Geist, Gespenst
gift	Geschenk
girl	Mädchen
girlfriend	Freundin
to give	geben, schenken, verteilen
to give up	aufgeben
glad	froh, glücklich, sich freuen
glass	Glas
to go	gehen, fahren, reisen
to go away	weggehen
to go on	weiter machen
to go shopping	Einkaufen gehen
to go swimming	Schwimmen gehen
goal	Ziel, Tor, Treffer
God	Gott
going to	vorhaben
good	gut
goodbye, good-bye	Auf Wiedersehen
grade	Note
grammar	Grammatik
grandfather	Großvater
grandmother	Großmutter
grass	Gras, Rasen
grateful	dankbar
great	großartig, toll, wichtig, super, groß, prima
greatly	stark, sehr
greedy	begierig
green	grün
to grind	mahlen, schleifen
grocer	Lebensmittelhändler
ground	Boden, Erde
to grow	wachsen
to grow up	aufwachsen, erwachsen werden
grown-up	erwachsen, Erwachsener
to grumble	murren, nörgeln

grumpy	misslaunisch, mürrisch
to guarantee	garantieren, bürgen
to guess	erraten, raten, abschätzen
guest	Gast
guilty	schuldig
gun	Gewehr, Pistole, Schusswaffe
habit	Gewohnheit
had better	wohl besser, Sie täten besser zu
hair	Haare
half	halb, Hälfte
half an hour	eine halbe Stunde
half past	halb
hall	Flur, Diele, Korridor, Saal, Halle
to hand in	einreichen, abgeben
to handle	handhaben, fertig werden mit, bewältigen
handsome	gut aussehend
handy	handlich
to hang	hängen, sich aufhängen
to hang up	aufhängen
to happen	geschehen, passieren, zufällig, durch Zufall
happy	glücklich, froh, fröhlich
hard	hart, schwer, kräftig
hardly	kaum
has	hat
hat	Hut
to hate	hassen, gar nicht mögen
to have	haben, besitzen, veranlassen
to have to	müssen
he	er
head	Kopf
headmaster	Schuldirektor
healthy	gesund
to hear	hören
heart	Herz
heartily	herzlich, aufrichtig, innig
heavenly	himmlisch
heavy	schwer
help	Hilfe
to help	helfen
helpful	hilfsbereit
hence	also, daher, deshalb
her	ihr, sie
here	hier, hierher
to hesitate	zögern
to hide	verstecken, sich verstecken
high	hoch, laut
highly	sehr empfehlend, höchst / sehr lobend, sehr
hill	Hügel
him	ihn, ihm
to hire	mieten, leihen, anstellen, in Dienst nehmen
his	sein
historic	historisch
to hit	schlagen
to hold	halten, abhalten, veranstalten
hole	Loch, Öffnung

holiday	Ferien, Urlaub
home	nach Hause, zu Hause, Heim, Zuhause
homework	Hausaufgaben
honest	ehrlich
to hope	hoffen
hopefully	hoffentlich
horrified	entsetzt
horse	Pferd
hospital	Krankenhaus
hot	heiß, warm, scharf gewürzt
hour	Stunde
hourly	stündlich
house	Haus
how	wie
how about	wie wäre es mit
however	jedoch, wie auch immer
how long	wie lange
how many	wie viele
how much	wieviel
how often	wie oft
hungry	hungrig
to hunt	jagen
hunter	Jäger
hurry	Eile
to hurry	sich beeilen, hasten
to hurt	verletzen, weh tun, schmerzen
husband	Ehemann
I	ich
ice-cream	Speiseeis, Eiskrem
idea	Idee
idle	faul
if	falls, ob, wenn
ill	krank, schlecht
to imagine	sich vorstellen, annehmen
immediate	sofort
immense	riesig, unermesslich
to implore	anflehen
impolite	unhöflich
important	wichtig
to impose	sich aufdrängen, aufzwingen, auferlegen
impossible	unmöglich
impressed	beeindruckt
impressive	eindrucksvoll, imponierend
to improve	verbessern
in	in
in addition	zusätzlich, außerdem, noch dazu
inclination	Neigung, Hang
inclined	geneigt
to include	einschließen, einbeziehen
in comparison	im Vergleich, verglichen mit
in conclusion	abschließend
in contrast	im Gegensatz
indeed	tatsächlich, wirklich
India	Indien
to induce	herbeiführen, bewirken, verursachen

inducement	Anreiz, Ansporn
to indulge	nachgeben, verwöhnen, frönen, gönnen, sich etwas erlauben
in fact	tatsächlich, in der Tat
infinite	unendlich
to inform	informieren, benachrichtigen
information	Information, Auskunft
in front of	vor
to injure	verletzen
injured	verletzt
in love	verliebt
in no time	im Nu
in order to	um ... zu
in other words	mit anderen Worten
to inquire	sich erkundigen
in short	kurz gesagt, kurzgefasst
inside	drinnen
to insist on	bestehen auf
in spite of	trotz, ungeachtet
to install	installieren, einrichten, einsetzen
instead of	anstatt, statt
instinct	Instinkt, Naturanlage
to instruct	unterrichten, anweisen
instruction	Anweisung, Befehl
in sum	zusammengefasst, zusammenfassend, insgesamt
intelligence	Intelligenz, Verstand
intelligent	klug, intelligent
in that case	in dem Fall
to intend	vorhaben, beabsichtigen
intense	heftig, intensiv
intention	Absicht, Vorhaben
interest	Interesse
to be interested in	interessiert sein an
interesting	interessant
in time	rechtzeitig
to introduce	vorstellen, bekannt machen
invitation	Einladung
to invite	einladen
to involve	beteiligen, hineinziehen, umfassen
to iron	bügeln
is	ist
island	Insel
isn't = is not	ist nicht
it	es
Italian	italienisch
its	sein
jail	Gefängnis
January	Januar
jeans	Jeanshose
job	Aufgabe, Arbeitsstelle, Beruf, Arbeit
joke	Witz, Scherz
juicy	saftig
July	Juli
to jump	springen
June	Juni
just	bloß, nur, einfach, wirklich, eben, gerade, mit Recht, gerecht

justly	gerechterweise, gerecht, mit Recht
to justify	rechtfertigen
keen on	begeistert, erpicht auf, interessiert an, verrückt nach
to keep	behalten
to keep from	hindern an, abhalten von, bewahren vor
to keep on	weitermachen, fortfahren, nicht aufhören, beibehalten
to keep to oneself	nicht gesellig, Einzelgänger sein
to keep s.o. waiting	warten lassen
keeper	Wärter
key	Schlüssel
to kill	töten
kind	liebenswürdig, nett, freundlich, gütig
kind of	eine Art, sozusagen, was für ein
kindness	Freundlichkeit, Güte
king	König
kitchen	Küche
kite	Drachen
kitten	Kätzchen
to kneel	knien
knife	Messer
to knock down	umwerfen, niederschlagen, niederwerfen, umstoßen
to know	kennen, wissen
ladder	Leiter
lady	Dame
lake	(Binnen-)See
to land	landen
language	Sprache
large	groß, umfangreich
last	zuletzt, letzte
late	spät, zu spät, verspätet
lately	kürzlich, neulich, vor kurzem
later	später
to laugh	lachen
to laugh at	auslachen
to lay	legen, stellen
lazy	faul, träge
to lead	führen
leaf, leaves	Blatt, Blätter
to lean	lehnen, stützen
to leap	springen
to learn	lernen, erfahren
to leave	weggehen, abfahren, verlassen, abreisen, lassen
leave	Erlaubnis
to leave off	ablassen
lecture	Vorlesung, Vortrag
left	links, übrig bleiben, übriggelassen
leg	Bein
to lend	borgen, leihen, verleihen
lesson	Unterrichtsstunde
to let	erlauben, lassen, vermieten, zulassen
Let's	Lasst uns
letter	Brief, Buchstabe
liable	dazu neigen, wahrscheinlich etw tun, haftbar
liberty	Freiheit, Recht, Erlaubnis
library	Bibliothek, Bücherei

to lie	liegen
to lie down	sich hinlegen
lift	Aufzug
light	Licht, Ampel, Lampe, hell, leicht
to light	anzünden, leuchten
like	wie
to like	mögen, gern haben
likewise	ebenso, gleichermassen, gleichfalls
line	Zeile, Linie, Wäscheleine
lion	Löwe
to listen	zuhören, horchen, anhören
little	klein, wenig, jung
to live	wohnen, leben
liver	Leber
living-room	Wohnzimmer
to load	beladen, laden
to loathe	verabscheuen
to lock	zuschließen, verschließen, zusperren, abschließen
lonely	einsam
long	lang
long ago	vor langem
to long for	sich sehnen nach
to look	gucken, aussehen, schauen, ansehen, sehen
to look after	aufpassen auf, sich kümmern um
to look at	ansehen, anschauen
to look for	suchen
to look forward to	sich freuen auf, mit Erwartung entgegensehen
to look like	aussehen, den Anschein haben
lorry	LKW, Lastwagen
to lose	verlieren
lost	verloren
lots of	viele
loud	laut
to love	lieben, sehr mögen, sehr gern haben
lovely	hübsch, reizend, wunderschön, herrlich, schön
low	niedrig, leise
lowly	bescheiden
lucky	glücklich, Glück haben
lunch	Mittagessen
lying	liegen
machine	Maschine, Apparat, Gerät
mad	zornig, wahnsinnig, verrückt
mainly	hauptsächlich
to maintain	behaupten
to make	machen, verursachen, veranlassen, zubereiten, anfertigen, bilden, bauen
man	Mann
to manage	zurechtkommen, schaffen, fertigbringen, verwalten, zuwegebringen
manager	Manager, Betriebsleiter, Direktor, Verwalter, Geschäftsführer
manner	Art und Weise
many	viel
map	Stadtplan, Landkarte
March	März
mark	Note, Zensur
married	verheiratet
to marry	heiraten

master	Herr
matchless	unübertrefflich, unvergleichlich
matter	Sache, Angelegenheit
may	können, dürfen
maybe	vielleicht
me	mich, mir
meal	Mahlzeit, Essen
to mean	meinen, vorhaben, bedeuten, beabsichtigen
meaning	Bedeutung
means	Möglichkeit, Mittel, Hilfsmittel, Geldmittel
meat	Fleisch
medal	Medaille
medicine	Medizin
to meditate	meditieren
to meet	sich treffen, kennenlernen
men	Männer
to mention	erwähnen
merely	lediglich, bloß, nichts als
mess	Durcheinander, Unordnung
method	Methode, System, Verfahren
mice	Mäuse
microwave	Mikrowellenherd
midnight	Mitternacht
might	könnte
mile	Meile (1,6 km)
milk	Milch
to mind	etwas dagegen haben, sich kümmern um, geneigt sein, sich entschließen, gib acht auf
mind	Lust, Absicht, Sinn, Meinung
mine	meine
mirror	Spiegel
to miss	verpassen, vermissen, verfehlen
missing	fehlend, verschwunden
mistake	Fehler, Irrtum
moment	Augenblick
Mommy	Mutti
Monday	Montag
money	Geld
monkey	Affe
month	Monat
monthly	jeden Monat, monatlich
morally	moralisch
more	mehr, weitere
moreover	außerdem, ferner, übrigens
morning	Morgen, Vormittag
mostly	hauptsächlich
mother	Mutter
mouse	Maus
mouth	Mund
to move	bewegen, umziehen
to mow	mähen
much	viel
Munich	München
music	Musik
musical	musikalisch

must	müssen
mustn't	dürfen nicht
my	mein
namely	nämlich
nap	Nickerchen
narrow	eng
natives	Eingeborene, Einheimische
naturally	natürlich, verständlicherweise
naughty	böse
near	nah, in der Nähe von
nearly	beinahe, fast
neat	ordentlich
necessary	notwendig
necessity	Notwendigkeit
to need	brauchen, benötigen
need	Notwendigkeit, Bedarf, Bedrängnis, Grund
need not	brauchen nicht, nicht müssen
to neglect	vernachlässigen, unterlassen
neighbour	Nachbar
neither	keine, weder ... noch
nervous	nervös, aufgeregt, ängstlich
never	nie
nevertheless	trotzdem, dennoch, nichtsdestoweniger
new	neu
newspaper	Zeitung
next	nächste, das nächste Mal, als nächstes
next to	neben
nice	nett, hübsch, schön
niece	Nichte
night	Nacht
nine	neun
no	nein, keine
nobody	keiner, niemand
noise	Geräusch, Lärm
noisy	laut, lärmend
noon	Mittag
no one	keiner
nor	auch nichts, noch
Normans	Normanen
nose	Nase
not	nicht
not at all	überhaupt nicht
nothing	nichts
to notice	bemerken
noticeable	erkennbar, wahrnehmbar
not yet	noch nicht
now	jetzt, nun
nowhere	nirgend wo
number	Nummer, Zahl, Ziffer
object to	ablehnen, missbilligen, Einspruch erheben, protestieren gegen
objection	Einwand, Einspruch, Protest
obligation	Verpflichtung, Verbindlichkeit
to oblige	verpflichten, zwingen
to observe	beobachten, bemerken
obviously	offensichtlich, deutlich, klar, offenbar, unverkennbar

occassion	Gelegenheit, Anlass, Grund
occasionally	gelegentlich
o'clock	Uhr
odd	merkwürdig, seltsam, komisch
of	von, an
of age	volljährig
of course	natürlich, selbstverständlich
of late	neuerlich
to offer	anbieten, zur Verfügung stellen
office	Büro, Praxis
officer	Beamte, Polizist
official	Beamter
often	oft
oil	Öl
old	alt
on	auf, an
once	einmal, einst, früher
once upon a time	es war einmal
one	einer, eine, eins
one day	eines Tages
only	nur, bloß, erst, einzig
only a few	nur wenige
only a little	nur wenig
on the contrary	im Gegenteil
on the one hand	einerseits
on time	pünktlich
to open	aufmachen, öffnen
open	offen, geöffnet, auf
opportunity	Gelegenheit, Chance
to oppose	entgegenstellen, bekämpfen, dagegen sein, entgegentreten
orange	Apfelsine, Orange, orangefarben
to order	befehlen, ordnen, regulieren
organ	Orgel
other	andere
otherwise	sonst, andernfalls
ought	sollen
our	unser
ours	unsers
ourselves	uns selbst
out	draußen, heraus, nicht zu Hause
outside	draußen, außerhalb von, nach draußen
over	über, vorbei, zu Ende, aus sein, oberhalb
over there	dort drüben
to overcome	besiegen, überwinden
to overhear	zufällig mitbekommen, zufällig hören, belauschen
overjoyed	überglücklich, entzückt, hocherfreut
to overtake	überholen, einholen
own	eigen
owner	Besitzer, Eigentümer
to pack	packen
page	Seite
to paint	anstreichen, malen, anmalen
pair	Paar
pancake	Pfannkuchen
pants	Hosen

paper	Papier, Zeitung
to pardon	verzeihen, entschuldigen
parents	Eltern
particularly	besonders, insbesondere
partly	zum Teil, teilweise, teils
to pass	bestehen, verstreichen, vergehen, reichen, weitergeben
to pass through	durch fahren
past	nach, vorbei, vorüber, vergangen
patient	Patient, geduldig
to pay	bezahlen, zahlen
pea	Erbse
pen	Füller
pencil	Bleistift
pen-friend	Brieffreund
people	Leute, Menschen
perfect	perfekt, vollkommen
to perform	aufführen, verrichten
perhaps	vielleicht, möglicherweise
periodically	regelmäßig
permission	Erlaubnis
to permit	erlauben
perpetual	ewig, ständig, unaufhörlich, ununterbrochen
perseverance	Ausdauer, Beharrlichkeit
to persist	unbeirrt fortfahren, bestehen auf, fortfahren zu tun
personally	persönlich
to persuade	überreden, überzeugen
to phone	anrufen, telefonieren
phone	Telefon
photo	Bild, Foto, Lichtbild
physics	Physik
piano	Klavier
to pick	pflücken
to pick up	aufheben
picnic	Picknick
picture	Bild
piece	Stück
pig	Schwein
pistol	Pistole
place	Ort, Platz, Stelle
to plan	planen, beabsichtigen
plane	Flugzeug
plant	Pflanze
plate	Teller
to play	spielen
player	Spieler
pleasant	angenehm
please	bitte, gefallen
pleased	freudig, zufrieden, erfreut
pleasure	Freude, Vergnügen
plenty of	viele
pocket	Tasche
poem	Gedicht
to point	zeigen
point:	
on the point of	im Begriff sein

point:	
There's no point in	Es hat keinen Zweck / keinen Sinn zu
pointless	sinnlos
police	Polizei
policeman	Polizist, Polizeibeamter, Schutzmann
police officer	Polizieibeamter
polite	höflich
politically	politisch
poor	schlecht, arm
popular	populär, beliebt
position	Lage, Position
possibility	Möglichkeit
possible	möglich, denkbar
possibly	möglicherweise, vielleicht
post office	Post, Postamt
to postpone	aufschieben, verschieben
pound	Pfund
to pour	gießen, schütten
power	Kraft
practical	praktisch
to practise	üben
precise	genau
to prefer	vorziehen, bevorzugen, lieber haben
to prepare	vorbereiten
present	Geschenk, Gegenwart, Präsens
to press	drücken, drängen, aufdrängen, bedrängen, pressieren
presumably	vermutlich, voraussichtlich, wahrscheinlich
to pretend	vortäuschen, vorgeben, sich ausgeben für, so tun als ob
pretty	hübsch, ziemlich, recht
to prevent	verhindern, vorbeugen
previous	vorhergehend
price	Preis
to print	drucken
prison	Gefängnis
privacy	Privatleben, Privatbereich, Zurückgezogenheit, das Alleinsein, die nötige Ruhe
privilege	Vorrecht, Sonderrecht, Vergnügen
prize	Gewinn, Preis
probable, probably	wahrscheinlich, vermutlich
problem	Problem, Schwierigkeit
to proceed	fortfahren, vorwärtsgehen
professor	Professor, Dozent
profit	Gewinn, Nutzen
programme	Programm, Sendung
prohibition	Verbot
project	Projekt, Plan, Vorhaben
to promise	versprechen
proper	korrekt, richtig, angebracht, geeignet, passend
to propose	vorschlagen, beabsichtigen
proud	stolz
to prove	beweisen, erweisen, zeigen
psychologically	psychisch, psychologisch
public	öffentlich
to pull	ziehen
to pull oneself together	sich zusammenreißen, sich zusammennehmen

pump	Pumpe, Luftpumpe
punctual	pünktlich
to punish	bestrafen
punishment	Bestrafung, Strafe
pupil	Schüler
purpose	Zweck
to push	schieben, schubsen, stoßen, drücken
to put	hinlegen, legen, stellen, tun, stecken, hintun, setzen, bringen
to put off	verschieben, aufschieben, auf die lange Bank schieben
to quarrel	streiten, zanken
queen	Königin
queer	eigenartig, seltsam, komisch
to question	Fragen stellen, ausfragen
question	Frage
quick	schnell, rasch
quiet	ruhig, leise, still
quite	ziemlich, ganz, völlig, gänzlich
rabbit	Hase, Kaninchen
race	Wettrennen, Wettlauf, Rennen
radical	radikal
to rain	regnen
rain	Regen
raincoat	Regenmantel
rainy	regnerisch
rapid	schnell, rasch
rare, rarely	selten
rather	ziemlich, etwas, eher
to reach	erreichen
to read	lesen, vorlesen
ready	fertig, bereit
realistic	realistisch
really	wirklich, eigentlich, tatsächlich
reason	Grund, Ursache
to rebuild	wieder aufbauen, wieder herstellen
to recall	sich erinnern, ins Gedächtnis zurückrufen
to receive	erhalten, bekommen
recently	neulich, vor kurzem
reciprocal	wechselseitig
to reckon	glauben, schätzen, rechnen
to recollect	sich erinnern an, sich entsinnen
to recommend	empfehlen, raten
record	Schallplatte, Rekord
to recover	sich erholen
red	rot
reflexive	rückbezüglich
to refrain	unterlassen, enthalten, Abstand nehmen
refreshing	erfrischend, erquickend
to refuse	ablehnen, abschlagen, verweigern
to regret	bedauern, bereuen
to reject	ablehnen, verwerfen
relative	Verwandter
reliable	zuverlässig
relieved	erleichtert, leichter zumute werden als
reluctant	widerwillig, abgeneigt
to rely on	sich verlassen auf

remain	bleiben, verbleiben, zurückbleiben, übrigbleiben, noch vorhanden sein
to remark	bemerken, äußern
to remember	sich erinnern an, daran denken, sich merken, behalten, sich ins Gedächtnis zurückrufen
to remind	erinnern
to rend	zerreißen
to repair	reparieren
to repeat	wiederholen
repeatedly	wiederholt
to reply	erwidern, antworten
to report	berichten
reportedly	angeblich, wie verlautet, es wird berichtet
to request	bitten, ersuchen
to require	benötigen, brauchen, fordern, verlangen
to resent	übel nehmen, verübeln
to resist	sich widersetzen, widerstehen, Widerstand leisten
to resolve	beschließen, erklären, lösen, Beschluss fassen zu
to respond	antworten, erwidern, reagieren auf, eingehen auf
responsibility	Verantwortung
to rest	ausruhen, erholen, lehnen gegen, stützen auf
result	Folge, Resultat, Ergebnis
to resume	wieder aufnehmen, wieder beginnen, fortfahren
to return	zurückgehen, zurückbringen, heimkehren, erwidern, wiederkehren, zurückkehren, zurückschicken
reward	Belohnung
to rid	befreien, freimachen von
to ride	reiten, fahren
ridiculous	lächerlich, unsinnig
right	richtig, Recht, Recht haben, gerade, sofort, passend, angemessen, gerade, sofort, also gut, rechts
right away	sofort
rightly	richtig, zu Recht
right now	gerade jetzt
to ring	läuten, klingeln
to ring up	anrufen
to rise	aufgehen, aufstehen, sich erheben
to risk	riskieren, wagen, aufs Spiel setzen
river	Fluss
road	Straße, Landstraße
to roar	brüllen, laut schreien
to rob	stehlen
robber	Räuber
to roll away	wegrollen
room	Zimmer, Raum
round	rund, um ... herum, in ... umher
to rub	reiben
rude	unhöflich, grob, ungebildet
rug	kleiner Teppich
ruler	Lineal
rules	Regeln, Vorschriften
to run	laufen, rennen
to run away	weglaufen
Russian	russisch
sad	traurig
safe	sicher, gefahrlos

salad	Salat
same	der-, die-, dasselbe, gleich
sandwich	belegtes Butterbrot
satisfied	zufrieden
Saturday	Samstag
to save	aufbewahren, retten, sparen, aufheben, bewahren
to say	sagen, erzählen, sprechen
scarcely	kaum, schwerlich
school	Schule
scientific	wissenschaftlich
to scold	ausschimpfen, schelten
scramble	Gerangel, Drängelei, Rangelei
to scream	schreien, brüllen
sea	See, Meer
to search	suchen
seaside	Meer, an der See, Meeresküste
season	Jahreszeit
seat	Sitzplatz, Sitz
to seat oneself	Platz nehmen
second	zweite
secret	Geheimnis, geheim
secretary	Sekretärin
to see	sehen, verstehen, erkennen, einsehen
to seek	suchen, erbitten
to seem	scheinen, erscheinen
seldom	selten
selfish	egoistisch, selbstsüchtig
self-pity	Selbstmitleid
to sell	verkaufen
to send	schicken, senden
sensible	vernünftig
sentence	Satz
to separate	trennen, lossagen, lösen, absondern
series	Serie, Reihe
serious	ernst, ernsthaft
to set	legen, setzen
to set fire to	anzünden
setting	niedergehend, untergehende
to settle	entscheiden, besiedeln, beruhigen, ansiedeln, niederlassen
to settle down	sich gemütlich machen
seven	sieben
several	einige, mehrere
severe	schwer, schlimm, streng
to sew	nähen
to shake	schütteln
shall	werden, sollen
shallow	flach
sharp	scharf, punkt
to shave	rasieren
she	sie
to shed	vergießen, verlieren
shelf	Bücherbrett, Regal, Bord
to shine	scheinen, strahlen
ship	Schiff
shirt	Hemd

shock	Schock, Schlag, Schicksalsschlag
shocked	schockiert, empört
shoe	Schuh
to shoot	schießen
shop	Geschäft, Laden
to shop	einkaufen
shopping bag	Einkaufstüte
short	kurz
shot	Spritze, Schuss
should	sollen
to shout	schreien, rufen
to show	zeigen
show	Veranstaltung, Show, Kino, Theater
shower	Dusche
to shrink	einlaufen, schrumpfen
to shut	schließen, zumachen
shy	scheu, schüchtern
sick	krank
sick of	satt haben, mehr als genug davon haben
side	Seite
sight	Blick, Anblick
to sign	unterschreiben
silent	still, ruhig, stumm
silly	albern, dumm, doof
similarly	genauso, ebenso, ähnlich, gleichartig
simple	einfach
since	seit, seitdem, da
sincere	aufrichtig, echt
to sing	singen
single	einzeln
to sink	sinken
sister	Schwester
to sit	sitzen, sich setzen
situation	Lage, Situation, Zustand
six	sechs
skirt	Rock
sky	Himmel
skyscraper	Wolkenkratzer, Hochhaus
to slay	erschlagen, töten
to sleep	schlafen
slice	Scheibe, Schnitte, Stück
to slide	gleiten, schlittern
to sling	schleudern
to slink	schleichen
to slit	aufschneiden, schlitzen
slow	langsam
small	klein
smart	klug, schlau
to smell	riechen, duften
to smile	lächeln
to smoke	rauchen
to snatch	greifen, entreißen, schnappen
to snow	schneien
snow	Schnee
so	also, so, deshalb, daher, so dass

soap	Seife
sock	Socke, Strumpf
so far	bis jetzt
soft	weich
to solve	lösen
some	einige, ein paar, etwas, irgendein, etwas
somebody	jemand
someone	jemand
something	etwas
sometimes	manchmal
somewhere	irgendwo, irgendwohin
son	Sohn
song	Lied
soon	bald
to soothe	beruhigen, lindern
sorry	traurig, Leid tun, Wie bitte, Es tut mir leid, Entschuldigung
sorry for	Leid tun, traurig um, bedauere
sort of	irgendwie, eine Art, etwas Derartiges, gewissermaßen
sound	Geräusch, solide, fest, vernünftig, gesund, ganz, kräftig, tüchtig
sour	sauer
south	Süden, nach Süden, südlich
to sow	säen
Spain	Spanien
spanking	Tracht Prügel, Klaps, die Löffel kriegen
to speak	sprechen, reden
special	speziell, besonder(s)
to specialize	sich spezialisieren
specific	bestimmt, genau
to speed	sich beeilen, beschleunigen, schnell fahren
to spell	buchstabieren
to spend	verbringen, ausgeben
spider	Spinne
to spill	verschütten
to spin	drehen, spinnen
to spit	spucken
to splash	bespritzen, plantschen
splendid	herrlich
to split	spalten, sich teilen
to spoil	verderben, verwöhnen
sports	Sport
to spread	ausbreiten, streichen
to spring	springen
spring	Frühling, Frühjahr
square	viereckig, Platz, Quadrat
stable	Stall
stairs	Treppe
stamp	Briefmarke
to stand	stehen, dulden, ausstehen
to stand up	aufstehen
to start	anfangen, beginnen, starten
station	Bahnhof, Haltestelle, Rundfunksender
to stay	bleiben, verbleiben
steady	ruhig, fest, beständig, standhaft, unerschütterlich
to steal	stehlen
to step	treten

to stick	stecken, kleben, hineinstecken, steckenbleiben, heften, befestigen
still	noch, immer noch, ruhig, still
to sting	stechen
to stink	stinken
stomach	Magen
stone	Stein
to stop	anhalten, aufhören, stoppen
store	Geschäft, Kaufhaus
story	Geschichte, Erzählung
straight	gerade, direkt, unmittelbar, geradewegs
strange	fremd, seltsam, merkwürdig, sonderbar
stranger	Fremder
strawberry	Erdbeere
street	Straße
strength	Kraft, Stärke
to stride	schreiten
to strike	schlagen
to string	aufreihen, spannen
to strive	sich bemühen, streben
strong	stark
to study	studieren, lernen
to stumble	stolpern
stupid	dumm, doof, blöd, dämlich
style	Stil
subject	Unterrichtsfach
to submit	beugen, nachgeben, unterwerfen
to succeed	Erfolg haben, gelingen
such	solch
suddenly	plötzlich
sugar	Zucker
to suggest	vorschlagen, andeuten, empfehlen
suitcase	Koffer
sum	Menge, Geldsumme
summer	Sommer
sums	Rechnen, Rechenaufgabe
sun	Sonne
to sunbathe	sich sonnen
Sunday	Sonntag
sunny	sonnig
sunshine	Sonnenschein
supermarket	Supermarkt
to support	unterstützen, ernähren
support	Unterstützung, Beistand
to suppose	annehmen, erwarten, meinen, vermuten
supposed to	sollen, es wird erwartet
supreme	höchst, oberst
sure	sicher
to surprise	überraschen
surprise	Überraschung
surprised	überrascht, sich wundern über
to surrender	sich ergeben
surrounded	umgeben, umstellt, umzingelt, eingekreist
survey	Untersuchung, Begutachtung, Vermessung, Marktstudie, Umfrage
to suspect	verdächtigen
to swear	fluchen, schwören

to sweep	kehren
sweet	süß
sweets	Süßigkeiten, Bonbons
to swell	schwellen, zunehmen
to swim	schwimmen
to swing	schaukeln, schwingen
to switch off	ausschalten, ausknipsen
Switzerland	Schweiz
systematic	systematisch
table	Tisch
tail	Schwanz
to take	nehmen, mitnehmen, dauern, wegbringen, annehmen, bringen
to take a walk	spazieren gehen
to take care of	kümmern um, sorgen für, aufpassen auf, acht geben
to take part in	Teilnehmen an
talent	Talent, Begabung
to talk	sprechen, reden
tall	groß, hochgewachsen, hoch
taste	Geschmack
tea	Tee
to teach	lehren, unterrichten, beibringen
teacher	Lehrer
to tear	reißen, zerreißen
technically	technisch
technology	Technologie, Technik
teeth	Zähne
telephone	Telefon
television	Fernsehen
to tell	erzählen, erklären, befehlen, sagen, mitteilen, berichten
temper	Zorn, Wut
to tempt	versuchen, in Versuchung führen
ten	zehn
to tend	dazu neigen, tendieren, Tendenz haben, gerichtet sein auf/nach
terrible	schrecklich, fürchterlich, furchtbar, unmöglich
test	Klassenarbeit, Test, Prüfung, Versuch
than	als
to thank	sich bedanken, danken
that	jener
the	der, die, das
theatre	Theater, Bühne, Schauspielhaus
their	ihre
theirs	ihres
them	sie, ihnen
then	dann
there	dort, da, dorthin, dahin
therefore	deshalb, daher
these	diese
they	sie
they're = they are	sie sind
thick	dick
thief	Dieb
thin	dünn
thing	Ding, Gegenstand, Sache
to think	meinen, glauben, denken
to think of	denken an

third	dritte
thirsty	durstig
this	dies, dieser, diese, dieses
thoroughly	gründlich, vollkommen
those	jene dort
though	obwohl
thousand	tausend
to threaten	drohen
three	drei
thrill	freudige Erregung, richtiges Erlebnis, Sensation, Spannung, das Spannende
thrilling	aufregend
to trouble	sich bemühen
through	durch, hindurch
to throw	werfen
to thrust	stoßen
Thursday	Donnerstag
thus	folglich, somit, daher
ticket	Eintrittskarte, Etikette, Fahrkarte, Fahrschein, Karte
to tickle	kitzeln
tidy	ordentlich, aufgeräumt
to tidy up	aufräumen
tight	eng, fest, stramm
till	bis
time	Zeit, Mal, Uhrzeit
times	mal
tiny	winzig, klein
tired	müde, erschöpft
to	zu, mit, vor, nach, in, um zu
today	heute
toe	Zeh
together	zusammen
tomorrow	morgen
tonight	heute Abend, heute Nacht
too	zu, auch, ebenfalls, außergewöhnlich, höchst, sehr, allzu
tortoise	Schildkröte
totally	völlig, total, ganz, gesamt
to touch	berühren
town	kleine Stadt, Stadt, Dorf
toy	Spielzeug, Spielsachen
traffic light	Verkehrsampel
train	Zug
tram	Strassenbahn
to travel	verreisen, fahren, reisen
to tread	treten
to treat	behandeln
tree	Baum
triangular	dreieckig
trick	Trick, Scherz, Spaß, Kunstgriff, Streich, Kunststück
tried	vor Gericht gestellt
trip	Reise, Ausflug, Tour
trouble	Schwierigkeit, Ärger
to trouble	beunruhigen, belästigen, sich Mühe geben, stören
trousers	lange Hosen
true, truly	wahr, aufrichtig, wahrhaftig, wirklich, wahrheitsgetreu
to trust	trauen, vertrauen, glauben, sich verlassen

truth	Wahrheit
to try	versuchen, ausprobieren, einen Versuch machen, probieren, durch Versuch feststellen, vor Gericht bringen
Tuesday	Dienstag
tune	Melodie
turn	an der Reihe sein
to turn	drehen, sich wenden, abbiegen, werden
to turn around	sich umdrehen
to turn out	sich herausstellen, sich ergeben
TV	Fernsehen, Fernsehapparat
twelve	zwölf
twenty	zwanzig
twice	zweimal
twins	Zwillinge
two	zwei
to type	tippen
typical	typisch
ugly	abstoßend, hässlich, widerwärtig
umbrella	Schirm
uncle	Onkel
under	unter
to understand	verstehen, begreifen, einsehen
understandably	verständlicherweise
to undertake	unternehmen, sich verpflichten
undoubtedly	zweifellos, unbestritten
unexpected	unerwartet
ungrateful	undankbar
unhappy	unglücklich, traurig
unique	einmalig, einzigartig
universal	allumfassend, universal
university	Universität
unless	es sei denn dass, vorausgesetzt
to unlock	aufschließen, aufsperren, öffnen
unluckily	unglücklicherweise
unpleasant	unangenehm
until	bis
unwilling	nicht bereit, nicht gewillt, abgeneigt, ungern
upset	aufgeregt, aufgebracht
to upset	umwerfen, verwirren, aus der Fassung bringen
upstairs	oben, nach oben
up till now	bis jetzt
up to now	bis jetzt
urge	Verlangen, Bedürfnis, Drang
to urge	drängen, eindringlich bitten, zwingen, vorwärtstreiben
urgent	dringend
us	uns
to use	gebrauchen, benutzen, verwenden
used to	gewohnt sein, pflegte zu tun
useful	nützlich
useless	nutzlos, untauglich
usually	gewöhnlich, meistens, normalerweise
utterly	völlig
vacation	Urlaub
to value	schätzen, hochachten, hochschätzen, Wert legen auf
very	sehr, rein, richtig, wirklich

to visit	besuchen, besichtigen
visitor	Besucher
vocabulary	Vokabeln
voice	Stimme
to volunteer	anbieten, sich freiwillig melden, aus freien Stücken tun
to vomit	erbrechen, ausbrechen, sich übergeben
to vote	wählen
to vow	geloben, feierlich versprechen, schwören
wager	Wette
to wait	warten
waiter	Kellner, Ober
to wait for	warten auf, erwarten
waitress	Kellnerin
to wake	aufwecken, erwachen, aufwachen
to wake up	aufwachen, aufwecken, wecken
walk	Spaziergang, Rundgang
to walk	zu Fuß gehen, laufen
walking stick	Spazierstock
wall	Wand, Mauer
to want	wollen, wünschen, mögen
to warn	warnen, ermahnen
warning	Warnung, Mahnung
was	war
to wash	waschen
wash	Wäsche
to waste	verschwenden, vergeuden
watch	Armbanduhr
to watch	beobachten, anschauen, zuschauen, sich etwas ansehen, sehen
to water	begießen
water	Wasser
to wave	winken
way	Art und Weise, Weg, weite Strecke
way of	Gelegenheit, Mittel, Verfahren, Weise ... zu
we	wir
weak	schwach
to wear	anziehen, tragen, anhaben
weary	müde, satt, überdrüssig
weather	Wetter
to weave	weben
Wednesday	Mittwoch
week	Woche
weekend	Wochenende
weekly	jede Woche, wöchentlich
to weep	weinen
weight	Gewicht
welcome	willkommen, keine Ursache
to welcome	begrüßen, willkommen heißen
well	gut, nun, gesund, wohl, gründlich, eigentlich
were	waren
wet	nass
what	was
What about	wie wäre es mit, Was hältst du von
What's the use of	Was nützt es
when	wann, als, wenn
whenever	jedes Mal wenn, so oft als

where	wo, wohin, woher
wherever	wo auch immer
whether	ob
which	welches
while	während
white	weiß
who	wer
whole, wholly	völlig, gänzlich, ausschließlich, durchaus, ganz
whom	wem, wen
whose	wessen
why	warum, weshalb
wicked	schlecht, böse, boshaft
wide	weit, breit
widow	Witwe
wife, wives	Ehefrau, Ehefrauen
will	werden, wird
willing	bereit, gewillt, bereitwillig, einverstanden
willpower	Willenskraft
to win	gewinnen, siegen
to wind	(auf)drehen, wickeln, aufziehen
wind	Wind
window	Fenster
wine	Wein
to wipe	wischen
wire	Draht
wise	weise, klug, schlau
wish	Wunsch, Verlangen
to wish	wünschen
with	mit, bei
within	innerhalb
without	ohne
wolf, wolves	Wolf, Wölfe
woman, women	Frau, Frauen
to wonder	möchte gerne wissen, erstaunt sein, sich überlegen ob, sich wundern, sich fragen, gespannt sein
wonderful	wunderbar
won't = will not	werden nicht, nicht tun werden
word	Wort
work	Arbeit
to work	arbeiten
worker	Arbeiter
workman	Arbeiter
world	Welt
to worry	sich sorgen, beunruhigen, sich Sorgen machen um/wegen
worth	wert, lohnen
worthwhile	lohnenswert
would	würde
would rather	möchter lieber
would sooner	möchte eher
to wring	wringen
to write	schreiben
writer	Schreiber, Autor
wrong	falsch, unrecht
year	Jahr
yearly	jährlich

to yell	brüllen, gellend schreien, laut anschreien
yellow	gelb
yes	ja
yesterday	gestern
yet	noch, schon
to yield	ergeben, nachgeben, sich fügen
you	du, dich, dir, ihr, euch, Ihnen, Sie
young	jung
your	dein, eure, Ihrer
yours	deins, eures
zoo	Tierpark, Zoo

34 Vokabelverzeichnis Deutsch-Englisch

Abend	evening
aber	but
abfahren	depart
Alkohol	alcohol
allein	alone
alles	all
als	than, as, when
als ob	as if
alt	old
am = an dem	on the
Ameise	ant
Amerika	America
andere(r,s)	different, other
anfangen	begin, start
anflehen	implore
Angst	fear, worry
Angst haben	be afraid
ankommen	arrive
anrufen	phone, call
ansehen	look at
anziehen	get dressed, dress 'self
Arzt	doctor
auch	also, too
auf	on, in
aufbleiben	stay up
aufhören	stop, discontinue
aufräumen	tidy up, clean up
aufstehen	get up, stand up
aus	out of, from
Auto	car
backen	bake
Bahn	tram, streetcar, train
bald	soon
Baustelle	building site
bedanken	decline, thank a person
bedienen	serve, help 'self
behaupten	maintain, claim, assert 'self, keep up, keep one's ground
Bein	leg
bekommen	get, obtain, receive
benehmen	behave
Bescheid sagen	inform, instruct, tell
besser	better
beste	the best
besuchen	visit, attend
betrachten	look at, consider, examine, regard

betreten	enter
Bett	bed
Bild	picture
bin	am
bis	until
bist	are
bitten	ask, beg
bleiben	stay, remain
Bleistift	pencil
Blume	flower
brauchen	need
brauchen nicht	need not, don't have to
Brief	letter
Brot	bread
Bruder	brother
Buch	book
da	since, as, there, because
dahin	there
Dame	lady
dann	then
daran	in it, to it
darf	may
das	the
dass	that
dein	your
denken	think, imagine
der, dem, den	the
deshalb	therefore
deutsch	German
die	the
Dienstag	Tuesday
dir	you
doch	yes
dorthin	there
draußen	outside
drei	three
du	you
dürfen	may, can, be allowed to, be permitted to
durch	through
durften	were allowed to, were permitted to, could
eigentlich	really, actually
einander	each other, one another
eine	a, one
Einbrecher	burglar
Einkäufe machen	go shopping
Eis	ice, ice-cream
er	he
erwachsen werden	grow up
erwarten	expect
erwartet	expected
es	it
essen	eat
euch	you
eure	your
fahren	drive, go, ride, travel

Fahrkarte	ticket
Fahrt	trip, journey
falls	in case, if
fangen	catch, seize
fehlen	be absent, be missing
Feier	celebration, party
feiern	celebrate
Fenster	window
fernsehen	watch television
finden	find
Fleisch	meat
fliegen	fly
Flugzeug	airplane, plane
folgen	follow
folgenden	following
fragen	ask
Frau	woman
Freitag	Friday
fressen	eat
freuen	be happy, enjoy 'self, rejoice
Freund	Friend
froh	happy, glad
früh	early
früher	earlier, formerly
fühlen	feel
führen	lead
Füller	pen
für	for
fürchten	be afraid
füttern	feed
gäbest	gave, would give
ganze	whole
geben	give
gebrochen	broken
Geburtstag	birthday
gefallen	please, like
gehen	go
Geld	money
genug	enough
gern	love to
Geschäft	shop
geschehen	happen
Gesicht	face
gestern	yesterday
ginge	went, would go
Haare	hair
haben	have
hätte	would have, had
Hand geben	shake hands
hassen	hate
Haus	house
Hausaufgaben	homework
heiraten	marry, get married
helfen	help
herumspringen	jump around

heute	today
heute abend	this evening
hier	here
hingehen	go there
hochkrabbeln	crawl up
Hochzeit	wedding, marriage
hören	hear, listen
hoffen	hope
hoffentlich	hopefully
holen	fetch, get
ich	I
ihm	him
ihn	him
ihr	her, you
immer	always
im Moment	at the moment
in	in
infolgedessen	therefore
ist	is
Jahr	year
je	ever
jede	each, every
jetzt	now
Juli	July
jung	young
Junge	boy
Juni	June
Kaffee	coffee
Kamera	camera
käme	came, would come
kämmen	comb
kann	can, is able to
Katze	cat
kaufen	buy
kein	no, not a
Kind	child
Kino	cinema, movies, theater
Kirche	church
Klasse	class
Klassenarbeit	(class) test
Klavier	piano
Kleid	dress
klein	small, little
König	king
können	can, be able to
kommen	come, get
kommenden	coming
krabbeln	crawl
krank	sick, ill
Krieg	war
Küche	kitchen
Kuchen	cake
küssen	kiss
lachen	laugh
länger	longer

lange	long
landen	land
lassen	leave, let
laufen	run, walk
laut	loud
leben	live
Lehrer	teacher
lernen	learn
lesen	read
letzte	last
Leute	people
lieb	dear, kind, nice
lieben	love
Loch	hole
machen	make, do
Mädchen	girl
Mann	man
Maus	mouse
mein	my
meinen	mean, think, believe
mich	me
Milch	milk
mir	me
mit	with
mitfahren	go along
mitgehen	go along, accompany
mitnehmen	take along
Mittwoch	Wednesday
möchten	would like, want
mögen	like, wish
Möglichkeit	possibility
im Moment	at the moment
Mond	moon
Montag	Monday
morgen	tomorrow
müde	tired
München	Munich
müssen	must, have to
mutig	courageous, brave
Mutter	mother
nach	after, following, to
nach Hause	home
nächste	next, following
nähen	sew
Nacht	night
nahe	near, close
Name	name
nehmen	take
nein	no
nett	nice
neu	new
Neues	new
nicht	not
noch	still
noch nicht	not yet

normal	normally
notwendig	necessary
nützlich	useful
ob	if, whether
oder	or
oft	often
Oma	grandmother
Onkel	uncle
Passagier	passenger
Pferd	horse
Polizei	police
Prüfung	exam, examination, test
putzen	clean, polish, scour
Rasen	grass, lawn
rasieren	shave 'self
rauchen	smoke
rechte	right
Regen	rain
Regenschirm	umbrella
regnen	rain
reisen	travel
reiten	ride
reparieren	repair
Reste	leftovers, remains
rufen	call, shout
sagen	say
Satz	sentence
schämen	be ashamed
Scheibe	slice
scheinen	seem, appear
schlafen	sleep
schneiden	cut
schnell	quick
schon	already
schreiben	write
Schuh	shoe
Schule	school
Schulhof	playground
Schwein	pig
Schwester	sister
schwierig	difficult, hard
schwimmen	swim
See	lake
sehen	see
sehr	very
sein	be, his
seit	since, for
selber	'self, oneself
selbst	'self
Selbstgespräche führen	talk to oneself
setzen	seat 'self, sit down
sicher	safe
sie	she, they, her, them
singen	sing

sitzen	sit
sofort	immediately, at once
Sohn	son
sollen	should, ought to
Sonntag	Sunday
spät	late
Spiegelbild	mirror image, reflection, see 'self in the mirror
spielen	play
sprechen	speak, talk
springen	jump
Stadt	city
ständig	continual, constant, permanent
stattdessen	instead of that
stattfinden	occur, take place
sterben	die
Straßenbahn	tram, streetcar
Stück	piece, slice
Stuhl	chair
Stunde	hour, lesson
suchen	look for, search, seek
täten	did, would do
Tag	day
tanzen	dance
Tennis	tennis
Tisch	table
tot	dead
tragen	carry, take, wear
treffen	meet, hit
trinken	drink
tun	do, make
überrascht	surprised, amazed
übersetzen	translate
Uhr	clock, o'clock
um	round, around, at, about, for
um zu	in order to
und	and
unglücklich	unhappy
uns	us
unser	our
unter	under
unterstützt	supported
Vater	father
Verben	verbs
verboten	forbidden, prohibited
vergessen	forget
verkaufen	sell
verlassen	abandon, leave, desert, depend on, forsake
verletzen	hurt, injure, wound
verletzt	hurt, injured
verlieben	fall in love
verlieren	lose
verpflichtet	obliged, committed, be s.o. duty
versprechen	promise
verständlich	understandable, clearly
sich verständlich machen	make 'self understood

verstecken	hide
verstehen	understand
viel	much, many
von	from, by
vorbereitet	prepared
vorstellen	imagine, introduce 'self, suppose
vorziehen	prefer, choose
wählen	vote, choose
wäre	would be, were
Wald	woods, forest
wann	when
war, warst	was
warten	wait
warum	why
was	what
waschen	wash
Wasser	water
wegbringen	take away
weil	because, as
Wein	wine
weinen	cry
weit	far
wenn	if, when, whenever
werden	become, will
werfen	throw
Wetter	weather
wie	how
wieder	again
wiederholen	repeat
wir	we
wird	will, become
wirklich	really
wischen	wipe
wissen	know, understand
Woche	week
wohl	indeed, probably, to be sure
Wolf, Wölfe	wolf, wolves
wollen	want to, want
würde	would
Zahn	tooth
Zahnarzt	dentist
zeigen	show
ziehen	pull
Zimmer	room
zu	to, too, for
Zucker	sugar
zu Fuß gehen	walk
Zug	train
zu Hause	at home
zum = zu dem	to the
zusammennehmen	pull oneself together, control 'self, make an effort, take care, gather up
zwei	two
zweimal	twice
zwingen	force

Index

Englische Übungsgrammatik
Lösungen zu den Übungen

Laura Miller

Inhaltsverzeichnis

1 Personal Pronouns

1. They, Their 2. He, He, him, his 3. They, them 4. you 5. Her 6. He, his 7. our, it 8. They, them 9. It 10. He, her 11. We, it 12. Her 13. His 14. Our 15. them, They 16. you 17. you 18. us 19. Our, them 20. He, him 21. Her 22. Their, They, them 23. her, She, it 24. his, He, They, them 25. us, Our, We 26. you, I, your, me, me 27. They, Their 28. them, him, her, her, He 29. He 30. her 31. them 32. They 33. him 34. I, my 35. It 36. you, you 37. your 38. She 39. his 40. We 41. our 42. They 43. us 44. his 45. She 46. We 47. They 48. them 49. their 50. your 51. She 52. He 53. it 54. him 55. your 56. He 57. your 58. you 59. them 60. you 61. us 62. you 63. It 64. their 65. her 66. it 67. you 68. him 69. our 70. his 71. Her 72. I 73. They 74. She 75. Its 76. We 77. She, it 78. He, him 79. They, them 80. She, it 81. He, it 82. she, them 83. he, them 84. He, her 85. They, it 86. it 87. They, them 88. They, it 89. She, them 90. He, it 91. They, him 92. you 93. you 94. We, them 95. They, them 96. him 97. her 98. She, him 99. you 100. Its 101. They 102. you 103. Her 104. I 105. We 106. She, us 107. your 108. It 109. them 110. you 111. it 112. She, his 113. you, it 114. our 115. He, it 116. you 117. He, us 118. him 119. you 120. her 121. I 122. He, them 123. you 124. They 125. her 126. you 127. hers 128. They 129. He 130. them 131. theirs 132. it 133. her 134. your 135. your 136. their 137. you 138. it 139. She 140. my 141. It 142. me 143. it 144. it 145. you 146. It 147. They, them 148. her 149. you 150. He, it 151. them 152. I 153. my 154. you 155. me 156. Her 157. their 158. We, it 159. He, him 160. She, his 161. us

2 Present Progressive

1. is barking 2. are getting 3. Are you writing 4. are running 5. are not singing 6. is growing 7. are not keeping 8. am feeding 9. are dancing 10. is washing 11. are shouting 12. am not saving 13. Is that boy speaking 14. is hoping 15. are riding 16. Is the girl giving 17. is closing 18. are fetching 19. are not repairing 20. are eating 21. is taking 22. is not flying 23. are coming 24. Are you reading 25. is walking 26. is arriving 27. are throwing 28. are tidying up 29. are having 30. is climbing 31. Is the dog looking 32. are feeling 33. are winning 34. are carrying 35. is not drinking 36. are standing 37. Am I saying 38. are changing 39. is cutting 40. is not collecting 41. are shutting 42. is following 43. am choosing 44. is seeing 45. Am I talking 46. is not running 47. is selling 48. are flying 49. Is my sister coming 50. is not giving 51. is showing 52. Is the girl getting 53. are living 54. Are you taking 55. are not sending 56.are calling 57. are playing 58. is ringing 59. am not putting 60. Is the man playing 61. are planning 62. are meeting 63. is trying 64. is not raining 65. is saving 66. Is the man telling 67. am moving 68. are wearing 69. is staying 70. am not getting 71. Are the girls putting 72. is using 73. are not clapping 74. is pushing 75. Is he living 76. is not having 77. is counting 78. are we flying 79. are asking 80. am copying 81. is not laughing 82. Are they running 83. are working 84. are swimming 85. is putting 86. are watching 87. are clapping 88. Are you learning 89. is helping 90. am cooking 91. are making 92. Is the baby crying? 93. are not listening 94. is sitting 95. am not taking 96. are sleeping 97. are not going 98. Are we saving 99. are buying 100. is shutting

3 Present simple - Present progressive

1. is barking, barks 2. have, is wearing, is wearing 3. go, go 4. leaves, is leaving 5. sits, am sitting 6. get up, are getting up 7. take, are taking 8. speak, are speaking 9. rings, is ringing 10. stop 11. drinks, is drinking 12. is Mike doing, is repairing 13. feed, are feeding 14. wash, are washing 15. play, plays 16. plays, am playing 17. are going, goes 18. see, are seeing 19. run, are running 20. get, gets 21. is sitting, sit 22. sleep, is sleeping 23. are having, have 24. take, are taking 25. am speaking, speak 26. play, are playing 27. is dancing, dance 28.wash, washes 29. does, do 30. is flying, flies 31. am watching, watches 32. are talking, talk 33. runs, is running 34. is getting up, gets up 35. sit, are sitting 36. Are you sleeping, sleep 37. see, am seeing 38. are buying, buy 39. am taking, take 40. wash, washes 41. takes, are taking 42. is flying, flies 43. speak, are speaking 44. are walking, walk, is walking 45. is waiting 46. gets 47. go 48. is pushing 49. is carrying 50. go 51. barks 52. eats 53. are playing 54. watches 55. is coming, are running 56. fly 57. stays 58. goes 59. is putting 60. are speaking 61. eat 62. watches 63. am writing 64. sit 65. swim 66. is riding 67. see 68. carry 69. are flying 70. wash 71. feed 72. is sleeping 73. gets 74. buy 75. is running 76. are taking 77. are writing 78. goes 79. carries 80. run 81. are buying 82. are sitting 83. get up 84. are taking 85. am running 86. watches 87. is putting 88. is carrying 89. play 90. are getting 91. is feeding 92. watch 93. are eating 94. fly 95. run 96. am closing 97. flies 98. are leaving 99. is holding 100. swim 101. are sitting 102. are riding 103. do 104. drink 105. does 106. wash 107. are standing 108. spell 109. are driving 110. watches 111. is running 112. am getting 113. eat 114. buys 115. are helping 116. read 117. wash 118. are feeding 119. goes 120. carry 121. are playing, play 122. is ringing, get up 123. walk, are walking 124. is sitting, sits 125. have, are having 126. are waiting 127. has, throws 128. is making 129. takes 130. help 131. drink, are drinking 132. is starting 133. repair 134. am running 135. am drawing, draw 136. is feeding, feeds 137. goes, is going 138. leave, is leaving 139. watch, are watching 140. He is coming now. ODER Now he is coming. 141. The boys often play tennis. 142. He is washing his face at the moment. ODER At the moment he is washing his face. 143. The teacher is waiting in the classroom now. 144. I always forget to eat my bread.

4 Question formation in the Present

1. Who is running home now? 2. Where is the boy running now? 3. When is the boy running home? 4. How is the boy running? 5. Why is the boy running quickly? 6. Is the boy running home now? 7. What is the boy doing now? 8. Who can run home now? 9. When can the boy run home? 10. Who is running home now? 11. Where are two girls running now? 12. How many girls are running home now? 13. When are two girls running home? 14. How are two girls running? 15. Why are two girls running quickly? 16. Are two girls running quickly? 17. What are two girls doing now? 18. Who must run home now? 19. Where must two girls run now? 20. Who is eating an apple now? 21. What am I eating now? 22. When am I eating an apple? 23. How am I eating an apple? 24. Why am I eating an apple quickly? 25. Am I eating an apple? 26. Where am I eating an apple? 27. What am I doing now? 28. Who can eat an apple now? 29. When can I eat an apple? 30. Who runs home every day? 31. Where does the boy run every day? 32. When does the boy run home? 33. How does the boy run? 34. Why does the boy run quickly? 35. Does the boy run quickly? 36. What does the boy do every day? 37. Who can run home every day? 38. When must the boy run home? 39. Who

runs home every day? 40. Where do two girls run every day? 41. How many girls run home every day? 42. When do two girls run home? 43. How do two girls run? 44. Why do two girls run quickly? 45. Do two girls run quickly? 46. What do two girls do every day? 47. Who can run quickly? 48. How can two girls run? 49. Who eats an apple every day? 50. What do I eat every day? 51. When do I eat an apple? 52. How do I eat an apple? 53. Why do I eat an apple quickly? 54. Do I eat an apple quickly? 55. What do I do quickly? 56. Who is coming? 57. How many birds are flying? 58. What are two birds doing? 59. When does the father come home? 60. What does the father do at night? 61. Where is the boy sitting? 62. Who is sitting in the kitchen? 63. What is the boy doing in the kitchen? 64. What is the girl drinking? 65. What is the girl doing? 66. What am I writing? 67. Who is writing a letter? 68. What am I doing? 69. Whose mother is here? 70. How is the boy running? 71. Where are the birds? 72. Who is talking? 73. What are the girls doing? 74. How many children are here? 75. Why is the baby crying? 76. Who eats cake? 77. What do the girls eat? 78. What do the girls do? 79. Where do the men eat? 80. Who eats in the kitchen? 81. What do the men do in the kitchen? 82. How many dogs bark every day? 83. When do three dogs bark? 84. What do three dogs do every day? 85. Can we drive the car? 86. Who carries many chairs? 87. What do you carry? 88. What do you do? 89. Who sees the tree in the morning? 90. What do I see in the morning? 91. What do I do in the morning? 92. When do I see the tree? 93. Who is sleeping in his bed/ in their beds? 94. What are the girls doing? 95. Where are the girls sleeping? 96. Who reads very slowly? 97. What does the child do? 98. How does the child read? 99. Who is driving to school? 100. What are the boys doing? 101. Where are the boys driving? 102. Who sells books every day? 103. What do I sell every day? 104. What do I do every day? 105. When do I sell books? 106. Who is talking too loudly? 107. How are you talking? 108. How many books can the tall man carry? 109. Who writes five books? 110. How many books do we write? 111. What do we write? 112. What do we do? 113. Are the women coming now? 114. Who writes letters? 115. What does the little girl do? 116. What does the little girl write? 117. Why are you sitting? 118. How many times must the dog bark? 119. Who is standing on a chair? 120. What are you doing? / What am I doing? 121. Where are you standing? 122. Does he live in a house? 123. Who is wearing a pullover? 124. What am I doing? / What are you doing? 125. What am I wearing? 126. Who often stands in the bus? 127. Where do the girls often stand? 128. What do the girls often do? 129. Who flies a plane? 130. What do I fly? 131. What do I do? 132. What is the cat eating? 133. What is the cat doing? 134. Does the little girl read books? 135. Can she read books? 136. Is the girl reading books? 137. Where are we arriving? 138. Do the children talk? 139. Can the children talk? 140. Are the children talking? 141. Do I always walk? 142. Am I walking? 143. Are we holding hands?

5 Some - any

1. some 2. anything 3. some 4. any 5. some 6. Something 7. some 8. anywhere 9. any 10. some 11. anything 12. Some 13. any 14. some 15. Some 16. any 17. some 18. somewhere 19. some 20. some 21. anything 22. Somebody 23. any 24. some 25. anything 26. some 27. any 28. some 29. anybody 30. something 31. somewhere 32. anywhere 33. some, some 34. any 35. some 36. any 37. somewhere 38. some 39. something 40. anywhere 41. some 42. anybody 43. Somebody 44. some 45. some 46. any 47. Something 48. anybody 49. Some 50. any 51. something 52. some 53. anywhere 54. anybody 55. some 56. any 57. somewhere

58. any 59. some 60. any 61. anywhere 62. some 63. Somebody 64. anything 65. some 66. anybody 67. some 68. Something 69. some 70. any 71. Somebody 72. any 73. some 74. some 75. somebody 76. any 77. something 78. some 79. anywhere 80. anybody 81. some 82. anything 83. some 84. anything 85. some 86. some 87. anybody 88. somewhere 89. anywhere 90. some 91. some 92. Somebody 93. any 94. Some 95. somewhere 96. anything 97. any 98. somewhere 99. some 100. anywhere 101. something 102. anybody

6 They're - there - their

1. Their 2. there 3. their 4. They're 5. there 6. their 7. their 8. They're 9. there 10. Their, their 11. They're 12. Their 13. They're 14. There 15. their 16. They're 17. Their 18. there 19. There 20. their 21. their 22. They're 23. there 24. They're 25. their 26. They're 27. their 28. their 29. They're 30. there 31. their 32. They're, their 33. They're 34. their 35. They're 36. there 37. their 38. They're 39. There 40. their 41. There 42. their 43. They're, their 44. They're 45. their 46. There 47. They're 48. their 49. Their 50. They're, there 51. their 52. They're 53. There 54. their 55. They're 56. Their 57. They're 58. They're 59. their 60. There 61. there 62. They're 63. Their 64. They're, their, there 65. they're, their, there 66. They're, their 67. there, there 68. They're, their

7 To - two - too

1. Two 2. too 3. two 4. too 5. to 6. two 7. to 8. too 9. Two 10. two 11. to 12. too 13. two 14. two, too 15. two 16. to 17. two 18. to 19. too 20. two 21. two, to 22. Two, too 23. two 24. to 25. to 26. two 27. to 28. two, too 29. Two 30. to 31. too 32. two 33. two, too 34. Two, to 35. two 36. two, too 37. to 38. two 39. to, too 40. Two 41. two 42. Two, too 43. to 44. two, too 45. two 46. to, two, too 47. two 48. two, too 49. Two, too 50. to 51. to, too 52. two, too 53. to 54. two, to, too 55. two 56. to 57. Two, too, too 58. two 59. too 60. two, too 61. too 62. to, two, too 63. two, to, too 64. Two, to, too 65. two, to, too

8 Much - many

1. many 2. much 3. many 4. many 5. much 6. much 7. many 8. much 9. Many 10. much 11. much 12. many 13. many 14. much 15. many 16. many 17. many 18. much 19. many 20. many 21. much 22. many 23. many 24. much 25. much 26. Many 27. much 28. many 29. many 30. much 31. Many 32. many 33. much 34. much 35. many 36. many 37. much 38. much 39. many 40. much 41. many 42. much 43. much 44. many 45. much 46. much 47. many 48. much 49. many 50. much 51. many 52. much 53. many 54. many 55. much 56. Many 57. much 58. many 59. much 60. many

9 Little - few

1. few / a few / only a few 2. little / a little / only a little 3. little 4. few / a few 5. little 6. little 7. few 8. few / a few / very few / only a few 9. little 10. little 11. few 12. little / a little / very little 13. Few / A few / Very few 14. few 15. little / a little / very little 16. little 17. few 18.

little 19. few / a few / very few 20. little 21. little 22. few 23. little 24. few 25. little / very little 26. little 27. few 28. few 29. little 30. little / a little / very little 31. few 32. little 33. few 34. little 35. few 36. little 37. few 38. little 39. few 40. few / a few / very few 41. Few /A few/ Very few 42. little 43. few 44. little 45. few 46. few /a few / very few 47. little 48. little 49. few 50. little 51. few 52. few 53. little 54. little 55. little 56. few 57. little 58. little 59. few 60. little

10 This - that - these - those

1. this 2. This 3. These 4. Those 5. Those 6. these 7. That 8. this 9. This 10. That 11. These 12. Those 13. those 14. these 15. that 16. this 17. that 18. this 19. This 20. that 21. those 22. these 23. those 24. these 25. This 26. That 27. That 28. this 29. these 30. This 31. these 32. That 33. those 34. that 35. this 36. Those 37. these 38. that 39. this 40. those 41. these 42. that 43. this 44. these 45. those 46. that 47. this 48. these 49. those 50. that 51. this 52. That 53. this 54. Those 55. these 56. These, this 57. those, that

11 Past tense

1. My sister usually saw Mr. Smith. 2. The boys were swimming 3. You often left ... 4. We sometimes took... 5. They always cleaned ... 6. My brother held... 7. The boy was running... 8. Did you often write... ? 9. The dogs always ate... 10. My brother always made... 11. We were driving... 12. The teacher came... 13. I was drawing... 14. My father had... 15. He was writing... 16. They always washed... 17. The baby slept... 18. I usually fed... 19. We always said what we did... 20. They often saw... 21. You always planned... 22. He was sitting... 23. They usually had... 24. He danced... 25. We always came... 26. The boys were laughing... 27. The girl always shook her head when she put ... 28. That boy carried... 29. We bought... 30. The boys usually played... 31. The father held... 32. She said, "You always stuck..." 33. Dogs always barked when they saw... 34. The child went to the door when it saw that its mother was coming. 35. Did he leave the house when you told... 36. The dogs barked because the men were running. 37. I made... 38. She got up... 39. You ate... 40. He drank water when he was thirsty. 41. Who knew... 42. He took... 43. We ate... 44. I knew what he wanted. 45. I saw... 46. When were you leaving... 47. The birds always flew. 48. You usually ran... 49. My father left his car at home when he drank. 50. She went... 51. Ben was laughing... 52. Mother and I counted... 53. Mary was saying... 54. Did she tell... 55. Were we putting... 56. Did I always turn... 57. Was father calling... 58. What did you say... 59. Did Robert always watch... 60. Did the girl shake... 61. Was I looking... 62. Were you reading... 63. Why did children always eat... 64. Did we always shout... 65. Were the babies laughing... 66. It was... 67. Tom saw... 68. John came... 69. A man and a girl were getting... 70. I did... 71. Linda showed... 72. We always left... 73. Peter had... 74. We were looking... 75. She took... 76. Mother went... 77. I counted... 78. Kate was cutting... 79. We put ... 80. Peter always waited... 81. The boys were sleeping... 82. They played ... 83. She wanted ... 84. We were singing... 85. Tom was riding... 86. He cleaned ... 87. Did they take ... 88. The men were repairing... 89. The women helped... 90. Mary washed... 91. She was eating... 92. Mother and Linda were counting... 93. The children left... 94. The women shook... 95. John told ... 96. The

boy was feeding... 97. They were eating... 98. Did they always eat ... 99. We listened... 100. The child sometimes stood... 101. Why were you laughing? 102. Father said ... 103. Barbara knew how big the baby was. 104. You and I were leaving... 105. I always bought ... 106. The cat was washing... 107. They shook hands when they said... 108. We were taking ... 109. The girls came... 110. I had... 111. Were you happy when you went ... 112. Did you like ... 113. My brother often flew. 114. She sometimes found... 115. Did the people always buy... 116. Were they answering your question then? 117. He held her hand when the dogs barked. 118. They cleaned the board when you told... 119. Did he watch you when you were swimming? 120. Their father put... 121. We bought ... 122. The people saw ... 123. Did you know... 124. Why did the children eat... 125. Mother and I said, "You were shouting... 126. Where were you going... 127. He told them, "You ate... " 128. The girl was wearing a pullover because it was cold. 129. When did you get... 130. My mother threw ... 131. You were standing ... 132. I went ... 133. Linda and Mary said... 134. Tina and I were watching ... 135. My brother was holding... 136. My father always bought... 137. I sometimes wrote ... 138. Helen and Jane were taking... 139. Did your father sing? 140. My sister and I carried... 141. You often threw... 142. I was playing... 143. Mother and I always fed... 144. Did I talk ... 145. Tom went... 146. We helped ... 147. Did you collect... 148. They were coming ... 149. I was holding... 150. Linda blew... 151. Were you dreaming? 152. Did he eat... 153. Could you come? 154. Did the girls work... 155. That was... 156. The lesson began... 157. We caught ... 158. Was he sleeping? 159. I was making ... 160. Susan wanted... 161. Jane and Tim liked... 162. Did your dog bark? 163. Could I read... 164. We cut... 165. Tom was swimming. 166. Was I pushing? 167. I hated ... 168. You shouted ... 169. We stayed in the house when it was hot. 170. Did your aunt ride... 171. The men carried... 172. I worked... 173. The monkey climbed... 174. You talked... 175. Were the Millers flying... 176. My mother was washing ... 177. We lived ... 178. Was the plane arriving... 179. The tree was growing. 180. Were we eating... 181. My brother called... 182. You were pulling... 183. They could see... 184. Was Diane drawing ... 185. You took... 186. Did we know... 187. Tom loved ... 188. The man cooked... 189. You looked funny. 190. The baby held... 191. My brother and I don't break ... 192. Does the cat climb ... 193. We like... 194. The dog hurts... 195. I am eating... 196. Do they work ... 197. The man feeds... 198. We meet... 199. Is father learning ... 200. The men don't cut ... 201. Do I sometimes read ... 202. Does your sister wash... 203. You are playing ... 204. The woman loves ... 205. My father and mother send... 206. Is the dog living ... 207. We can talk ... 208. I don't help... 209. Your brother often comes... 210. Is the lady drinking ... 211. You eat ... 212. Does she sing... 213. My father is lighting... 214. Are the girls shouting? 215. Our cat doesn't forget ... 216. Do we sweep... 217. My mother doesn't hear ... 218. The girl can feel ... 219. You don't carry... 220. Am I wearing... 221. Tom and Jean work ... 222. My brother reads ... 223. Are we collecting... 224. My sister is riding ... 225. Are you running ... 226. I blow... 227. The cat is shaking... 228. Do you fetch ... 229. Do we want ... 230. The man doesn't start... 231. Does the girl swim... 232. The dog pulls ... 233. The girl doesn't keep... 234. We are selling... 235. Do they stand... 236. Does he often call... 237. Is your brother buying... 238. Her mother doesn't cook... 239. The lady gives... 240. The women are speaking... 241. The doctor arrives... 242. Do you cry ... 243. Is he holding ... 244. John and Barbara take... 245. We are shouting... 246. They buy ... 247. Does he laugh ... 248. Are you making... 249. Yes, I make... 250. The dog barks when it sees ... 251. We always eat... 252. You feed... 253.

Are you shouting... 254. Does your brother go ... 255. Father is helping... 256. They are laughing when I see... 257. He runs into the room when he sees me. 258. Does he drink... 259. The cat shakes its head when it stands. 260. We are dancing today. 261. My mother puts... 262. I am looking... 263. Do you laugh when Tom tells... 264. He is holding her hand while he says... 265. Do I see... 266. Does he sometimes carry ... 267. We hold ... 268. They come... 269. The man leaves... 270. Linda and I make ... 271. Does the lady run... 272. Is the baby crying? 273. When does the cat eat... 274. Does he leave ... 275. My brother and sister are standing ... 276. I am shaking... 277. When do you tell ... 278. That man is taking ... 279. Don't I keep... 280. Are Linda and Sandy walking? 281. My mother and I don't pay for our bread today. 282. I am going... 283. They feed ... 284. Aren't you coming ... 285. The dog is running... 286. I choose... 287. Isn't the boy doing... 288. Are you helping mother today? 289. Karen and I buy... 290. You don't leave... 291. I am not shouting ... 292. Don't the girls stay... 293. Is the woman speaking... 294. You drink ... 295. The girl doesn't make... 296. Tom and I are eating...

12 Past simple - Past Progressive

1. She opened the window, looked out, and saw her mother. 2. The dog was barking when I came home. 3. When did I see you last? 4. You were blowing your... 5. He flew to ... 6. Were they riding a ... 7. I often swept the ... 8. While we were sleeping, the dogs were barking. 9. Did you meet her... 10. She was singing a ... 11. When I saw mother, she was buying bread. 12. He left his... 13. I always brought him... 14. We were holding hands when mother came in. 15. Was he feeding the ... 16. We were digging a ... 17. Did she always hide her ... 18. You were running too ... 19. Two people were shaking hands when the third person shouted. 20. The cat always slept in ... 21. My sister was telling me... 22. My mother was reading a book when I phoned yesterday. 23. You always woke me... 24. The children were taking the ... 25. Did he learn his ... 26. We usually spread butter ... 27. We were wearing old ... 28. Was she beginning to ... 29. The children grew so ... 30. The children were running around when the teacher called them. 31. The dog broke its ... 32. The children were freezing in ... 33. Did the tree get enough... 34. Did mother and I come quickly... 35. The woman was lying in ... 36. While one girl was reading, the other girl was writing. 37. The woman paid for ... 38. Were you standing in the cold while he was drinking tea? 39. The boy was winning the ... 40. We often sold our... 41. Did the men always show the ... 42. They were singing while mother was washing the dishes. 43. I always rang the... 44. The man and I were speaking for ... 45. You often bit my ... 46. Was I cutting the cake when you came in? 47. While the boy was running, his sister was sleeping. 48. He always ate too much until he became ill. 49. In the picture she was falling down ... 50. Did the men often choose the ... 51. Mother was cutting the cake when father came home. 52. Her nose often bled in... 53. Were we buying shoes ... 54. The men were selling their ... 55. You often stole my... 56. They were driving to ... 57. Did he always go to ... 58. Father and I usually gave the... 59. Two days ago the dog barked, bit the child and ran away. But then we found it. 60. The dog and cat were fighting when... 61. The girl caught the ... 62. While the man was cooking, the woman was getting everything ... 63. Did the old man always forget his ... 64. I was feeling sad ... 65. The balloon burst when... 66. My brother and I put our ... 67. The boy was still sleeping when we woke up. 68. You were writing letters when I saw you... 69. Did the teachers teach you... 70. My teacher always let me... 71. The child was

crying and was looking for ... 72. She always sold apples ... 73. I was digging a ... 74. Did the cat sometimes sit in... 75. The man was saying goodbye ... 76. We always spent our ... 77. Did I lose my ... 78. You were taking a... 79. The birds built a... 80. Was she doing her ... 81. You sometimes drank milk ... 82. I was giving a ... 83. Were they shaking their ... 84. He always spelt (spelled) his ... 85. Yesterday I phoned my sister, packed my things and drove to... 86. The cat always caught a ... 87. The man was drawing a ... 88. Did the girl always find her ... 89. You sometimes bought a ... 90. I was fighting a ... 91. The bad boy always stole money ... 92. Were the children hiding when... 93. You were riding a horse while your sister was washing the car. 94. Did the woman usually sleep so... 95. We were standing in... 96. I sometimes lay in ... 97. Did the birds fly to ... 98. The teacher was shutting her book when the pupils came in. 99. The boy always won when ... 100. Did we begin to talk ...

13 Question formation in the Past

1. How many houses did he see? 2. Who saw two houses? 3. What did he see? 4. What did he do? 5. Who was eating pudding? 6. What were you doing? 7. What were you eating? 8. Where did I sing a song? 9. Who sang a song in the kitchen? 10. What did I sing in the kitchen? 11. What did I do in the kitchen? 12. How many houses were Mother and I building? 13. Who was building two houses? 14. What were Mother and I doing? 15. What were Mother and I building? 16. Who was writing a letter? 17. What was Linda writing? 18. What was Linda doing? 19. Whose apple was I biting? 20. What was I biting? 21. What was I doing? 22. How many words did you write? 23. Who wrote ten words? 24. What did you write? 25. What did you do? 26. Why did he give you the present? 27. What did he do because he loved you? 28. What were the three girls singing this morning? 29. How many girls were singing a song this morning? 30. Who was singing a song this morning? 31. What were the three girls doing this morning? 32. When were the three girls singing a song? 33. How did I read the book? 34. Who read the book loudly? 35. What did I read loudly? 36. What did I do? 37. When did the little boy know the answer? 38. Who knew the answer last week? 39. What did the little boy know last week? 40. Where were you sitting? 41. Who was sitting on a chair? 42. What were you doing? 43. Why did Tom and I run? 44. Who ran because we were late? 45. What did Tom and I do because we were late? 46. What did Mother hang up? 47. Who hung up my dress? 48. What did Mother do? 49. Why did Linda and Gary ring us up? 50. Who rang us up because they had not seen us? 51. What did Linda and Gary do because they had not seen us? 52. For whom (For who) did Mother buy a cat? / Whom (Who) did Mother buy a cat for? 53. Who bought a cat for father? 54. What did Mother buy for father? 55. What did Mother do for father? 56. Who began to read? 57. What did I begin to do? 58. What did I do? 59. How was the cat walking? 60. Who / What was walking very quietly? 61. What was the cat doing very quietly? 62. What was the cat doing? 63. When were you reading the book? 64. Who was reading the book when I phoned? 65. What were you reading when I phoned? 66. What were you doing when I phoned? 67. When was the woman selling books? 68. Who was selling the books last night? 69. What was the woman selling last night? 70. What was the woman doing last night? 71. With whose balls were the dogs and I playing?/ Whose balls were the dogs and I playing with? 72. Who was playing with the children's balls? 73. What were the dogs and I doing with the children's balls? 74. What were the dogs and I playing with? / With what were the dogs and I playing?

75. How did you eat? 76. Who ate too quickly? 77. What did you do too quickly? 78. How was I working? 79. Who was working very slowly? 80. What was I doing very slowly? 81. Where did my brother drive his car? 82. Who drove his car to his sister? 83. What did my brother drive to his sister? 84. What did my brother do? 85. Why did we eat ice-cream? 86. Who ate ice-cream because it was a hot day? 87. What did we eat because it was a hot day? 88. What did we do because it was a hot day? 89. Who shook their heads? 90. What did the girls shake? 91. What did the girls do? 92. Where did you throw the ball? 93. Who threw the ball in the garden? 94. What did you throw in the garden? 95. What did you do in the garden? 96. Where was I walking? 97. What was I doing? 98. How many dog biscuits were the dogs eating? 99. Who was eating two dog biscuits? 100. What were the dogs eating? 101. What were the dogs doing? 102. What did the little dog catch? 103. Who caught a ball? 104. What did the little dog do? 105. Who was flying in a plane? 106. In what were the boys and I flying? / What were the boys and I flying in? 107. What were the boys and I doing in a plane? 108. Who went for a swim on Sunday? 109. When did Tom and Dick go for a swim? 110. What did Tom and Dick do on Sunday? 111. Where did the children take their toys? 112. Who took their toys to their mothers? 113. What did the children take to their mothers? 114. What did the children do? 115. Why was the baby boy wearing a pullover? 116. Who was wearing a pullover because it was cold? 117. What was the baby boy wearing because it was cold? 118. What was the baby boy doing because it was cold? 119. For how many hours did I swim? 120. Who swam for two hours? 121. What did I do for two hours? 122. Where were the books lying? 123. What was lying on a table? 124. Who broke the pencil? 125. What did you break? 126. What did you do? 127. Why did Linda and Bob hold hands? 128. Who held hands because they loved each other? 129. What did Linda and Bob do because they loved each other? 130. Whose hand did Father and I hold? 131. Who held mother's hand? 132. What did father and I hold? 133. What did father and I do? 134. Where did the boy find the ball? 135. Who found the ball under the tree? 136. What did the boy find under the tree? 137. What did the boy do under the tree? 138. Where did Mother and I hang the picture up? 139. Who hung the picture up in the living-room? 140. What did Mother and I hang up in the living-room? 141. What did Mother and I do in the living-room? 142. Where did I go every week? 143. Who went to school every week? 144. What did I do every week? 145. When did I go to school? 146. How many apples was the girl buying? 147. Who was buying two apples? 148. What was the girl doing? 149. What was the girl buying? 150. Why did Ben and I learn the words? 151. Who learnt the words because the teacher told us to? 152. What did Ben and I learn because the teacher told us to? 153. What did Ben and I do because the teacher told us to? 154. When did you give me a book? 155. Who gave me a book yesterday? 156. What did you give me yesterday? 157. Whom (Who) did you give a book yesterday? 158. What did you do yesterday? 159. How did Mother sleep? 160. Who slept poorly? 161. Where did the cat take a mouse? 162. Who took a mouse to its mother? 163. What did the cat take to its mother? 164. What did the cat do? 165. What did his uncle carry? 166. Who carried the chair? 167. What did his uncle do? 168. When did you go to Bonn? 169. Who went to Bonn last year? 170. Where did you go last year? 171. What did you do last year? 172. How did the children run? 173. What did the children do? 174. Who ran quickly? 175. When did my sisters and I meet the man? 176. Whom (Who) did my sisters and I meet two years ago? 177. What did my sisters and I do two years ago? 178. Who met the man two years ago? 179. Why were you laughing? 180. What were you doing because you were happy? 181. Who was laughing? 182. Whose cars were the men selling? 183. What were the

men selling? 184. What were the men doing? 185. Who was selling their cars? 186. Who bought milk? 187. What did my father buy? 188. What did my father do? 189. What did you see yesterday? 190. Who saw the house yesterday? 191. When did you see the house? 192. What did you do yesterday? 193. Whose banana did the monkeys eat? 194. Who ate the child's banana? 195. What did the monkeys eat? 196. What did the monkeys do? 197. When did I feed the cat? 198. Whom (What) (Who) did I feed every day? 199. What did I do every day? 200. Who fed the cat every day? 201. How many words did the women and I speak? 202. What did the women and I do? 203. Who spoke ten words? 204. What did the women and I speak? 205. How were you laughing? 206. Who was laughing very loudly? 207. What were you doing very loudly? 208. Who walked home yesterday? 209. Where did Susan walk yesterday? 210. What did Susan do yesterday? 211. When did Susan walk home? 212. When were the men eating in the kitchen? 213. Who was eating in the kitchen last month? 214. Where were the men eating last month? 215. What were the men doing in the kitchen? 216. What were the men doing last month? 217. Why were the old women sitting down? 218. Who was sitting down? 219. What were the old women doing because they were lazy? 220. Where were the children and I riding horses? 221. What were the children and I riding at the farm? 222. Who was riding horses at the farm? 223. What were the children and I doing at the farm? 224. What did the boy hold? 225. What did the boy do? 226. Who held a book? 227. How many books was I reading? 228. What was I doing? 229. Who was reading twelve books? 230. What was I reading? 231. Where were the children quiet? 232. Who was quiet in the supermarket? 233. What did my father sometimes tell? 234. Who sometimes told a story? 235. What did my father sometimes do? 236. What was Linda throwing? 237. What was Linda doing? 238. Who was throwing a ball? 239. Where were the men standing? 240. Who was standing at the door? 241. What were the men doing at the door? 242. How many balls did the boys throw? 243. Who threw four balls? 244. What did the boys do? 245. What did the boys throw? 246. Who drew pictures? 247. What did my sister and I draw? 248. What did my sister and I do? 249. Who was selling cars? 250. What were the boys doing? 251. What were the boys selling? 252. Whose car did you see? 253. Who saw Linda's car? 254. What did you do? 255. What did you see? 256. To whom (To who) were we reading a book?/ Who (Whom) were we reading a book to? 257. Who was reading a book to the girl? 258. What were we reading to the girl? 259. What were we doing? 260. Why was I reading the book? 261. What was I reading? 262. When did they have lunch? 263. For whom (who) was Tom cooking?/Whom (Who) was Tom cooking for? 264. What was Tom doing for his sister? 265. Whose ball were you catching? 266. Who was catching Linda's ball? 267. What were you catching? 268. What were you doing? 269. When was I making a cake? 270. What was I making yesterday afternoon? 271. What was I doing yesterday afternoon? 272. How did Father and I speak? 273. Who spoke too quietly? 274. What did Father and I do too quietly? 275. How were the men working? 276. Who was working quickly? 277. What were the men doing quickly? 278. Where were you walking? 279. Who was walking at the park? 280. What were you doing at the park? 281. How were we driving? 282. Who was driving very fast? 283. What was the girl holding? 284. Whose book did I take? 285. What did I do? 286. Who took Ken's book? 287. For whom (who) were Linda and Dick buying toys?/Whom (Who) were Linda and Dick buying toys for? 288. What were Linda and Dick doing for their children? 289. Who was buying toys for their children? 290. What were Linda and Dick buying for their children? 291. Who was driving home? 292. Where were the man and his wife driving? 293. What were the man and his wife doing? 294. Where was the cat hiding? 295. What was the cat doing under the tree? 296. Who was driving the car? 297. What was I driving? 298. What was I doing? 299. How did the dogs bark? 300. What did the dogs do loudly? 301. For whom (who) was I washing the plates?/Who (Whom) was I washing the plates for? 302. What was I washing for you? 303. What was I doing for you? 304. Whose dog was the man feeding? 305. What was the man doing? 306. Who was feeding the boy's dog? 307. What was the man feeding? 308. Who was playing in the park? 309. Where were the dogs and cats playing? 310. What were the dogs and cats doing in the park? 311. How many songs were you hearing? 312. What were you doing? 313. Who was hearing ten songs? 314. What were you hearing? 315. Who was talking on the phone? 316. What were you doing on the phone? 317. Where were you talking? 318. When did my father and I drink milk? 319. What did my father and I drink before school? 320. What did my father and I do before school? 321. Who drank milk before school? 322. Where did I burn my finger? 323. What did I burn on the hot plate? 324. What did I do? 325. What did we give the poor people? 326. Whom (Who) did we give clothes? 327. What did we do? 328. Who gave the poor people clothes? 329. What were we cleaning? 330. Who was cleaning the kitchen? 331. What were we doing? 332. Who was writing many sentences? 333. What were the girls doing? 334. What were the girls writing?

14 Past - Present Perfect

1. visited 2. met, did he meet 3. did not play, played 4. Have you ever seen 5. have never heard 6. had 7. has just given 8. took 9. came, broke 10. have you played 11. fed 12. wrote 13. repaired 14. went 15. have just bought 16. has written 17. did not see, saw 18. have you worn 19. has he written 20. Did you see, didn't see, saw 21. Have you often seen, haven't seen, have often seen 22. Didn't I see, saw 23. Have they already eaten 24. did not sleep 25. Haven't we seen 26. has he been waiting, has been waiting 27. did they buy, bought 28. have not spoken, spoke 29. have not done, have played 30. took 31. Have we answered 32. Did you write 33. Haven't I seen 34. were playing 35. bought 36. Didn't he visit 37. haven't gone 38. Did our friends eat, ate 39. Was I 40. Didn't he ride, rode 41. flew 42. Didn't I work, worked 43. Didn't you drive 44. Did the lady go, went 45. Did I do, did 46. have been working 47. Haven't you ever seen, have not seen, have seen 48. Hasn't he seen, hasn't seen, has seen 49. Did they sit, didn't sit, sat 50. has been wearing 51. Did you go, went 52. Has it eaten 53. You did not watch 54. have not seen 55. did he go, went 56. Didn't we see 57. went 58. Haven't they drunk 59. have already fed 60. Has my sister gone 61. did not go 62. Haven't you seen 63. Did father and mother go 64. have never seen 65. did not eat 66. Have you ever heard 67. saw 68. did you drive, drove 69. has been sleeping 70. Didn't they phone, phoned 71. Haven't they read 72. have never stolen, stole 73. have just gone 74. stole 75. Have you already washed 76. did not buy 77. Have I ever seen 78. saw 79. did not see 80. have not read, read 81. did they live, lived 82. Haven't I spoken 83. went 84. Haven't they just come 85. did not run 86. was not talking 87. Were you reading 88. were not playing 89. Haven't you found 90. haven't the people eaten 91. did not sleep 92. have watched 93. has never been 94. did not drive 95. have not seen 96. Were you sleeping 97. wasn't 98. has not written 99. Haven't they gone 100. did not wash

15 Comparison of adjectives

1. smaller 2. the biggest 3. happier 4. more exciting 5. the most interesting 6. as lazy as 7. cold 8. more helpful 9. noisier 10. the eldest / the oldest 11. more 12. not as dark as; not so dark as 13. cheaper 14. the highest 15. big 16. shorter 17. the most thrilling 18. as unhappy as 19. more careful 20. the most popular 21. louder 22. wonderful 23. the bluest 24. as special as 25. more interesting 26. the hottest 27. colder 28. stupid 29. the most difficult 30. as free as 31. lazier 32. the busiest 33. sweet 34. dirtier 35. old 36. not as large as/ not so large as 37. the quickest 38. later 39. special 40. angrier 41. the worst 42. as hungry as 43. nicer 44. the hungriest 45. fewer 46. more thrilling 47. better 48. not as surprised as / not so surprised as 49. the loudest 50. more expensive 51. good 52. more popular 53. the oldest 54. as early as 55. more useful 56. the youngest 57. more exciting 58. expensive 59. cleaner 60. not as sunny as/ not so sunny as 61. the brightest 62. more dangerous 63. clever 64. more careful 65. the most 66. as tidy as 67. worse 68. bad 69. cleverer / more clever 70. many 71. more interesting 72. as difficult as 73. the longest 74. more boring 75. bad 76. more difficult 77. the cleverest 78. not as funny as/ not so funny as 79. more exciting 80. interesting 81. more expensive 82. little 83. the loveliest / the most lovely 84. less 85. terrible 86. the easiest 87. more brilliant 88. far 89. more terrible 90. the quietest / the most quiet 91. terrible 92. more expensive 93. farther 94. the most wonderful 95. younger 96. silly 97. more 98. the best 99. faster 100. the funniest 101. older 102. modern 103. hotter 104. happy 105. prettier 106. busier 107. the least 108. quieter 109. popular 110. the strongest 111. more stupid / stupider 112. bigger 113. the most surprised 114. thirstier 115. the most brilliant 116. the dirtiest 117. the luckiest 118. cool 119. sillier 120. tidy 121. the warmest 122. the most dangerous 123. the most useful

16 Adverbs / Adverbials

1. happy; fast 2. nice 3. quickly 4. quiet; carefully 5. angrily 6. well 7. pretty; quickly 8. noisy 9. slowly 10. nice 11. quickly 12. loudly; angry 13. fast; fast 14. hard; carefully 15. sad; stupidly 16. good; well 17. loudly 18. young; happily; wonderful 19. popular; slowly 20. hungrily 21. stupid; quickly 22. brilliant 23. dirty; thirstily 24. dangerous 25. lazily 26. quickly 27. happy; nicely 28. terrible 29. boringly 30. easily 31. slow; slowly 32. angry; angrily 33. slowly; slow 34. interesting; interestingly 35. bad; badly 36. busy; busily 37. good; well 38. fast; fast 39. lazy; lazily 40. quickly; quickly 41. good 42. correctly 43. typical 44. polite; polite 45. tidily 46. good 47. unhappy 48. exciting 49. happy; exciting 50. quiet; quietly 51. angrily; angry 52. funny; funnily 53. nice; nicely 54. slowly; slow 55. poor; poorly 56. happily; happy 57. fast 58. angry; quickly 59. careful; hard; noisily 60. terrible; tidily; carefully 61. boringly; poorly 62. well 63. hard; quickly 64. pretty; happily 65. fast 66. sweet; sadly 67. quietly 68. hard 69. fast; slowly 70. She has often been here. 71. We never go for a walk. 72. They never take a walk before breakfast. / Before breakfast they never take a walk. 73. We went to the shop yesterday. / Yesterday we went to the shop. 74. My father never works hard at home. / At home my father never works hard. 75. The young man often swims in the morning. / In the morning the young man often swims. 76. She will ride a bicycle to the shop carefully. / She will carefully ride a bicycle to the shop. 77. Ben has seldom read a book. 78. Today you have sung three songs in your room. / You have sung three songs in your room today. 79. We never find our books on the table. 80. She always

comes to Cologne at 12 o'clock. / At 12 o'clock she always comes to Cologne. 81. Yesterday they went to the zoo quietly. / Yesterday they quietly went to the zoo. / They went to the zoo quietly yesterday. / They quietly went to the zoo yesterday. / They went to the zoo yesterday quietly. 82. Tomorrow I will open the door noisily. / I will open the door noisily tomorrow. / I will noisily open the door tomorrow. / Tomorrow I will noisily open the door. 83. Last year you seldom helped us. / You seldom helped us last year. 84. We saw them in the kitchen this morning. / This morning we saw them in the kitchen. 85. The old lady seldom goes out in the evening. / In the evening the old lady seldom goes out. 86. She always goes for a swim after school. / After school she always goes for a swim. 87. I shall run to the doctor quickly. / I shall quickly run to the doctor. 88. She arrived at the station yesterday. / Yesterday she arrived at the station. 89. She has often forgotten things. 90. I have seen her at the circus this afternoon. / This afternoon I have seen her at the circus. 91. At the office she works busily. / She busily works at the office. / She works at the office busily. 92. I must go to bed at 8 o'clock. / At 8 o'clock I must go to bed. 93. We shall visit you next week. / Next week we shall visit you. 94. Mike always eats chocolate during the lessons. / During the lessons Mike always eats chocolate. 95. They always go for a walk on Saturdays. / On Saturdays they always go for a walk. 96. They often buy sweets at the supermarket. / At the supermarket they often buy sweets. 97. Mr. Potter quickly finished his meal. / Mr. Potter finished his meal quickly. 98. The old woman climbed the stairs slowly. / The old woman slowly climbed the stairs. 99. The boys went for a swim in the sea before lunch. / Before lunch the boys went for a swim in the sea. 100. At 8 o'clock they have breakfast in the kitchen. / They have breakfast in the kitchen at 8 o'clock. 101. We always spend our holidays in London. 102. We carefully planned our holidays. / We planned our holidays carefully. 103. She often sunbathed on the beach. / On the beach she often sunbathed. 104. Tim quickly closed the window. / Tim closed the window quickly. 105. I was at home yesterday. / Yesterday I was at home. 106. We saw her in the bus this morning. / This morning we saw her in the bus. 107. She did her homework slowly. / She slowly did her homework. 108. We shall drive carefully. 109. I quickly ran to the bus stop. / I ran to the bus stop quickly. 110. They always went to school at 8 o'clock. / At 8 o'clock they always went to school. 111. She never talked to me angrily in the morning. / In the morning she never talked to me angrily. / She never talked to me in the morning angrily. 112. We have often sung a song noisily in the bathroom. / We have often sung a song in the bathroom noisily. / In the bathroom we have often sung a song noisily. 113. He never got up at 5 o'clock. 114. The lady sat in the sun every day. / Every day the lady sat in the sun. 115. The men always sang songs happily at church. / At church the men always sang songs happily. / The men always sang songs at church happily. 116. The children clapped their hands loudly during the show. / The children loudly clapped their hands during the show. / During the show the children clapped their hands loudly. / During the show the children loudly clapped their hands. 117. We usually wash our faces quickly in the bathroom in the morning. / In the morning we usually wash our faces quickly in the bathroom. / In the morning we usually wash our faces in the bathroom quickly. 118. We will always take the dog for a walk before school. / Before school we will always take the dog for a walk. 119. The children will have seen the cats often by tomorrow. 120. The boys were happily eating apples in their room in the afternoon. / In the afternoon the boys were happily eating apples in their room. / In the afternoon the boys were eating apples in their room happily. 121. I would never have gone to that house at night. / At night I would never have gone to that house. 122. My sister had sometimes cleaned her room fast on Saturday. /

On Saturday my sister had sometimes cleaned her room fast.

17 Question Tags

1. aren't they 2. is he 3. don't we 4. didn't I 5. haven't you 6. does she 7. aren't there 8. has it 9. doesn't it 10. did they 11. hasn't it 12. are they 13. isn't it 14. do we 15. isn't it 16. have they 17. are you 18. didn't she 19. haven't I 20. doesn't she 21. isn't it 22. has it 23. aren't we 24. do they 25. didn't I 26. isn't it 27. does she 28. hasn't she 29. is it 30. don't they 31. did they 32. aren't they 33. have they 34. is he 35. didn't we 36. hasn't he 37. aren't they 38. does he 39. is he 40. has he 41. can't she 42. is he 43. don't they 44. will she 45. wouldn't they 46. don't we 47. can't we 48. had we 49. was I 50. aren't you 51. didn't she 52. did we 53. are they 54. would he 55. don't we 56. haven't I 57. have you 58. won't we 59. will you 60. aren't they 61. would she 62. won't you 63. doesn't he 64. would we 65. weren't you 66. are they 67. wouldn't we 68. did he 69. aren't you 70. can they 71. haven't I 72. are you 73. won't she 74. can we 75. didn't I 76. are they 77. wouldn't I 78. do we 79. were you 80. hasn't he 81. did it 82. wouldn't we 83. will you 84. wouldn't I 85. aren't they 86. have we 87. weren't you 88. hadn't she 89. would we 90. did you 91. weren't they 92. do I 93. will he 94. did we 95. am I 96. wouldn't it 97. have we 98. wouldn't you 99. hadn't I 100. could they 101. hadn't we 102. had you 103. did she 104. wouldn't he 105. have they 106. aren't we 107. had it 108. won't you 109. could I 110. haven't they 111. do you 112. will we 113. can't it 114. did you 115. wouldn't they 116. will I 117. does she 118. wouldn't you 119. were they 120. don't I 121. would he 122. haven't you 123. haven't we 124. do I 125. will they 126. didn't we 127. has he 128. hadn't you 129. does he 130. won't they 131. did you 132. can he 133. couldn't she 134. would they 135. don't we 136. won't we 137. had you 138. isn't he 139. hasn't it 140. doesn't he 141. would she 142. hadn't we 143. wouldn't you 144. will they 145. wouldn't I 146. did I 147. hasn't he

18 If-clauses

1. were 2. could have helped 3. takes 4. will give 5. does not speak 6. would have come 7. would know 8. will repair 9. would have won 10. did not know 11. have 12. would help 13. would have shot 14. will invite 15. will you do 16. would he do 17. would drink 18. would we have done 19. could not have come 20. would you do 21. would have drunk 22. does not learn 23. would have bought 24. will you do 25. spoke 26. did not speak 27. would have spoken 28. would have come 29. could they give 30. did not eat 31. would help 32. drives 33. saw 34. will run 35. will have to pay / must pay 36. had had 37. would they have gone 38. could have held 39. see 40. give 41. had caught 42. found 43. had not thrown 44. will he be able to come / can he come 45. would be 46. could have driven 47. will have to go / must go 48. would they have hidden 49. did not feed 50. teaches 51. would have written 52. would you buy 53. would have flown 54. had seen 55. had asked 56. sees 57. ate 58. would read 59. saw 60. would I have found 61. would have given 62. could have eaten 63. help 64. will he go 65. had not eaten 66. could you eat / would you be able to eat 67. did not live 68. would be 69. would have seen 70. had looked 71. will have to wait / must wait 72. catches 73. did not talk 74. could have visited 75. had helped 76. could he win / would he be able to win 77. will be able to catch / can catch 78. had taken 79. would have won 80. runs 81.

ran 82. would have thrown 83. will they come 84. would pay 85. catch 86. would she have drunk 87. did not speak 88. would see 89. will get 90. would have bought 91. will be able to go / can go 92. gives 93. would have been 94. had known 95. had read 96. would eat 97. flew 98. would have given 99. bought 100. will shout 101. could show / would be able to show 102. had gone 103. will come 104. left 105. could have read / would have been able to read 106. hears 107. could have hurt 108. would not be 109. do not eat 110. can drive / is able to drive 111. had known 112. ran 113. will drive 114. did not have 115. would have said 116. would have had to eat 117. would see 118. will have to talk / must talk 119. would be 120. eats 121. had found 122. would you go 123. would have brought 124. threw 125. brings 126. asks 127. likes 128. would she buy 129. had played 130. tried 131. would have been 132. had seen 133. will eat 134. had 135. would have had to drive 136. can catch / is able to catch 137. must phone / will have to phone 138. did not have 139. would have taken 140. do not take 141. would know 142. can use / is able to use 143. do not see 144. would have read 145. came 146. would have played 147. would have had to help 148. would run 149. had had 150. will have to give / must give 151. had come 152. would she use 153. was / were 154. buys 155. did not know 156. takes 157. will call 158. would have read 159. did not talk 160. would buy 161. will laugh 162. would have taken 163. would they sing 164. hides 165. held 166. had seen 167. will have to say / must say 168. can help / am able to help 169. would have had to pay 170. do not bring 171. saw 172. comes 173. does not shut 174. will hear 175. would wear 176. drank 177. had allowed 178. sees 179. would shout 180. was / were 181. does not wake 182. would not have been 183. will phone 184. would run 185. would have had 186. rises 187. had caught 188. does not hide 189. would not have fallen 190. will have 191. left 192. wants 193. had not broken 194. would ring 195. He could have helped you if he had wanted to. 196. If you gave him the book now, he could translate it. 197. If I were you, I would wash my hands. 198. He would still have got (caught) the train if he had found his ticket. 199. If he comes late, we will not go to the cinema. 200. I would have given Paul the letter if I had seen him. 201. If we did that, he would be happy. 202. I would see Susan if I went to school. 203. If we had seen the letter, we would have read it. 204. If he sees the cake, he will eat it. 205. If he had seen Linda, he would have given her money. 206. If I see him, I will give him the letter. 207. We would have gone soon if we had not come so late. 208. I would have helped father if I had seen him. 209. If the woman came, we would laugh. 210. If we visit them (her), we will take a flower along. 211. If they sell the house, they will get much money. 212. If I had seen the children, I would have laughed. 213. If the man were here, he would help me. 214. If he had been at home, he would have caught the burglar. 215. If you come, you will see my horses. 216. If I stop now, I can go to bed. 217. If I were you, I would go to bed. 218. If she had gone to bed earlier, she would not have been so tired. 219. If you go to the doctor, you will not like it. 220. If we had found the camera, we would have taken pictures. 221. I could have helped her if she had asked. 222. He would speak with us if we phoned him. 223. If they come, we will drink coffee. 224. We would write letters if we had pencils. 225. If you hide, we will find you. 226. He would have been able to give you the chair if he had known it. / He could have given you the chair if he had known it. 227. If I had slept long, I would not have been so tired. 228. We could have driven there if the weather had been better. 229. If I had seen you, I would have been happy. 230. You would sleep if you had beds. 231. If he shows us the picture, we will show him our pictures, too. 232. I would bake a cake if I had sugar. 233. If we help him, it will go much quicker. 234. If he had bought that, he would have been unhappy. 235. They could have seen the king if they had come sooner. / They would have been able to see the king if they had come sooner. 236. If he had a girl friend, he would go dancing. 237. If he had done his homework, he wouldn't have got a "5" in the test. 238. If he hadn't wanted to go home, he wouldn't have said good-bye. 239. If we liked to walk, we wouldn't take the bus. 240. If we didn't like to walk, we would take the bus. 241. If they hadn't wanted to walk, they would have driven a car. 242. If they had wanted to walk, they wouldn't have driven a car. 243. If he weren't (wasn't) so quiet, I could hear him. 244. If I had done my homework yesterday, I wouldn't have gone to the city. 245. If I hadn't done my homework yesterday, I would have gone to the city. 246. If he didn't sit at home in the afternoon, he would see his friends in the afternoon. 247. If he had stayed at home, he could have watched TV. 248. If he didn't stay at home, he couldn't watch TV. 249. If he stayed at home, he could watch TV. 250. If he didn't buy many things, he would have much money. 251. If he hadn't bought many things, he would have had much money. 252. If I ran quickly, I would get the bus. 253. If I ran quickly, I could get the bus. 254. If I had run quickly, I would have got the bus. 255. If I had run quickly, I could have got the bus. 256. If I didn't run quickly, I wouldn't be very fast. 257. If I had run quickly, I would have won the game. 258. If I hadn't run quickly, I wouldn't have won the game.

19 Question formation

1. Who is this? 2. What is she selling? 3. When can you see her? 4. What does she sell? 5. When does she sell the newspaper? 6. What is Mr. Jones? 7. What is he doing? 8. Where does he often drive? 9. Where are Peggy and Jill walking? 10. What do they often do? 11. Who often walks to work? 12. Do they go to work by bus? 13. Where is Mr. Summers sitting? 14. Does he sometimes watch the children? 15. What does he do? 16. Where can he sleep? 17. Who is driving her car? 18. Where do Mike and Joe live? 19. Who lives in London? 20. Are they asking people about their jobs? 21. Who lives in London? 22. What are Mike and Joe doing? 23. Who is asking people about their jobs? 24. When is Mrs. Pritchard closing the supermarket? 25. What can Mr. Carter catch? 26. When do Mike and Joe get up? 27. Who gets up at seven o'clock? 28. Is Mike watching the people? 29. Who can go to work by train? 30. Why does Mr. Jackson drive to London? 31. What does Mr. Jackson do because he works there? 32. How many children does Mr. Summer see? 33. Whom (Who) does Mrs. Black sell a newspaper? 34. How many girls walk to work? 35 Where do two girls walk? 36. Who watches Mr. Summers? 37. Whom (Who) do three children watch? 38. Did he usually read to them? 39. Was he reading a book? / Wasn't he reading a book? 40. Who is writing a letter? 41. Did you write one yesterday? 42 What do mother and I always eat on Sunday? 43. What do my father and mother often do? 44. Where did Lois and Terry buy that? 45. What can the man feed? 46. What did they do yesterday? 47. Can he swim well? / Can't he swim well? 48. When was I wearing a pullover? 49. Do father and mother drive a car? / Don't father and mother drive a car? 50. Who is standing at the window? 51. At how many boys did my brother throw the books? / How many boys did my brother throw the books at? 52. When were you wearing a blouse? 53. Who rings them up every evening? 54 How many boys wrote a letter? 55. What do we do every afternoon? 56. Whose sister told me a story? 57. What do Tom and Carol always eat at school? 58. Can you/we give me/you that book? / Can't you/we give me/you that book? 59. Where are they running? 60. What did the animals do? 61. When did mother and I/you go to the supermarket? 62. What were my brothers singing? 63. What does my sister hear every morning? 64. Does my/your brother

drink tea? / Doesn't my/your brother drink tea? 65. Who was helping the women? 66. Where did the man drive me/you? 67. Whom (Who) does the man take along in his car? 68. Why do I/you hate that music? 69. Who always carries my/your books? 70. Whom (Who) do I/you help with her homework? 71. When did the three birds fly? 72. Why was the child crying? 73. What is the man driving? 74. Who is washing the dishes? 75. Where does the girl work? 76. When do the children go to the seaside? 77. Why didn't we/you want to sit there? 78. What did the girls take? 79. Where do I/you ride a horse? 80. Whom (Who) did the woman give an apple? 81. Why is his boy helping him? 82. Who is cleaning the windows? 83. What do the cats always eat? 84. What is the boy eating? 85. Who brought his hat? 86. To whom (who) does the baby walk? / Whom (Who) does the baby walk to? 87. What are Linda and Tom picking? 88. When were the men playing football? 89. Where was I/were you eating a cake? 90. When does the baby cry? 91. Who/What plays on the floor? 92. Whom (Who) are you/am I telling a story? 93. Why did Ted and I/you want to go to the beach? 94. What did the woman drink? 95. Where were the three children playing? 96. What was barking at the cat? 97. Whose toy did the child take? 98. Who took Ben's toy? 99. What did the child do? 100. What did the child take? 101. Where does the man put his hat? 102. What does the man put on a chair? 103. Who puts his hat on a chair? 104. What does the man do? 105. Why will the people come? 106. Who will come because we asked them? 107. What will the people do because we asked them? 108. Who was running to the bus? 109. Where were we running? 110. What were we doing? 111. Why is he cutting your dress? 112. Whom (Who) have you often seen? 113. Who has often seen my sister? 114. What have you often done? 115. What are you blowing up? 116. Who/What caught a ball? 117. What did the dog do? 118. What did the dog catch? 119. Whom /(Who)/What was the woman holding yesterday? 120. What was the woman doing yesterday? 121. When was the woman holding the baby? 122. What does my brother do every day? 123. Who catches a ball every day? 124. What does my brother catch every day? 125. When does my brother catch a ball? 126. What will their parents hear? 127. Who will hear the cars? 128. What will their parents do? 129. Who goes to school every day? 130. What do my friends do every day? 131. When do my friends go to school? 132. Where do my friends go every day? 133. Whom (Who) do you take to a show every week? 134. Who takes Linda to a show every week? 135. Where do you take Linda every week? 136. When do you take Linda to a show? 137. What do you do every week? 138. Where can my brothers run after school? 139. Who can run home after school? 140. When can my brothers run home? 141. What can my brothers do after school? 142. Is my sister buying a new car? 143. What did we do yesterday? 144. Who threw the paper to them yesterday? 145. What did we throw to them yesterday? 146. To whom (To who) did we throw the paper yesterday? Whom (Who) did we throw the paper to yesterday? 147. When did we throw the paper to them? 148. Whose sister has washed his shirts? 149. What has Tom's sister washed? 150. What has Tom's sister done? 151. Who has washed his shirts? 152. Whose sister do we ring up every day? 153. Who rings Jean's sister up every day? 154. What do we do every day? 155. Whom (Who) do we ring up every day? 156. When do we ring up Jean's sister? 157. When must the children go to school? 158. Who must go to school tomorrow? 159. What must the children do tomorrow? 160. Where must the children go tomorrow? 161. When must my father wake Mother up? 162. Was I riding the pony when you saw me? / Wasn't I riding the pony when you saw me? / Were you riding the pony when I saw you? / Weren't you riding the pony when I saw you? 163. What will Linda be holding tomorrow? 164. Who will be holding an apple tomorrow? 165. What will

Linda be doing tomorrow? 166. When will Linda be holding an apple? 167. What had the men done? 168. Who had heard a car? 169. What had the men heard? 170. Does the cat eat from his hand? 171. Who has seen many dogs? 172. What have the children done? 173. What have the children seen? 174. What were Jim and I taking? 175. Who was taking a test? 176. What were Jim and I doing? 177. When have they taken a trip? 178. Who has taken a trip today? 179. What have they done today? 180. What have they taken today? 181. What have they done? 182. What/Whom/(Who) has Mr. Smith held? 183. Who/What drinks milk? 184. What does the cat do? 185. What does the cat drink? 186. Why did Bob and Mary run home? 187. Whose blouse was blue? 188. With whom (who) will I/you walk home tomorrow?/ Whom (Who) will I/you walk home with tomorrow? 189. Who will walk home with you tomorrow? 190. What will I do with you tomorrow? 191. Where will I walk with you tomorrow? 192. When will I walk home with you? 193. Are you helping me now? / Am I helping you now? 194. Where are you walking? / Where am I walking? 195. Who is walking to the supermarket? 196. What are you doing? 197. Who was eating an apple? 198. What were Linda and I/you taking? 199. Who was taking a bus? 200. What could Linda and I do? 201. What could Linda and I take? 202. Who could take a bus? 203. Can he help you/me today? 204. What were Mother and I/you holding? 205. What could Mother and I have held? 206. What could Mother and I have done? 207. How many girls do I/you always see? 208. Who always sees three girls? 209. What do I always do? 210. Whom (Who/What) do I always see? 211. How many sandwiches have I always eaten? 212. What have I always eaten? 213. Who has always eaten two sandwiches? 214. What have I always done? 215. Did Mary go to the supermarket? 216. When did the boy see the dog? 217. What did the boy see the day before yesterday? 218. What did the boy do the day before yesterday? 219. Does the dog often bark? 220. With whom (who) is Mr. Smith talking? /Whom (Who) is Mr. Smith talking with? 221. How many books will you/I read tomorrow? 222. Who will read three books tomorrow? 223. What will you/I read tomorrow? 224. When will you/I read three books? 225. What will you/I do tomorrow? 226. With whom (who) are we/you walking? / Whom (Who) are we/you walking with? 227. Who is walking with Tom? 228. Whom (Who) should we/you help? 229. Who should help Mother? 230. What should we do? 231. Who is talking to her sister? 232. Who is here? 233. Who has been here? 234. When will we/you run to school? 235. Who will run to school after breakfast? 236. Where will we/you run after breakfast? 237. What will we/you do after breakfast? 238. Where did he run after lunch? 239. Who ran to the station after lunch? 240. When did he run to the station? 241. What did he do after lunch? 242. Who throws balls every day? 243. When does my brother throw balls? 244. What does my brother do every day? 245. What have they given her? 246. Who has given her a book? 247. What have they done? 248. Whom (Who) have they given a book? 249. Why am I happy?/Why are you happy? 250. How often did they speak to her? 251. What did they do to her four times? 252. How many trees were growing near the river? 253. What did the dog do? 254. What did the dog shake? 255. What would the dog have done? 256. What would the dog have shaken? 257. What has the dog done? 258. What has the dog shaken? 259. What does the dog do? 260. What does the dog shake? 261. What can the dog do? 262. What can the dog shake? 263. Where are we/you hiding? 264. Who is hiding in the bedroom? 265. What are we/you doing in the bedroom? 266. Where were we/you hiding? 267. Who was hiding in the bedroom? 268. What were we/you doing in the bedroom? 269. Where will we/you be hiding? 270. Who will be hiding in the bedroom? 271. What will we/you be doing in the bedroom? 272. When did we/you drink milk? 273. Who drank milk yesterday? 274. What did we/you do yesterday? 275. When do we/you drink milk? 276. Who drinks milk every day? 277. What do we/you do every day? 278. When have we/you drunk milk? 279. Who has drunk milk every day? 280. What have we/you done every day? 281. When would we/you drink milk? 282. Who would drink milk every day? 283. What would we/you do every day? 284. When should we/you drink milk? 285. Who should drink milk every day? 286. What should we/you do every day? 287. When will we/you drink milk? 288. Who will drink milk every day? 289. What will we/you do every day? 290. When had we/you drunk milk? 291. Who had drunk milk every day? 292. What had we/you done every day? 293. What did they take? 294. Who took an apple? 295. What did they do? 296. How many books did she buy? 297. What did she buy? 298. Why did I/you tell you/me a story? 299. Who stood in the classroom? 300. Where did the two men stand? 301. How many men stood in the classroom? 302. What did the two men do in the classroom? 303. Where did he go? 304. What do they eat? 305. Who ran home? 306. When did I/you go swimming? 307. Why did you/I help me/you? 308. How many girls bought books? 309. Who bought books? 310. What did two girls do? 311. What did two girls buy? 312. Where were we/you flying a kite? 313. Who was flying a kite at the beach? 314. Who can help you/me? 315. Whom (Who) can the old man help? 316. What can the old man do? 317. When will we/you be visiting them? 318. Who will be visiting them on Sunday? 319. What will we be doing on Sunday? 320. Whom (Who) will we be visiting on Sunday? 321. Do you like him? 322. What does he eat every day? 323. When will she call him? 324. Who will call him at 3 o'clock? 325. What will she do at 3 o'clock? 326. Whom (Who) will she call at 3 o'clock? 327. When did Mother go to Bonn? 328. With whom (who) will we/you talk tomorrow? 329. What will we do tomorrow? 330. Who will talk with him tomorrow? 331. Did Don take his pullover with him? 332. Where are you/am I running? 333. Who is running to the bus stop? 334. How many apples do I/you always eat every week? 335. Who always eats six apples every week? 336. What do I/you see? 337. What had I seen? 338. Who had seen the red pencil? 339. What had I done? 340. What would I see? 341. Who would see the red pencil? 342. What would I do? 343. Who has cars? 344. When did the supermarket open? 345. What did the supermarket do at 2 o'clock? 346. Can I/you come to visit you/me? 347. Where are they walking? 348. Who is walking to the window? 349. Whom (Who) is he looking at?/At whom (who) is he looking? 350. How often did I/you sing that song? 351. What did I/you do twice? 352. How often would I/you sing that song? 353. Who would sing that song twice? 354. What would I/you do twice? 355. How often had I/you sung that song? 356. Who had sung that song twice? 357. What had I/you done twice? 358. What does she often do? 359. Did they wear hats yesterday? 360. What did they buy last week? 361. How did she run? 362. What did she do? 363. Why did the child hide behind the door? 364. Where will she go tomorrow? 365. Who will go to school tomorrow? 366. What did we/you listen to? / To what did we/you listen? 367. How many children are running down the street? 368. Who is running down the street? 369. Where are five children running? 370. What are five children doing? 371. What did they always do? 372. What did they always feed? 373. Who forgot to take his pullover? 374. What did I forget to take? 375. Why had they given her money? 376. Who had given her money? 377. What had they given her? 378. Whom (Who) had they given money? 379. What had they done? 380. Who would give her money? 381. What would they give her? 382. Whom (Who) would they give money? 383. What would they do? 384. Who would have given her money? 385. What would they have given her? 386. Whom (Who) would they have given money? 387. What would they have done? 388.

When will you/I be driving there? 389. What will you be doing on Sunday? 390. What has she done? 391. What has she drawn? 392. How many pieces of cake does he eat every day? 393. What does he do every day? 394. Where did we/you swim? 395. What did we do? 396. When are you/am I buying a new blouse? 397. Who is buying a new blouse tomorrow? 398. Who speaks to me every day? 399.a. Who saw the birds on the tree? b. How many boys saw the birds on the tree? c. What did the three boys see on the tree? d. Where did the three boys see the birds? 400. a. Who has driven two cars to Bonn? b. What has Mother done?/What has mother driven to Bonn? c. How many cars has Mother driven to Bonn? d. Where has Mother driven two cars? 401.a. Who is sitting on the chair? b. Whose sister is sitting on the chair? c. Where is father's sister sitting? 402 a. How many boys would eat ten pieces of cake if you baked cake? b. Who would eat ten pieces of cake if you baked cake? c. How many pieces of cake would the five boys eat if you baked cake? d. What would the five boys eat if you baked cake? e. What would the five boys do if you baked cake? 403.a. Who always gives you books to read? b. Whom (Who) do we/you always give books to read? c. What do we/you aways give you/us to read? 404. a. Who must go home now? b. Where must I go now? c. When must I go home? d. What must I do now? 405.a. Who was eating apples in the garage? b. What were the boys eating in the garage? c. Where were the boys eating apples? d. What were the boys doing in the garage? 406. a. Who had thrown toys on the floor? b. What had the children thrown on the floor? c. Where had the children thrown the toys? d. What had the children done? 407.a. Who will buy Susan five new books? b. Whom (Who) will father buy five new books? c. How many new books will father buy Susan? d. What will father buy Susan?/What will father do? 408. Who will be flying to London tomorrow? b. Where will my brother be flying tomorrow? c. When will my brother be flying to London? d. What will my brother be doing tomorrow? 409.a. Whose sister took Mike's car? b. What did Pat's sister take? c. Whose car did Pat's sister take? d. What did Pat's sister do? 410. a. Who would have given you many books if you had asked? b. Whom (Who) would the men have given many books if you had asked? c. What would the men have given you if you had asked? d. What would the men have done if you had asked? 411.a. Who goes to Rome every summer? b. Where do they go every summer? c. When do they go to Rome? d. What do they do every summer? 412. a. Who has drunk a glass of milk? b. What have I/you drunk? c. What have I/you done? 413.a. Who was sitting on a chair in the kitchen? b. How many boys were sitting on a chair in the kitchen? c. On what were three boys sitting in the kitchen? d. Where were three boys sitting on a chair? e. What were three boys doing? 414 .a. Who sees four trees? b. What does he see? c. How many trees does he see? 415. a. Who is going to Berlin tomorrow? b. Where am I/are you going tomorrow? c. When am I/are you going to Berlin? d. What am I/are you doing tomorrow? 416. a. Who wrote twenty letters yesterday? b. Whose sister wrote twenty letters yesterday? c. What did Jane's sister write yesterday? d. When did Jane's sister write twenty letters? e. What did Jane's sister do yesterday? 417. a. How long can they talk today? b. When can they talk for two hours? c. What can they do today? 418. a. Who will go to the beach next week? b. Where will the class go next week? c. When will the class go to the beach? d. What will the class do next week? 419. a. Who helps me/you every day? b. Whose brother helps me/you every day? c. Whom (Who) does John's brother help every day? d. When does John's brother help me/you? e. What does John's brother do every day? 420. a. Who is playing football? b. How many boys are playing football? c. What are two boys playing? 421. a. Who has bought three pullovers? b. How many pullovers have the girls bought? c. What have the girls bought? d. What have the girls done? 422. a. What/Who saw our dog yesterday? b. Whose dog did the cat see yesterday? c. What did the cat see yesterday? d. When did the cat see our dog? 423. a. How many dogs would have barked loudly if they had seen the cats? b. What (Who) would have barked loudly if they had seen the cats? c. How would the ten dogs have barked if they had seen the cats? d. What would the ten dogs have done if they had seen the cats? 424. a. Who always eats six bars of chocolate? b. How many girls always eat six bars of chocolate? c. How many bars of chocolate do the three girls always eat? d. What do the three girls always eat? e. What do the three girls always do? 425. a. Who will be eating our food when you arrive tomorrow? b. What will we be eating when you arrive tomorrow? c. What will we be doing when you arrive tomorrow? 426. a. Who can help you tomorrow? b. Whom (Who) can mother and I help tomorrow? c. When can mother and I help you? d. What can mother and I do? 427. a. Who should drive the car into the garage? b. What should the man drive into the garage? c. Where should the man drive the car? d. What should the man do? 428. a. Whose brother will go to school? b. Who will go to school? c. Where will my brother go? d. What will my brother do? 429 a. Who would work very hard every day if they had a job? b. How would the men work every day if they had a job? c. When would the men work very hard if they had a job? d. What would the men do every day if they had a job? 430. a. Who is throwing a ball into the air? b. What is the girl throwing into the air? c. Where is the girl throwing a ball? d. What is the girl doing? 431 a. Who often laughs at his two brothers? b. At how many brothers does the boy often laugh?/How many brothers does the boy often laugh at? c. At whom (who) does the boy often laugh?/Whom (Who) does the boy often laugh at? d. What does the boy often do? 432. a. Who was writing ten sentences? b. How many sentences were the men writing? c. What were the men writing? d. What were the men doing? 433. a. Who / What had sold ten apples? b. How many apples had the supermarket sold? c. What had the supermarket sold? d. What had the supermarket done? 434. a. Who said a word? b. What did mother say? c. What did mother do? 435. a. Who will read a book tomorrow? b. What will father read tomorrow? c. When will father read a book? d. What will father do tomorrow? 436. a. Who would go to your party if Linda went there, too? b. To whose party would Tom go if Linda went there, too?/ Whose party would Tom go to if Linda went there, too? c. Where would Tom go if Linda went there, too? d. What would Tom do if Linda went there, too? 437. a. Is father reading? 438. a. Who always reads books? b. What does father always read? c. What does father always do? 439. a. Who often read books when he was a boy? b. What did father often read when he was a boy? c. When did father often read books? d. What did father often do? e. What did father often do when he was a boy? 440. a. Who often washes our/his cars? b. Whose cars do we/you often wash? c. What do we/you often wash? d. What do we/you often do? 441. Where are we/you running? 442. Who is running to school? 443. What are we/you doing? 444. Who has eaten his sandwich? 445. What has he done? 446. Who is eating his sandwich? 447. What is he doing? 448. Who would go to work if he had a job? 449. What would he do if he had a job? 450. Who had gone to work when he had a job? 451. What had he done when he had a job? 452. Why is Linda sitting there? 453. Will we give you the paper? 454. Whom (Who) have they taken to school? 455. Who has taken you to school? 456. What have they done? 457. Who had taken you to school? 458. What had they done? 459. Who would take you to school? 460. What would they do? 461. Who had helped you very often last year? 462. What had we done very often last year? 463. Who would help you if you asked us? 464. What would we do if you asked us? 465. With whose brother has mother spoken?/ Whose brother has mother spoken with? 466. Who has spoken with Tom's brother? 467. What has Mother done? 468. Who is speaking with Tom's brother? 469. What is Mother doing? 470. What will the girls feed? 471. Will his sister swim next week? 472. When is mother flying to Berlin? 473. Who is flying to Berlin tomorrow? 474. What is Mother doing tomorrow? 475. Who has flown to Berlin very often? 476. What has Mother done very often? 477. Where is Jerry sleeping now? 478. Who is sleeping on a sofa now? 479. What is Jerry doing now? 480. Who has slept on a sofa very often? 481. What has Jerry done very often?

20 Verb tenses

1. had been sleeping 2. had written 3. will have broken 4. Have you been 5. were drinking 6. would not always steal 7. usually drive 8. would have bitten 9. usually caught 10. had sometimes had 11. sleeps 12. always understood 13. Has he got 14. Was the wind blowing 15. have spoken 16. had left 17. will meet 18. was blowing 19. would have forgotten 20. would keep 21. will have begun 22. bought 23. are sleeping 24. fall 25. were riding 26. Have we spoken 27. had had 28. are riding 29. have sometimes got 30. were holding 31. will have begun 32. ate 33. would steal 34. often understood 35. heard 36. have been 37. take 38. was drinking 39. flies 40. am reading 41. was driving 42. was selling 43. had often left 44. is driving 45. were eating 46. call 47. caught 48. got 49. had always had 50. goes 51. will be singing, meet 52. had found, would have given 53. have been speaking 54. caught, could eat / would be able to eat 55. has not seen 56. would be riding 57. was running, had to talk 58. Are you drawing 59. will know, hear 60. were saying, could build / were able to build 61. have slept, will get up 62. had been swimming 63. would buy 64. Is David taking 65. collect, collects 66. goes 67. have just seen 68. was sitting, saw 69. watch, are listening 70. had helped, would have got 71. come, will hear 72. knew, would understand, have said 73. have been talking 74. had hoped, would be writing, came 75. will be drinking, find 76. would have been burning, had not caught 77. was doing, said, would play 78. had talked, had to go, could finish 79. heard, said, will be 80. Have you seen 81. had spoken, would have known 82. take, will make 83. will be leaving 84. bought, would eat 85. did not buy 86. does not like 87. will have cleaned, come 88. thought, had seen 89. has been swimming 90. had not eaten 91. had given 92. strikes 93. has grown 94. have been flying 95. was putting, saw 96. am lying 97. drew 98. opened, had taken 99. forgets, will sleep 100. are repairing 101. saw, had been learning 102. has, will buy 103. had learnt, would have had 104. has done, is playing 105. was washing, rang 106. ran, would catch 107. come, will build 108. come, will have drawn 109. came 110. were doing 111. had helped, went 112. had read, would have known 113. arrived, was telling 114. run 115. Does your cat run 116. Was he drinking 117. did not catch 118. buys 119. Did you know 120. does not understand 121. takes 122. will have left 123. Did you see 124. is not cleaning 125. Was he cleaning 126. walk 127. Are you taking 128. has taught 129. Does your dog sometimes bite 130. has not taught 131. Was, were 132. eats 133. had not written 134. does not like 135. Is your mother making 136. saw 137. have already asked 138. Were the girls singing 139. has given 140. Does he drink 141. sometimes drink 142. were eating 143. would have eaten, had found 144. always carries 145. often feeds 146. would cut, held 147. Would your sister know, met 148. will hide 149. Can he drive / Is he able to drive 150. had caught, would have thrown 151. usually thought 152. will be holding 153. would have eaten, had kept 154. does not usually drive 155. Would you eat, bought 156. does not often speak 157. sometimes brought 158. feeds 159. Would he sell,

drew 160. were shutting 161. Will you be wearing 162. will they have read 163. spent, will go 164. is driving 165. bought 166. will often draw 167. heard 168. were selling 169. Has she spoken 170. goes 171. Did you play 172. is 173. has already started 174. were washing 175. caught 176. is reading 177. did you arrive 178. has been crying 179. have known 180. left 181. had to talk 182. were still talking 183. has always worked 184. will go 185. don't want 186. lives 187. has helped 188. is cooking 189. saw 190. caught 191. has been raining 192. Is your father working 193. am trying 194. is talking 195. has not seen 196. taught 197. was still working 198. broke 199. has broken 200. were not wearing 201. was washing 202. did not visit 203. has been playing 204. phoned 205. are reading 206. met 207. went, bought 208. is helping 209. go 210. began, has been working 211. sings 212. will have fed 213. spent 214. drinks, drank 215. have been writing 216. have been playing 217. would buy 218. has never eaten 219. would have driven 220. am taking 221. will fly / will be flying 222. will have shut 223. Haven't you written 224. would read 225. were drawing 226. had already found 227. will meet 228. were stealing 229. could sweep / were able to sweep 230. will swim 231. have been sweeping 232. would hide 233. is washing 234. have been reading 235. would have worn 236. has never torn 237. Haven't you found 238. lost, Have you seen. 239. have not seen 240. Did you watch 241. have not heard, had 242. got, was 243. has just moved 244. have you been 245. Did he see 246. saw 247. Will you read 248. will not read / won't read 249. gave 250. came 251. was not / wasn't 252. have known 253. told 254. has never forgotten 255. is swimming 256. would drink 257. have taught 258. was buying 259. Have they ever sold 260. did not learn 261. have been sitting 262. will have begun 263. have sung/have been singing 264. are biting 265. flies 266. Are you leaving 267. has never written 268. did not hear 269. had to drive 270. were 271. Have you ever stuck 272. Did she play 273. have been doing 274. had already paid 275. did not see 276. will hide 277. were holding 278. has that man shaken 279. has been teaching 280. would put 281. could feed / were able to feed 282. will be building 283. had to catch 284. has never made 285. have been standing 286. are running 287. could throw / was able to throw 288. will see 289. did not go 290. will be holding 291.b. 292.c. 293.a. 294.d. 295.b. 296.b. 297.d. 298.c. 299.b. 300.a. 301. He is eating many apples. 302. He had eaten many apples. 303. He would be eating many apples. 304. He ate many apples. 305. He will have been eating many apples. 306. He will eat many apples. 307. He would have eaten many apples. 308. He has been eating many apples. 309. He eats many apples. 310. He had been eating many apples. 311. He would eat many apples. 312. He was eating many apples. 313. He has eaten many apples. 314. He would have been eating many apples. 315. He will be eating many apples. 316. He will have eaten many apples. 317. What will he be eating? 318. What would he eat? 319. What was he eating? 320. What has he eaten? 321. What is he eating? 322. What had he eaten? 323. What would he have been eating? 324. What will he eat? 325. What will he have been eating? 326. What does he eat? 327. What would he be eating? 328. What had he been eating? 329. What would he have eaten? 330. What will he have eaten? 331. What has he been eating? 332. What did he eat? 333. He hasn't eaten many apples. 334. He won't be eating many apples. 335. He wouldn't eat many apples. 336. He doesn't eat many apples. 337. He hadn't been eating many apples. 338. He won't have eaten many apples. 339. He wouldn't have been eating many apples. 340. He didn't eat many apples. 341. He hasn't been eating many apples. 342. He won't eat many apples. 343. He wouldn't be eating many apples. 344. He wasn't eating many apples. 345. He won't have been eating many apples. 346. He isn't eating many apples. 347. He hadn't eaten many apples. 348. He wouldn't have eaten many apples. 349.

They will drive quickly. 350. They would be driving quickly. 351. They drove quickly. 352. They have been driving quickly. 353. They will have driven quickly. 354. They would have been driving quickly. 355. They are driving quickly. 356. They had been driving quickly. 357. They would drive quickly. 358. They drive quickly. 359. They will have been driving quickly. 360. They have driven quickly. 361. They would have driven quickly. 362. They were driving quickly. 363. They will be driving quickly. 364. They had driven quickly. 365. How have they driven? 366. How will they have been driving? 367. How did they drive? 368. How would they be driving? 369. How had they driven? 370. How will they be driving? 371. How would they have driven? 372. How had they been driving? 373. How will they drive? 374. How would they have been driving? 375. How do they drive? 376. How have they been driving? 377. How would they drive? 378. How were they driving? 379. How will they have driven? 380. How are they driving? 381. They won't have driven quickly. 382. They haven't been driving quickly. 383. They wouldn't drive quickly. 384. They aren't driving quickly. 385. They hadn't driven quickly. 386. They wouldn't have been driving quickly. 387. They won't (= will not) drive quickly. 388. They weren't driving quickly. 389. They won't have been driving quickly. 390. They don't drive quickly. 391. They wouldn't be driving quickly. 392. They haven't driven quickly. 393. They won't be driving quickly. 394. They wouldn't have driven quickly. 395. They hadn't been driving quickly. 396. They didn't drive quickly. 397. How won't they have been driving? 398. What hasn't the man been doing? 399. Where wouldn't the girls have gone? 400. Who hasn't taken a test?

21 Relative Clauses

1. whose 2. which 3. who 4. whom (who) 5. whose 6. whom (who) 7. which 8. whom (who) 9. whose 10. whom (who) 11. which 12. whom (who) 13. whose 14. which 15. who 16. whom (who) 17. who 18. whom (who) 19. whose 20. which 21. which 22. which 23. who 24. who 25. which 26. whom (who) 27. which 28. whom (who) 29. whose 30. which 31. who 32. which 33. whose 34. who 35. which 36. who 37. whose 38. whom (who) 39. whose 40. we visited 41. we drank with our food 42. we stayed at 43. we slept in 44. who has ten children 45. who filled a bag with their best apples 46. which Sam carried 47. they looked at 48. who was walking by himself 49. the two brothers were taking to town 50. we live in 51. we saw on the street 52. we ate from 53. who was walking through a street in London, which had dresses in it. 54. he saw 55. whose shop it was 56. he had been talking to 57. mother worked in 58. who wanted to buy the dress mother had put in the window, mother had put in the window 59. whose friend talked to her 60. whom they could give the money to, whose blouse was on a chair 61. they had heard of, they had given him 62. we worked in 63. we had gone to 64. whose bike was broken 65. we had heard 66. who was washing her face 67. Peter whom (who) he had helped said "thank you." / He had helped Peter who said "thank you." 68. The pictures which we were looking at were interesting. / We were looking at the pictures which were interesting. 69. Mrs. Green whose house we lived in asked Tom to lunch. / Mrs. Green in whose house we lived asked Tom to lunch. 70. The man who ate a cake is here. 71. We took the apple which was lying on the table. 72. Linda whom (who) they had taken home waved good-bye. 73. You could see Mr. Twain whose books Ken has read. 74. We could talk to the woman who was writing a letter. 75. The dog whose ear was dirty could not hear. 76. We saw the boys whom (who) you had played with. / We saw the boys with whom (who) you had played. / We saw the boys you had played with. /You had

played with the boys whom (who) we saw. 77. Dick whom (who) we had brought home said "hello." 78. You can speak to Linda who is reading the newspaper. 79. They saw Mary Ann and me whom (who) Father played with. / They saw Mary Ann and me with whom (who) Father played. 80. The songs which we were listening to were funny. / The songs to which we were listening were funny. / The songs we were listening to were funny./We were listening to the songs which were funny. 81. The woman who has eaten an apple is there. 82. Linda has stolen the money which was lying under the chair. 83. We saw the Beatles whose records Tom has heard. 84. The cat whose eye is bad cannot see. 85. Peter and Sue whom (who) Jenny helped said "thank you." / Jenny helped Peter and Sue who said “thank you.” 86. Mr. Black whose house we live in will ask Laurie to lunch. / Mr. Black in whose house we live will ask Laurie to lunch. 87. John is running to his brother who gave him the bike. 88. Mr. Green whose shop is in Cologne sells many things. 89. They drive along the street which is very busy. / The street they drive along is very busy. / The street which they drive along is very busy. 90. Uncle John whom (who) Bob helps with the work eats fish every day. 91. That is the man who took my car which is 5 years old. 92. The man whom (who) I see is eating a sandwich. / The man I see is eating a sandwich. / I see the man who is eating a sandwich. 93. The girl who is my sister always drinks water./The girl who always drinks water is my sister. 94. The dog which is running down the street is black. 95. The chair which I am sitting on is blue. / The chair on which I am sitting is blue. / The chair I am sitting on is blue./I am sitting on the chair which is blue. 96. I am reading the letter which is from my father./The letter which I am reading is from my father. 97. The little boy whom (who) my mother is holding is crying. / The little boy my mother is holding is crying./My mother is holding the boy who is crying. 98. The man whose car I drove gave me a book. 99. The woman whose husband stood up was talking then. 100. The child whose arm was broken cried. 101. The child whose shoe was open was young. 102. The man whose coat was black talked to me. 103. The girl whose birthday it was was happy. 104. The boy who had his own coat ran home. 105. The man whom (who) I gave the book to is my father. / The man to whom (who) I gave the book is my father. / The man I gave the book to is my father. 106. His sister whom (who) he bought a present for is 32. / His sister for whom (who) he bought a present is 32. 107. The supermarket which the ice-cream was in was open. / The supermarket in which the ice-cream was was open. 108. The shop he was walking to was closed. / The shop to which he was walking was closed. / The shop which he was walking to was closed./He was walking to the shop which was closed. 109. The woman he was talking with had a book. / The woman with whom (who) he was talking had a book. / The woman whom (who) he was talking with had a book. 110. The tables which the chairs were between were red. / The tables between which the chairs were were red. / The tables the chairs were between were red./The chairs were between the tables which were red. 111. The table the man was lying on was at the doctor’s. / The table which the man was lying on was at the doctor’s. / The table on which the man was lying was at the doctor’s. / The man was lying on the table which was at the doctor’s. 112. A man who was a neighbour questioned her. 113. The woman who was his mother rang him up. 114. The man who is very good drives a Mercedes. 115. A house which was very old burnt down last night. 116. The sock which wasn’t clean fell to the floor. 117. The man they’ve caught stole money. / The man whom (who) they’ve caught stole money. 118. The man she loved gave her a ring. / The man whom (who) she loved gave her a ring. 119. The money he took was on the table. / The money which he took was on the table. 120. The man I know did this. / The man whom (who) I know did this. 121. I ate the food which made me ill. 122. We had been waiting for the bus which was full. / The bus which we had been waiting for was full. 123. The knife we cut our bread with is long. / The knife which we cut our bread with is long. / The knife with which we cut our bread is long. / We cut our bread with the knife which is long. 124. I was talking to the girl who was my cousin. / The girl I was talking to was my cousin. / The girl whom (who) I was talking to was my cousin. / The girl to whom (who) I was talking was my cousin. 125. The man who is my father is nice. / The man who is nice is my father. 126. John is talking to his sister who asked him to come home. 127. The chair was expensive. I sat on the chair. 128. He likes the girl. The girl's mother is now talking. 129. The man is our uncle. We took the books to the man. 130. Can you see the man? The man is helping Jane. 131. We helped the woman. The woman's car had stopped. 132. They talked to the child. He had taken a banana from the child. 133. The girl ran away. The girl was looking at the dress when I saw her. 134. Penny walked to her mother. I was reading Penny's book. 135. The boy threw the ball. They had seen the boy playing football. 136. The animal was a cat. The animal had eaten the cake. 137. The baby had no mother. They heard the baby crying. 138. The person was Tom. I had seen the person. 139. The man was father. I had helped the man. 140. The animal was a hamster. The animal had left its cage. 141. Rosemary ran to her father. I have found Rosemary's letter. 142. We spoke with the man. You had taken a book from the man. 143. The shoes were new. She had the shoes on. 144. Rita went to the man. The man's car was dirty. 145. The man walked away. The man was looking at the car when we saw him. 146. The girl gave me a ball. You had watched the girl. 147. The girl was sad. The girl's mother had left the house. 148. If I had the camera, I would take a photo. You gave me the camera. 149. The man was his father. He gave the book to the man. 150. The woman carried two books. I saw the woman. 151. The bird cried for help. The bird's tail was in the cat's mouth. 152. If they knew the man, they would tell their mother. The man had phoned. 153. The men ate their lunch. They were working with the men. 154. The people asked me questions. You showed the picture to the people. 155. If he had understood the woman, he would have told his mother. The woman had called. 156. The shop was closed yesterday. I bought the chair from the shop. 157. The girl fell from her bike. The girl was looking at you. 158. The man turned around. I saw the man walking down the street. 159. The book told about cats. She was reading the book when you came. 160. The radio is now broken. We were listening to the radio today. 161. If I wore the dress, I would make her happy. She sold me the dress. 162. He likes the girl. The girl's mother is now talking. 163. Is the man our uncle? We took the books to the man. 164. Can you see the woman? The woman is helping Jane. 165. The man wrote down our names. We had spoken with the man. 166. Did the cat catch a mouse? The cat's ball rolled away. 167. Were the babies hungry? The babies were crying. 168. We heard the girls. The girls' mothers had gone shopping. 169. The shop cost much money. We had bought the shop. 170. The horses walked slowly. We rode the horses. 171. Why did the dog bark? He was holding the dog. 172. Didn't you see the man? The man gave me the camera. 173. Did the ball roll away? She was playing with the ball. 174. Have you seen the letters? They've written the letters. 175. When'll the cake be cool? They're making the cake. 176. Isn't that the biggest fish? We've caught the fish. 177. Did the cat forget him? He fed the cat. 178. Won't you be staying at the house? They live in the house. 179. What was the day like? You dreamt about the day. 180. Where's the book? She's been reading the book. 181. The dogs grew quickly. They gave us the dogs. 182. Didn't he hear the noise? The dog made the noise. 183. Will the picture be pretty? They're drawing the picture.

22 Passive

1. Letters are written by me. 2. A book was written by him. 3. A picture will be drawn by her. 4. The light has been found by him. 5. A friend will be met by you. 6. Her house had been sold (by her.) 7. His letters were torn up (by him.) 8. A radio has been stolen by the man. 9. The car is usually driven by the lady. 10. Bob is beaten by the cook. 11. The thief was caught by the policeman. 12. – 13. The shop is visited by professors. 14. A letter has been written by Linda. 15. I had been met at the station by some friends. 16. The ball is always blown up by Jim. 17. The boys were waited for by the man. 18. Such a song had never been heard of by the girls. 19. All the cake has just been eaten up by the boys and girls. 20. The monkey was laughed at by the children. 21. The boy was looked after by an old man. 22. The project was talked about for a long time (by people.) 23. The lions are fed at noon by the keeper. 24. Yesterday they were fed at noon by him. 25. The water is carried to a higher place by pumps. 26. He was expected to come at three o'clock (by us.) 27. The house is carefully cleaned by Jim. 28. The walls are beautifully painted by Betty. 29. The baby has been cared for every day by Mac. 30. The curtains had been washed well by John. 31. A lecture will be given next week by the doctor. 32. The injured man was taken to the hospital (by the doctor.) 33. He is called Ted by his friends. 34. All the bread has been eaten by the mice. 35. Our windows will be cleaned tomorrow by the man. 36. Those letters will be typed by the secretary. 37. A new edition of the book is now being printed (by them.) 38. He is being visited in hospital by many people. 39. Fruit was being stolen from the apple trees by thieves. 40. The lady at the counter was seen by my father. 41. His books are brought to school by the boy. 42. Her sums have been done by the girl. 43. The next book will be found more interesting (by you.) 44. Seven languages were spoken by the clever man. 45. The ball had been thrown quickly by Bob. 46. Eight words will now be written by me. 47. Many fingers are pointed at Tom by the old women. 48. The lady at the counter was helped by him. 49. The clothes were hung up by the boy. 50. Much money is given to the church by him. 51. The setting sun has been seen by the old man. 52. Bad words had been spoken by him. 53. The train was stopped by robbers. 54. The suitcases are being packed by his wife. 55. Police officers have often been seen by them. 56. The money had been found by a little girl. 57. Birds are fed by many people. 58. My hand will be held by my boyfriend. 59. The men were being watched by the little girl. 60. Letters were written by two friends. 61. That book has been read by the teachers. 62. Apples are eaten every day by my sister. 63. The ball has often been thrown by the boys. 64. Will the letter be opened by the men? 65. Her father and mother are helped by the little girl. 66. Their children would be driven home by the farmers. 67. The doors had been shut by the doctor. 68. The cars were stolen (by you.) 69. A dress is often worn (by you.) 70. A picture is being painted by the artist. 71. Our radio was being repaired by them. 72. The windows will have been cleaned by this afternoon (by her.) 73. His table is being sold by them. 74. The books had often been found (by you.) 75. The book can be read (by me.) 76. When was the milk drunk by the boy? 77. New balls are being thrown by my brother. 78. A car had been driven by us yesterday. 79. Was a table bought (by them)? 80. The cake will have been eaten by tomorrow (by you.) 81. How will the street be found (by them)? 82. A ball must be blown up by my sister. 83. The dishes would have been broken (by you.) 84. — 85. Where is your money hidden (by you)? 86. A song was being sung by my sisters. 87. Why will those books be kept (by them)? 88. A book was being hidden by my brothers. 89. — 90. The forks will have been put away by tomorrow (by us.) 91. I would have been bitten by the

dog. 92. A cake must be brought by Linda. 93. Where are such clothes bought (by you)? 94. Was a chair broken (by them)? 95. The ball would be bought by my father. 96. A pen had been found (by them) yesterday 97. When was the man eaten by the lion? 98. A new dress is being worn by my mother. 99. Where are such pictures seen (by you)? 100. A nice song would be heard by the man. 101. — 102. Was a car driven (by them)? 103. A new car was being bought by father and mother. 104. An answer will have been found by tomorrow (by us.) 105. A big cake is being eaten by my sister. 106. Why will the cat be bitten (by him)? 107. A dress had been worn yesterday (by my sister.) 108. Chairs would have been brought (by us.) 109. When was the book put on the shelf by the lady? 110. The ball must be caught (by them.) 111. The plates will be taken to mother (by me.) 112. Are his cats fed by the boy? 113. Coffee was being drunk by the men. 114. My cold would certainly be caught by the babies. 115. Have the presents been bought by mother? 116. Were the tables being carried by the children? 117. The two patients can be rung up by the doctor. 118. Will those books be read by the lady? 119. John is being followed everywhere by gangsters. 120. The clock can't be seen from here (by me.) 121. A dress has just been bought in London (by me.) 122. I am being taught to swim (by him.) 123. His homework will have been finished at 9 o'clock (by him.) 124. My dinner was eaten very quickly (by me.) 125. While the dog was being fed in the kitchen (by me), a mouse was caught in the garden by the cat. 126. The books had been corrected very carefully by the teacher. 127. We were taken to the zoo last week by father. 128. Television is watched every evening (by many people.) 129. We will be told the reason soon (by them.) 130. He was allowed three minutes to get ready (by her.) 131. I have never been taught how to ride a bicycle (by anyone.) 132. The money must be paid by the end of the month (by you). 133. The cakes should be fetched before the shops close (by you). 134. The house must be painted in the summer (by him). 135. The letter should have been written yesterday (by you). 136. The medicine must be taken every three hours (by you). 137. Tickets should be bought before you get on the tram (by you). 138. Tickets can no longer be bought from the driver (by you). 139. If the dog's tail had been pulled (by me), I would have been bitten (by it). 140. A broken walking stick was found near his body (by them). 141. The policeman was taken to Mr. Brown's house (by that man). 142. Some burnt papers had also been found there (by them). 143. The man couldn't be caught for a long time (by them). 144. Janet is given a pen by the teacher. A pen is given to Janet by the teacher. 145. I was offered a cup of tea by Aunt Jane. A cup of tea was offered to me by Aunt Jane. 146. Thousands of dolls were sold to the visitors (by the shops). 147. They have just been taught a song by the teacher. A song has just been taught to them by the teacher. 148. The girls were told a nice story by father. A nice story was told to the girls by father. 149. They were shown the rooms (by the owner). The rooms were shown to them (by the owner). 150. Many letters were written to the German girls (by the English girls). 151. I was shown a nice picture by father. A nice picture was shown to me by father. 152. I have just been given a book by mother. A book has just been given to me by mother. 153. I have just been given the book (by him). The book has just been given to me (by him). 154. He will be shown pictures by the little girl. Pictures will be shown to him by the little girl. 155. The children were told a nice story (by me). A nice story was told to the children (by me). 156. I was shown my room (by the woman). My room was shown to me (by the woman). 157. They are always given presents (by us). Presents are always given to them (by us). 158. Mary has been sold new shoes by Linda and me. New shoes have been sold to Mary by Linda and me. 159. Their mothers were written a letter by Dick and Hank. A letter was written to their mothers by Dick and Hank. 160. You would be brought the books by father. The books would be brought to you by father. 161. Their brothers were sung a song by John and Tom. A song was sung to their brothers by John and Tom. 162. Father has been given many books by Tina and me. Many books have been given to father by Tina and me. 163. John has been thrown three balls by Tom and me. Three balls have been thrown to John by Tom and me. 164. Their dogs were fed a bone by Ken and Dave. A bone was fed to their dogs by Ken and Dave. 165. Tom has been thrown a ball (by the boys). A ball has been thrown to Tom (by the boys). 166. Our mother is always shown the books (by Linda and me). The books are always shown to our mother (by Linda and me). 167. Their sisters will have been sold some books (by the boys). Some books will have been sold to their sisters (by the boys). 168. Jane is being given new records by Dick. New records are being given to Jane by Dick. 169. Were the girls told the story (by the woman)? Was the story told to the girls (by the woman)? 170. His father was shown many pictures (by the little boy). Many pictures were shown to his father (by the little boy). 171. The ball was thrown to Mary by Tom. 172. The house was being shown to the new guest (by mother). 173. It will be given to you later by Sally. 174. She was given a prize (by them). A prize was given to her (by them). 175. Were you offered a job (by them)? Was a job offered to you (by them)? 176. All the money has been given to the workers (by them). 177. Were you shown all the rooms (by them)? Were all the rooms shown to you (by them)? 178. He has been offered a cup of tea (by them). A cup of tea has been offered to him (by them). 179. John was promised a new car for his birthday (by them). A new car was promised to John for his birthday (by them). 180. Were you given enough money (by them)? Was enough money given to you (by them)? 181. I was lent that book for the weekend (by someone). That book was lent to me for the weekend (by someone). 182. Many people have read that book. 183. What will you (they) give the child? 184. Father and mother blew the toy up. 185. Does the man always hold the dogs? 186. Did the thieves steal the car? 187. Bad students will win no prizes. 188. Lions often eat this meat. 189. Such men have often said silly things. 190. She said that a young lady would sing a German song. 191. The good king had made all the people happy. 192. Those men have never made bad mistakes. 193. Tom will bring the gifts for our friends. 194. The boys found the missing bag. 195. They (You) are preparing the meal now. 196. Two men were carrying the suitcases. 197. They will soon forgive you. 198. People (They, You) no longer sell such things. 199. They (You) will give us a lesson tomorrow. 200. They gave her a prize. 201. Did they offer you a job? 202. They gave all the money to the workers. 203. Did they show you all the rooms? 204. They have never taught students how to do that. 205. They (You) sold the house for six thousand pounds. 206. They will arrest him soon. 207. Where do you (they) keep the sugar? 208. The trees hid the house. 209. Did the child break the toy? 210. Does that class often sing those songs? 211. Where will they (you) take the bad man? 212. Those men have sold my sister books. 213. The silly men laughed at many songs. 214. My father looked after the house. 215. Does my sister often catch the balls? 216. Did my sister write the letter? 217. Many people have driven that car. 218. When will they feed the lions? 219. Do they (you) sing that song every Sunday? 220. That girl often wears those two dresses. 221. The man would have hit the ball. 222. Two men heard the girl's song. 223. Boys have often seen the pigs. 224. We (You, People, They) always eat the apples right away. 225. The bad boy beat the dogs. 226. With what does the woman sweep the floors? 227. When did the girl sew the dresses? 228. How many hands am I holding? 229. They have dug a big hole quickly. 230. Father will bring the newspaper upstairs. 231. Workmen still find old bombs every year. 232.

How do thieves steal money? 233. The man was lighting the candles when I left. 234. The car has broken the balls. 235. Why did he show you the rooms? 236. How often does their father shake the children? 237. That city is building skyscrapers every year. 238. How many slices of bread has he eaten tonight? 239. Is the owner riding the horse at the moment? 240. The boy was choosing his words carefully. 241. Yes, they will meet us at the station. 242. The dogs would have bitten the girls if they had come near. 243. How long have the thieves hidden the money? 244. You would cut your finger soon if you kept on. 245. When will they give you the prizes? 246. Where did the hunter shoot the deer? 247. The wind will have blown the leaves tomorrow. 248. The little girl fed the birds. 249. The teacher could hear their voices if they spoke louder. 250. That player had caught eight balls.

23 Reported Speech

1. He said that he had gone home at 2 o'clock the previous day (the day before). 2. He said that he would go home... 3. He said that he always went... 4. He said that he had been going home... 5. He said that he wanted to go... 6. He said that he had wanted to go... 7. He said that he had to go... 8. He said that he had had to go... 9. He said that he would have to go... 10. He said that he had to go... 11. He said that he would be going... 12. Peter asked Jim if he would send it back the next day (the day after, the following day). 13. John said to Jane that she had forgotten to send him a present. 14. John asked George if his dog bit. 15. Jim said to Dave that he should take ... 16. John told Jim not to tell Mary. 17. Tom said that his brother had gone home. 18. Mary asked Dick if he was laughing at her. 19. Jim asked Linda to go with him. 20. Bill asked Harry how much he had paid for his coat. 21. Mary told Bill to find her a nice book. 22. Ann told Jim that that piece of cake was for him. 23. Fred told Helen that she had put her umbrella in his car the previous day (the day before). 24. Father told Mother to give Jim... 25. Father told Mother that he would see Jim the following day (the next day; the day after). 26. Mary asked Bill if he had heard the... 27. Mary asked Bill to open the window. 28. Fred said that he was going to the city that day and that he would fly to London in two days time (two days after; two days later). 29. Mary asked Jim where he had hidden her shoe. 30. Bill asked Ann how long they had known each other. 31. The man told the girl that he would ring her father up if he caught her there again. 32. Jim said to Tom that he had seen him there two years before. 33. Mary asked Father if he had bought the books up to that time. 34. Linda said that she would be going to school the next year (the following year; the year after). 35. Jim told Mary to talk louder. / Jim asked Mary to talk louder. 36. John said that his sister had flown to New York the previous week (the week before). 37. Mary asked if they would come... 38. Mary asked if they should be there ... 39. Father told Bill that he couldn't have a car. 40. Mother told Linda that she was sorry that she couldn't help her... 41. The thief warned the boy that he would kill him if he shouted. 42. Your father promised us that he would go to the zoo with us. 43. Bill maintained that he wanted to marry Betty. 44. Sue responded that she had known them when they had been young. 45. Tom and Lucy proudly said that they had done everything themselves. 46. The Taylors complained that they had had a... 47. Dotty asked us if we had been at ... 48. The men asked their wives if they had really gone there the previous night (the night before). 49. Peter said that he promised to be ... 50. The girl asked me if I would help her the following day (the next day; the day after). 51. She asked him if he had read the newspaper the previous day (the day before). 52. They said to us that we should walk slowly if we didn't want to

fall. 53. He told us to look at the shops and not to talk so loudly. 54. She said that she had bought that dress two days before (two days earlier). 55. He asked her if she saw... 56. She asked him if he was flying to Moscow the following day (the next day; the day after). 57. He said that he had read 20 books that year and that the previous year (the year before) he had read only 15 but that the next year (the following year; the year after) he would certainly read more. 58. The boy told the policeman that he couldn't see them then (at that time). 59. She said to the boy that she had cleaned the kitchen twice that day. If he thought that she was going to clean it again because he had broken the dish, then he was wrong. She would wait until the next day (the following day; the day after). 60. Mary said that she was going to the cinema the next day (the following day; the day after). 61. Mary told Jim that he could have dinner with them that evening. 62. Mary said that they would go to the beach when they had had lunch. 63. Mary said that she didn't like cats but that she liked dogs. 64. Mary told Jim to come quickly and to see what she had done. 65. Mary asked Jim when they would arrive. 66. Mary said that she hadn't finished her homework the previous day (the day before) because she had been so tired after the party two days earlier (two days before). 67. Mary said that her aunt lived in that house over there. 68. Mary said to Jim that he should close the window before he left. 69. Mary said that Jim had to hand in his book and then he could go home. 70. Mary asked her mother at what time the party would start. 71. John said to Paul that they could see the rabbits if they walked quietly. 72. Mary said that she had been at the cinema the previous day (the day before) and that she had to visit her grandmother the following day (the next day; the day after). 73. She said that Susan would be in Bonn that afternoon. 74. My boss asked me if I was going home... 75. They told us that they would be playing cards after they had had lunch. 76. Father told Mike to wipe his shoes before he came in. 77. The woman asked us why we hadn't washed the cups. 78. Mary said that she hadn't seen anyone there two hours before. 79. I said that Mary and Peter were coming that day and that Bill was not leaving until the next (the following) Wednesday (the Wednesday after). 80. Aunt Jane said to Peter that he should switch the light off and close the door before he left... 81. We asked the stewardess when the plane arrived... 82. The policeman asked the boy what his name was. 83. You said to us that we should take our coats... 84. You said to us that we had held ... 85. He said that he had to go... 86. The doctor asked the man if his toe hurt. 87. Father asked us how far we were walking that day. 88. The woman said that she would play... 89. The doctor asked Marie why she hadn't taken her baby to the hospital the previous week (the week before). 90. The teacher told us to leave the building. 91. Mother said to you that you had done... 92. The men asked the girls if they had gone there the previous day (the day before). 93. Martha said to me that I should not work... 94. The old woman said that her sister had lived there two years before. 95. The captain said to his men that they couldn't leave if the weather didn't change. 96. He said that he would come as soon as he had finished the book he was reading. 97. Mrs. Jones said that she would help him if she could. 98. Their daughter said to them that she was not going to school that day. 99. Her mother asked us why we hadn't tried... 100. He asked her if she could come. 101. He said to us that we should get out of his house... 102. She asked him if he wanted... 103. My mother asked me if I was washing my face. 104. John told us that someone had broken into his house the previous night (the night before). 105. Jane said to us that she was glad to hear that we were so... 106. She told her to have ... 107. Linda told Dave (said to Dave) that they hadn't seen... 108. Dave asked Linda what she had been doing. 109. I said to her that I had something to show her. 110. She said that nothing ever grew in her... 111. He said to his mother that he was going away the next day (the following day; the day after). 112. They said that they had a lift but that it very often didn't work. 113. The small boy said that he had an English lesson the following day (the next day; the day after) and that he hadn't done his homework up to that time. 114. The boy said that he was going fishing with his father that... 115. Mrs. Small said that she would wait until her boy came in but she hoped that he wouldn't be... 116. The policeman asked the man what his name was. 117. The boys asked the girls if they had come there the previous day (the day before). 118. Mother told him to look... 119. You said to us that we should take our dogs for a walk at that time (then). 120. They said to her that she had written... 121. You asked me when I would come home the following day (the next day; the day after). 122. She told us that we would see two dogs if we went there. 123. He said to you that you would have seen the word if you had read... 124. You said that he hadn't eaten the apple after he had stolen it. 125. He said to me that I could go to the zoo with him in two days time (two days after; two days later) if I was helping my mother then (at that time). 126. He asked his wife if she wanted him to come... 127. He said that he promised that he would be home... 128. Judy told Bill that she would miss him... 129. Fred told Helen that he had lost his key but that he had found hers. 130. George said that he thought that he had left it on his desk. 131. He explained that he had missed... 132. John asked Mary what she was doing. 133. John asked Peter how the film had ended. 134. George asked Mary why his food wasn't ready. 135. The waitress asked the lady if she would like tea. 136. Tom asked Jane if she could catch... 137. We answered that he was sitting over there. 138. Ruth told Ken not to drink .../Ruth said to Ken that he shouldn't drink.../Ruth ordered Ken not to drink... 139. They asked us if we hadn't bought a tree up to that time. 140. They said that he had sat there for two hours at that time (then). 141. Linda asked them where they would sleep the following day (the day after; the next day). 142. Tom said to Peggy that he would forget the words again if she taught (had taught) him the words that day. 143. He said that he spent all his money... 144. Bob said to Dolly that she should hold his book. / Bob told Dolly to hold his book. 145. They said to us that we had thrown the chair away three years before. 146. She said to me that she would not say that if she were (was) me. 147. She said that she swam... 148. Linda said to Bob that she had to show him the book the following day (the next day; the day after). 149. They said to us that we had sat there two days before. 150. Linda said that then (at that time) the men had shot five birds there that afternoon. 151. They told me that I had not sat there the day before (the previous day). 152. We said that we would not bring you there... 153. Tom said to Becky that he would not go with her if it weren't... 154. Bill said that he was learning... 155. Ben said to Linda that she would see Carter if she flew to New York in two days time (two days later; two days after). 156. She said that she knew all the people there. 157. Tom asked them when they would go the following year (the year after; the next year). 158. They said that he had been wearing a brown coat the previous day (the day before). 159. Ruth told Mac to sing... 160. Tom told Linda not to drive.../Tom said to Linda that she shouldn't drive.../Tom ordered Linda not to drive... 161. They said that he had been feeding the deer the previous day (the day before). 162. Ben asked Peggy when she had ridden... 163. Linda said that she had cut her finger two days earlier (two days before). 164. Mother told Father that she would not ask him to go if she could go. 165. Mom said that they had found ten toys unter the chairs there at that time (then). 166. She said that she loved her new... 167. John said to Linda that she should take... 168. Linda said that she had to sell her books in two days time (two days later; two days after). 169. Linda told Tom not to blow... 170. Jenny told her boyfriend that she hadn't kept his ring. 171. The man said to his sister that he had bought two dresses for her that week. 172. Richard asked his mother what she had done two weeks before. 173. Bob said to Susan that she shouldn't begin to read. 174. My brother asked Linda if she always threw her books... 175. Tom reported that he wouldn't go... 176. Bob said to Linda that he had known her... 177. Susan told Jenny to buy tomatoes that day. 178. Linda said to me that she would hold my book there. 179. The boys asked us if we had sold our car. 180. Cathy replied that she was drinking milk then (at that time). 181. Tom asked Peggy to give him her pen. 182. Carl told Susan that she hadn't thought of that the previous day (the day before). 183. The woman told her husband that she would be singing that song two days later (in two days time; two days after). 184. Tom said to Peggy that she should catch that ball. 185. Daniel said that he often took... 186. The girls said to their mothers that they had been running to school when they had seen them. 187. My sister asked me when I would wake up the following day (the day after; the next day). 188. Cathy told Ben that she didn't understand what he had said. 189. Mary asked Peter at what time he got up. 190. The mother told her girl that she could go to school when she was... 191. Tom said that he had visited the British Museum while he had been on holiday that year. 192. Mother told us to hurry up or we would be late... 193. The girl told me that I would have to take the dog out every day if I had a dog. 194. The girl asked her boyfriend why he hadn't stayed at home the previous night (the night before). 195. The doctor said to Miss Smith that he thought that he had seen her before. 196. The teacher said to us that we should open our books and (should) begin... 197. Jim told Linda that he hadn't seen anyone there two hours before. 198. The man asked his daughter if she had seen his pen. 199. The lady asked me if I liked... 200. Bill told Mary that she had left her umbrella in his car the previous day (the day before). 201. The man asked the children if they had been to the zoo that week. 202. Mary said that she had seen the car accident but she denied that she had caused it. 203. The children asked if they could take... 204. Peggy asked Tom if he was coming to her party the next day (the following day; the day after). 205. Dan asked Linda if she had told his sister... 206. The boys asked their father if they had to go to the doctor's the next day (the following day; the day after). 207. Judy said to Tom that she had gone there earlier than he. 208. Linda said that she would go... 209. Dan said that he had heard... 210. Tom said to his mother that they went ... 211. Andrea said that they had seen... 212. Ann said that Linda and she had thrown her the ball two days before. 213. Susan said to father that he would buy a car the following week (the week after; the next week). 214. Tom said to Jane that he was sure that he had left her book on his desk. 215. Father warned the girls not to stay too long or they would have to go... 216. The teacher told us that we wouldn't understand what he (she) was (had been) saying if we didn't work... 217. Mary reported that she had been at home the previous day (the day before) and that she was going to the zoo the next day (the following day; the day after). 218. John replied that he had visited his uncle three weeks before. 219. She said to father that she was leaving the next day (the following day; the day after). 220. Linda told Dick that she would be with him as soon as she was ready. 221. Dan explained that they would go... 222. The teacher told the children that they had played very much that day. 223. They shouted that he was washing... 224. Father said to Linda that she couldn't go... 225. Tom's sister replied that he always came... 226. The boys said that they would be taking the test the following day (the next day; the day after). 227. Their father said to the girls that they had gone to church the previous day (the day before). 228. The neighbour said to Tom that he had seen him often. 229. The teacher said that the boy would be going... 230.

She replied that she had been there... 231. They said to Tom that they didn't want to see him then (at that time). 232. The daughter answered that she had come home that day. 233. Tom said to Betty that he wanted to marry her. 234. Mother said to Linda that she hadn't played... 235. d.) 236. d.) 237. d.) 238. a.) 239. b.) 240. a.) 241. d.) 242. d.) 243. b.) 244. a.) 245. c.) 246. b.) 247. b.) 248. a.) 249. a.) 250. b.) 251. c.) 252. c.) 253. d.) 254. b.) 255. b.) 256. a.) 257. c.) 258. d.) 259. b.) 260. c.) 261. c.) 262. c.) 263. a.) 264. b.) 265. c.) 266. a.) 267. a.) 268. He said to Linda, "You will be home soon." 269. He asked, "Don, please help me." 270. He agreed, "Yes, Nancy, your dress is nice." 271. He asked Peggy, "Were you here yesterday (a day ago)?" 272. He said to the people, "Be quiet." 273. We asked Tom, "Don't go with Dick tomorrow." 274. You said, "We were very quiet today." 275. Linda asked us, "Have you been to London yet?" 276. They said, "Linda helped us the day before yesterday." 277. You asked us, "Will you see Tom tomorrow?" 278. They said to us, "Run to the bus this morning." 279. We said, "Yes, Linda, you can write a letter." 280. She ordered, "Tom, write a book." / She ordered Tom, "Write a book." 281. You asked us, "Are you going shopping tomorrow?" 282. You said, "Tom will be helping you the day after tomorrow." 283. I told the boy, "Don't pick the apples here." 284. They told me, "You must take the bus tomorrow." 285. We asked them, "Will you have to drink... " 286. They said, "Yes, Linda, it would have been better if you had gone to school earlier." (It would be better if you went to school earlier.) 287. The man said, "I drove the car yesterday." 288. The lady said, "Tom, please pick up your coat." 289. The boy asked, "Will Linda be coming tomorrow?" 290. The man said, "Dan, sit down." (The man told Dan, "Sit down.") 291. The woman said, "The wind was blowing very strongly here yesterday." 292. The teacher asked us, "Will you be flying to America the day after tomorrow?" 293. Peter asked us, "Did you go by train yesterday?" 294. The doctor asked the child, "What did you do to the dog yesterday?" 295. Dan told Jenny, "It is your turn to feed the cat tomorrow." 296. They asked Don, "Are you building the garage now?" 297. My girlfriend said, "Yes, I'll come to your house next Friday." 298. The students asked the teacher, "Will you know the result of the test the day after tomorrow?" 299. I asked my sister, "Do you always bind these flowers?" 300. Father asked Linda, "Did you draw a picture yesterday?" 301. The boys asked the girls, "Do you want to dig a hole tonight?" 302. The Smiths said, "We bought the table last week." 303. The girl told me, "I cut my finger today." 304. Our friends asked us, "When will you be meeting the people tomorrow?" 305. The man asked me, "Have you begun to write the letter yet?" 306. They told us, "We will drive to the city tomorrow." 307. We asked the policemen, "Did you catch the thief last month?" 308. Tom's uncle asked him, "Why did you fight with the other boy the day before yesterday (two days ago)?" 309. Mother asked the boy, "Did you bite this apple?" 310. The stranger asked Carl, "What did you find two days ago (the day before yesterday)?" 311. I told Mary, "I am bringing you your milk now."

24 Reflexive Pronouns

1. herself 2. ourselves 3. herself 4. yourselves 5. each other 6. ourselves 7. themselves 8. yourself/yourselves 9. myself 10. herself 11. themselves 12. myself 13. herself 14. myself 15. ourselves 16. himself 17. ourselves 18. herself 19. yourselves 20. ourselves 21. yourself/yourselves 22. herself 23. himself 24. ourselves 25. myself 26. themselves 27. yourself 28. themselves 29. myself 30. yourselves 31. yourself 32. each other 33. himself 34. herself 35. myself 36. myself 37. yourselves 38. themselves 39. myself 40. themselves 41. herself

42. myself 43. himself 44. myself 45. themselves 46. myself 47. herself 48. yourself 49. each other 50. himself 51. myself 52. herself 53. yourself/yourselves 54. herself 55. itself 56. himself 57. ourselves 58. themselves; each other 59. — 60. — 61. I settled myself down... 62. — 63. We prepared ourselves... 64. — 65. The dog proved itself... 66. — 67. — 68. The girls dressed themselves... 69. — 70. They settled themselves... 71. — 72. — 73. Did you shave yourself... 74. I hurt my hand myself. 75. — 76. Did the children behave themselves? 77. I cut my finger myself. 78. — 79. The girls dressed themselves. 80. The little children enjoyed themselves very much. 81. The children were ashamed of themselves. 82. We had to wash ourselves quickly. 83. The children hid themselves. 84. The girl talked to herself. 85. Did you hurt yourself? 86. The courageous children asserted themselves. 87. The boy cut himself. 88. Behave yourself! 89. Does the boy have to shave himself already? 90. Did you sew it yourself? 91. Can I make myself useful? 92. Did you want to do it yourself? 93. The ladies introduced themselves. 94. They looked at themselves in the mirror. 95. I seated myself. 96. Help yourself to a piece of cake. 97. The boy and the girl fell in love. 98. We saw each other through the window. 99. I wanted to look at the city by myself. 100. I introduced the ladies. 101. You should help each other. 102. The crying mothers had to pull themselves together. 103. Did his wife support herself or her husband? 104. The boy hurt himself. 105. The girl traveled all by herself. 106. We thought of each other constantly.

25 Future

1. does the show start 2. arrives 3. starts 4. start 5. close 6. open 7. must you read / do you have to read 8. does the train leave 9. you are going shopping 10. is going 11. Are you going 12. he is doing 13. am taking 14. is John taking a walk 15. is your child starting 16. am going 17. is father working 18. are you doing 19. are your friends coming 20. are driving 21. am planning to wash 22. are you going 23. Will you be 24. will certainly snow 25. will go 26. Will we see 27. will drive 28. will you take 29. will make 30. will we do 31. will father be 32. will cry 33. will you cook 34. will have 35. will you wear 36. will have 37. will eat 38. will/shall be landing 39. will be starting 40. will/shall probably be sleeping 41. will be sleeping 42. will be coming 43. will be reading 44. will be wearing 45. will be working 46. will be arriving 47. will be going 48. will be going 49. will be going 50. will/shall be seeing 51. will be raining 52. will be arriving 53. Is he going to meet 54. are you going to tell 55. Are you going to play 56. is going to rain 57. is going to get married 58. are they going to visit 59. aren't we going to feed 60. Is your brother going to wash 61. Are the men going to stop work 62. am going to buy 63. Is your sister going to drive 64. are you going to be 65. Isn't your friend going to phone 66. are you going to study 67. are going to buy 68. will all be taking / are all taking 69. is going to have to take / will have to take 70. Will church start / Will church be starting / Does church start 71. will get 72. will be walking 73. Is he flying / Is he going to fly 74. won't be dying / won't die 75. are going to take 76. are going to take 77. will grow up 78. are going to have / will have 79. does Elvis arrive 80. is staying / will stay / is going to stay / will be staying 81. I will/shall help you this evening. 82. The marriage/wedding will be taking place in June. 83. War is going to come. 84. Your train leaves at 8 o'clock this coming Tuesday. 85. When are you going to church tomorrow? 86. I am taking the test/examination this coming Wednesday. 87. We will be landing on the moon in ten years. 88. My brother will show the people how they must drive. 89. The baby thinks its mother is going to feed it. 90. In America the Fourth of July celebration starts at 9

p.m. 91. We will be sleeping longer tomorrow. 92. Will you phone us when you have arrived home? 93. Dan is driving/traveling to Bonn on Friday. 94. The cat hopes that the mouse is going to come out of the hole. 95. We will be getting married tomorrow. / We are getting married tomorrow. 96. a. 97. a./b. 98. b. 99. a./b. 100. a. 101. a./b. 102. b. 103. a. 104. b. 105. a./b. 106. a./b. 107. a. 108. b. 109. a. 110. a./b. 111. b. 112. a. 113. b. 114. a./b. 115. a./b. 116. a.

26 Auxiliaries

1. can kill / is able to kill 2. can walk / is able to walk 3. could work / was able to work 4. will not be able to see 5. can see / are able to see 6. has been able to talk 7. would be able to play 8. Have you been able to talk 9. Will you be able to watch/Can you watch 10. may come / might come 11. might have come / may have come 12. may be / might be 13. may have seen / might have seen 14. might eat 15. might have done 16. may have read / might have read 17. may go / can go / are allowed to go / are permitted to go 18. may not go / can not go / are not allowed to go / are not permitted to go / are forbidden to go 19. may go / can go / will be permitted to go / will be allowed to go 20. Are you always allowed to go / Are you always permitted to go 21. May I smoke? / Can I smoke? / Am I allowed to smoke? / Am I permitted to smoke? 22. Has he really not been allowed to read / Has he really not been permitted to read 23. may not drink / can not drink / are not allowed to drink / are not permitted to drink / are forbidden to drink 24. Have they never been allowed to paint / Have they never been permitted to paint 25. have never been allowed to do / have never been permitted to do 26. Would he be allowed to see / Would he be permitted to see 27. have to do / must do 28. don't have to do / need not do 29. was forced to go / was compelled to go 30. will have to leave / will be forced to leave / will be compelled to leave / must leave 31. have often had to run / have often been forced to run / have often been compelled to run 32. would have had to shoot / would have been forced to shoot / would have been compelled to shoot 33. have had to work / have been forced to work / have been compelled to work 34. was forced to go / was compelled to go / had to go 35. would have to brush / would be forced to brush / would be compelled to brush 36. had had to eat / had been forced to eat / had been compelled to eat 37. would not be forced to get up / would not be compelled to get up / would not have to get up 38. would have had to go / would have been forced to go / would have been compelled to go 39. should have come / ought to have come / was to have come / was expected to have come / was supposed to have come 40. should help / ought to help / will be expected to help / will be supposed to help / will have to help 41. would be expected to go / would be supposed to go / would have to go 42. should do / ought to do / are to do / are expected to do / are supposed to do / have to do 43. was to arrive / was expected to arrive / was supposed to arrive 44. have always been expected to comb / have always been supposed to comb / have always had to comb 45. would not have been expected to help / would not have been supposed to help / would not have had to help 46. had been expected to go / should have gone / ought to have gone / was to have gone / was expected to have gone / was supposed to have gone 47. would be expected to wash / would be supposed to wash / would have to wash 48. will be expected to take / will be supposed to take / will have to take / should take / ought to take 49. need not bring / don't have to bring 50. is no need to bring / isn't any need to bring 51. was not necessary to bring / is not necessary to bring 52. need not come / don't have to come / won't have to come 53. would be necessary

to come 54. would have been no need to come / wouldn't have been any need to come 55. can 56. need not 57. must 58. must 59. should / ought to 60. must not 61. may / can 62. must 63. should / ought to 64. must 65. must not 66. need not 67. must 68. must not 69. need not 70. may / might 71. must 72. should / ought to 73. must not 74. must 75. must 76. should / ought to 77. may / might 78. need not 79. may / can 80. will not be necessary 81. was not allowed to / was forbidden to / was not permitted to 82. Have you never been expected to / Have you never been supposed to / Have you never had to 83. Would they be able to 84. will have to / will be forced to / will be compelled to/must 85. would have been no necessity to / wouldn't have been any necessity to/would have been no need to/wouldn't have been any need to 86. Have you been allowed to / Have you been permitted to 87. is their duty 88. did not have to 89. will have to / will be forced to / will be compelled to 90. Would they be able to 91. have to 92. have had to / have been expected to / have been supposed to 93. is his duty 94. did not have to 95. Would you be able to 96. will have to / will be forced to / will be compelled to 97. Have they ever been expected to / Have they ever been supposed to / Have they ever had to 98. is your duty to 99. have never had to / have never been expected to / have never been supposed to 100. will have to / will be forced to / will be compelled to 101. would have been no necessity to / wouldn't have been any necessity to/would have been no need to/ wouldn't have been any need to 102. has to 103. were forbidden to / weren't allowed to / weren't permitted to 104. Would he be able to 105. a/c 106. c 107. a/b 108. a/c 109. a 110. b/c 111. a/c 112. possibility 113.duty, obligation 114. necessity 115. compulsion 116. permission 117. ability 118.duty, obligation 119. necessity; compulsion 120. prohibition 121. possibility 122. necessity; compulsion 123. possibility 124. duty,obligation 125. compulsion 126. permission 127. necessity 128. necessity 129. ability 130. I will be able to help you. 131. We have not had to wash the curtains every week. 132. The baby will really have to go to bed. 133. Father said I will not be allowed to go (will not be permitted to go; will be forbidden to go) swimming tomorrow. 134. We weren't to drink so much water. / We weren't supposed to drink so much water. / We weren't supposed to have drunk so much water. / We shouldn't have drunk so much water. 135. We will have to be going now. 136. You were to wash the dishes. / You were supposed to wash the dishes. / You were expected to wash the dishes. / You ought to have washed the dishes. / You should have washed the dishes. / You were supposed to have washed the dishes. / You were expected to have washed the dishes. / You were to have washed the dishes. 137. The children won't have to be so quiet. 138. Has he been able to walk without help? 139. The plane will have to land soon. 140. You were not allowed to touch the pictures! / You were forbidden to touch the pictures! / You were not permitted to touch the pictures! 141. We won't be able to see the sun at night. 142. I have been forced to do my homework every day. / I have been compelled to do my homework every day. / I have had to do my homework every day. 143. Won't you be able to write your name? 144. You were to go to bed. / You were supposed to go to bed. / You were expected to go to bed. / You should have gone to bed. / You ought to have gone to bed. / You were expected to have gone to bed. / You were supposed to have gone to bed. / You were to have gone to bed. 145. Would Tom be permitted to go with us? / Would Tom be allowed to go with us? 146. could not walk / was not able to walk. 147. may go / might go 148. will have to do / will be forced to do / will be compelled to do / must do 149. need not buy / do not have to buy 150. could (not) / were (not) able to 151. shouldn't / ought not to / aren't supposed to 152. ought not 153. need not / don't have to 154. were allowed to / were permitted to 155. will have to / will be forced to / will be compelled to / will be expected to / will be supposed to 156. had / were forced 157. may have gone / might have gone 158. would not have had to go / would not have been forced to go / would not have been compelled to go 159. should / ought to / are to / (are to be doing) / are expected to / (are expected to be doing) / are supposed to (are supposed to be doing) 160. had to / was forced to / was compelled to 161. will not be allowed to go / will not be permitted to go / will be forbidden to go / are not allowed to go / are not permitted to go / are forbidden to go / may not go / cannot go 162. will have to / must / will be forced to / will be compelled to 163. need not / doesn't have to. 164. might be 165. will you have to go / will you be forced to go / will you be compelled to go 166. could hardly understand / was hardly able to understand 167. must wear / have to wear 168. was not allowed to go / was not permitted to go 169. would not have to paint 170. could have helped / would have been able to help ; couldn't help / wasn't able to help 171. may / can / are allowed to / are permitted to 172. must not / are forbidden to / are not allowed to / are not permitted to / may not 173. could not / was not able to 174. Can / Are you able to ; cannot / am not able to ; can / will be able to 175. had to / was forced to / was compelled to 176. must / has to ; need not / does not have to 177. cannot / is not able to ; will be able to /can 178. was allowed to / was permitted to / could 179. May / Can / Am I allowed to / Am I permitted to ; may not / cannot / are not allowed to / are not permitted to / are forbidden to ; will be allowed to / will be permitted to / may / can 180. don't have to / need not 181. must not / are forbidden to 182. will have to / will be forced to / will be compelled to /must 183. may / can / are allowed to / are permitted to 184. must / has to 185. could not / were not able to ; Can / Are you able to 186. should / ought to / are expected to / are supposed to 187. may / might 188. should / ought to / is supposed to / is expected to / is to / has to 189. may have cried / might have cried / may have been crying / might have been crying 190. I can not swim. / I am not able to swim. 191. When I was two years old, I could not swim (I was not able to swim). 192. When I am 80 years old, I will not be able to swim. 193. Until my grandmother died, I could go (was able to go) to her every Sunday. 194. Can you play the piano? / Are you able to play the piano? 195. He has been able to speak for five years. 196. She could already walk (She was already able to walk) when she was one year old. 197. They (You) will be able to drive home in two hours. 198. I may not be here at 5 o'clock. 199. I might not take the airplane. 200. She may have gone earlier. 201. They (You) were afraid that wolves might be in the woods. 202. That might not have happened if she had been here. 203. You may have been in the kitchen. 204. They (You) were afraid that he might not go. 205. She thought that he might be dead. 206. It might rain. 207. May I go? / Can I go? / Am I allowed to go? / Am I permitted to go? 208. You may not smoke in the tram. / You must not smoke in the tram. / You are not allowed to smoke in the tram. / You are not permitted to smoke in the tram. / You are forbidden to smoke in the tram. 209. When I was ten years old, I was allowed to (was permitted to) go to another city alone. 210. You will be allowed to (will be permitted to) get married when you are 18. 211. For the past year I have been allowed to (have been permitted to) go to bed at 10 p.m. 212. If he was 18, he would be allowed to (would be permitted to) vote. 213. We were not allowed to (were not permitted to / were forbidden to) talk too loudly. 214. You did not help me; therefore you may not (cannot / are not permitted to / are not allowed to / are forbidden to) have an ice. 215. Children are not allowed to (are not permitted to / are forbidden to / may not / must not) enter the building site. 216. The passengers were not allowed to (were not permitted to / were forbidden to) leave the airplane. 217. The dress may not be (must not be) washed too often. 218. You may not (cannot / are not allowed to / are not permitted to) go home yet. 219. I must (have to) go shopping. 220. You must (have to / are forced to) go to the doctor's. 221. He had to (was forced to) stay home. 222. He will have to (will be forced to/ must) fly to Munich tomorrow. 223. Have you ever had to (Have you ever been forced to / Have you ever been compelled to) eat grass? 224. You need not (don't have to) go yet. 225. Yes, I must (have to / am forced to) go now. 226. You should be (ought to be / are to be / are expected to be / are supposed to be / have to be) home at 8 p.m. 227. He should not (ought not to / is not to) speak (talk) so loudly. 228. When she is 18, she has to (will have to / will be expected to) celebrate her birthday. 229. I should not have (ought not to have / was not to have / was not expected to have / was not supposed to have) done that. 230. You should have (ought to have / were to have / were expected to have / were supposed to have) helped us. 231. They (you) were to have (were expected to have / were supposed to have / should have / ought to have) come yesterday. 232. I really should not (ought not to / am not to / am not supposed to) go there. 233. He must (has to) eat in order to live. 234. You don't have to (need not) do that if you don't want to. 235. I didn't have to go (It wasn't necessary for me to go) along yesterday. 236. We won't have to go (It won't be necessary for us to go) by bus if we have a car. 237. She must go (has to go) to the dentist twice a year. 238. He might come tomorrow. 239. You may not (must not / are not allowed to / are not permitted to / are forbidden to) leave the room. 240. He said he could (would be able to) come tomorrow. 241. We need not be (don't have to be / It isn't necessary for us to be) there early. 242. You shouldn't eat (ought not to eat / aren't supposed to eat / aren't to eat) so much. 243. Was he allowed to (Was he permitted to) go swimming yesterday? 244. You'll have to get up (You'll be forced to get up / You'll be compelled to get up /You must get up) early tomorrow. 245. If he came now, would you then be permitted to (would you then be allowed to) go with me? 246. If he had been here, he might have gone with us. 247. I could have helped (I would have been able to help) you if you had told me. 248. When did you have to go (were you forced to go) to bed yesterday? 249. I should have helped (ought to have helped / was to have helped / was expected to have helped) her. 250. What can (may) I write? 251. She was expected to (was supposed to / was to) help. 252. Will you have to (Will you be forced to / Will you be compelled to) read the book? 253. We have been forbidden to smoke here. 254. It won't be necessary to (There won't be any need to / There will be no need to) sell the car. 255. We may drive (travel) tomorrow. 256. We will be able to come (We can come) tomorrow. 257. He might have written. 258. Would they be allowed to (Would they be permitted to) visit us tomorrow? 259. We might have helped. 260. He will be able to read next year. 261. You should have gone (ought to have gone / were supposed to have gone / were to have gone) to bed earlier. 262. I may be ill (sick) tomorrow. 263. I might have come if you had asked me. 264. When I was ill (sick), I had to stay (was forced to stay / was compelled to stay) in bed. 265. The doctor said I would be allowed to (would be permitted to) get up three days later ; then I would be able to eat normally again. 266. Children under 18 years of age are not allowed to (are not permitted to / are forbidden to) drink alcohol. 267. I cannot help (am not able to help) you at the moment because I have to (am supposed to / am to) clean up my room. 268. He said that he could not come (was not able to come) because he had to (was forced to) clean the windows. 269. He should have cleaned (ought to have cleaned / was to have cleaned / was supposed to have cleaned) the windows; but instead of that he went swimming. 270. Do we have to do (Must we do) that; is it really necessary? 271. Why won't you be able to come (Why can't you come) next week? 272. I am not allowed to (I am not permitted to / I am forbidden to) because it is my duty to play with my little brother. 273. Would you be allowed to come (Would you be permitted to come) if my sister played with your brother? 274. Hopefully she will soon be able to go home. 275. Last year she could not (was not able to) speak yet. 276. We may be able to go tomorrow. 277. He might have been allowed (permitted) to go. 278. We may not go (cannot go / are not allowed to go / are forbidden to go / are not permitted to go) there. 279. He was allowed to go (was permitted to go) home yesterday. 280. May we see (Can we see / Are we allowed to see / Are we permitted to see) the child? 281. He will be allowed to (will be permitted to) travel to London next year. 282. As (Because) no tram came, I had to (was forced to / was compelled to) walk. 283. You will have to (will be forced to) stay home tomorrow morning because your mother is ill (sick). 284. They (You) should really have been (ought really to have been / were really expected to have been / were really supposed to have been / really were to have been) home yesterday. 285. He should really be (He really ought to be) here at 5 p.m. tomorrow. 286. Because (As/ Since) it is raining, I must (have to) take an umbrella. 287. The man with the broken arm asked, "When will I be able to write again?" 288. You should have gone (ought to have gone / were to have gone / were supposed to have gone) to the dentist on Monday. Why weren't you there? 289. We weren't allowed to (weren't permitted to / were forbidden to) sit on the table at school. 290. She should make (is to make / is supposed to make) her bed, but she doesn't have to (need not) tidy up her room. 291. If I had lost the book, I would have been forced to (would have had to / would have been compelled to) buy a new one. 292. I am not allowed to (am not permitted to / am forbidden to / may not) jump on the bed at home. 293. d) 294. b) 295. d) 296. c) 297. b) 298. c) 299. a) 300. c) 301. a) 302. d) 303. a) 304. c) 305. d) 306. c) 307. c) 308. a) 309. d) 310. c) 311. d) 312. c) 313. d) 314. b) 315. b) 316. c) 317. c)

27 Gerunds

1. seeing 2. to see 3. waiting 4. not to touch 5. to lock; going 6. not to speak 7. smoking 8. showing; to work 9. walking; to let 10. playing; doing 11. overhearing 12. smoking 13. to smoke 14. going; saying 15. He has improved his French by learning... 16. Alfred succeeded in defeating... 17. Father could not help laughing heartily. 18. I insist on your coming at once. 19. I did not mind his opening the window. 20. Tommy, stop talking! 21. Father is fond of reading the... 22. After having returned from school, Tom did... 23. The girl got an expensive stamp by paying a great... 24. Before going to school, we say... 25. Nobody can be put into jail before having been tried. 26. He left the room without saying a word. 27. Charles got a prize for having written the... 28. After having arrived in London, Tom... 29. Swimming is healthy. 30. The Normans continued speaking French. 31. He finished speaking and... 32. We are looking forward to reading your... 33. They don't allow smoking in ... 34. He is thinking of leaving his job and going to... 35. He was accused of stealing cars. 36. Do stop talking; I am trying to finish a... 37. The police accused him of setting fire to the house, but he denied having been there. 38. I couldn't help laughing. 39. Traveling by ship is more pleasant than traveling by... 40. I have always liked learning poems. 41. I prefer walking. 42. Billy was very proud of having won a... 43. I have finished writing a... 44. I don't mind your going alone. 45. Nobody will prevent you from doing that. 46. You can't accuse him of being lazy. 47. After having finished his work, he... 48. Tom frightened me by banging the... 49. You may depend on my coming in time. 50. Please excuse my being in a great hurry. 51. Seeing is believing. 52. I hate listening to such talk. 53. Monika is proud of being a German. 54. What is the meaning of... 55. Writing books is ... 56. She remembers

going to... / She remembers having gone to ... 57. Did you remember to lock... 58. After spending two days arguing about where to go for their holidays, they decided not to go anywhere. 59. He said, "I'm terribly sorry for keeping you waiting." 60. The teacher began by telling us ... 61. Would you like to come to... 62. What about buying two... 63. When would you like to start? 64. Let's wait until it stops raining. 65. He succeeded in climbing out... 66. Remember to bring your balls. 67. What about having a... 68. After spending/ having spent a week in the cottage, he decided that he didn't really enjoy living in... 69. The town was captured without a shot being fired. 70. You still have a lot to learn if you'll forgive my saying so. 71. Why do you keep on looking back? 72. Is he afraid of walking home... 73. We regret his having given an impolite answer. 74. Do you remember hearing that.../Do you remember having heard that... 75. What about coming with... 76. The story was so interesting that the girls stopped talking to listen to it. 77. We are interested in going to the cinema. 78. They don't allow girls to wear trousers... 79. They don't allow girls wearing trousers... 80. Did she remember to phone you... 81. Do you understand our having phoned them yesterday? 82. She watched TV before doing her... 83. Could they imagine your being / having been on television? 84. Please forgive them for having hurt you. 85. Linda, stop eating! 86. Mr. Smith didn't permit talking in... 87. I sewed my dress without using a... 88. After having gone to school for one year, I could write... 89. Do you think you'll succeed in getting up at 5 a.m.? 90. They'll always prefer drinking milk to drinking rum. 91. He didn't mind my reading his book. 92. Would they mind helping him... 93. Does he feel like cleaning his room? 94. Helping you wash... 95. Would you mind telling me... 96. They didn't allow their children to watch television. 97. Sally, stop running! 98. After having taken English for four years, she could... 99. Riding a boat... 100. He was suspected of shooting the man. 101. I'll always dislike writing letters. 102. I didn't mind their smoking... 103. I read her letter before writing an... 104. Did you remember to buy shoes... 105. During their walk they stopped to have a... 106. They don't permit running in... 107. He regrets her going / having gone home. 108. I am interested in collecting stamps. 109. Do you remember climbing / having climbed trees... 110. I understand his having helped her. 111. They will, of course, succeed in getting a good mark. 112. Do you feel like going to bed? 113. Can you imagine my drinking / having drunk oil? 114. He did his homework without asking his... 115. I regret their having left us so soon. 116. Do you remember reading that.../Do you remember having read that... 117. After having slept for two hours, we... 118. He is interested in reading many books. 119. Do they feel like going for a picnic? 120. They washed their hands without using soap. 121. Are you proud of being a... 122. We don't allow cheating on... 123. We understand her running / having run away from home. 124. Would he mind showing... 125.... the children stopped playing in the snow to see it. 126. I'll succeed in writing a book. 127. Could he imagine your sitting / having sat on a camel? 128. I love riding a pony. 129. She had seen him often before talking to him. 130. Please forgive me for being / having been late. 131. He always liked helping his... 132. We won't permit our boy to smoke at... 133. Do they always remember to go to... 134. They didn't mind our talking loudly. 135. Watching birds is an... 136. He does most of the talking. 137. She likes working in the office. 138.... had stopped helping him. 139.... stopped to help us. 140.... stopped helping his... 141. I always like seeing a... 142. Right now I'd prefer to be alone. 143. I dislike taking such... 144. He avoided meeting her... 145. ... he kept on talking. 146. Would you like to go for... 147. I want you to read that... 148. I remember seeing / having seen the... 149. My mother always expects me to make my bed. 150. If you don't stop making that... 151. I couldn't help feeling sorry... 152. I like playing records. 153. Will you please remember to bring me... 154. Why can't you help me to make the... 155. My brother's trying to draw a... 156. If we stop to buy a... 157. Don't try to move your ... 158. ... she hadn't remembered to phone him... 159. I can't help singing that... 160.... to remember going / having gone to... 161. I'm fond of drawing pictures and I'd like you to draw one, too. 162. I hope you enjoyed watching the film. 163. Did you forget to write the... 164.... stopped crying. 165. ... we stopped to help her. 166. She wants to go for... 167. He prefers eating chocolate ... 168. ... kept on walking. 169. He avoided seeing me ... 170. She would hate to hurt her... 171. We did not mind going to... 172. ... he finished writing the... 173.... Susan to read the... 174. Please try to tell me... 175. I'd like to hear that... 176. Don't forget to write your ... 177. Stop talking when... 178. Father hates being late. 179. I couldn't help crying when... 180. Try talking without ... 181. ...regret taking/having taken Susan's ... 182. Father used to take the... 183. We advised him to go to... 184.... we'll forget to leave on time. 185. We were used to going to... 186. We used to go to... 187.... required us to tell them... 188.... try going to... 189. We stopped to help the... 190. I was used to working late... 191. I advised writing a ... 192. My sister likes taking pictures... 193.... me to learn the...

28 Participles

1. ...pictures taken long ago. 2. The girl, waiting for the bus, was.... 3. Knowing that we had... 4.... desk, writing a letter. 5. Snatching his coat, the boy ran out ... 6. ... and found ourselves surrounded... 7. The woman, waiting at the bus stop, was very... 8. ... outside, lying in the sunshine. 9.... pictures drawn by a... 10. I found the girls acting very... 11. After having finished /After finishing her homework, ... 12. ... brother, riding a bicycle. 13. Seeing the spider,... 14. Knowing that the... 15. If asked her name and address, the little girl couldn't ... 16.... cake baked by... 17. ... us in the coming year. 18. We like children swimming. 19. Not seeing the baby, I... 20. ... because of her screaming child. 21. Though paying / Though having paid for the lesson,... 22. We found the stolen car. 23. Seeing that she wouldn't catch the bus, the girl stopped running. 24. Yelling that she was late, the teenager ran... 25. The boy, writing a letter, didn't... 26. ... cars given to us... 27. Feeling lonely, I went... 28. ... while listening to... 29. ... found her mother sleeping. 30. Hoping to get more... 31. Saying good-night to the children, the mother left... 32. After having eaten / After eating our meal,... 33. Looking through... 34. While taking a... / The man sang while taking a shower. 35. Though wanting to go... 36. Seeing the mouse, the... 37. ... cat sitting in a tree. 38. If taken at once, the medicine will... 39. Not being told/Not having been told exactly... 40. ... man riding on... 41. ... found the doctor helping him. 42.... horse, ridden by ... 43. After saying / After having said "good-bye", our friends drove away. 44. Taking his money, the man went to the shop. 45. Having closed the door, the man locked it. 46.... boy hiding from them. 47.... baby held by its mother. 48. ... away, leaving the ... 49. Not feeling good, the child... 50. The work having been completed, the... 51. Having gone to bed... 52. After having bathed / After bathing the baby, the mother put it to bed. 53. Catching / Having caught the ball, the player ran to... 54.... bird caught by ... 55. Having rained, the ... 56.... found themselves surrounded by... 57. Though expecting her child to phone in the evening, the mother waited... 58. Taking a pencil, the child drew... 59. Thinking it would... 60. Having taken her shower, the woman went to bed. 61. After having

finished / After finishing their job, the men ate... 62. Not wanting to be late, the man... 63. If drunk too quickly, the cold milk will... 64. Until coming here, I didn't... 65. Climbing on a chair, the baby started... 66.... dirt, swept under... 67. After drinking / After having drunk her milk, the girl was happy. 68. Thinking the baby... 69. Opening the door, the woman looked outside. 70. ... sour unless drunk at once./ Unless drunk at once, the milk... 71. When painted, the house looked pretty. 72. Though having started / Though starting her homework early, the girl wasn't... 73. After having been baked / Having been baked, the cake was... 74. ... pictures taken long ago. 75. Not knowing where to turn, the driver... 76. Not having worked hard for the test, the children were... 77.... wind, as if held back... 78. The sky being so dark, we... 79. After having caught / After catching / Having caught the bird, the cat... 80.... die unless given the medicine... 81. The rain finished, we... 82.... till having heard that ... 83. Though eating twice as much as anyone else, the girl didn't... 84. If performed faithfully every day, the exercises will help you lose weight. 85. Not wishing to be alone, the... 86.... homework, written the... 87. After having been read / After being read/Having been read, the book was returned... 88. Not seeing where we... / Not being able to see where ... 89. Having thrown the ball,... 90. ... night, each going his... 91. Hoping to be invited... 92. The music being so loud, ... 93. ... leg, swinging it around / Holding his child by its leg, the father swung it around. 94. If forced to eat, the child will vomit. 95.... dress, especially sewn for her. 96. The tree having been cut / being cut down, .../ After having been cut / After being cut down, the tree was made... 97. Not being able to buy anything cheap, the woman went... 98. Expecting you to be... 99. Though watered every day, the garden dried... 100. I cried, hiding my... 101. Having understood the sentences, the children were happy. 102. Not being able to go to sleep, I ... 103. Expecting to be hit, the... 104. After having slept / After sleeping / Having slept for a long time, the woman felt better. 105. If practised every day, the English words will ... 106. Not wanting to impose, the visitors didn't... 107. Though having studied very hard, the pupil failed... 108. We heard her talking to... 109.... time taking care... 110.... piano being played by... 111.... baby sleeping quietly. 112. A dog came running up... 113. ... me standing at... 114. After having eaten / After eating her food, Tina left... 115. We cleaned up, singing as we worked. 116. Opening the door, the father saw... 117. Having seen so many churches, the tourists no longer... 118. My mother heard me speaking with the man. 119. I'll have my hair cut next week. / I'm getting my hair cut next week. 120. The man kept his car running. 121. Can the boy make himself understood? 122. I heard my name being called. 123. She wants the room cleaned up (tidied up) by this evening. 124. I feel the ants crawling up my legs. 125. The man had his shoes repaired. 126. I want it taken away immediately. 127. I had my tooth pulled last week. 128. We will have our car washed next week. 129. Having been fed the best meat, the cat didn't want to eat the leftovers from the table. 130. The boy came home, followed by his friends. 131. After eating breakfast, I go to school. 132. After having eaten breakfast, I went to school. 133. Father reads the newspaper while eating his food. 134. My brother brushes his teeth before going to bed. 135. When looking out of the window, the people saw... 136. Until having turned the radio on, I couldn't... 137. Though thinking his friends were gone, the man phoned... 138. After hearing the music in the morning, we.../After having heard the music in the morning, we... 139. The man sang in the bathroom while washing his face. 140. Before leaving the room, you... 141. Before having driven away, the man gave... 142. While being driven in a car, the famous man looked.../While driven in a car, the famous man looked... 143. If taken every day, the medicine will... 144. Though having been given tickets, they didn't.../Though given tickets, they didn't... 145. Having bought a CD, the girls listened.../After having bought a CD, the girls listened.../After buying a CD, the girls listened 146. After having taken her jeans off, she ... 147. After having been taken off, the jeans... 148. Feeling sad, I cried. 149. Not knowing his telephone number, I couldn't... 150. Being tired, the woman went... 151. The car, going too fast, hit the man. Going too fast, the car hit the man. 152. Driven too fast, the car couldn't stop. 153. I saw the road, leading to Bonn. 154. I talked to a man, wearing a coat. 155. Having been driven home, the girl was home early. Driven home, the girl was... 156. The books, stolen from the shops, are gone. Stolen from the shops, the books were gone. 157. They saw the child eating cake. 158. We saw the dog being fed. 159. Having done her homework, the girl watched TV. 160. The homework having been done quickly, the girl still...

29 The infinitive with and without "to"

1. go 2. to help 3. to tell 4. to be 5. to leave 6. tell 7. to get 8. to go 9. to get 10. to wear 11. go 12. to let 13. to be 14. to return 15. jump 16. to see 17. to want 18. to help 19. come 20. to open 21. to leave 22. to walk 23. wear 24. to bake 25. to pass 26. go 27. to load/load 28. to stop 29. to tell 30. to go 31. to read 32. leave 33. to tell 34. to do 35. to take 36. strike 37. to enter 38. to be 39. to come 40. use 41. to rain 42. to read; to write 43. to go on 44. take 45. to remind 46. to understand 47. to open 48. work 49. to go 50. to go 51. to stop 52. to be 53. to go 54. write 55. to see 56. to help 57. to do 58. to know 59. to come 60. go 61. eat 62. to catch 63. to write 64. blow 65. to do 66. to be 67. tell 68. to come 69. put 70. to go 71. come 72. to swim 73. to open 74. to marry 75. to be 76. drink 77. to work 78. to write 79. to hurry 80. to wear 81. to be 82. to be 83. eat 84. to get 85. to stay 86. to come 87. pay 88. to drink 89. to swim 90. to marry 91. do; do 92. to pass 93. I showed him how to write his name. 94. The teachers decided where to have their picnic. 95. We were pleased to hear that you were coming. 96. I bet she'd be surprised to get a letter! 97. How often have we told you not to say that word? 98. Did he understand how to get to Bonn? 99. Did they tell you when to come? 100. We didn't remember whether to come today or tomorrow. 101. We had hoped to have left early. /We had hoped to leave early. 102. Did the children know where to buy pancakes? 103. Has he remembered what to ask them? 104. We forgot which road to take. 105. Has the new mother found out when to bathe the baby? 106. Did the boy forget how to unlock the door? 107. Has the girl understood why it is important to brush her teeth? 108. Did you decide whom to tell the story? 109. We were sorry to hear that you had been ill. 110. I'd be glad to shake his hand. 111. Has the man discovered what to take home? 112. Did they ask where to meet us? 113. Do the children know which man to ask for help if they are lost? 114. I would be delighted to go with you! 115. He was surprised to see his son driving a car. 116. They must have decided whether to eat now or later. 117. I found out whom to ask for money. 118. Did you ask to take John with you? 119. How did you know whether to speak or to stay silent? 120. We would be delighted to visit them. 121. Did your teacher tell you which words to learn? 122. I wonder when to phone her. 123. They showed us whom to help. 124. She didn't know where to turn for help. 125. Has the man thought of what to give his wife for her birthday? 126. The last person to be outside is a donkey. 127. She supposed him to be sleeping. 128. We found it to be very difficult to do. 129. The only person to finish the race was a big boy. 130. Did you estimate it to cost too much? 131. We considered that

matter to be finished. 132. It was difficult for me to write a letter in German. 133. Are you ready to take the test? / Are you prepared to take the examination? 134. I expect him to be nice. 135. The people would hate you to be late. 136. Do you promise to help me tomorrow? 137. He would be happy to have your picture. 138. We would like you to come again soon. / We want you to come again soon. 139. You don't have to go there tomorrow. / You need not go there tomorrow. 140. I would like my son to be a doctor. 141. The man asked me to help him. 142. I would love to go with you. 143. Would you prefer to drink wine? 144. The woman asked to speak to you. 145. He is looking for a possibility to get there. 146. You seem to be growing up so quickly. 147. I implore you to help me. 148. Would you be surprised to meet her here? 149. We are waiting for the rain to stop. 150. He chose to go along.

30 Adverbial clauses

1. When Carl turned the radio off, we... / Carl turned the radio off so that we couldn't... 2. After Carl had turned the radio off, we couldn't ... 3. After Tom had eaten ten pieces of cake, his... 4. Although/Though Father was very busy, he... 5. ... money so that we can... 6. If I had gone to school earlier, I would... 7.... mother so that she would... 8. When/Whenever Dan was not nice, he was bad. 9.... corner until/till you come. 10.... chair so that it... 11. After the baby had climbed onto the chair, it... /... chair so that it... 12. The tree died, although/though/after we had watered it. 13.... now so that we can... 14. If she had 20 Euro, she would... 15.... paper so that you can... 16. Since/Because Mother bought a dishwasher, we... 17. Since Daniel moved to Bonn, he ... 18. Although/Though the food smelled bad, the women ate it. 19. Since/As/Because it was raining, we... 20. Since/As/Because/When/ Whenever we were very tired, we... 21. If he went to school, he... 22. ... stop, when/ although/though/since/because she couldn't ... 23. When/Whenever/ Since/Because Susan got a "2", she... 24. While Mother was cooking, Father... 25. Since/As/Because Harry wanted to write letters, he bought paper. 26. Since/Because Linda liked the colour red, she bought... 27.... sports that he won... 28. Whenever/When we come to town, we... 29.... pretty that she became... 30. Although/Though we helped him, he got... 31.... tests that he always... 32.... twice since she moved... 33. ... time that I must... 34.... person that everyone ... 35. ... cinema that we had ... 36. Because Dan liked cars, he... 37. While we were talking on the phone, the... 38. Although Tom wanted a new car, he... 39. Since White knocked the bar down, Lee... 40. Until Dick bought a Ford, he... 41. Don was such a stupid person that he... 42. If Ben helped his mother, she... 43. Whenever we see our friends, we ... 44. After Linda had got the bad test back, she cried. 45. Tom is so tall that he... 46. ... loudly so that we... 47. Since Tom talked to me yesterday, I... 48. Before you could take the bus, you... 49. When Father had a cold, he... 50. ... written so many letters that her... 51.... passed since we... 52.... book so that I... 53. If they had finished reading the book, they... 54. Though she hadn't started to read the book, she... 55. After we had read the book, we... 56. When it gets dark, we... 57. Because he ate too much, he... 58.... book because it... 59. When the desks are dirty, we... 60. When Helen left the room, the... 61. ... happy because he... 62. ... dark because/when it was raining. / When it was dark it was raining. 63. ... play when Robert ... 64. He cried because he... 65. When he reached... 66. He failed, though he... 67. If you are good, you... 68. If you walk quickly, you... 69. Though you walk quickly, you... 70. If you want to grow tall, you... 71. Though you want to go home, you... 72.... dirty, though it was... 73. If he wants to go to the university, he... 74.

...policeman if I got... 75. He got lost, though he had... 76. If Mother went to the grocer's, she ... 77. She was happy, though she got... 78. If we go home now, we... 79. When it strikes 8, we... 80. ...ill because you... 81. Though he is a teacher, he... 82....cried because she had... 83. If you are good, you... 84. When/Because the film was over, we... 85. If they all go, we will.../Because they all go, we will also go. 86....suddenly because/ when a person... 87. If I met the film star, I... 88. If you did your lessons, you... 89. Though she tried very hard, she failed. 90....time because she failed... 91. If he works hard, he ... 92. Because they had worked hard, they... 93. When some people had got in, the ... 94. Since/As/Because the girls didn't study, they ... 95. Until/ Although/Though/When/Till I was three years old, I couldn't talk. 96....quickly so that he... 97. Since/As/Because the lady was standing, I... 98. Although/Though she looked like 16, she... / She looked like 16, although/though she was... 99. When/Because/ As/Since the boy saw the mouse, he... 100. ...was so very tired that she... 101. Because/As/Since/When it was dark, we ... 102. Although/Though it was dark, we... 103. Because/Since/As it was dark, we lit candles so that the children... 104....radio so that I could... / When/Since/Because I turned off the radio, I could ... 105. They were so very tired that they went... / Since/ Because/As/Whenever they were very tired, they... 106. Although/ Though it was raining, the children ... 107. When we went swimming, it ... / We went swimming because/since/while/whenever it was so hot. 108. ...records, although/ though he had little money. /Since/Because he bought records, he had... 109....ring while/when I was reading... 110....phone because/ since/after I had heard... / Before I went to the phone, I had... 111. ...grade, although/though he had... 112. Since/As/Because I have no dress to wear, I... 113. Since/Because/As we bought a dishwasher, we... / ...dishwasher so that we don't... 114. While Mother was preparing the food, the... 115. It was so cold that the... 116. Although/Though it was rainy, we had ... 117....hard so that they should... / Since/As/Because the girls worked hard, they... 118....over because/since it is her... 119....voice that she had... 120. If they installed a new traffic light, a lot... 121. Before 122. until 123. while 124. After/ Since/As/Because 125. since